Leadership in Education

*Organizational Theory
for the Practitioner*

Leadership in Education

Organizational Theory for the Practitioner

Russ Marion
Clemson University

Merrill
Prentice Hall

Upper Saddle River, New Jersey
Columbus, Ohio

Library of Congress Cataloging-in-Publication Data

Marion, Russ.

  Leadership in education : organizational theory for the practitioner / Russ Marion.

    p. cm.

  Includes bibliographical references and index.

  ISBN 0-13-016744-4

  1. Educational leadership. 2. School management and organization. 3. Organizational

sociology. I. Title.

  LB2806 .M365 2002

  371.2—dc21   2001021414

Vice President and Publisher: Jeffery W. Johnston
Executive Editor: Debra A. Stollenwerk
Assistant Editor: Dan Parker
Editorial Assistant: Mary Morrill
Production Editor: Linda Hillis Bayma
Design Coordinator: Diane C. Lorenzo
Cover Designer: Andrew Lundberg
Cover art: SuperStock
Production Manager: Pamela D. Bennett
Production Coordination: Carlisle Publishers Services
Director of Marketing: Kevin Flanagan
Marketing Manager: Krista Groshong
Marketing Coordinator: Barbara Koontz

This book was set in Guardi Roman by Carlisle Communications, Ltd. It was printed and bound by R.R. Donnelley & Sons Company. The cover was printed by The Lehigh Press, Inc.

Pearson Education Ltd., *London*
Pearson Education Australia Pty. Limited, *Sydney*
Pearson Education Singapore Pte. Ltd.
Pearson Education North Asia Ltd., *Hong Kong*
Pearson Education Canada, Ltd., *Toronto*
Pearson Educación de Mexico, S.A. de C.V.
Pearson Education—Japan, *Tokyo*
Pearson Education Malaysia Pte. Ltd.
Pearson Education, *Upper Saddle River, New Jersey*

10 9 8 7 6 5 4 3 2 1
ISBN 0-13-016744-4

ABOUT THE AUTHOR

Russ Marion grew up in North Carolina and received four degrees in education and educational administration from the University of North Carolina at Chapel Hill. He has been a public school teacher, a school principal, and a program director in the North Carolina Department of Education. He is currently a professor of educational leadership at Clemson University in South Carolina where he teaches several courses in organizational theory. Marion's research interests include organizational theory, school finance and student achievement, and nonlinear social dynamics. He has published articles on organizational theory and finance in journals such as *Journal of Education Finance, The British Journal of Management in Education, Emergence: A Journal of Complexity Issues in Organizations and Management,* and *The Journal of School Leadership.* In addition to this text, Russ Marion has also written *The Edge of Organization: Chaos and Complexity Theories of Formal Social Systems.*

To my wife, Gail, and daughter, Cathy.
This dedication is small return compared to all they have
put up with while I wrote this book.

PREFACE

This is an organizational theory book for educators. Its applications, discussion questions, activities, research questions, case studies, and content (as well as its omissions) were selected with public and private K–12 administrators, higher education administrators, and preservice administrators in mind. It draws from the literature on organizations of all types, but it focuses that literature on the specific experiences of education.

The book will examine three major paradigm shifts in organizational theory. The first emerged in the early years of the 20th century. It represents a shift away from a survival-of-the-fittest model, in which powerful tycoons single-handedly carved corporate empires, to a model guided by scientific principles and impersonal regulation. The theories of this paradigm are called, collectively, Closed Systems theory. They include the Machine and the Human Relations theories. The second shift appeared in the 1960s; it rejected the Closed Systems assumption that organizational behavior was an inhouse product and embraced an Open Systems assumption that behavior is strongly influenced by external environments. Like Closed Systems theory, however, this perspective assumed that theory spawns law-like prescriptions for leadership action. Contingency theory is one of the better-known products of the Open Systems movement. The third shift began about 1970. It preserved the Open Systems assumption about environment, but added that organizational events are largely unpredictable and ungeneralizable—theory cannot spawn law-like prescriptions for leadership action. This movement is called anti-positivism (Donaldson, 1996). (It is also called postmodernism.) Popular spin-offs of this movement include Strategic Choice theory, Culture theory, and Institutionalism.

Along the way there were background shifts that interacted with these major shifts. There was, for example, a shift from bureaucratic control structures to decentralized control in the 1980s that was related to anti-positivism. In earlier decades of the 20th century, there was a shift from an impersonal, mass movement perspective of organization (Spencerian evolution) to a model in which intelligent behavior made a difference in organizational productivity (Scientific Management).

This typology of theories is consistent with those of other writers. Scott (1987), for example, also divides 20th-century theory into closed and open perspectives. He further divided closed theories into closed rational and closed natural and divided open theories into open rational and open natural (see Fig. 1 for comparison).

This book contains three parts, one for each of the major paradigms of the 20th and 21st centuries. The first part covers Closed Systems theories, the second covers Open Systems, and the third covers anti-positivism. Each part concludes

SCOTT'S TYPOLOGY		TYPOLOGY FOR THIS TEXT	
		Pre-20th Century	Spencer's Social Darwinism
Closed:	Rational Type I • Scientific Management • Bureaucracy • Administration theory	**Closed: (Part One)**	Machine Theory • Scientific Management • Bureaucracy • Administration theory
	Natural Type II • Human Relations		Human Relations • Human Relations Structuralism — a transitional theory
Open:	Rational Type III • Contingency	**Open: (Part Two)**	Open Systems • Contingency theory
	Natural Type IV • Strategic Choice • Population Ecology • Critical theory • Institutional	**(Part Three)**	Anti-Positivist • Strategic Choice • Population Ecology • Culture theory • Critical theory • Institutionalism • Complexity theory

FIGURE 1 Comparison of Scott's (1987) typology of organizational theories with the typology adopted for this textbook.

with a cumulative summary. The Closed Systems material is summarized at the end of Chapter 4 (a section on leadership), Closed and Open Systems are summarized in Chapter 7's discussion of conflict, and the entire text is summarized at the end of the book by the chapter on change.

Theories, Topics, and Organization

This book is organized by macrotheories, microtheories, and topics. Distinctions between macro- and microtheories are based on level of generality: Macrotheories are the most generalizable, microtheories are the least. Topics are what theories are about—their subject matter.

Macrotheories are defined at two levels of generality: The more generalizable macrotheories are Closed Systems theory, Open Systems theory, and anti-positivism (the book's parts are organized around these levels). Specific macrotheories include Machine theory, Human Relations theory, Structuralist theory, Contingency theory, Strategic Choice theory, Population Ecology theory, Culture theory, Critical theory, Institutionalism theory, and Complexity theory. The book's chapters are constructed around this more specific level of generality (see Fig. 2).

Microtheories, by contrast, are even more specific theories about specific topics: James Burns, for example, wrote of a specific (micro) theory of leadership that he called Transformational Leadership. Hersey and Blanchard developed Situational Leadership, another microtheory. Microtheories are hierarchically subsumed within the context of given macrotheories; thus, Situational Leadership is based on the premises of Contingency theory which, in turn, is influenced by Open Systems theory.

Topics are the subject matter of macro- and microtheories. This book will cover a number of topics, including leadership, decision making, motivation, organizational structure, organizational change, and organizational conflict.

The chapters in this text are organized by topics *and* chronologically by macrotheory. Chapter 6, for example, is about leadership (topic) and about Contingency theory (macrotheory), and Chapter 8 is about decision making and learning, and about Strategic Choice theory. This multidimensional structuring is possible because macrotheories (the second-level ones, such as Contingency and Human Relations) tend to have major topical themes—thus, Contingency theory is largely (although not exclusively) about leadership, and Strategic Choice theory is largely about decision making and organizational learning.

Macrotheories do, of course, make observations about other topics (for example, while Strategic Choice theory—Chapter 8—is primarily about decision making and learning, it also deals with issues such as structure and communication). These topics are woven around the respective themes as appropriate.

Chapter 7 (which concludes the positivistic theories) and Chapter 14 (the final chapter) depart from this topic-theory schema. Chapter 7 pulls together cross-theory literature on conflict; Chapter 14 does the same for change. Chapter 7 lays a summary of the positivistic theory literature (both Closed and Open Systems) on top of a discussion of conflict. It explains how different positivistic paradigms

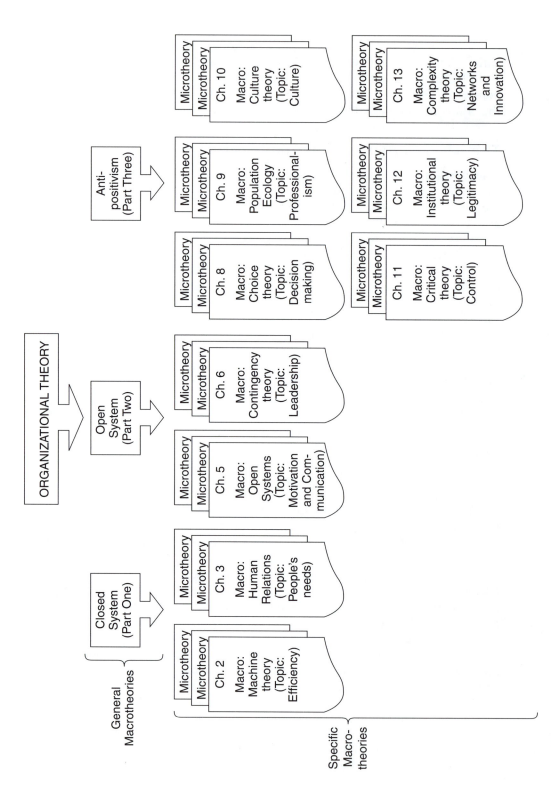

FIGURE 2 This textbook is organized by macrotheory, microtheory, and topics. Chapter 4 on Structuralism is not categorized because it represents a transition between the Closed and Open perspectives.

have influenced perceptions of conflict in the 20th century. That is, Chapter 7 discusses conflict in educational systems *and* summarizes the first two parts of the book. Chapter 14 presents the argument that this textbook, ultimately, is about change; thus, the placement of this material as the final chapter provides an opportunity not only to talk about this important subject but to summarize the themes developed in the entire book as well.

Pedagogy

Marshall McLuhan, the 1960s counterculture guru, said there are two types of media: hot media and cool media. Hot media are full of information; they overload the senses to the point that the individual is incapable of interacting with what he or she is learning. If you were to arrive at an automobile accident with injuries, your attention would likely be so riveted on the scene that you would fail to properly notice other things going on around you. The scene is so full of information that you could not attend to anything else. You are ripe for a secondary accident. Cool media, by contrast, are more interactive; they invite you to participate in the information, to process it, critique it, and apply it. Cool media engage the imagination. The telephone is a cool medium (except when used while driving); the television is a hot medium. Books are cool media; movies are hot. Discussions are cool media; lectures are hot media.

This textbook is written to be both hot and cool: It will at times overstimulate students with information, and at other times it will engage students interactively. The hot media are important, for there are a number of theories one needs to absorb, but it is equally important that students explore the ideas and decide what they mean for their personal leadership styles.

The book is likewise attentive to the academic versus the practical implications of theories. Theories are little more than ivory tower artifacts if they cannot be translated into guides for actual leadership behavior. Some of the theories discussed in this book are more practitioner-oriented than others, but we (I write to engage the student personally—we explore together) will constantly keep the practitioner side of theory before us.

There are several vehicles for delivering cool media and practical applications. Each chapter begins with a list of objectives that reflect expected student outcomes (as opposed to chapter intent). The objectives are implemented through roundtables (or discussion questions), suggested research topics, activities, and case studies (all of which I have "field-tested" and refined in my own graduate classes). These are embedded within the text, so students must periodically shift from hot media (the readings) to cool media (the discussions, activities, and research topics)—and from academic to practical. Instructors could also use these activities for large- or small-group discussion, or as portfolio assignments. Students are encouraged to develop a diary based on questions presented at the end of each chapter. Diary entries are reflections on ideas discussed in the given chapter. Every diary assignment has one common question: Students are asked to explain how their perceptions of leadership have evolved since the previous chapter's readings. Many of the roundtable and diary questions ask students to consider what they must do to enhance their personal leadership skills. Finally, each chapter concludes with brief reviews of recommended readings that students might pursue for further information on the ideas developed in the chapter.

This book, then, represents an effort to bridge the theoretical and practical, to place theory within broad historical and philosophical contexts, and to help students see patterns in the material they are examining. It is written in a style that avoids the didactic and tedious and seeks to be accessible, interesting, and easy to read. And, perhaps most importantly, it seeks to engage and involve students rather than merely to teach them, to challenge them to use the ideas in the text to develop their personal leadership styles. I hope students will come away from this book with more than knowledge; I hope they come away with new behaviors.

Acknowledgments

I would like to thank Philip L. Arbaugh, Western Maryland College; R. Wilburn Clouse, Vanderbilt University; Mary Jane Connelly, University of Tennessee; Gene Gallegos, California State University, Bakersfield; Larry W. Hughes, University of Houston; Richard M. Jacobs, Villanova University; Kathy Peca, Eastern New Mexico University; and Michael D. Richardson, Georgia Southern University, for their insightful remarks as they reviewed the manuscript. I would also like to thank Jeff Martin and Bonnie Snyder for their invaluable comments as I was developing this text.

References

Burns, J. M. (1978). *Leadership*. New York: Harper & Row.

Donaldson, L. (1996). *For positivist organization theory: Proving the hard core*. London: Sage Publications.

Hersey, P., & Blanchard, K. H. (1993). *Management of organizational behavior: Utilizing human resources* (6th ed.). Englewood Cliffs, NJ: Prentice Hall.

Kuhn, T. S. (1970). *The structure of scientific revolutions* (2nd ed.). Chicago: The University of Chicago Press.

Lawrence, P. R., & Lorsch, J. W. (1967). *Organization and environment*. Cambridge, MA: Harvard University Press.

McLuhan, M. (1964). *Understanding media: The extensions of man*. New York: McGraw-Hill.

Scott, W. R. (1987). *Organizations: Rational, natural, and open systems* (2nd ed.). Englewood Cliffs, NJ: Prentice Hall.

Vroom, V. (1964). *Work and motivation*. New York: John Wiley.

DISCOVER THE COMPANION WEBSITE ACCOMPANYING THIS BOOK

The Prentice Hall Companion Website: A Virtual Learning Environment

Technology is a constantly growing and changing aspect of our field that is creating a need for content and resources. To address this emerging need, Prentice Hall has developed an online learning environment for students and professors alike—Companion Websites—to support our textbooks.

In creating a Companion Website, our goal is to build on and enhance what the textbook already offers. For this reason, the content for each user-friendly website is organized by topic and provides the professor and student with a variety of meaningful resources. Common features of a Companion Website include:

For the Professor—

Every Companion Website integrates **Syllabus Manager™**, an online syllabus creation and management utility.

- **Syllabus Manager™** provides you, the instructor, with an easy, step-by-step process to create and revise syllabi, with direct links into the Companion Website and other online content without having to learn HTML.

- Students may log on to your syllabus during any study session. All they need to know is the web address for the Companion Website and the password you've assigned to your syllabus.

- After you have created a syllabus using **Syllabus Manager™**, students may enter the syllabus for their course section from any point in the Companion Website.

- Clicking on a date, the student is shown the list of activities for the assignment. The activities for each assignment are linked directly to actual content, saving time for students.

- Adding assignments consists of clicking on the desired due date, then filling in the details of the assignment—name of the assignment, instructions, and whether it is a one-time or repeating assignment.

- In addition, links to other activities can be created easily. If the activity is online, a URL can be entered in the space provided, and it will be linked automatically in the final syllabus.

- Your completed syllabus is hosted on our servers, allowing convenient updates from any computer on the Internet. Changes you make to your syllabus are immediately available to your students at their next logon.

For the Student—

- **Topic Overviews**—outline key concepts in topic areas

- **Web Links**—a wide range of websites that provide useful and current information related to each topic area

- **Readings**—suggested readings for further study of certain aspects of the topic areas

- **Trends and Issues**—links to relevant sites about the trends and issues of educational administration

- **Education Resources**—links to schools, online journals, government sites, departments of education, professional organizations, regional information, and more

- **Electronic Bluebook**—send homework or essays directly to your instructor's email with this paperless form

- **Message Board**—serves as a virtual bulletin board to post—or respond to—questions or comments to/from a national audience

- **Chat**—real-time chat with anyone who is using the text anywhere in the country—ideal for discussion and study groups, class projects, etc.

To take advantage of these and other resources, please visit the *Leadership in Education: Organizational Theory for the Practitioner* Companion Website at

www.prenhall.com/marion

BRIEF CONTENTS

CONTENTS

Leadership in Education

*Organizational Theory
for the Practitioner*

PART ONE

Closed Systems Theory

Closed Systems theory, the subject of the next two chapters, is about efficiency and effectiveness. That is, it presumes that an organization's dominant, if not only, goal is productivity, and any other organizational outcomes are either secondary or illegitimate. Closed Systems theory is a relatively old theory that generally only appears in serious academic discussion as a historical artifact, but one can see very new manifestations of it in public debates about the direction of education. Modern accountability legislation, which holds educators directly and exclusively responsible for student achievement, assumes that public education can focus on achievement without distraction from external goals or characteristics. School boards often implement policies that prohibit activities not related to basic achievement (such as fluoride swish or interpersonal skills instruction) or that prescribe time-on-task. All such activities reflect a Closed System bias, one that implies that public education's solitary focus is efficiency and effectiveness (as measured by achievement tests), and that administrators and teachers need only implement definable and rational efficiency/effectiveness strategies to achieve those goals.

Closed Systems theory gets its name from the underlying presumption that organizations are self-contained entities largely untainted by external forces or issues, and that efficiency is served by controlling internal activities. This does not mean that organizations ignore demands from customers or raw material providers; it means that such demands are believed to be resolved by organizational effectiveness and efficiency. Were public education a closed system, it would not need to foster racial equality or deal with student health issues, for neither of these problems relates directly to educational efficiency and effectiveness. Breakfast and lunch grants for indigent students would be judged in terms of their effect on educational productivity (measured as student achievement). Students would be uniformly capable of achievement, and failure would be attributable to their lack of effort. Education's goal would be clear, untainted, and unambiguous: achievement productivity.

The Closed Systems perspective of organization was dominant at a crucial time in the development of the modern school structure, and its influence is felt to this day. This body of theory evolved and incubated during the last 30 years of the 19th century, and achieved maturity during the first two decades of the 20th century. During these years, Horace Mann successfully sold the common school concept in the United States and the National Education Association developed the basic rationale for high school education (the famous report of the Committee of Ten and the later report of the Commission on the Reorganization of Secondary Education). Modern organizational patterns and polity of public education took root. The very rationales underlying public education were installed as part of our cultural mindset, rationales such as the need to produce successful adults, to provide productive workers for the modern workforce, and to produce an enlightened citizenry. The Closed Systems mindset pervaded the worldview of the society that developed the structure and rationale of 20th-century public education; thus, it was inevitable that Closed Systems assumptions would influence that development and would be evident in its structure even today.

Two broad macrotheories lie within the Closed Systems rubric. The first, and earliest, is called Machine theory (sometimes referred to as Classical theory). Machine theory is in turn composed of three lesser macrotheories—Scientific Management, Administration Management, and Bureaucracy theory. We will discuss these theories in the next chapter. The second, and later, closed macrotheory is known as Human Relations theory; it is discussed in Chapter 3. Chapter 4 deals with Structural theory, a transitional theory that bridges the closed and open perspectives of organization.

CHAPTER 1

Roots of Modern Organizational Theory

OVERVIEW AND CHAPTER OBJECTIVES

There were no organizational theorists or sociologists per se before the 20th century; or rather, organizational theory and sociology were not defined as specific academic subjects before that time. Humans have been interested in the nature and dynamics of their organizations and other social structures since the time of the great Greek civilizations, however, and probably even before then. Those who studied organizational theory or sociology in these early years did so under the guise of philosophy, politics, economics, or even biology.

However, we shall not review the earliest thoughts on this subject in this chapter—those of Plato, Aristotle, and others—but will instead focus on the rise of modern perceptions of organization and social structure. The first such theory of organization that we will examine is called Social Physics, which appeared in the mid-1700s. The second of the early theories was popular in the late 1800s; it was called Social Darwinism. First, however, we will define theory.

In this chapter, students will:

- Struggle with questions about whether we can sufficiently control our futures to make organizational planning a worthwhile endeavor.

- Begin to develop a code of ethics that will serve them as leaders and as academics.

- Begin to develop a worldview about the role of conflict and cooperation in organizations.

- Refine their understanding of social causation.

- Begin to develop a definition of leadership.

INTRODUCTION TO THEORY

You need to understand something about theory, for doing so will clarify important issues that many students don't grasp until well into their doctoral studies (if then). Theory is not reality; it is our best shot at describing reality. This obviously is not a complicated notion (although its meaning for theory can become rather sophisticated), but for some reason teachers don't always get around to letting students in on this fact. Theory is a worldview, a paradigm, a philosophy, a way of understanding reality. A person who adheres to one theory will draw one set of conclusions about reality; one who adheres to another will draw different conclusions. The two people may approach research differently, they may ask different questions, and they certainly would draw different conclusions about their observations. Is one right and the other wrong? Not necessarily. Even when the premises underlying one's theory are in error, one might still make useful deductions about reality. Often different theories look at different parts of reality, but even when they look at the same reality, one can learn from them.

In a previous book, I illustrated this with the familiar folk tale of three blind men attempting to describe an elephant (Marion, 1999). One blind man in this story feels the tail and says the elephant is like a rope. The second feels the elephant's flank and concludes it must be like a wall. The third feels the trunk and says it is like a tree. Each man focuses on different perspectives and creates different explanations of elephant. A test of model goodness is its generalizability; thus, the tree model, if reasonably accurate, should work for the opposite end of the mammoth, but of course it doesn't. Our blind scientists could argue that the elephant is so complex that theorists must focus on just one part of the animal at a time. When the different models are restricted to their intended uses, they are reasonably appropriate. Still, these models are problematic because they do not impart a full sense of elephant, and the blind scientists will inevitably be bothered by the lack of connection among the theories.

As a folk tale, the story ends here; as a metaphor, we will follow events in the blind culture a bit further. Eventually some other blind man or woman reconciles the shortcomings of the original models by creating a new one that focuses on, say, skin texture, a feature that is constant over much of the elephant. There is the matter of the elephant's feet and soft tissue (eyes, inside the ears, etc.), but these are conveniently labeled inconsequential. The new model is more generalizable, although its detractors argue that, in addition to the problem of feet and soft tissue, it ignores structure—the focus of the original theories. The critics, however, are branded as old-fashioned and eventually their arguments are all but forgotten. Over time scientists learn more and more about skin texture, but increasingly the problem of the feet and soft tissues stands in the way of further understanding. When the difficulties become intolerable, someone revives the structural arguments and, with brilliant insight, produces a model that connects texture and structure. Understanding in the blind culture is advancing.

The moral of the story is simple: Reality is an elusive commodity and the best one can hope for is closer and closer—or maybe just varying—approximations of it. We may never arrive at absolute and total reality, and even if we did, our "blindness" would likely prevent us from confirming our arrival. Nonetheless, our models serve us well, for we eventually learn to ride our elephants and use them for work. Theory-building is a process of building and rebuilding, with each cycle illuminating different corners of the darkness.

The story of the blind men and the elephant hints at yet another characteristic of theory. Theories experience long periods of stasis that are occasionally punctuated by sudden change. During the tenure of a given theoretical perspective, scientists build on its basic premises, and knowledge about the world slowly increases as a result. At some point, however, people get tired of their existing theories or, more likely, they come to realize that there are too many holes in them, and they move on to some other theory. Thomas Kuhn, author of *The Structure of Scientific Revolutions* (1970), calls this a "paradigm shift." A paradigm shift is a major change in the way a culture perceives reality—imagine the impact of Copernicus and his heliocentric theory of the universe on such things as religion, for example. In organizational theory, the social upheaval that occurred in Western society in the 1960s was associated with significant changes in the way we perceived formal organization. Liberal politics and rebellion against scientific sociology created another major shift in the way we perceive organizational behavior in the 1980s. Each of these shifts significantly influenced the way we think about reality and about ourselves.

Some popular writers in the organizational behavior field propose that a paradigm shift is any change in the way we approach a problem—they use terms such as "thinking outside the box" to illustrate what they mean. This is not "paradigm shift" as Kuhn intended it; rather, it is a buzz word that has devolved into little more than a cliché. It's like saying a ripple in a pond is a tidal wave, or someone creates earthquakes by jumping up and down. Paradigm shifts are more significant than thinking outside the box to solve a localized problem.

Theory and Practice

One of my students recently raised an interesting question. We were about halfway through a survey course on administration theory and she was trying to relate the material to the behaviors and activities of business leaders in her community. She teaches business education and knows most of the business CEOs in her town. Her question was simple: She wanted to know how theory was reflected in the practice of administrators in education and in business. Administrative practice, to her, appeared to be an undifferentiated dynamic. Administrators all seemed to do the same things—they told people what to do, assured the availability of resources, organized workflow, negotiated contracts, and such. All the theories we had discussed until that point in the class seemed logical to her—she appreciated their value—but she couldn't quite grasp *why* they were valuable. She didn't see any administrators with whom she was familiar analyzing worker readiness and tailoring leadership behavior accordingly, as proposed by Hersey and Blanchard (Chapter 6). She didn't see much concern about the subtle nuances of worker motivation (Chapter 5)—workers in her experience either performed as expected or they were fired. She didn't have a problem with the theories, for they were good models for leadership behavior, but she could not see how they related to practice. It was a good question, and there are several answers.

First, she is right, managers don't go around saying, "What would Hersey and Blanchard do in this case?" or "Lawrence and Lorsch say I ought to behave this way under this circumstance." Rather, administrative behaviors are influenced by the general premises underlying given theoretical perspectives, particularly those premises that were prevalent at the time an organization's leaders were trained or when the organization was first created. Managers who were prepared during the heyday of Contingency theory (1960s and 1970s) are likely to tailor their behaviors to organizational contingencies ("These workers are not achievement-oriented, so I need to manage more authoritatively;" or "Our workflow is sufficiently stable that we don't need to spend a lot of money on a complex departmental structure"). Organizations that emerged during the 1980s, when Culture theory was popular, are likely to invest power in the worker and to provide perks such as daycare and gyms. The influence of theory is not necessarily conscious—often it can be identified simply as "the way we do things around here"—but it is usually there.

Second, organizational theory is as much about describing and reflecting what is going on in organizations as it is about finding ways to improve organizational behavior. It is as much descriptive as it is prescriptive. Administrative approaches to leadership are a product of the times and are influenced by general societal beliefs and sensibilities. In the 1950s, women had "women's jobs" (secretaries, nurses, teachers, etc.). Our sensibilities on this issue have changed significantly since then, administrative behavior has adjusted accordingly, and all this is accompanied by something of a "feminization" of organizational theory. Organizational theorists probably have been somewhere in the vanguard of this movement, but they have also been swept along a movement that is bigger than themselves. So theories don't just influence administrative behavior, often they describe or reflect what is happening in society and its organizations.

Third, a good course in organizational theory will expand your unconscious (or semi-conscious) repertoire of administrative behaviors and solutions. It will provide you with lots of ways to approach a given situation. It will organize your thoughts about organizational dynamics. Your professors want you one day to say (not in words, but in your behavior), "I remember talking about change in Dr. Theorist's class; she said that change is a complex process and is influenced by a number of different organizational dynamics. I've got a great speech on the new curriculum prepared, but what else do I need to be doing to get it properly implemented?" "That math teacher is really in a rut. What are some motivational strategies we discussed in Dr. Theorist's class?" "My teachers' garbage cans need filling; I'm going to find the money to send at least some of them to a conference." "It's crazy to put together these detailed plans for where we will be five years from now—things change too unpredictably. How can I approach this planning process more effectively?" You may not remember the details of theories themselves, but if the material in this text can influence and expand your "autonomic" leadership behavior, it has done its job.

This book is written with these points in mind. It is organized to expand your repertoire of leadership behaviors and understandings. It is devoted not just to telling you about theories, but to getting you to think about them. What do they mean? How do they apply to practice? Do you agree with them? How are they interrelated? What is their value?

One final point: Theories fall in and out of favor. They are popular among theorists for a few years, then are thrown aside for new theories. So, one might ask, why teach the old theories? Why not just focus this text on the more current and influential theories that dominate space in our journals and discussion at our conferences? I could talk here about history and background orientation—all the usual (and persuasive) arguments about history and the emergence of knowledge, but the more immediate reason has to do with practitioners. It's not about what goes on in our arcane academic debates, but about what goes on in our principals' and deans' offices. Educational leaders still need to understand the power of social interactions, and the strategies of efficiency, so this book teaches about the Machine theory movement of the 1910s and '20s, and about the Human Relations movement of the 1930s and '40s. The organizational sciences of the present focus on the idiosyncratic nature of organization, the anti-positivistic side of administration, but most anti-positivists admit there is at least some relationship between contingency and outcome, so we teach Contingency theories of the 1960s and 1970s. The old theories haven't become unusable just because academics have moved on to new perspectives, and the behaviors they describe haven't disappeared from work environments just because the theories have disappeared from our journals. Practitioners can benefit from what past theories have to offer, so we should teach them. New theories underscore the limitations of older theories and give us new ways to understand organization. New theories help us do an even better job of leading. But the new theories do not, and should not, stand alone.

PHYSICS AND SOCIETY

A theory of social organization known as Social Physics appeared shortly after Newton wrote *Principia,* during the infancy of the Industrial Revolution. This theory, predictably, took its cues from Newton's theories. As we shall see throughout this book, it is not at all unusual for social scientists to borrow from the theories of the physical sciences. Scientific "paradigms" define a worldview, or a way of perceiving reality, and as such their influence tends to infuse social perceptions in general—including perceptions of organization.

Newtonian physics is about motion, like the motion of a pendulum. Certain dynamic states are called "attractors;" attractors draw surrounding motion toward themselves. The back-and-forth motion of a pendulum, for example, is an attractor; if one places a pendulum near its back-and-forth attractor trajectory, it will naturally move to that state. Motion on an attractor is said to be stable and at equilibrium. Other dynamic states are called "repellors": states that repel motion.

Social physicists used similar terms and concepts to describe social structure. Social behavior gravitates to certain social attractors such as family life and governmental structures. Similarly, social structure is repelled away from other types of social behavior, such as crime or incest. Social structures are stable and at equilibrium with one another; there is, for example, an equilibrium relationship between the responsibilities assumed by family and those assumed by government.

Despite its obvious naiveté, Social Physics, like the Newtonian physics that sired it, introduced ideas into our culture that influence our thinking even today. One such idea involves stability and equilibrium. Organizational theorists and philosophers in the 20th century have debated, often heatedly, whether social structures are stable and at equilibrium, or patently unstable. Philosophers in the 1920s from what is called the Chicago School of thought (which included such noted thinkers as Albion Small and John Dewey) argued that social structure never rests, that any semblance of stability is, in reality, a fleeting period of transition lying between two periods of dynamic change. Talcott Parsons, a sociologist from the 1940s and 1950s, proposed a stability view of society that was far more sophisticated than, but otherwise similar to, that of Social Physicists. Dynamic equilibrium (a more active form of stability) is a key concept in Open Systems theory. Indeed, much of organizational theory presumes some form of stable relationships among actors—that's why (at least in part) we call these things we are studying *organizations:* they are organized, stable systems. A group of theorists we will call anti-positivists, by contrast, reject notions of stability that imply generalizations across groups. The Social Physicists defined the debate, and we still struggle with it today.

Newton and Social Physics underscore yet another important element of the Western mindset: its ideas about causality. Newton's physics is premised on assumptions of relatively simple relationships between cause and effect. This is not to imply that Newtonian physics and its primary tool, calculus, are themselves in any way simple. Rather, it suggests that physical behavior is functionally, directly, and almost exclusively related to relatively few input variables. The volume of gas in a cylinder is functionally, directly, and exclusively related to pressure and temperature. One can determine the trajectory of an object given knowledge of its position and velocity. This is what I mean by relatively simple relationships between cause and effect. Outcome is not complicated by impossibly large numbers of inputs, events aren't muddled by circular effects (at least not after equilibrium is achieved), and effects can be traced to definable causes.

This defines not only our scientific mindset, but our social mindset as well. Even today we assume that events have causes, even when logic would tell us otherwise. When bad things happen to us, we often ask ourselves what we did wrong to cause our misfortune. We believe if we had only done something differently we would not have suffered the outcome we experienced. Teachers seek to understand the causes of misbehavior in a given student; principals try to predict the outcomes of their actions or believe that they can control organizational futures with certain definable behaviors. We assume that our problems, our behaviors, and our futures are products of simple, identifiable causes.

A growing number of organizational theorists are disputing this mindset, however. They argue that outcomes are the product of complex interactions among multiple actors, and that cause/effect is circular and nonlinear instead of one-way and linear. Parents socialize children *and* children socialize their parents. Futures cannot be controlled by simple acts, nor can student behavior be explained with simple models. To these theorists, Newton deluded us about causation—a fact that we are beginning to find is even true in physics (see Prigogene, 1997; and Marion, 1999, for example). Organizational perspectives have been significantly "complexified" in recent years. Strategic Choice theorists have argued that organizations define their own reality, Garbage Can theorists argue that decisions are often derived illogically, and Population Ecologists argue that organizations have multiple goals, many of which have little to do with organizational effectiveness and most of which are poorly specified. The real world, they say, is much crazier than the orderly universe in which Newton and Social Physicists led us to believe.

ROUNDTABLE

This book is more than a repository of information. It focuses on stimulating you to interact mentally with organizational theories, to critique various theoretical perspectives, to apply theory to practice, to make connections among different theories, and to figure out what theory means for school administrators. One of the vehicles by which this is accomplished is the "Roundtable" discussion question. You are encouraged to debate these Roundtable questions in small groups, then to debate the group's positions with those of other groups in your class. Other vehicles that you will find scattered throughout the book are "Activities" (games, simulations, questionnaires, and experiments that underscore or explore given points); "Research Topics" (that outline possible research papers you can develop—most are appropriate for class projects but some are intended to stimulate thesis projects); "Case Studies" (that tell stories to help you understand theories in practical context); and "Diary" (that helps you structure your conclusions about each chapter). Following is the first of the Roundtable discussion questions.

Administrative behavior all too often confirms the power of the Newtonian mindset in Western culture. Planning, for example, is premised on the Newtonian/Social Physics assumption that social organizations are stable and predictable, and consequently that the future can be controlled. Planning is something of a sacred rite in administration—leaders establish their 'virility' (speaking without reference to gender) with their prowess at planning (how many of you have seen new administrators initiate their tenure with strategic planning efforts?) The cultural genes we inherited from Newton and the Social Physicists (among others—I must state that it is too simple to attribute this mindset to just one or two causes) say that planning is good and productive; modern logic suggests it may be overrated. The lessons of modern organizational theorists suggest that organizational dynamics are far too ambiguous and unstable to be planned. So which is right? Are we wasting our time in endless planning meetings and cluttering our shelves with useless five-year plans, or are our planning activities keeping our schools strong, pertinent, and productive? Does all this have any implications for the nature of planning in education?

HERBERT SPENCER AND SOCIAL DARWINISM

Social Darwinism exists on something of a different logic plane than Social Physics. It has a somewhat different view of causation than did Newton, although it does not violate the spirit of Newton's view. Otherwise, Social Darwinism just doesn't talk about the same ideas that Newton discussed, so we can't really say that Social Physics "evolved" into Social Darwinism. Social Darwinism dominated our beliefs about social dynamics in the last half of the 19th century, and even had significant influence over events that occurred in the 20th century. Consequently, Social Darwinism exerted important influence over the way organizations were run during this period of time.

Social Darwinism, obviously, is based on Darwin's theories of natural selection in biology (again, social science takes its cues from general science). Darwinism attributes biological structure to a series of mutational accidents, the most effective of which survive. In a sense, natural selection is a sieve that screens out disorder (ineffective structure) and permits only the passing of order. A species that develops effective attributes can compete successfully, thus increasing the likelihood that its structure will survive. Social structures, according to Social Darwinism, likewise "mutate," and the more effective changes pass into the culture, while less effective mutations die.

Causation, according to Darwin, is a blind process; in this he agreed with Newton. Events (causes) occur randomly and produce their inevitable outcomes. The major difference between the two views is that there is no "judging" of outcomes in Newtonian causality. A given cause may produce a useful effect or an effect that is not useful, but once that effect occurs, there is no further action based on benefits associated with the outcome. The Newtonian cause/effect process serves no end— a drinking glass is not round because round is comfortable to the human hand, it is round because gravity (cause) makes it that way. This is called "efficient causation." Darwinian outcome, by contrast, occurs randomly as does efficient causation, but only survives if it serves a useful purpose. Nobody (God or otherwise) initiates the cause/effect cycle in the Darwinian scenario, so there is no pre-decision that certain biological features are needed and others are not. Causes happen randomly just as they do in Newtonian logic, but their outcomes are judged by external agencies and survive only if they pass muster.

The English philosopher Herbert Spencer adopted Darwin's theories for social explanation in the mid-19th century. Indeed, it was Spencer, not Darwin, who coined the famous phrase, "survival of the fittest." Spencer maintained that social change, like biological change, is "judged" for its usefulness by impartial forces, and that only the fittest social structures survive and thrive.

Two different models of social evolution can be found in Spencer's work. His "organismic" model proposes that the parts of a social system interact and cooperate much as do the interdependent organs of a biological system. His "organic" model, by contrast, likens social events to interspecies competition, a view that is more in tune with Darwin's natural selection models than is the cooperation (organismic) proposal. Spencer favored his conflictive (organic) description of sociology, and warned against incautious use of the organismic model.

These models lead one to radically different conclusions about social structure. One would conclude from the organismic model that society is consensual and interdependent. This perspective sounds a lot like the mechanistic models of Social Physicists, particularly their views on stability and social equilibrium. The organic model, on the other hand, is a competition model, and leads to conclusions about variety, divergence, and conflict in society and organization.

Competition or Cooperation

It is rather odd that Spencer would offer such divergent views of society, or that he could even deduce a cooperative, or organismic, model from the works of Darwin. But he did, and herein lies a puzzle that social scientists have struggled with for decades: Is social behavior best described as cooperative or conflictive? The free market philosophy so cherished in Western cultures, particularly the United States, favors a conflict or competition model of economics. Business and politics are described as dog-eat-dog worlds, and public institutions, such as education, must compete with one another for limited financial resources and public favor. Even so, it is hard to imagine how anything positive could emerge from a system in which every personal and corporate gain comes only at the expense of another, or how unity of purpose emerges out of ruthless competition.

Even so, Spencer's organic model of social dynamics, the competition model, is probably more widely accepted than is his organismic, or cooperation model. Organizational structure, for example, is commonly interpreted in terms of power and struggle over scarce resources; this view is evident, for example, in the works of Population Ecologists such as Michael Hannan and John Freeman (1977). There have been voices who advocate a cooperative view of organization, however; sociologists Talcott Parsons and Edward Shils (1951), for example, echoed Spencer's organismic model when he proposed that social structures were basically stable and at equilibrium relative to one another. Open Systems theorists of the 1960s and 1970s opted for a more cooperative view of organization, as have recent Complexity theory models.

ACTIVITY

A game called Prisoner's Dilemma can help clarify issues raised by Spencer's "indecision" about cooperation or competition, and I encourage students to find a partner and play a few rounds. Prisoner's Dilemma is a zero sum game in that one wins only at the expense

TABLE 1.1   Prisoner's dilemma.

	Prisoner A Rats	Prisoner A Doesn't Rat
Prisoner B Rats	A gets 3 years B gets 3 years	A gets 5 years B gets 0 years
Prisoner B Doesn't Rat	A gets 0 years B gets 5 years	A gets 1 year B gets 1 year

of someone else. Ostensibly, then, it would seem to favor a competition perspective of organizational behavior; as you shall see, that is not necessarily the case. The game is fairly simple to play. Imagine that you and your game partner have been arrested on suspicion of theft. The two of you are taken to separate rooms in the police station for questioning. Each of you is asked to provide evidence against your partner; you are told that by doing so you could get a lighter sentence. You are informed that your partner is being offered the same options, however. If you tell on your partner and your partner does not tell on you, he or she will get a heavy sentence of five years in prison and you will get off scott-free. If both of you tell on each other, the prison officials will compromise and give both of you three years; if neither of you rat, both of you will get one year in prison on lesser charges. What do you do? Do you betray your partner and go for total freedom? If your partner is equally ruthless, both of you will get three years instead. Do you trust your partner and go for the one-year sentence? You could wind up with five instead. You don't know what your partner will do, and herein lies the dilemma. The problem can be illustrated as a contingency table, as shown in Table 1.1.

You and your playing partner should mark your decisions secretly on paper, then compare decisions. But there is one more catch: The game is not played just once. You will play it repeatedly, comparing decisions after each round. Thus, if you betray your partner in one round of play, he or she will remember it in the next round. Your score for each round is the number of years in prison you would have gotten, and your score for the game is the total number of years across rounds. About 25 rounds should be sufficient, and the winner is the person who accumulates the least number of years in prison. You may want a separate person to call a surprise end to play—if players know when the rounds are to end, they will inevitably go for betrayal on the last round, knowing there will be no retribution.

Play the game several times, and each time try a new strategy. You might, for example, play one game as a betrayer, then try another as a cooperator. Try making random decisions (to keep your partner off guard). Try a tit-for-tat strategy in which your first play is cooperation (nonbetrayal), but subsequent rounds mimic the immediately preceding behaviors of your partner. Try a forgiving variation of tit-for-tat in which you occasionally forgive your partner's betrayal. Try changing partners each round. At the end of play, revisit the question raised by Spencer's variations of Social Darwinism: Is society basically competitive or cooperative? You are encouraged to consider this issue now and as you study the next few chapters of this text. Consider in particular how the answer to this question affects organizational leadership style and how the answer relates to organizational productivity, innovation, and change.

The Impact of Social Darwinism

During the latter half of the 19th century and even into the 20th century, Social Darwinism affected businesses' decisions, economic philosophy, public policy, and social welfare issues. In particular, it provided corporate magnates with a strong argument against governmental intrusion into their affairs. They argued, quite successfully, that governmental laws would only disrupt the economic selection process and would perpetuate the existence of weak and nonproductive businesses. Social welfare legislation was similarly perceived: Society will weed out the weak if left to its natural designs. The result was exploitation and social injustice. We all have seen pictures of grimy children posing before the mineshafts in which they worked from dawn to dusk, or have heard stories of pregnant women delivering their babies while on the job. (Coincidentally, it was at this same time that the great educator Horace Mann argued for universal, common schooling and an educated citizenry; this would seem to contradict the more elitist attitude implied by Social Darwinism. An interesting study could be made of whether Social Darwinism and Mann's common school movement, both powerful social forces of the time, were compatible or contradictory.)

Probably the worst offense of Social Darwinism was perpetuated by the politics of Nazism, however. Hitler and his supporters liberally applied survival of the fittest logic to justify their racial cleansing policies—policies that resulted in the deaths of over six million Jews and other peoples.

What caused the degeneration of Social Darwinism into such moral dilemma? The validity of the Darwinian perspective has survived numerous assaults and maintains its descriptive potency to this day. Yet how can we tolerate a theory that spawns such excesses? The answer is in the assumptions. Both Darwin and Spencer made an untenable assumption about evolution, and it was this assumption that led to the problems. Correct the assumption, and the excesses will disappear. The incorrect assumption they made is that the sieve of natural selection will produce ever *better* life forms (or, in the case of Spencer, ever better social forms); that, like microcomputer makers, nature is forever producing improved versions of its products. If this were true, then the Nazis were right (albeit immoral): nature should be left to its weeding. The assumption is not true, however, and the Nazis and 19th-century social policy were wrong.

What *is* the ultimate life form on Earth? Humans? What about cockroaches? They've been around a lot longer than we have, and if that nuclear winter ever arrives, they'll probably be the survivors. What is the principle threat to human survival? We, as humans, probably are a major threat to our own existence ("I have seen the enemy, and it is us"—Pogo), but I suspect that an even bigger threat is posed by "lowly" bacteria and viruses. These are life forms that can barely be called life, yet they threaten the very existence of the king of the hill. Who can say that an inhabitant of Wall Street is a higher life form than a Bushman of Africa? The Bushman's capacity to thrive on what to us would be barren land is legendary. Plunk Wall Streeters down in Bushman country, and their stocks and bonds will contribute little to their survival. Obviously, we need a revised definition of what natural selection does.

The answer is simple: natural selection produces a life or social form that is adequate for survival *in its environment*. Such a life (or social) form is not the best possible form (for "best" is an indefensible, relative term), nor is it necessarily better than previous forms. Fit systems are good survivors; they can efficiently and effectively glean resources from their surroundings, but they are not best. There are no superior men, no superior races, no ultimate social structures. Natural selection maintains survival congruency with environment, that's all. We needn't put up with self-serving excesses to accept the tenets of natural selection.

Natural selection died as a major force in organizational theory in the early 20th century; it did so partially because of its excesses. It reappeared briefly in the 1950s, this time without its superiority complex. It resurfaced again in the 1970s and 1980s under the title "Population Ecology" to become a major macrotheory in organizational studies. We will discuss this "improved" variation (I am aware of the contradiction) in Chapter 9.

Theory and Morality

The story of Darwinian excesses is an interesting history lesson, but it also says legions about morality and theory, and it calls on us as school administrators to struggle with difficult moral issues of practice. Theory-building is a quest for understanding, but what if that quest leads us to answers that are harmful to some, as happened with Social Darwinism? Should we cherish knowledge regardless of whom it harms? Should we assume that knowledge will ultimately serve the greater good? Policy-makers in the 19th century assumed, based on Spencerian theory, that a laissez-faire relationship between industry and government would ultimately serve the betterment of society; they apparently assumed either that the harm inflicted on workers by this policy was necessary, or they ignored the harm altogether. A truth that transcended individual existence was, after all, at work to improve society.

The fact that a given theoretical perspective causes harm to individuals should have encouraged caution, however. One should be particularly cautious when a theory serves the interests of those with the power to act on its implications, for those perpetuating the theory and benefiting from its ramifications are easily blinded to mistaken perceptions. Theoreticians and practitioners have a responsibility to impartially scrutinize the assumptions underlying their theoretical guides for weaknesses (something we should do regardless of moral dilemmas, of course). Indeed, this is an important role for the academicians in a society. Social Darwinism and its excesses have become testimony to this.

The issue of morality in theory-building is more complex than these introductory observations suggest, however. A theory's implications can indeed be injurious in the short run but helpful in the long run; there are times when we must do difficult things for ultimate gain. Economic theory, for example, demands that nations sometimes implement austerity policies, with all the attendant misery this can create, in order to maintain a healthy long-term economy. Social theory requires that we inflict the "misery" of schooling on our young, all for the ultimate benefit of children and society. Short-term pain is not proof of immoral or flawed theory, it is instead a flag that requires attention, a caution that obligates us to carefully scrutinize and, when necessary, revise our models.

Theory can actually serve to protect against excesses. Researchers have, at times, studied questions society would consider inappropriate or unpopular, such as questions of IQ and race, or (in one recent controversial case) natural selection and rape. Academics are charged with finding the truth, but society often penalizes those whose efforts lead them to unpopular conclusions. How do we deal with such dilemma? Do we not serve society best by allowing its academics the latitude to ask the questions they wish, even when those questions may be unpopular or even deliberately biased? Theoretical stricture provides protection against such scientific excess without the hazards of popular restraint. Theory forces academicians to ground their conclusions in solid explanation. There is no credible theory that satisfactorily explains why one race would be genetically more or less intelligent than another, for example, and research that makes such a claim must defend itself against the glaring absence of rationale. Lack of theoretical support suggests that such findings may be attributed to any of a number of causes, such as culturally biased testing or unequal access. Researchers who ask these questions should not be sanctioned for seeking knowledge, but they should be expected to support generalizations and should not subject our morality to ungrounded claims.

Some argue that theory should go a step further and cater to our sense of morality. Educator and philosopher George Counts (1932) argued, for example, that curriculum should reconstruct history to serve our perceptions of a just future. Postmodernists argue that reality is of our own making and we should consequently create perceptions of reality to serve justice, that theory should be united with struggles for social and moral change (Horkheimer, 1972). In an overview of postmodernist Critical theory, Jermier (1998) stated that social scientists take sides on important issues even when they strive for impartiality. Since scholars cannot rid themselves of normative content, he concluded, they should openly deal with their partiality. The arguments are compelling but one must, of course, provide safeguards to ensure that such license does not produce excesses every bit as dangerous as those of Social Darwinism.

THE PUNCTUATION OF SOCIAL DARWINISM

Theory experiences periods of stasis punctuated by periods of rapid change. Stasis refers to a worldview, a generalized perception of reality and propriety, what Thomas Kuhn (1970) has called a "paradigm." A paradigm both limits and enables research and theory-building—limits because it discourages questions that are not encompassed by the paradigm, and enables by focusing and unifying research. Long association with given paradigms is punctuated by periodic, often dramatic, periods of change, or punctuation. The rise and fall of Social Darwinism, at least as it relates to theories of organization, is our first good illustration of paradigm and punctuation. Social Darwinism had a significant impact on the way organizations were structured and run during the last half of the 19th century, and social scientists of the day built their basic tenets into a rather sophisticated model of social behavior. By the beginning of the new century, however, Social Darwinism was faltering under the weight of its moral dilemmas. Predictions and behaviors derived from Social Darwinism were causing difficult-to-resolve problems. Further, Darwinism is an epic theory. It speaks of mass movements and national events. Individual humans are lost in all this epic-ness; indeed, humans are mere flotsam, fuel, in this grand picture of events. Predictably, this was to rub our collective egos a bit raw. People wanted to know how they, personally, could affect organizational life. What activities of leadership, for example, would produce improved organizational productivity? How can school principals improve the achievement of their student wards? How can superintendents and school boards foster educational effectiveness? Spencer's talk of natural selection and evolution was fine, but where are the implications for leadership behavior?

Furthermore, progress in the late 19th and early 20th centuries demanded a more down-to-earth, hands-on approach to management. Industry and technology were advancing at a tremendous rate; it was the gilded age of bigger and better. The old age of the heroic magnates who "single-handedly" amassed great fortunes and massive industries by ruthlessly climbing to the top of the natural selection mountain was passing. The mature industrial revolution needed greater efficiency; it needed strategies for systematizing and consolidating its gains. Natural selection provided no guidance about how to accomplish this.

This is the ambiance against which the stories in the next chapter emerge.

Incidentally, in the Prisoner's Dilemma game, how long did it take you to realize that attempting to "beat" your opponent (competition strategy) caused you to rack up a lot of years in prison? This suggests that cooperation is a better strategy for accomplishing one's personal desires, and, I argue, even suggests that cooperation is a better model of evolution than is survival of the fittest. Do you agree? Why?

Diary

You are encouraged to start a diary of reflections on the readings and exercises in this course and to make entries in that diary after each chapter is completed. This diary might be expanded into a portfolio that includes evidence that you have mastered certain skills and concepts. The last section of each chapter will offer recommendations for topics to discuss in your diary. The idea is for you to articulate your leadership persona, to stake out your position on a variety of leadership issues, and to identify ways in which theory can inform leadership behavior. The diary is a codification of personal and class debates: it will help you organize your thoughts, formulate questions and issues about the material in each chapter, remember the key issues that were developed in each chapter, and help you mature your leadership and management styles.

In your diary entry for this chapter, summarize your thoughts on the Roundtable discussions that were proposed. You are also encouraged to reflect on the following questions (and on any other thoughts that you may have struggled with as you read the chapter, of course):

- What is the relationship between theory and practice?
- What do "equilibrium," "stability," "attractors and repellors," and "motion" have to do with understanding organizations and leadership?
- Is causation indeed blind, as Newton has argued? Is it focused on improvement in an accidental sort of way, as Darwin argued? Or do we make our own futures, as most of us want to believe?
- Should social scientists shy away from asking questions that are morally reprehensible?
- How do you think schools should be run? Reflect on some general principles that guide your thoughts about organizational leadership. How should a leader relate to faculty and staff? How should one implement change? How do you motivate people? How does a leader deal with conflict? What is the role of leadership in a school? We will ask this leadership question at the end of each chapter. Concentrate on using the training provided in this course to modify your leadership personality.

Recommended Readings

Kuhn, T.S. (1970). *The structure of scientific revolutions* (2nd ed.). Chicago: The University of Chicago Press.

This short but powerful book should be on the "must read" list of every academic. Kuhn, a science historian, proposes that scientific knowledge has accumulated over the centuries in sudden surges, rather than incrementally as most people believe. He calls these surges "paradigm shifts," or precipitous revisions in, or new insight about, nature. A paradigm shift (such as the shift to a Copernican universe and to Einstein's relativity) marks the onset of a new mindset about scientific reality. Once accepted, the new reality develops and grows, and much of science revolves around that reality and will reject research that does not reflect the prevailing dogma. The mindset shapes the very questions asked about nature, and leads us to ignore or belittle evidence that fails to support the current theory.

Research Journals and Trade Magazines for Organizational Theory

Students of organizational theory will find journals and trade magazines indispensable to their study. They are typically the most up-to-date source of current thought available. The contents of journals and trade magazines will reflect patterns of organizational thought. At present, Critical theory and Institutional theory are popular and you will find many articles devoted to these subjects. In the 1980s, Culture theory was popular; in the 1970s, it was Contingency theory. Journals will reflect the paradigm of the day, and it is interesting to track the evolution of theory in their pages.

Let me offer a few hints on using journals to do research. This is the way I do it; perhaps your professor will use a different strategy and you should discuss that with him or her. The start of a research project is often daunting. You possibly know relatively little about the subject you want to research, which makes matters even more difficult. Without knowing who some of the major writers in a subject are, it is difficult to know how to get started. There are "tricks of the trade," however.

First, identify the theoretical period in which your topic was popular, if indeed it was limited to a certain period in time, and begin in journals for that period. If you are looking for works on Selznick's Institutionalism, for example, you will look in the journals published in the 1940s and 1950s. If you are interested in the modern revisions of Institutionalism, go to journals from the 1980s and 1990s. If you are interested in decision making, the subject is timeless and you would start in the present.

Go to the end of the period (or a little beyond) and work backward. You will depend heavily on the reference section of different studies. Since researchers can't provide references that weren't yet written, you will finish your literature review more rapidly by working backward instead of forward.

Peruse the table of contents of the most recent journal for the period you are researching. When you find something that looks promising, jot down a quick reference and read the abstract for the article. If that looks promising, examine the article's references.

You are looking for several patterns in all this. First, you will try to define the time period during which researchers were interested in this subject, if you haven't already done so. Second, you will try to get a handle on the different approaches to the subject. If, for example, you are doing research on Contingency theory, you will discover that early researchers struggled with definitions of environment, whether it was best measured as external events (such as market instability) or as internal manifestation of external environment (nature of raw material, for example). Third, identify researchers who seem to be the major writers on the subject. Who does everyone seem to reference? Fourth, identify articles by these major writers. Begin with the major writers, then look at some of the less central ones.

Following are a few of the important journals and trade magazines with which you should be familiar. Your professor will likely add to this list for it is hardly complete. For a more complete discussion of journals in educational administration and organizational theory, refer to *Cabell's Directory of Publishing Opportunities in Education* (1998). This two-volume set is updated every few years, and is arguably the definitive source of information about journals in education.

AASA Professor
AASA Professor, published by the American Association of School Administrators, includes articles on general administration and supervision, summaries of research, practical applications of research, and topics in higher education.

Administrative Science Quarterly
Administrative Science Quarterly, published by the Johnson School of Management at Cornell University, is one of the more prestigious journals in organizational

theory. *ASQ* publishes papers on organizational behavior and theory, sociology, social psychology, strategic management, economics, and industrial relations. It publishes qualitative papers, quantitative work, and purely theoretical papers. A review of books important to the field is included.

Education Week
Education Week, published by Editorial Projects in Education, Inc., is a weekly newspaper of current events for elementary and secondary school educators.

Educational Administration Abstracts
Educational Administration Abstracts, published by Sage Publications, is a comprehensive and convenient source of research abstracts in educational administration. Entries are organized by subject and descriptor, and alphabetically by author. Concise summaries of contents are provided. The fourth issue of each year contains the cumulative author and subject indexes for the year. There are over 1,000 entries per year.

Educational Administration Quarterly
Educational Administration Quarterly, published by Sage Publications, provides current information on research and practice in Educational Administration. Topics include restructuring, leadership strategies, administration leadership, decision making, and school politics. *EAQ* is consistently listed among the top 10 journals in the *Social Sciences Citation Index*.

Educational Leadership
Educational Leadership is the official publication of the Association for Supervision and Curriculum Development. *Educational Leadership* is known for its theme issues on current educational trends.

Educational Management & Administration
Educational Management & Administration, published by Sage Publications, publishes articles on management, administration, and policy in education. Articles include critical discussions, accounts of new methods, analysis of theory and practice, developments and controversial issues, research reports and analyses from researchers, practicing managers, and administrators.

Human Relations
Human Relations, published by Sage Publications, was inaugurated in the mid-1900s as an outlet for the pioneering works of Human Relations theorists. Its original editorial board and early contributors included some of the best known theorists from that era—E. A. Shils, Douglas MacGregor, Kurt Lewin, Lester Coch, and John French, to name a few. Two issues per year provide reviews of books that are important to the field.

The Journal of Management Education
The Journal of Management Education, published by Sage Publications, prints original research on teaching management and organizational behavior. It covers such areas

as human resources, organizational behavior, public administration, management consultation, gender issues, organizational culture, organizational communication, and industrial and labor relations.

Organization

Organization, published by Sage Publications, contains articles on organization theory and behavior, strategy and strategic management, human resources, management and employment relations, comparative and international management, organizational sociology and psychology, and organizational economics. It also includes a book review section.

Phi Delta Kappan

Phi Delta Kappan is the publication of Phi Delta Kappa, International, a fraternity for educators. It addresses policy issues for educators at all levels. It includes the well-known Gallup/PDK Annual Survey of Public Attitudes toward Public Education in its September issue.

The School Administrator

The School Administrator, published by the American Association of School Administrators, publishes articles on educational management, administration and supervision, the principalship, and the superintendency. The articles address issues of practical application of research.

References

Cabell, D. W. E. (1998). *Cabell's directory of publishing opportunities in education* (5th ed.). Beaumont, TX: Cabell Publishing Company.

Counts, G.S. (1932). *Dare the school build a new social order?* New York: John Day.

Hannan, M., & Freeman, J. (1977). The population ecology of organizations. *American Journal of Sociology, 82,* 926–964.

Horkheimer. (1972). Traditional and critical theory. In *Critical theory: Selected essays* (pp. 188–243). New York: Seabury Press.

Jermier, J.M. (1998). Introduction: Critical perspectives on organizational control. *Administrative Science Quarterly, 43*(2), 235–256.

Kuhn, T.S. (1970). *The structure of scientific revolutions* (2nd ed.). Chicago: The University of Chicago Press.

Marion, R. (1999). *The edge of organization: Chaos and complexity theories of formal social organization.* Newbury Park, CA: Sage.

Parsons, T., & Shils, E.A. (Eds.). (1951). *Toward a general theory of action.* Cambridge, MA: Harvard University Press.

Prigogine, I. (1997). *The end of certainty.* New York: The Free Press.

CHAPTER 2

Managing Tasks

Closed Systems theory and the efficiency movement of the early 20th century were logically inevitable byproducts of the Industrial Revolution. That revolution had spawned the assembly line and standardization, and factory owners wanted to squeeze even greater returns out of their machines. The result was a "scientific" search for efficient production techniques, efficient management procedures, and efficient organizational structure. Efforts in these three areas produced, respectively, the fields of Scientific Management, Administration Management, and Bureaucracy theory. Scientific Management, which was championed by researchers such as Frederick Taylor, Frank and Lillian Gilbreth, and others, studied details of the production process in order to shave wasted effort. Administration Managers, notably Henri Fayol and Mary Parker Follett, sought strategies such as command unity, division of work, and centralization of decision making, for making the administration process more efficient. Bureaucracy theory, which is indelibly linked with the work of German sociologist Max Weber, proposed organizational structures that enabled efficiency, reduced conflict, and made it possible to coordinate the massive governmental and private sector organizations that emerged in the 20th century. Collectively, these theories are referred to as Machine theory.

Machine theory derives its name from the perception that its models ignore worker needs and conceptualize organization and leadership much as one would approach the management of machinery. One might consider this a rather inhumane approach to management, but we shall see that this reputation is not entirely justified. Indeed, Machine theory's focus on worker concerns likely helped to spawn a large middle class in Western society and the concurrent reversal of economic and social dynamics that had led philosophers such as Karl Marx and Thomas Malthus to predict rampant

21

poverty and worker revolution. Nonetheless, one can certainly see where the nomen, Machine theory, comes from, for these models focus rather heavily on workflow strategies for improving worker efficiency. The models seek ways to make workers produce more, although not, as is often assumed, by making them work harder. It does explore ways to make business more efficient, but it does not necessarily do so at the expense of human need. Indeed, the theorists who framed these models recognized that inhumane exploitation would work against the goal of productivity rather than advancing it.

Although these theories evolved a century ago at the end of the 19th and beginning of the 20th centuries, they are potent forces even today, at the beginning of the 21st century. One modern offspring of the Machine theory movement, ergonomics, is of particular interest in this age of computers. Ergonomics is the science of efficient workstations. Its interest is in producing chairs, desks, data entry procedures, and such that maximize productivity, realizing that the health of the human operator is a key element of efficiency. In government, business, and education, bureaucracy is still the preferred style of organization, although there is now evidence that this structural archetype is replaceable (we will examine this evidence in the chapter on culture). Even so, the fingerprints of our Bureaucracy legacy are clearly evident in the way we organize and run schools.

And no matter how "modern" and sophisticated our theories have become, we cannot escape the necessity for efficient and effective production, whether that production is cars or education. Efficiency and effectiveness are subjects we will visit repeatedly throughout this book, and they inevitably will lurk behind most definitions of leadership to be developed during the course of this study (Chapter 11, which is about moral leadership, will provide the only exception). Machine theory may be "old social science," but social scientists have found it a challenge to escape its precepts.

In this chapter, students will:

- Understand the principles of Scientific Management.
- Explore how Scientific Management has influenced the institution of education.
- Critique a scientific approach to decision making.
- Develop strategies for efficient leadership.
- Examine different perspectives on the nature of communication in efficient organizations.
- Examine and critique Bureaucracy theory.
- Explore the impact of bureaucracy on educators.
- Refine their definitions of the role of leadership in education.

FREDERICK TAYLOR AND THE SCIENTIFIC MANAGEMENT MOVEMENT

Industrialist Frederick Taylor is considered the father of Scientific Management, but Taylor was hardly the only actor in its development. Contractor Frank Gilbreth and his wife, Lillian, developed the idea of motion study and of the closely related fatigue study; they even used the budding technology of motion pictures in their analyses. (Classical movie buffs should recognize the Gilbreths: the film, *Cheaper by the Dozen,* was based on their rather large family). J. Sellers Bancroft, of William Sellars & Company in Philadelphia, studied metal-cutting techniques as early as 1869 (several years before Taylor began his studies), and those studies probably influenced Taylor's subsequent work on the same subject (Wrenge & Greenwood, 1991). Captain Henry Bancroft, also of William Sellars & Company, developed proposals about a foreman's responsibilities that likely influenced Taylor's notion of "functional foremanship." Documents from Midvale Steel Company (where Taylor did his early work) suggest that Charles Brinkley, a chemist at Midvale, developed time study and piece-rate practices before Taylor even arrived at Midvale (Midvale Steel Company of Philadelphia, 1917). Taylor and Scientific Management, then, did not emerge from a vacuum and Taylor did not single-handedly create Scientific Management. Clearly, however, his work brought this "science" to its maturity, and it was Taylor who popularized its ideas; for that reason, we call him its father.

Frederick Taylor was born in Germantown, Pennsylvania (a suburb of Philadelphia), in 1856. Taylor grew up in wealth under the tutelage of a mother whose child-rearing practices were based on "work, and drill, and practice" (Copley, 1923, p. 52). A story told by one of his childhood friends illuminates something of Taylor's personality and helps us understand where Scientific Management originates. The story has to do with how Taylor played croquet:

> [Croquet was] . . . a source of study and careful analysis with Fred, who worked out carefully the angles of the various strokes, the force of the impact, and the advantages and disadvantages of the understroke, the overstroke, etc. (Copley, 1923, p. 57)

Taylor approached management in the same way: carefully working out the advantages of competing workflow strategies and personnel policies. His almost neurotic attention to detail and efficiency translated into his influential theory of management.

Taylor's early experiments with Scientific Management began in the 1870s in the Midvale Steel Company in Philadelphia. In the subsequent two decades, the principles he derived from these experiments were successfully implemented in other steel mills and in industries as diverse as construction, armament production, paper production, link belt production, and apparel manufacturing. These experiments explored strategies for improving production procedures and for managing worker implementation of efficient procedures.

Early in his tenure at Midvale, Taylor observed that production procedures were based on individual intuition and learned habits, and that procedures varied from worker to worker. He argued that production procedures should be standardized around methodology proven to be efficient. One should determine which metalworking tool was most efficient at rough milling, for example, and should mandate its use for all initial cutting. With the support of management, he sought answers to questions such as, "How deep can a saw cut into metal without stalling, and what type of saw blade will cut the deepest?" "What is the optimal speed at which saws should be drawn through metal?" and "What is the optimal tension on the belt drive of a metal boring machine?" Later in his career he would experiment with questions such as, "What can be done to improve the performance of golf drivers and putters (he obtained patents on these answers—golfers will recognize the Taylor-Made brand of clubs)?" "What is the optimal temperature to which metal should be heated when it is forged?" and "What is the best shovel size for shoveling coal (he concluded that a man could work most efficiently with a shovel that scooped up 21.5 pounds of rock; subsequently, the Wyoming Shovel Works began selling a "scientific shovel" based on this conclusion)?"

Taylor's questions were not generated haphazardly; they emerged out of careful observation of operating procedures. To accomplish this "careful observation," Taylor proposed a procedure called "time and motion study." Operating procedures are first analyzed to determine their component activities (select saw blade, feed blade through the metal, draw the saw at a given speed and depth, for example). Each component of the process is carefully analyzed and timed (Taylor and his associates developed forms and a special stopwatch for performing these measurements). The researcher then experiments with different strategies for each activity, again carefully measuring how long it takes to perform the activity with each variation. Different types of saw blades might be tested in cutting metal, for example. Such experiments often led to the development of improved technology—new types of saw blades might be suggested, or new ways to feed the blade might be found.

Discovering the most efficient methods for performing a task was only half the battle, however; Taylor knew that management techniques had to be developed for assuring that standardized procedures were implemented. He consequently developed four managerial activities. The first involves careful bookkeeping to track productivity and to provide ongoing data for analysis. The second requires careful planning of workflow procedures before they occur (some would say that this was his most valuable contribution to effective organizational management).

The third activity was what he called functional foremanship. Traditionally, a single foreman had been responsible for all aspects of workflow on a shop floor. Taylor recommended that the responsibilities be divided among five different foremen: (1) the instruction card man, responsible for daily planning and instructions; (2) the time man, responsible for keeping track of employees' time; (3) the inspector, who assures product quality; (4) the gang boss, who sets up and communicates the procedures that are issued on the instruction cards; and (5) the disciplinarian, who tracks worker performance and adjusts wages accordingly (Wrenge & Greenwood, 1991).

Worker Incentives

The fourth element of Taylor's management plan deals with worker motivation. Early in his career, Taylor had experienced difficulty convincing workers to adopt the changes he implemented. Workers preferred their old way of doing things and resented his efforts at change. He tried piece-rate wages, but found that it failed to promote quality work. Further, this strategy simply caused worker resistance because of the implicit wage cuts associated with piece rate (if piece rates were set above current productivity levels, workers felt, correctly, that their wages had been cut). Taylor's solution was to submit daily written instructions to workers detailing tasks and time allowances for each task. Workers who met the daily goals were given extra wages, while those who fell short were given ordinary wages for the day. This solution worked reasonably well, although it penalized workers whose failure to meet goals was related to factors beyond their control, such as equipment failure or late arrival of raw materials.

Taylor's attention was drawn to this issue of worker incentive while he was a foreman at Midvale Steel Company by a rather interesting and dramatic set of incidents; these events have implications that we will refer to when we discuss Human Relations theory. The source of these events was something called "soldiering." According to Taylor's account:

> As soon as I became gang boss [at Midvale], the men who were working under me and who, of course, knew that I was onto the whole game of soldiering, or deliberately restricting output, came to me at once and said, "Now Fred, you are not going to be a damn piece-rate hog are you?" I said, "If you fellows mean you are afraid I'm going to try to get a larger amount from these lathe . . . . Yes, I propose to get more out." . . . They said, "We warn you, Fred, if you try to bust any of these rates we will have you over the fence in six weeks." . . . Now that was the beginning of a piecework fight which lasted for nearly three years . . . in which I was doing everything in my power to increase the output of the shop, while the men were absolutely determined that output should not be increased. (*Taylor's famous testimony,* 1926, p. 122)

In his later reflections, Taylor admitted that the men he supervised at Midvale were poorly paid. In particular they weren't paid to produce more, so they had little incentive to work harder. That didn't deter his efforts, however. He tried hiring hard-working men, but his recruits quickly succumbed to social pressure to soldier like their co-workers. When Taylor intensified his insistence upon increased productivity, machines began "mysteriously" breaking, and Taylor retaliated by charging workers for breakage even when breakage was clearly accidental. Eventually the workers capitulated and began producing what Taylor considered to be a fair day's work, but his painful experience sufficiently impressed him that it influenced his subsequent proposals on wage incentives.

Scientific Management and Social Justice

It seems odd to speak of social justice after discussing such harsh methods of management as Taylor's "war" on soldiering, but indeed Taylor was concerned about worker welfare. His concern wasn't necessarily altruistic, however. Rather, he felt that if workers did not share in the wealth produced by increased productivity, they would resist productivity initiatives (as they had in the soldiering story), and that resulting worker unrest would hamper economic advances.

In the opening sentence of the first chapter in his landmark 1911 book, *Principles of Scientific Management,* Taylor states, "The principal objective of management should be to secure the maximum prosperity for the employer, coupled with the maximum prosperity for each employee" (p. 1). He believed that this was the most important aspect of his entire management philosophy, and he called it a "Mental Revolution" (Wrenge & Greenwood, 1991). Scientific Management, he argued, required a mental revolution among workers—dramatic new attitudes about work—and a mental revolution on the part of management—on their duties toward workers. "Scientific management involves a complete mental revolution on the part of the working man . . . [and an] equally complete mental revolution on the part of [management] . . . toward their fellow workers." (Taylor's Famous Testimony, 1926, p. 103). This "mental revolution" that Taylor advocated was an important element in the development of a strong middle class in America and Europe (although it is undoubtedly accurate to emphasize that Taylor was an advocate of such egalitarian principles rather than their progenitor).

ROUNDTABLE

Should Scientific Management have been imported into fields such as public education, however? Are there differences among organizations, their tasks, their products, their raw materials, and their workers, that make some more suitable than others for Taylor's principles, and is public education one of those exceptions? We will develop answers to such questions later in this book; for now, I would encourage you to grapple with the issue of Scientific Management in education. The idea is to try to "discover" what later theorists have discovered, to probe the chinks in Scientific Management and in the Closed Systems perspective, generally. The following questions should help guide your thinking:

- To what degree is public education, its organizational structure, its management, and its control, influenced by Scientific Management principles?
- How else could public education be structured? This question is meant to foster a sense of how a given "worldview" or "paradigm" can constrain one's perception of how things can be done. Paradigms often prevent us from exploring alternative ways of performing a task, just as expectations often prevent one from realizing that his or her lost keys may be in the unexpected rather than the expected place. To get you started on this question, you might think about how hospitals are organized. You might also consider why hospital and public education structures differ as they do when both developed at about the same time.
- In what ways is Scientific Management unsuitable for use in public education? Consider tasks, raw materials, workers, and products. There is an underlying assumption ultimately at fault here: what is it?

Decision Making from a Taylorian Perspective

John Dewey is responsible for a decision-making model that is still popularly taught to teachers and school administrators (I most recently heard it offered as a process for making decisions in team teaching settings). Dewey, like Machine theorists, evoked a "scientific method" in his approach to workflow (in Dewey's case, the workflow is public education instruction). He felt that education should be based on the experiences of life and on scientific investigation. Dewey's decision-making model was not intended to be an administrative tool, it was intended as a model to be used by children as they explore their environment, but has been adapted for administrative decision making. Although Dewey rejected kinship with Machine theory, his decision-making strategy (as applied in organizational theory) is strikingly related to Scientific Management precepts, and consequently will be presented as a decision-making model in the spirit of Machine theory.

The model is a recipe of sorts for decision making, and looks something like this:

1. Identify a problem, one that demands a decision and action.
2. Analyze the problem; understand its underlying dynamics and motivations thoroughly. Don't assume that the surface features reflect what is really going on. For example, if teachers are threatening to strike for increased wages, ask whether the underlying problem is indeed wages or is it related to other factors, such as low morale.
3. Brainstorm possible solutions to the problem. Here anything and everything goes on the table without critique. What may appear "off the wall" at first blush may turn out to be a good solution on later reflection.
4. Analyze each possible solution; consider pros and cons.
5. Choose a decision after all have been analyzed.
6. Implement the decision and monitor its effects. The impact of the decision may reveal or produce new problems that need to be cycled back into step 1 of the model.

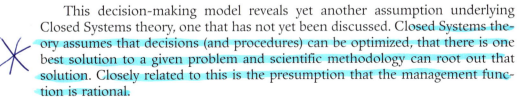

This decision-making model reveals yet another assumption underlying Closed Systems theory, one that has not yet been discussed. Closed Systems theory assumes that decisions (and procedures) can be optimized, that there is one best solution to a given problem and scientific methodology can root out that solution. Closely related to this is the presumption that the management function is rational.

Optimization is grounded in the Closed System's assumption that all relevant variables in a problem can be discovered and controlled. Problems are not unduly complicated by multiple goals and complex causation; thus, scientific thinking can produce clear understanding and the best possible decisions. The closely related notion of rationality suggests that, because goals and causations are manageable, problems can be logically solved. That is, if efficiency is the only organizational concern, and if science can answer all questions of efficiency, then solutions to problems can be clearly mapped and rational decisions can be formulated.

ROUNDTABLE

This model obviously makes useful points and you should appreciate them. However, I encourage you to critique the assumptions of each point in the model. What dynamics might teachers and school administrators bring to the decision-making table that undermine the effectiveness of this model? How do you think subsequent 20th-century theorists will conceptualize the issue of decision making? Under what conditions might the model be useful and under what conditions is it not useful? We will revisit decision making several times throughout this textbook, and will be addressing these questions at those times.   ■

LEADERSHIP FUNCTIONS

In the early years of the 20th century, managers primarily focused on the production process and considered humans to be adjunct to that process. They sought to make their machinery ever more efficient and productive, and likewise sought to forge work groups that were ever more efficient and productive. The stories we have been telling—Frederick Taylor's soldiering experience and his time and motion studies, Frank and Lillian Gilbreth's use of cinema to study fatigue—are testimony to this. Leaders were perceived as practical scientists who were thoroughly familiar with the production process and who were able to wring every last ounce of productivity out of that process.

Taylor and his colleagues focused primarily on the workflow of an organization; the nuts and bolts of efficient production, so to speak. Other theorists in the first half of the 20th century were interested in issues of management at higher organizational levels, issues such as organizational structure and coordination. Organizational theorists James March and Herbert Simon (1958) labeled these efforts "Administration Management theory."

French industrialist Henri Fayol was perhaps the earliest and most famous proponent of Administration Management theory. Unlike Taylor, whose experiences led him to write about production processes, Fayol's observations reflected his experiences as a top executive in the French mining industry. His principle contribution to the management field was *Administration Industrielle et Générale* (or *General and Industrial Management*), published in 1916 and first translated into English in 1929. In this book, Fayol proposed five basic functions of management—planning, organization, command, coordination, and control. These functions, according to Fayol, are universally applicable across many different types of organizations, including business, government, military, and religious organizations. Fayol developed a comprehensive list of 14 management principles from these five general principles. Fremont Kast and James Rosenzweig (1970) summarize these principles as:

1. Division of Work. The principle of specialization of labor in order to concentrate activities for more efficiency.
2. Authority and Responsibility. Authority is the right to give orders and the power to exact obedience.
3. Discipline. Discipline is absolutely essential for the smooth running of business, and without discipline no enterprise could prosper.
4. Unity of Command. An employee should receive orders from one superior only.

5. Unity of Direction. One head and one plan for a group of activities having the same objectives.

6. Subordination of individual interests to general interests. The interest of one employee or a group should not prevail over that of the organization.

7. Remuneration of Personnel. Compensation should be fair and, as far as possible, afford satisfaction both to personnel and the firm.

8. Centralization. Centralization is essential to the organization and is a natural consequence of organizing.

9. Scalar Chains. The scalar chain is the chain of superiors ranging from the ultimate authority to the lowest rank.

10. Order. The organization should provide an orderly place for every individual. A place for everyone and everyone in his place.

11. Equity. Equity and a sense of justice pervade the organization.

12. Stability of Tenure of Personnel. Time is needed for the employee to adapt to his work and to perform it efficiently.

13. Initiative. At all levels of the organizational ladder zeal and energy are augmented by initiative.

14. Esprit de corps. This principle emphasized the need for teamwork and the maintenance of interpersonal relationships. (p. 66)

Fayol insisted that these principles should not be rigidly applied to all situations and that they were subject to modification and expansion. "For preference," he wrote in *General and Industrial Management*, "I shall adopt the term principles whilst dissociating it from any suggestion of rigidity. Seldom do we have to apply the same principle twice in identical conditions: allowance must be made for different changing circumstances." (Fayol, 1949, p. 19)

Administrative Management theory was expanded considerably in the 1920s and 1930s, and is even the inspiration (whether consciously or not) for popular perspectives on management today. In 1937, Luther Gulich and Lyndall Urwick proposed a number of Fayol-sounding principles, including proposals that one top executive should be the source of authority in an organization, there should be a unity of command, and wages should be linked with responsibility. Today there are management gurus who propose activities for effective leadership that sound a lot like the old Fayol system, activities such as being proactive, being goal-oriented, prioritizing, self-renewal, thinking win/win, and cooperation.

Communication and Administration Management

Perhaps one of the more famous Administration Management theorists, after Fayol, was a social worker from Boston, Mary Parker Follett. Follett wrote from her vast knowledge of governmental organizations and business management. Her writings were unique in that she considered organizational dynamics to be driven as much by social and psychological processes as by economic ones. While Fayol wrote of the power of position, Follett wrote of the situational nature of power (Hofstede, 1984). Follett is categorized as a Machine theorist because she wrote in the tradition of, and was a contemporary of, this school, but her perspectives on organization fit comfortably in the Human Relations tradition as well.

Follett advocated "the acceptance of authority, the importance of lateral coordination, the integration of organizational participants, and the necessity for change in a dynamic administrative process" (Kast & Rosenzweig, 1970, p. 67). In 1932, Follett summarized her views as four principles:

- Coordination through direct contact between persons involved.
- Coordination in the early stages.
- Coordination as the reciprocal relating of all factors in the situation.
- Coordination as a continuing process.

Even a cursory comparison of these points with Fayol's principles reveals significant differences. In particular, she differed with Fayol on the matter of communication. Fayol (and other Machine theorists) felt that managers—the rational and scientific wizards of the organization—should be firmly in control of communication; thus, communication should flow through a hierarchy. If a worker needed to tell something to another worker, he or she passed the message through one or more bosses (in reality, workers rarely had anything of importance to say in this scenario, so upward communication was often a moot point). Follett, by contrast, proposed direct rather than hierarchical coordination of activities. If two people at the same hierarchical level needed to talk with one another, they should do so. Similarly, Follett advocated the distribution of power and authority throughout the lower ranks of the hierarchy. In short, she proposed that organizations could obtain greater efficiency if they relaxed their insistence on strict class structure (referring to their hierarchical control structures) and by loosening their control over interaction and decision making.

It is typically assumed that other Machine theorists of the period focused on hierarchical communication to the exclusion of horizontal communication (interaction among workers at the same level of authority). Owens (1995), for example, wrote that Follett's principles "clashed with the typical classical preoccupation with hierarchical communication and control" (p. 285). Kast and Rosenzweig (1970) wrote that "Her [Follett's] ideas . . . on the importance of lateral communication . . . differed substantially from those of other writers" (p. 67). These claims are largely accurate; Fayol's summarizing principles give no hint to the contrary, and Weber (whom we will discuss momentarily) made vertical communication one of the cornerstones of the ideal bureaucracy. However, they are not entirely true; Fayol, at least, was aware of the drawbacks in the hierarchical communication structures that Follett would later emphasize.

In his book, *General and Industrial Management,* Fayol developed a principle known as the "gangplank concept." He observed that two positions in a hierarchy, each of which is separated from the top position in an organization by 10 nonoverlapping hierarchical levels, could only communicate with one another by transmitting messages through 20 different levels of authority. The originator would have to communicate upward to the CEO through 10 levels of authority; the CEO, in turn, would forward the communication down 10 levels to the recipient. This, he argued, would "inconvenience many people, involve masses of paper, lose weeks or months to get to a conclusion less satisfactory generally than the one which could have been obtained via direct contact . . . " (Fayol, 1949, p. 35). This problem could be resolved, he proposed, if a "gangplank," or direct channel of communication, could be established linking the two horizontal positions. This is strikingly similar to Follett's proposals about direct coordination, and suggests that, in the years prior to the Human Relations movement, theorists were at least tentatively beginning to modify the strict, machine-like conceptualization of organization.

ROUNDTABLE

It was popular during the heyday of Closed Systems theory to go one step beyond Fayol and Follett with handbooks that prescribe detailed management behavior. A Canadian institute called the Lincoln Extension Institute, Inc., for example, wrote a series of training books for factory foremen between the mid-1920s and the mid-1950s. These books, published by the H.W. Hill Printing Company, bore such titles as *The Forman—His Job* (1930), *The Workman—His Development* (1948), *The Foreman—His Leadership* (1942), *The Foreman—His Personality* (1945), and *General Factory Control* (1940). The 1930 book, *The Forman—His Job*, written by Col. E.C. Peck (who wrote many of the books in this series), included a checklist for effective supervision; parts of that checklist are presented below. Assume this was written as a checklist for effective supervision in an educational organization and critique it. Identify the underlying Machine theory assumptions and discuss their weaknesses. The task may not be particularly easy, and your first reading of the checklist may leave you feeling that it is rather reasonable. If so, does this suggest that we, today, are still somewhat under the influence of the Closed Systems worldview, and how so? Are there elements of that worldview that should indeed be applicable for effective supervision—then and today?

Roundtable Specimen: Select Items from Col. E. C. Peck's "How Do You Rate as a Supervisor?"

These questions were intended to be rated as "Always," "Usually," or "Seldom." Users counted the responses in each rating category to obtain supervisory profile scores. The text associated with the scale said that "[The Rating Check-list (sic)] will give you a good estimate of your qualifications as a supervisory executive. It will also guide you by letting you know wherein your weaknesses lie. You can refer to it constantly for guidance. [It will help you understand your] possibilities in your advance up the executive scale" (p. 126; the scale itself is on a foldout sheet following that page).

Sample questions include:

Do I know all the rules and regulations that are necessary to me?

Do I obey the rules and regulations?

Do I avoid any show of favoritism or partiality among the men?

Do I consider the workers as individuals?

Am I fair in my dealing with every man as well as with other foremen?

Do I help both old and new workers willingly when they need it?

Do I try to anticipate their gripes?

Do I reprimand only when necessary?

Am I usually cheerful?

Do I represent management to the workers?

Do I make decisions myself instead of running to the boss?

Am I constantly alert for shortcuts that will help my men and the plant?

Am I aware of costs and am I trying to keep them down?

Do I refuse to take any legalized graft (nylons, cigars, butter)?

Do I conduct myself in a manner which commands respect at all times?

Do I get all the facts on a situation before reaching a decision?

Do I avoid excesses such as continued heavy drinking, profanity, etc.?

Do I try to advance myself by study?

Am I alert to the safety and health of my workers?

BUREAUCRACY THEORY

Bureaucracy evokes thoughts of unpleasantries—long lines, rude behavior by employees, endless forms and red tape, and being passed from department to department to complete a simple task. Bureaucracy has indeed been guilty of such public relations excesses; but bureaucracies have also been indispensable to government, the military, and business for over a century. The increasing complexity of organizations during the late stages of the Industrial Revolution rapidly overtaxed the coordinating capacity of personal, or patriarch-like, managers. The Henry Fords and Cornelius Vanderbilts of business could no longer manage organizations by the strength of their personality and charisma; personalized management styles had to be replaced with more depersonalized and rational strategies. We may not like bureaucracy, but we learned during the early decades of the 20th century that we need it.

The German sociologist, Max Weber (pronounced Mahx Vay'ber), is indelibly associated with the development of Bureaucracy theory. Weber's work in this area is only a small (albeit important) part of his broader interest in the development of Western civilization, however. He wrote, for example, of the influence of religion on the rise of capitalism, and he rejected the Marxian emphasis on economics in social dynamics. Because of Weber's contributions to understanding of the roles of religion, ideology, economics, charismatic leaders, and industrialization in the development of Western society, he has been called the father of modern sociology.

Weber's work with Bureaucracy theory can best be understood within the larger context of his sociological proposals. Weber wrote that there are three types of authority:

- Traditional authority—resting on an established belief in the sanctity of immemorial traditions and the legitimacy of those exercising authority under them.

- Rational-legal authority—resting on a belief in the "legality" of patterns of normative rules and the right of those elevated to authority under such rules to issue commands.
- Charismatic authority—resting on devotion to the specific and exceptional sanctity, heroism, or exemplary character of an individual person, and of the normative patterns of order revealed or ordained by him (Weber, 1947, p. 328).

Traditional authority is that which is vested in royalty or feudal leadership. Charismatic authority is vested in leaders who capture public imagination and devotion, such as Gandhi or Dr. Martin Luther King, Jr. Rational-legal authority is grounded within the legal system of a nation. Weber argued that only the traditional and rational-legal authority structures are sufficiently stable to afford long-term governance, and that, while charismatic leadership may serve to initiate or strengthen a governance structure, it must eventually be replaced by traditional or rational-legal authority. For example, India won its independence from Great Britain under the charismatic leadership of Mohandas Gandhi. The nationalistic fervor and unity that he inspired, however, were not sufficient for the more mundane, ongoing governance of a large and complex polity, thus his charismatic leadership was replaced in the 1950s by a rational-legal authority structure.

Bureaucracy, according to Weber, is the most efficient form, thus the highest expression, of rational-legal authority. Weber's Bureaucratic theory, however, is not a blueprint for organizational control; rather, he saw it as an "ideal type" or generalized model of governance. It is not "ideal" in the normative sense; rather, it represents the most salient features of his solution to the need for efficient control of large, complex systems. Weber felt that an "ideal model" provides organizations something against which to evaluate their own needs and structures.

Richard Hall (1963) has distilled six dimensions from Weber's conceptualization of bureaucracy:

1. A division of labor based on functional specialization.
2. A well-defined hierarchy of authority.
3. A system of rules covering the rights and duties of positional incumbents.
4. A system of procedures for dealing with work situations.
5. Impersonality of interpersonal relations.
6. Promotion and selection based on technical competence.

Weber suggested that division of labor serves to compartmentalize components of the organizational task, thus allowing each to be performed by persons or groups with specialized knowledge and skills about the given component. The responsibilities of each person or group, then, are well defined and clearly delineated from other responsibilities. This reduces the possibility of redundancy and interpersonal conflict over relative responsibilities and increases efficiency. Further, offices within the hierarchy have clearly defined authority over lower-level offices, and are in turn supervised by clearly specified, higher-level offices. Since responsibilities and authority are carefully defined, the system can be coordinated with rules and procedures rather than through personal supervision;

this permits more efficient operation and, again, tends to blunt interpersonal conflict. Finally, appointment and promotion are based on impersonal, thus rational, appraisal of merit.

Critique of Bureaucracy Theory

Perhaps the first critique of Bureaucracy theory in anyone's mind is the very impersonality that Weber advocated. Impersonality is useful when it translates into fairness; it is quite another thing when it becomes uncaring abuse of position. Weber himself was concerned about the potential for this, and spoke of participants being reduced to "cog[s] in an ever-moving mechanism," and of imprisoning humanity in an "iron cage" (1947, p. 228). Closed Systems theory gave Weber the license to organize his models solely around the efficiency needs of the organization. Such systems are not crafted to "interface" effectively with environmental elements, such as clients. Bureaucracy theory provides keys to the internal environment but fails to provide keys to the external environment. Clients and their problems, in other words, are expected to conform to the existing bureaucratic structure rather than vice versa, and where this conformity fails, the client is not served. At best, the client is frustrated and angered by the need to jump through bureaucracy's impersonal hoops—hoops that, to the client, makes no sense, but that are entirely rational within the Closed Systems perspective. This is Weber's "iron cage."

Sociologist Robert Merton defines one variation of this problem. His logic begins with a Machine theory premise: human variability must be reduced to increase predictability and efficiency (see Fig. 2.1). In bureaucracies, human variability is controlled by rules. Clearly defined rules (reliability) provide the impersonal authority for decisions needed to solve problems, which in turn reinforces the need for rules. Put more prosaically, impersonal rules serve to solve problems efficiently and, consequently, to increase service to, and decrease conflict with, clients. Merton argues, however, that this ideal model spawns unanticipated consequences that thwart what bureaucracy is intended to achieve. Bureaucratic rules and procedures encourage rigid behavior by bureaucrats, which leads to, rather than controls, difficulty with clients. As we said earlier, clients resent jumping through what are, to them, unfriendly and illogical hoops, and when their problems are unique, the rigid structure is unable to help clients. Conflicts with clients, in turn, cause organizational members to increase rigidity as a way of defending their authority and behavior. This cycles back into increased rigidity of rules and feeds a vicious cycle of conflict and rigidity.

This is known as "goal displacement." Goal displacement occurs when the organization becomes focused on the path to its outcome rather than the outcome itself: when the means become the end. Bureaucracies tend to supplant the efficiency function of rules with a defense function. Closed Systems theory assumes a single-minded focus on efficiency. Without this singular focus, when some other goal or goals creep into the mix, the whole deck of cards is compromised. The very structure that Weber proposed for achieving efficiency, however, serves to create just such a competing goal: defense of the organization by

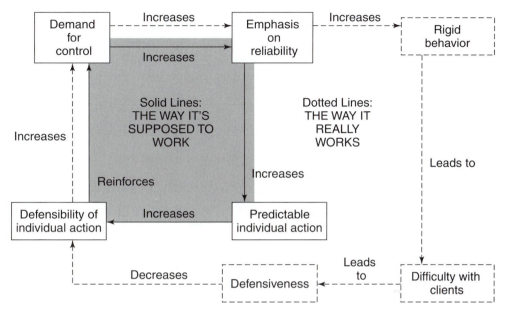

FIGURE 2.1   The Merton model of bureaucratic behavior.

From James G. March and Herbert A. Simon, *Organizations* (New York: Wiley, 1958), p. 41. Copyright © 1958 by Blackwell Publishers, Ltd. Adapted by permission.

enforcing and refining rules. The rules become less a tool of efficiency and more a tool of control and survival.

The same rigidity can lead to internal organizational problems as well, according to organizational theorist Alvin Gouldner. Gouldner proposed a model of unintended consequences that begins just where Merton's began, with bureaucratic emphasis on control and predictability (see Fig. 2.2). This leads to emphasis on impersonal rules and, in turn, decreases visibility of power relationships—that is, rules decrease the need for personal supervision. The decreased dependence on supervisory power relationships fosters reduced interpersonal tension, thus reinforcing the dependence on rules.

That's the way it's supposed to happen: impersonal rules reduce internal conflicts and enhance predictability, control, and efficiency. What actually happens, according to Gouldner, is that rules, which are intended to define a baseline for behavior, in reality establish maximum behavior. Workers do only what is expected of them by the rules. Organizational goals are consequently short-changed, thus forcing increased supervision; increased supervision sparks increased tension, and increased tension solidifies dependence on rules.

School principals who require teachers to sign-in in the morning, who draw a red line under the last name at 8 a.m. in order to impartially sanction late

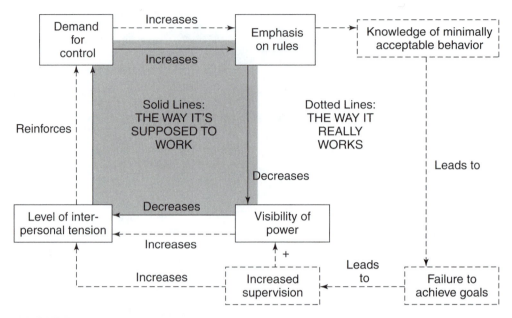

FIGURE 2.2   The Gouldner model of bureaucratic behavior.

From James G. March and Herbert A. Simon, *Organizations* (New York: Wiley, 1958), p. 45. Copyright © 1958 by Blackwell Publishers, Ltd. Adapted by permission.

teachers, and who monitor to assure that teachers don't leave in the afternoon before 3:30, will likely experience what Gouldner is talking about. The principal's general goal may be to foster professional commitment, and the rule is implemented to assure that teachers will be at school before and after classes. It may have just the opposite effect, however. If the teachers feel demeaned, they may interpret the rules as maximum standards and arrive only moments before 8 a.m. and will be standing at the door waiting to leave at 3:30. The professional atmosphere goal is consequently unmet and the principal may feel the need to increase supervision; this exacerbates interpersonal tensions and leads to more rules. In another example, a principal may implement a dress code intended to improve the moral climate of a school by prohibiting students from wearing T-shirts with obscene messages. However, students will inevitably test the boundaries of such rules, and the dress code becomes the boundary standard rather than the minimal standard. Perhaps it doesn't technically prohibit, say, obscene pictures, so there is an increase in this problem, to which the principal responds with revised rules. The morality goal is unmet, and the atmosphere is ripe for increased supervision and tension and for additional rules.

ROUNDTABLE

This is a topic that warrants further class discussion. We all agree that rules are necessary, but how can we avoid the problems of which Gouldner warns? We tend to think of the Department of Motor Vehicles or the Internal Revenue Service when we think of bureaucracy, but school systems are bureaucracies as well. How do Merton's and Gouldner's cautions apply to education? In what ways do we do some of the same things that so anger us about the IRS or DMV?

Hyperrationality

The dependence and proliferation of rules explicit in the bureaucracy model of organization can also lead to what is called "hyperrationalization," or conflicting goals. If a principal enforces a rule banning head wear, but another rule requires head wear in classes that prepare food, the rules conflict with one another. Such a simple dilemma can be worked out by allowing exceptions, of course, but hyperrationalization typically involves more complex problems than this.

To illustrate, let's say that a given rule is either enforced or it is not enforced; that is, a given rule is either "on" (enforced) or "off" (not enforced). Imagine a set of such rules in a given setting. If the rules are independent of one another (let's call this a $k = 0$ state in which each rule is dependent on the status of 0 other rules), then optimal enforcement can be readily achieved—simply turn each rule "on." If, on the other hand, $k = 2$ (each rule is dependent on the status of exactly two other rules; see Fig. 2.3), and if some rules conflict with others (the "on" status of one rule forces the "off" status of another, for example), irreconcilable problems can arise. Further, these problems tend to cascade throughout the network, with one conflicting problem leading to yet another. Incompatibilities such as this are called "conflicting constraints." When the level of interdependency among actors or rules is even moderately high, a few conflicting constraints can generate an irreconcilable mess. That is the hyperrationality dilemma. It occurs when rules proliferate unchecked and when rules are created without careful consideration of how each new rule fits into the larger network of regulations.

Diary

- Given what you have learned in this chapter, what are some important functions of leadership? In what way does your answer change your answer to the leadership question in your diary entry for Chapter 1?
- Identify errors in the Closed Systems perspective.
- Try to put yourself in the shoes of a manager from the late 19th and early 20th centuries to understand the appeal of Scientific Management. Certainly the ultimate appeal was profit, but I believe there was a more individualistic, siren-like attraction inherent in this philosophy. What might it have been?

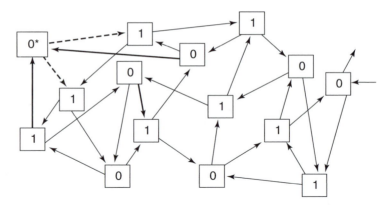

FIGURE 2.3 A network of rules, with k = 2 (each rule is dependent on the states of 2 other rules). 1 indicates an "on," or implemented, rule, and 0 indicates an "off," or unimplemented, rule. For example, the unit in the upper left corner (with asterisk) represents a rule that is not implemented because of the nature of its interaction with two other rules (linked to it by arrows); had these three rules all been compatible, the asterisked rule could have been on. The off state of the asterisked rule, in this case, enables two other rules to be achieved (follow the arrows leading away from the asterisked box). Rules can interact in complex ways—a rule can be on only if another is off, for example, or a rule may depend on the interactive status of two other rules. Such complexity is magnified across a network like the one suggested in this figure.

- Scientific Management is about efficient operation. For what functions of the educational operation is this philosophy appropriate? What specifically are some strategies for making an administration office more efficient?
- Review the discussion of Mary Parker Follett. Do you think women bring a unique, feminine perspective to the study of organization? Explain.
- Most would agree that the institution of public education is a bureaucracy. What sort of problems does this pose for the professionals (faculty and administrators) who must function within this governmental bureaucracy?
- Perhaps the most glaring problem underscored by Gouldner's and Merton's models of bureaucracy is the absence of an effective link with the environment. Explain.

Recommended Readings

Frymier, J. (1987). Bureaucracy and the neutering of teachers. *Phi Delta Kappan,* 9–14.

Jack Frymier, of Phi Delta Kappa, International, an educational fraternity, argues that teacher creativity and productivity are stifled by bureaucratic rules and authoritarian administrators. He argues that the problem with education is not insufficient control, as state legislators often argue, but too much control.

Hall, R. (1968). Professionalization and bureaucratization. *American Sociological Review, 33*(1), 92–104.

Hall, a noted authority on organizational bureaucracy, has provided an excellent summary of the major elements of bureaucracy theory, along with a categorization and definitions of professionalism in this readable article. He discusses what he calls "professionalization," or the process by which a discipline achieves professional status. Hall examines professionalization within the context of organizational structure and studies the relationships among bureaucracy, structure, and professionalization. This article is particularly pertinent to educators, since education functions within what Hall calls the "heteronomous bureaucracy," or a bureaucracy of professionals (governmental services are a major example).

Wrenge, C.D., & Greenwood, R.G. (1991). *Frederick W. Taylor, The father of Scientific Management: Myth and reality.* Burr Ridge, IL: Irwin.

A thorough, well-written biography about the life of Frederick Taylor. Organizational theory textbooks, like those in most disciplines, tend to perpetuate myths and incorrect information about historical personages and events. They do this, in part, because they derive information from each other, and once a mistake enters academic traffic, it is hard to correct. Misinformation is also propagated by incomplete or selective coverage of lives and events. This is the case with Frederick Taylor. Few realize that Taylor was genuinely concerned about worker welfare, and have heard only of his "demeaning" mechanistic philosophy. This less flattering view was current as early as the 1920s, and worker strikes are known to have erupted when it was even rumored that plant managers were considering adoption of Taylorian principles. Unfortunately, academics have done little to correct this misperception in the intervening years. The best way to protect against such errors is to read the original texts for one's self. The second best way is to read authors who have themselves visited the original documents. Wrenge and Greenwood fall into this latter category.

References

Copley, F.B. (1923). *Frederick W. Taylor: Father of scientific management.* New York: Harper & Brothers.

Fayol, H. (1949). *General and industrial management* (Constance Storrs, Trans.). London: Sir Isaac Pitman & Sons, Ltd.

Hall, R.H. (1963). The concept of bureaucracy: An empirical assessment. *American Journal of Sociology, 69,* 32–40.

Hofstede, G. (1984). *Culture's consequences: International differences in work-related values* (Abridged edition). Beverly Hills, CA: Sage Publications, Inc.

Industrial relations, final report and testimony submitted to Congress by the Commission on Industrial Relations. Document No. 415, 64th Cong., 1st Sess. (1914) (Testimony of Frederick W. Taylor).

Kast, F., & Rosenzweig, J. (1970). *Organization and management*. New York: McGraw Hill Book Company.

March, J.G., & Simon, H.A. (1958). *Organizations*. New York: Wiley.

Midvale Steel Company of Philadelphia. (1917). *Fiftieth anniversary: 1867–1917*.

Owens, R.G. (1995). *Organizational behavior in education*. Boston: Allyn & Bacon.

Taylor, F.W. (1911). *Principles of scientific management*. New York: Harper & Brothers.

Taylor's famous testimony before the special house committee. (1926). *Bulletin of the Taylor Society, 11*(3-4), 95–196.

Weber, M. (1947). *The theory of social and economic organization* (A.H. Henderson & Talcott Parsons, Trans.). Glencoe, IL: Free Press.

Wrenge, C.D., & Greenwood, R.G. (1991). *Frederick W. Taylor, the father of scientific management: Myth and reality*. Burr Ridge, IL: Irwin.

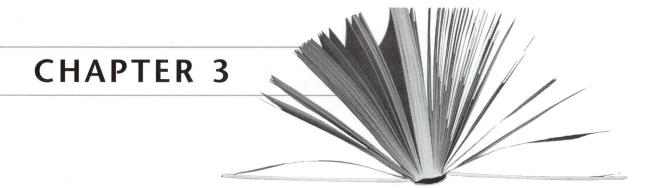

CHAPTER 3

Supervising People

The Human Relations movement was about workers and their needs. It began, roughly, in the 1920s (although its roots run a bit deeper), reached maturity in the 1930s, and was of particular importance in organizational theory through the 1950s. Important conclusions that emerged out of this movement are still taught to aspiring educational administrators and still influence the way managers deal with their employees. Human Relations theory relates organizational performance to personal and social needs and behaviors; it seeks to understand those behaviors and to increase organizational productivity with effective human relations intervention. Human Relations is classified as a Closed Systems theory because of assumptions of unitary goals (efficiency and effectiveness), but its proponents were more sensitive to environmental influences than were proponents of Machine theory (for example, one of its major advocates, Elton Mayo, was concerned about the effects of workers' home lives on plant productivity).

Several currents of thought influenced the Human Relations movement. The works of Freud, Jung, and others on the human psyche were important in defining the movement, and are particularly evident in the pioneering human relations work of Elton Mayo. Sociologist Vilfredo Pareto's work with logical and nonlogical thinking, social systems, equilibrium, the function of language, and the circulation of elites provided the theoretical framework for the important Hawthorne studies (see Kast & Rosenzweig, 1970). Spencer's notion of organismic systems is evident in much of the writings on human relations. We have already considered the contributions of Mary Parker Follett and Henri Fayol to principles of decentralized decision making, control, and communication.

41

This chapter examines Human Relations theories and their applications to modern educational leadership. It will look first at Elton Mayo's famous work with the Hawthorne studies in Cicero, Illinois, and how the results of this study influence leadership behavior even today. We will move from there to a discussion of three traditional lines of study in Human Relations theory. Some of the earliest of these studies examined human motivation and worker psychology. These studies included what is arguably the most widely taught model of human motivation in organizational theory: Maslow's Hierarchy of Needs. The second line of research in Human Relations dealt with the nature and influence of informal groups, or naturally emerging social groups in organizations and in communities. The third research tradition in Human Relations theory examined the dynamics of organizational change. It proposed that workers are more receptive to change when they participate in decision making about the change.

In this chapter, students will:

- Examine the premises and implications of Human Relations theory.

- Apply psychological models of human motivation and behavior to educational settings.

- Critique Maslow's work from a woman's perspective.

- Explore whether the psychological models of behavior accurately explain the motivation of teachers.

- Examine employee satisfaction, and try to explain why teachers so often "burn out."

- Develop leadership strategies for preventing low morale and burnout among teachers.

- Build personal techniques for dealing effectively with school and community informal groups.

- Develop a facility for fostering change in educational settings.

- Understand the shortcomings of a Human Relations approach to change.

- Refine their definitions of the function of leadership in education.

ELTON MAYO AND THE HUMAN RELATIONS MOVEMENT

Human Relations theory is usually attributed to the work of the industrial psychologist Elton Mayo. Mayo was born in 1880 in Australia, and in 1911 he received an Honours Degree, Bachelor of Arts in Philosophy from the University of Adelaide in Australia. Mayo's father was a physician and Mayo himself received medical training, although he left that training because of anxieties about his career commitment (a problem of esteem that plagued Mayo's early years). In part because of this skirmish with medicine, however, Mayo was drawn to the infant field of psychiatry and showed considerable aptitude for working with people. Mayo's subsequent work in management psychology was clearly influenced by this interest. There is even evidence that he provided psychiatric counseling to employees in plants where he consulted, and "indeed, the record seems clear that Mayo had an extraordinary capacity to touch people who were in distress and for whom a healer was a godsend" (Trahair, 1984, p. 2).

Mayo argued that management policies (such as Scientific Management) that fail to consider the human condition tend to disrupt an individual's organic equilibrium. This problem exacerbates, or is exacerbated by, poor social experiences in the worker's home environment. Mayo proposed that such disruptions cause unhealthy mental states, which result in unbalanced vital signs such as elevated blood pressure or pulse rate. These mental states, in turn, lead to reduced productivity.

Mayo sought ways to restore organic balance and re-establish the equilibrium in organizational life. One of his primary lines of research dealt with worker fatigue. He argued, for example, that workers who were on their feet for extended periods of time needed periodic rests to maintain organic balance and be fully productive. At the Continental Mills in Philadelphia (makers of woolen fabrics), Mayo implemented 10-minute rest periods during which workers lay on cots with their feet elevated. He found that workers were less fatigued at the end of the day, and he claimed to have improved plant productivity by 30% and reduced worker turnover significantly. When the foreman in one department decided unilaterally to stop allowing breaks, productivity declined, thus supporting Mayo's conclusions.

The Hawthorne Plant Studies

In 1928, the Hawthorne Works of the Western Electric Company in Cicero, Illinois (near Chicago), began a series of studies that soon would advance Mayo's reputation and career, and that would set the stage for the maturation of Human Relations theory (contrary to popular assumption, Mayo was not the author of these studies). The Western Electric Company, which made telephone equipment at its Cicero plant, was known for its enlightened and experimental approach to management.

The first of the Hawthorne studies was inspired by the work of Frederick Taylor and Scientific Management rather than by Human Relations. The researchers asked the very Taylorian question: Does room lighting affect productivity? With the help of a research service, the National Research Council, company leaders sought to determine the lighting level required for optimal productivity at minimum cost. The results were puzzling, for there seemed to be no relationship, but there was change. Mayo later reviewed these findings and observed that:

> The conditions of scientific experiment had apparently been fulfilled—experimental room, control room; changes introduced one at a time; all other conditions held steady. And the results were perplexing. . . . Lighting improved in the experimental room, production went up; but it rose also in the control room. The opposite of this: lighting diminished from 10 to 3 foot-candles in the experimental room and the production again went up; simultaneously in the control room, with illumination constant, production also rose. (Mayo, 1945, p. 69)

The researchers concluded that a number of psychological variables had intervened in this initial study, so they conducted a more carefully controlled and involved follow-up analysis. They asked six female employees who assembled telephone relays to participate in this experiment (hence it is called the Relay Room experiments). The women's productivity was first evaluated under original work conditions to establish baseline information. To control for extraneous variation (particularly fatigue), participants were then placed in a test room away from their regular departments. Productivity was carefully recorded as the experiment progressed; data were also collected on room temperature and humidity, medical histories, eating and sleeping habits, and conversations in the workroom. The women were unsupervised; instead, there was a research observer in the room who arranged work and tried to maintain a spirit of cooperation.

Changes were introduced into this Relay Room experiment one at a time. A pay incentive program was tried first, followed by 5-minute (and later 10-minute) rest pauses twice a day, then light lunches were provided twice a day, the workday was shortened by a half, then a whole, hour, and the work week was shortened to 5 days. Productivity increased significantly after each stage of the analysis, and remained high for some time after the women returned to their original working conditions.

Why did productivity rise so dramatically? Survey responses from the women indicated that they were motivated by six conditions. In the order of importance, these are:

1. Small groups
2. Type of supervision
3. Earnings
4. Novelty of the situation
5. Interest in the experiment
6. Attention received in the test room (Luthans, 1992)

Interviews with the women revealed that their attitudes toward work in the experimental room differed from their attitudes under the original work conditions. They felt a responsibility for their fellow employees, they liked working without supervision, they developed satisfying friendships and rituals among themselves and even made a ceremony (with cake and ice cream) of the periodic medical exams, they celebrated birthdays, and they helped each other when fatigued (Trahair, 1984).

It is interesting that novelty is fourth on the list of reasons cited by the women. Researchers have deduced the famous "Hawthorne Effect" from this study, which states that subjects will perform better than usual in novel situations (it's also called the placebo effect). Many social scientists likewise attribute the productivity in this (and the original lighting) phase of the Hawthorne study to the special attention given the participants, and to the novelty of the situation (Luthans, 1992). Novelty, however, was not cited by the participants as the most important reason for increased productivity: it followed three issues related to working conditions. What many have traditionally been taught about these experiments, it turns out, does not agree entirely with the facts of the case.

In March of 1928, the manager of the project at Cicero consulted with Mayo on the results from the Relay Room study. Mayo had been looking for an opportunity to advance his research on organic equilibrium, so he was immediately attracted to the project. After reviewing the research reports, he suggested that the company correlate productivity figures with blood pressure and pulse rate data from the women. He argued that productivity is a function of organic equilibrium and could be explained using vital sign indices. The most productive woman in the group did indeed exhibit such equilibrium, but the vital signs data were less predictive of productivity in the remaining subjects. Their output was better described by work habits and general constitution. Nor could the results explain the uncooperative nature of two women who had to be replaced in the study.

Eight months after the Relay Room tests began, Western Electric decided to conduct interviews of supervisors in the plant. Mayo was consulted on the project, and he made a number of recommendations for the interview process. He recommended an indirect interview method, for example, in which interviewers probed for information rather than asking leading questions. He suggested that the results of this phase of the project be used to train supervisors. The interviews were so revealing that Western Electric expanded them to include all 40,000 Western Electric employees—a massive undertaking. The interviewers asked structured questions about employee likes and dislikes, and answers were recorded verbatim.

Some respondents in the study tended to focus obsessively on limited concerns; the researchers attributed this to mental problems brought on by work conditions, fatigue, or stress at home. Researchers also observed patterns of behavior that were related to social relationships within the plant, and this led them to focus their attention on work groups. What they found surprised them. Work groups were deliberately manipulating work conditions and management perceptions of work productivity. For example, the workers in a group often led foremen to believe that tasks were far more difficult to master than they actually were in order to restrict demand for productivity. Researchers concluded that supervisors had less influence over work output and practices than they thought.

Mayo explored the interview study results with a study of 14 male volunteers in what was called the Bank Wiring Observation Room (BWOR). These men operated under normal working conditions with a supervisor, normal working hours, and no exceptional amenities—unlike the conditions in the earlier Relay Room study. Observers did nothing but record what the men said and did. They identified two friendship groups among the subjects. Like the social groupings in the original interviews, these groups managed to control productivity among their members. In follow-up interviews, the researchers discovered that the men feared that if they worked too hard, management would increase expectations or reduce pay rates.

The men controlled productivity with a number of tactics. They had, for example, a practice they called "binging": if anyone violated group work norms, he could be hit hard on the shoulder by another worker. The men also manipulated member behaviors with general social pressures, such as ostracism.

Researchers concluded that productivity was more a function of social conditions than of physical conditions—in stark contrast to the economic motivation assumed by Scientific Management. As Richard Trahair, one of Mayo's biographers, put it, "changes in the technical organization often attacked routines of human association that give value to work. In response, workers protected themselves against such attacks with what appeared to be illogical sentiments and practices" (1984, p. 228).

The Western Electric studies were disrupted in 1932 by economic conditions associated with global recession. By 1936, conditions improved and Western Electric introduced a counseling program based on the results of the earlier interviews. Educated counselors, or "personnel men," were hired; their job was to provide workers with a non-threatening outlet for their problems.

Mayo was associated with the Hawthorne project for the rest of his career (he died in 1949 after publishing his last article on Human Relations that same year). Although the project was authored by Western Electric and the National Research Council, Mayo was indelibly associated with it. In addition to his significant participation in the research, Mayo published extensively on the research and defended the findings against its critics. Because of his significant participation in the research, we often mistakenly, but perhaps appropriately, attribute the study exclusively to Mayo.

THREE TRADITIONS IN HUMAN RELATIONS RESEARCH

Three general categories of research can be identified within the Human Relations tradition. Each of these movements bears clear imprints of the pioneering work of Elton Mayo. The first is a set of studies that dealt with the psychological needs structure of humans; the second examined social structures called informal groups; and the third set explored organizational change. We will discuss each of these in turn.

Motivation and Worker Psychology

The term "motivation" is not typically found in the Scientific Management literature, which suggests that the mechanical worldview of that time blinded its proponents to the notion that workers were anything other than "economic men," or persons who are motivated by physical rewards. The earliest studies of worker motivation didn't appear in the organizational theory literature until the 1920s. These early studies were derived from the writings of Sigmund Freud and Carl Jung. They suggested that motivation is the property of the individual and management can manipulate the psychological state to benefit productivity.

Abraham Maslow's Hierarchy of Needs Perhaps the most famous psychological study to emerge out of the Human Relations movement was Abraham Maslow's Hierarchy of Needs. Maslow's needs-motivation hypothesis was based on his work as a clinical psychologist and on analyses of the personalities of great people such as Eleanor Roosevelt, Thomas Jefferson, and Albert Einstein. He did not intend for it to be used to describe workplace motivation, and only began to write of its potential for understanding organizational motivation 20 years after his original (1943) paper on the subject.

Maslow argued that humans have five types of needs: physical needs, safety needs, love needs, esteem needs, and self-actualization needs. Physical needs are those basic things we need to survive, such as air, water, food, sleep, and sex. Safety is freedom from external threats to physical or emotional survival. Love represents a caring relationship with others, a sense of belonging and affiliation; and esteem refers to respect, power, and status. Self-actualized people are self-fulfilled and have realized their potential.

Maslow organized these needs hierarchically in a priority order such that lower level needs must be largely satisfied before an individual seeks higher level satisfaction (see Fig. 3.1). Thus, a drowning person is deprived of an important physical need and will grab anything, even, say, a shark, in an effort to relieve the deprivation. Only when he or she reaches the surface does concern about the threat to safety represented by the shark exert itself.

Maslow emphasized that one need does not have to be fully satisfied (indeed, no need is ever fully satisfied) before the next level is sought, and that people move among various levels of the hierarchy at different times in their lives. Motivation, he further argued, derives from deprivation of need, not its satisfaction.

The first three levels of need, physical, safety, and love, are called *deficiency needs.* Maslow argued that if these needs are not met, the individual will not experience healthy psychological growth. The next two levels are called *growth needs;* gratification of these helps individuals develop their potential.

Luthans (1992) has translated Maslow's hierarchy into a content model of work motivation. Luthans identified the lowest level of need in a work environment as basic needs, such as pay (see Fig. 3.2). The second level (Maslow's safety needs) is associated with such things as seniority plans, union activity, and severance pay. Luthans called the third level belonging needs; this includes a need

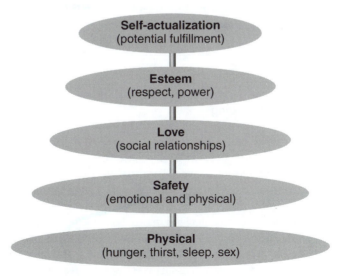

FIGURE 3.1   Maslow's Hierarchy of Needs.

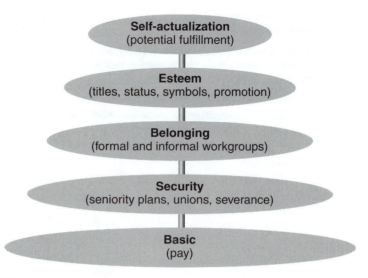

FIGURE 3.2   Luthans' modification of Maslow's hierarchy.

From Fred Luthans, *Organizational behavior,* 6th ed. (New York: McGraw-Hill, Inc., 1992), p. 158. Copyright © 1992 by McGraw-Hill, Inc. Adapted by permission.

for formal and informal group relationships. The esteem level refers to titles, status symbols, promotion, and recognition. The fifth level, self-actualization, is not further defined by Luthans—he accepts Maslow's definition of this need. Like Maslow's model, Luthan proposes a hierarchical relationship among these organizational needs. Unsatisfactory pay structures in an organization, for example, motivate workers to focus on their physical level needs and prevent them from seeking protection against loss (security needs), group participation (belonging needs), title and status (esteem needs), or self-actualization.

ROUNDTABLE

Reformulate Maslow's model (and Luthan's derivation) to describe motivation in an educational setting.   ■

Variations and Critiques of the Needs Hierarchy   Some researchers have argued that different types of organizational experiences provide different types of incentives for their employees—motivation in church settings is different from motivation in factory settings, for example. Clark and Wilson (1961) proposed three such incentives: materialistic incentives, or tangible rewards; solidarity incentives, or intangible rewards derived from the act of association; and purposive incentives, which are intangible rewards associated with the goals of the organization. They further argue that different people are motivated by different incentives. That is, motivation is not necessarily structured hierarchically; rather, motivation is a mat-

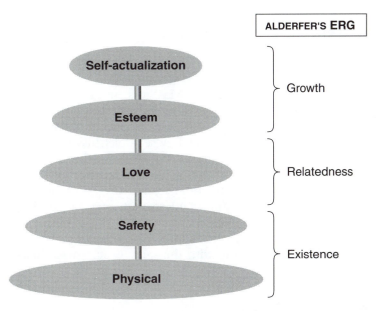

FIGURE 3.3   Luthans' comparison of Maslow's hierarchy and Alderfer's ERG theory. From Fred Luthans, *Organizational behavior,* 6th ed. (New York: McGraw-Hill, Inc., 1992), p. 161. Copyright © 1992 by McGraw-Hill, Inc. Adapted by permission.

ter of personal preferences and personalities. A father can be drowning but still be motivated by concern about the welfare of another family member, for example.

ROUNDTABLE

Do you agree? Does this invalidate Maslow's hierarchy (can a husband be more concerned about his wife's safety than his own, for example)? What is the dominant type of incentive in education, and how does this perspective contribute to your critique of Maslow?   ▪

Clayton Alderfer (1972) attempted to deal with the problems in Maslow's model with a variation he called the ERG theory (Fig. 3.3). Alderfer agreed with Maslow in the value of distinguishing between different types of need and with the need to distinguish generally between lower and upper level needs, but he felt that strict hierarchy and prepotency (the precedence of lower over upper level needs) were indefensible. Alderfer's model collapses Maslow's five needs to three: existence, relatedness, and growth (hence ERG). Existence needs are those that are related to survival; relatedness refers to the need for social relationships; and growth needs are concerned with personal development. Alderfer conceptualized each of these needs as a continuum, thus basic satisfaction of a given need simply intensifies desire for more satisfaction (needs are never satisfied and people don't move from need to need). Further, like Clark and Wilson (last paragraph), Alderfer argued that different people jump into the needs structure at different places—some seek growth, for example, even when their physical needs are largely unmet.

Maslow and Women   Maslow's hierarchy was a subject of Carol Shakeshaft's and Irene Nowell's (1984) feminist critique of organizational theory. Shakeshaft and Nowell argued that Maslow's model is androcentric; that is, it was shaped by male-oriented bias. "The effect of his conceptualization of the levels of need which motivate people," they wrote, "lead women to believe that their self-actualization is prescribed by sex-role fulfillment or sex-role denial; it leads men to devalue the experience of hearth and home; and it denies both sexes participation in the full range of human expression" (p. 194). Shakeshaft and Nowell argued that women would restructure and redefine Maslow's needs, that needs and attainments important to men may not be important to women. Further, they continued, Maslow overlooked the feminine experience and how it might offer a different path to self-actualization; instead, he expected that women would achieve completion with the same experiences that motivate men.

 ## ROUNDTABLE

Shakeshaft's and Nowell's conclusions were based on selected passages from Maslow's work, which follow. You are encouraged to determine if Maslow's bias did indeed favor the male experience. If so, how would you restructure the needs for the feminine experience? Could it be that Shakeshaft's and Nowell's arguments are oblique restatements of the conclusions of Clark and Wilson (1961), rather than a call to revamp Maslow's hierarchy? Support your answer.

The first of Shakeshaft's and Nowell's proof texts come from Maslow's book, *Motivation and Personality* (1970); Maslow describes the esteem need in this way:

> These are, first, the desire for strength, for achievement, for adequacy, for mastery and competence, for confidence in the face of the world, and for independence and freedom. Second, we have what we may call the desire for reputation or prestige . . . status, fame and glory, dominance, recognition, attention, importance, dignity, or appreciation. (p. 45)

They then quote from Maslow's description in a 1968 article of the self-actualized woman:

> Now that females, at least in the advanced countries, have been emancipated and self-actualization is possible for them also, how will this change the relationship between the sexes? (p. 149)

Quoting again from Maslow's book, *Motivation and Personality*:

> It is possible for a woman to have all the specifically female fulfillments (being loved, having the home, having the baby) and then without giving up any of these satisfactions already achieved, go beyond femaleness to the full humanness that she shares with males, for example, the full development of her intelligence, of any talents that she may have, and of her own particular idiosyncratic genius, of her own individual fulfillment. (p. xvii) ■

Two Sides of the Human Personality   A second model of motivational psychology in the Human Relations literature is related to ancient debates about human nature. One of the pillars of many Christian denominations is the notion that man is born in sin, that the fall of Adam and Eve doomed mankind to evil. In large part because of rich religious heritage, this "man is bad" notion is tattooed on the Western mindset, affecting even the way we manage organizations and react to work.

Philosophers of the Enlightenment period in Western culture argued, by contrast, that sin is not inherited, that humans are born with blank slates (Rousseau's *carte blanc*), and that a proper life experience will create a good person on that slate. Man, if left to natural design, is good; if one becomes evil it is because society corrupted the developmental slate and not because of natural tendencies.

This "man-is-good/man-is-bad" debate is at the core of Human Relation theorist Douglas McGregor's (1960) conceptualization of motivation. The man-is-bad thesis, which he labeled "Theory X," maintains that workers are inherently lazy, indolent, mean-spirited, and opposed to work. Theory X is the foundation on which Machine theory is created, according to Knowles and Saxberg (1967). They summarized their argument in the following six principles of Frederick Taylor's Scientific Management:

1. The employee is a "constant" in the production equation. The implication here is that man has a fixed nature.

2. The employee is an inert adjunct to the machine, prone to inefficiency and waste unless properly programmed.

3. The employee is by nature lazy; only managers honor the "hard work" creed of the Protestant Ethic.

4. The employee's main concern is self-interest. At work, this is always expressed in economic values.

5. Given appropriate expression, these values will make man fiercely competitive among his peers as an accumulator of financial rewards.

6. Man (at least the working man) must therefore be tightly controlled and externally motivated in order to overcome his natural desire to avoid work unless the material gains available to him are worth his effort (p. 22).

McGregor argues that the man-is-good philosophy (Theory Y), by contrast, sees workers as basically cooperative, caring, friendly, industrious, and responsible. Where humans are lazy and indolent, it is not because their nature is so constructed, it is because their organizational experience has made them that way. Theory Y is reflected in the work of Human Relationists such as Elton Mayo and Abraham Maslow. Knowles and Saxberg wrote, for example, that Mayo considered the evil instinct perception an inadequate basis for understanding human emotions, that people react to a total organizational environment and must be understood within that total context. Similarly, Maslow focused on providing an organizational atmosphere in which people can grow and develop their potential, and considered the human needs to be at least neutral in value rather than evil.

Theory X motivation requires that managers organize the productive enterprise around economic goals, and that they organize and control worker behavior with rewards and punishment. Theory Y managers recognize and develop the human potential, they develop worker capacity to assume responsibility, and they provide an environment in which workers can achieve their goals. Theory X educational administrators motivate with threats and close supervision, by requiring that weekly lesson plans be submitted for review, with sign-in and sign-out sheets for faculty, with punitive evaluation procedures, and through fear ("It is much safer to be feared than loved. . . . For it may be said of men in general that they are ungrateful, voluble, dissemblers, anxious to avoid dangers, and covetous of gain"—Niccolo Machiavelli in *The Prince,* Chapter 17). Theory Y administrators motivate with trust, with shared responsibility, by encouraging risk-taking and creativity, and with collaboration and collegiality.

Hygienic Motivators Hygienic Motivator model is a third important model of psychological motivation in the Human Relations literature. In 1959, Frederick Herzberg published the results of a study of job satisfaction among 200 engineers and accountants in Pittsburgh (Herzberg, Mausner, & Snyderman, 1959). Herzberg asked respondents about conditions in which they felt particularly good about their work and when they felt exceptionally bad. The responses clustered into two categories; the first he labeled "motivating factors," the second, "hygienic factors" or "dissatisfiers." He wrote in his 1966 book on the subject:

> Five factors stand out as strong determiners of job satisfaction—achievement, recognition, work itself, responsibility and advancement—the last three being of greater importance for lasting change of attitudes. These five factors appeared very infrequently when the respondents described events that paralleled job dissatisfaction feelings . . . When the factors involved in the job dissatisfaction events were coded, an entirely different set of factors evolved. These factors were similar to the satisfiers in their unidimensional effect. This time, however, they served only to bring about job dissatisfaction and were rarely involved in events that led to positive job attitudes. Also, unlike the "satisfiers," the "dissatisfiers" consistently produced short-term changes in job attitudes. The major dissatisfiers were company policy and administration, supervision, salary, interpersonal relations and working conditions. (p. 72–74)

Herzberg and his associates labeled the second group of this set of factors the "hygienic factors" to suggest that they refer to maintenance strategies, or activities aimed at preventing dissatisfaction. By themselves, they cannot produce motivation; that is the role of the first set of factors.

ROUNDTABLE

Public school teachers tend to "burn out" after a decade or so in the teaching profession; anybody in higher education knows professors who achieved tenure then quit publishing. What are administrators doing to contribute to such burnout—that is, what are leaders doing or not doing that disrupts the psychological motivation of faculty? ▪

Herzberg's findings have been the subject of numerous followup studies, many of which attempted to replicate his results in other populations. Sergiovanni (1967) tested Herzberg's theory in a school setting. The motivators that emerged were a sense of achievement, recognition for good work, challenging and interesting work, and a sense of responsibility for one's work. The hygienic factors in Sergiovanni's study included pleasant interpersonal relationships on the job, nonstressful and fair supervision, reasonable policies, and an administrative climate that does not hinder. Hackman and Oldham (1976) attempted to identify the psychological states that underlie motivation. These include:

> Experienced meaningfulness: "The extent to which a person perceives work as being worthwhile or important, given her or his system of values."
> Experienced responsibility: "The extent to which a person believes that she or he is personally responsible or accountable for the outcomes of efforts."
> Knowledge of results: "The extent to which a person is able to determine on a regular basis whether or not the outcomes of her or his efforts are satisfactory." (p. 57)

Hackman and Oldham (1976) identified five ways that leaders can build these psychological states. They are reported by Sergiovanni (1992) as:

- Use more of their talents and skills (skills variety).
- Engage in activities that allow them to see the whole and understand how their contributions fit into the overall purpose or mission (task identity).
- [Help teachers to] view their work as having a substantial and significant impact on the lives or work of other people (task significance).
- [Allow teachers to] experience discretion and independence in scheduling work and in deciding classroom arrangements and instructional procedures (autonomy).
- Get firsthand, and from other sources, clear information about the effects of their performance (feedback) (p. 61).

Communication and Informal Groups

The second major line of research in the Human Relations tradition is about informal groups. In Chapter 2, we learned of Frederick Taylor's difficulty with "soldiering," or the attempt by workers to control productivity. Taylor's comments on the incident were quoted in the last chapter and are reproduced below:

> As soon as I became gang boss [at Midvale], the men who were working under me and who, of course, knew that I was onto the whole game of soldiering, or deliberately restricting output, came to me at once and said "Now Fred, you are not going to be a damn piece-rate hog are you?" I said, "If you fellows mean you are afraid I'm going to try to get a larger amount from these lathe . . . Yes, I propose to get more out." . . . They said, "We warn you, Fred, if you try to bust any of these rates we will have you over the fence in six weeks." . . . Now that was the beginning of a piecework fight which lasted for nearly three years . . . in which I was doing everything in my power to increase the output of the shop, while the men were absolutely determined that output should not be increased. (Taylor's famous testimony, 1926, p. 122)

Taylor was experiencing the "informal group," a phenomenon that would become a centerpiece of Mayo's work at the Western Electric plant in Cicero. An informal group differs from a formal group in that the former has no formally prescribed roles and relationships. An informal group may evolve out of a formal relationship, but it need not do so. Informal groups have two broad functions: (1) they provide a social outlet for their participants; and (2) they provide participants greater control over their environments than they would have individually.

The informal group's social function derives from the human need to interact with others. It serves to increase self-esteem and job satisfaction. One of the early studies in group dynamics, for example, examined work group structure and satisfaction among carpenters and bricklayers working on a housing development (Van Zelst, 1952). The researchers first assigned laborers to work groups randomly, then later allowed groups to form naturally. The natural arrangement resulted in reduced building cost and lowered worker turnover. As one worker on the project put it, "The work is a lot more interesting when you've got a buddy working with you. You certainly like it a lot better anyway" (p. 183).

The informal group's ability to control its environment has been the subject of considerable research and, among managers, consternation. The early research on the subject assumed that informal groups threaten the achievement of formal organizational goals. Taylor's story on the previous page illustrates this concern: the informal group opposed Taylor's efforts for increased productivity. Western Electric's famous study in the bank wiring observation room concluded that informal group pressure hampered productivity. Later work on the subject, however, concluded that informal groups can have a more neutral impact on authority and can even serve to enhance the attainment of organizational goals.

Typically, an informal group has a central personality to whom the group looks for leadership. This person (or, sometimes, persons) typifies the intent and nature of the informal group and helps to keep the group together. Informal groups characteristically have expectations or norms about group behavior and a set of definitions about "what ought to be," or values (a common perception of what is appropriate and what is inappropriate in the world). A former student of mine, for example, reported that an informal group of primary grade teachers in her elementary school had an unspoken rule that teachers in a given grade level must cover a defined amount of curricular material by the end of each school year (a group norm or value). If too little material was covered, subsequent teachers had to backtrack in order to bring students up to the level of work expected of their grade level; too much coverage infringed on the curricular turf of subsequent grade level teachers. A group of farmers in a community where I was once a school principal had a rule that any member who had a farm implement to sell must offer it within the group before seeking an outside buyer. Group norms could be as simple as requiring regular attendance at social gatherings or as complex as requiring specific political or professional behavior and attitudes. Group leaders are the only group members permitted the latitude to break rules—perhaps this serves to enable change and adaptation—but that latitude does have bounds, and unacceptable violation poses hazards to the ability of the leader to maintain his or her position.

Informal groups enforce their norms by a variety of means. First-time or simple infractions may be dealt with by prodding the miscreant. If the deviant behavior continues, sanctions increase in intensity. The harassment becomes more serious and will eventually lead to deprivation of benefits associated with group membership and even harsh ostracism. The story of the primary grade teachers' informal group previously mentioned illustrates this theory. A new teacher came to the school one year and was, of course, invited into the group. At the end of the first year that teacher failed to complete the amount of material required by the group. Her colleagues reacted by kidding and with "lectures" on expected behavior. When the failure reoccurred the second year, the teacher was ostracized by the other teachers. During her third year at this school, the principal decided not to give her tenure or to rehire her for a fourth year. Normally, such an action by the principal would have elicited opposition from the other teachers and support for the affected teacher—members of the group stuck together. They were silent in this case, however; the deviant teacher had violated their norms and, consequently, was not supported when the principal moved to fire her.

Sociologist George C. Homans (1950) has argued that informal groups emerge within an organization because of the activities they perform, the sentiments they develop toward others in the organization, and their interactions with one another. As the model in Figure 3.4 suggests, these factors are mutually dependent and are sensitive to change in any element of the model.

People in a work environment necessarily engage in each of these behaviors to varying degrees—they interact during activities and develop certain sentiments relative to the work and their co-workers. When the activities foster affirming interactions, positive sentiments tend to emerge. These sentiments reinforce the work and the interactions, thus unleashing a spiraling dynamic that culminates in some level of equilibrium. This equilibrium is the informal group. As Homans' dynamic evolves, group members become increasingly more alike in their sentiments and their interactions, and their identity with the group strengthens. Along the way, the group develops norms of group behavior. Deviants from these norms are sanctioned, and conformers are rewarded with the benefits of group membership.

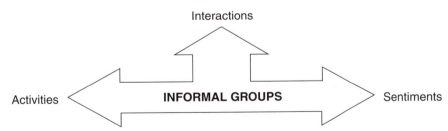

FIGURE 3.4 George Homans' model of informal group dynamics.
From P. Hershey and K. H. Blanchard, *Management of organizational behavior: Utilizing human resources,* 6th ed., p. 63. (Upper Saddle River, NJ. Prentice Hall, Inc.) Copyright © 1993. Copyrighted material adapted by permission of the Center for Leadership Studies, Escondito, CA 92025. All rights reserved.

A number of researchers have provided fascinating insights into the dynamics of informal groups. S.E. Asch (1963), for example, examined the power that informal groups have over individual behavior. Groups of eight college students were recruited by Asch. Seven members of each group conspired with the researcher to give a rather obviously wrong answer to a task (matching the length of a line to the length of one of three other lines). The eighth, unenlightened member was the last to perform the task; fully one-third of these unsuspecting subjects conformed to the wrong answers of the conspirators. Group pressure distorted their perceptions of reality. In a similar fashion, informal groups shape the perceptions and values of their membership.

Peter Blau (1974) calls this a "contextual effect." A contextual effect occurs when the opinion of the group affects that of an individual. Stephen Cole (1969) observed this phenomenon among public school teachers. He found that a teacher's predisposition to engage in a labor strike is influenced by the attitudes of his or her colleagues: if the prevailing view in a school is to strike, the predilection of an individual who previously had not been disposed to strike will often align with that of the group.

In the 1950s, Donald Roy published a series of articles on the effect that informal groups have on workflow in organizations. One particularly famous study involved a battle between machine operators and management in a particular factory over access to the tool room (Roy, 1954). Machine operators liked to get a head start on their next job by accessing the "tool crib" in the tool room for their setup tools ahead of time. A tool crib attendant was responsible for keeping up with the tools and dispensing the setups. Management instituted a rule prohibiting advance access to tools because they wanted to discourage the practice of keeping tools at the machines rather than in the tool crib. The machine operators opposed the new rule, arguing that the tool crib attendant often couldn't find tools when they were needed (undoubtedly because tools were being kept at the machines, but that's beside the point). They got around the rule by exchanging paperwork for the setups without actually turning in the tools, and the crib attendants cooperated with the machine operators in their subterfuge. Management countered by issuing an "exclusion rule" prohibiting machine operators from entering the crib area. This was enforced for only 10 days before conditions reverted to normal practice. In this story, the machine operators and crib attendants constituted an informal group that opposed management control and who cooperated with one another to find ways of circumventing management controls. By doing so, they were able to improve their productivity, but their subterfuge sometimes created allocation problems. The author concluded that this was a case of a "nonrational" work group opposing a "rational" management; but the result, ironically, was improved productivity.

In a study conducted again during the early 1950s (and published in 1963), Joseph Bensman and Israel Gerver (1963) examined the use of the "tap" by workers in an airplane factory. A tap is a tool used to recreate threads in a bolt or screw hole. Use of the tap was strictly prohibited in this factory except under the instructions of an engineer because of the possibility that a tapped bolt could vibrate loose and jeopardize airplane safety. A worker could even be fired on the spot for possessing one. Regardless, use of the tap was widespread in this company. It was a mark of status to own one, and new workers were routinely taught how to use them. There was general collusion to cover up the fact, and the collusion extended even to inspectors and foremen who were reluctant to report violations because of the severity of the penalty. This behavior emerged largely because the alternative was reduced productivity. If a hole in a wing attachment were improperly aligned, for example, the entire assembly would have to be taken apart and a new wing used—a day or more could be lost. A quick tap could solve the problem and keep the task moving. An interesting ceremony was associated with norm enforcement. If a worker was caught using the tap, the foreman was obligated to respond. He would go through the formality of dressing down the offender in public and deliver a lecture on the safety issue along with an admonition never to do it again. The worker was obligated to accept the reprimand and to commit to reform.

Informal Groups in Education   Educational leaders deal with informal groups at two levels: those in the school and those in the community. Administrators can influence the emergence, the activities, and the continuance of informal school groups, but to do so, it helps to better understand why a given group exists. Greenberg and Baron (1993) identify six reasons why informal groups emerge:

1. Mutual benefit, a desire to attain shared goals by influencing such things as school policy, administrative decision making, politics, or the actions of other groups.
2. Security, or protection against a common enemy.
3. To socialize with others.
4. For self-esteem; as Van Zelst (1952) noted, members in satisfying relationships feel good about their work.
5. Mutual self-interest, or the opportunity to share personal interests such as hobbies.
6. Physical proximity or access; groups often form because people have regular access to one another.

At first blush, it would seem that the first two reasons are potentially problematic for school leaders, but that is not necessarily true. The group's mutual concern could just as easily be related to positive educational issues as to negative ones. An administrator, then, should focus on the nature of a group's impact rather than its reason for existing.

As mentioned earlier, administrators often assume that an informal group's behavior is contrary to the best interests of the organization when reality may be just the opposite. In Donald Roy's (1954) story of the machine operators and the tool crib, for example, managers in the plant were concerned about the rational disposition of tools while the effect of the operator's subterfuge was increased productivity. As is often the case in a complex work situation, simple, seemingly rational rules cannot fully anticipate the mix of dynamics and unanticipated consequences that impact effective production. We shall argue in the chapter on Complexity theory that interactive systems can work out these complexities naturally, as if by an invisible hand—complexities that are well beyond the ken of "rational" managers to comprehend. The informal group can be an important part of this emergent phenomenon, and managers who feel they can do a better job underestimate the usefulness and potency of informal groups. Stating this more colloquially: administrators should be wary of assuming that behavior contrary to their "rational" rules is counterproductive, and should be wary of assuming that the administrator should control everything.

Nonetheless, the impact of an informal group on organizational outcomes can indeed be harmful for the organization. If a given group breeds unhealthy conflict and angry feelings in an organization, if it is self-serving to the point of unfairness, if it breeds mediocrity or poor morale, then leaders are obligated to intervene.

A word of caution, however: confrontation with an informal group can be a daunting task, and there are numerous examples of leaders who have lost such battles. There are times when a head-on confrontation is inevitable or desirable; leaders should firmly resist unethical, self-serving demands, for example, or should quickly deal with activities that threaten morale. For many other situations, however, subtlety and tact are more prudent.

Leaders can influence informal group activity in two ways: (1) by fostering the emergence of strong, positive informal groups to offset the deleterious impact of more negative groups; and (2) by quietly disrupting the activities of negative groups. Greenberg and Baron's six reasons why informal groups evolve provide clues about how to foster new informal groups. Emergence can be encouraged by arranging schedules and office or class assignments to bring together people who have a strong commitment to a positive educational environment (groups emerge because of proximity or access). The leader can provide support (resources or other forms of expressed interest) for the goals of select personnel and provide opportunities for them to collaborate on their interests (mutual benefit). Leaders can provide opportunities for personnel to share hobbies (self-interest; this one may seem an odd recommendation, but remember that positive group relationships foster job satisfaction).

Groups can be disrupted in similar fashion. Perhaps the most effective strategy is to encourage members of a problem group to get involved in more positive groups—to siphon away the power base of harmful groups. Schedules and office assignments can be manipulated to make it harder for groups to access one another. If the negative group has any interests that could benefit the school, the administrator could support those interests. Members can be co-opted, given formal responsibilities that require them to affirm beneficial educational outputs.

Disruption of informal groups can backfire, particularly when used by leaders who are, themselves, self-serving or motivated by a desire to control rather than a desire to improve the social and work environment. Informal group behavior can enhance productivity as discussed above, and leaders who focus on control rather than effectiveness may lose this benefit. Disruption can breed active resentment and resistance, thus thwarting effectiveness goals altogether. The leader could lose the battle, thus placing himself or herself in an unfortunate position.

Community-based informal groups are more difficult to influence, but they are responsive to some of the same strategies one uses with groups within the organization. Community-based informal groups include the group of retirees who meets every Saturday morning at the local restaurant, the women who gather in church circle meetings, the tennis or bridge groups, the sports parents, and the booster club. Community groups, like their school counterparts, exist to socialize and to control, and they have the typical leader and norm governance structure. Often they are active in politics and governance of a community, and are inevitably interested in some aspect of school functioning. Occasionally they grow so large that they assume a pseudo-formal status as a political action group or a formal support group. They can be either a thorn in the flesh or a gold mine of support for school personnel.

ROUNDTABLE

I leave it to you to come up with strategies for dealing with community-based informal groups. It would help to do a little research in your community to find out something about one or more groups. Where do they meet? Who are their leaders and what are their norms? What are their agendas for education? What is their power base and how can (or do) they affect the educational organization? What can administrators do to help the community-based informal group become an ally of education, and what can they do that will alienate that group? How should administrators respond when a group emerges with an agenda that is clearly inimical to schools?   ■

Change: The Human Relations Approach

A third major line of research in the Human Relations tradition involved organizational change. Perhaps the most pervasive assumption about change—both during the Human Relations period and now—is that management can alter organizational activities by providing workers with appropriate information, such as the rationale for the change and instructions about new activities. A stirring speech at the beginning of the school year by a superintendent or a dean, along with a couple of workshops, is believed to be sufficient to launch a radically new instructional approach; or pointing out subordinates' shortcomings is sufficient to elicit more acceptable behavior. Studies of the relationship between communication skills and change have not entirely supported this assumption, however. In 1964, for example, Robert Kahn reported that the communication skills of foremen in an appliance factory were unrelated to change except where the foremen possessed significant power in the organization. Katz and Kahn (1966) argued that communication is effective in clarifying ambiguous tasks, but is otherwise ineffective in producing organizational change. Other theorists, starting with the Human Relationists, will likewise argue that complex changes require much more than mere rationality and instructions.

One school of Human Relations thought focused on the role of the individual's psychology in the change process. Their assumption in doing so was that general operational change can be affected by altering the personalities, attitudes, and motivations of the people who will implement change. Elton Mayo, for example, spent much of his early career exploring strategies for re-establishing the "organic equilibrium" of workers, including efforts to counsel individuals. Katz, Sarnoff, and McClintock (1956) found that when people were counseled about their motivations and prejudice, they became more tolerant of other races. It became rather popular among businesses in the 1940s and 1950s to have counselors on staff for helping workers (remember the psychologist in the movie *Miracle on 34th Street?*).

The logic of such an approach to change is rather tortured, however. As Katz and Kahn (1966) observed,

> . . . to approach institutional change solely in individual terms involves an impressive and discouraging series of assumptions. . . . They include at the very least: the assumption that the individual can be provided with new insights and knowledge; that these will produce some significant alteration in his motivational pattern; that these insights and motivations will be retained even when the individual leaves the protected situation in which they were learned and returns to his accustomed role in the organization; that he will be able to adapt his new knowledge to that real-life situation; that he will be able to persuade his coworkers to accept the changes in his behavior which he now desires; and that he will also be able to persuade them to make complementary changes in their own expectations and behavior. (p. 391)

And of course there is still the likelihood that the boss' "diagnosis" of the individual is wrong. It is, after all, easier to blame problems on subordinates than to deal with fundamental problems in the system or in one's leadership style.

Other Human Relations theorists examined the impact of informal groups on the change process, and this research proved somewhat more productive. The premises behind this school of thought emerged out of the Western Electric study and the observations of work group influence over productivity. The Relay Room experiments, for example, suggested that workers influence the success or failure of organizational initiatives. Both the Relay Room experiments and the BWOR experiments underscored the importance of group decision making to productivity.

Kurt Lewin (1952) popularized an approach to change that is based on the power of informal groups. During World War II, he sought ways to convince housewives to serve less popular cuts of meat, such as beef hearts and kidneys. He recruited six groups of Red Cross workers for his experiments: half were subjected to lectures on the subject and the remaining three were involved in discussions and group decision making. A subsequent follow-up evaluation of the two groups revealed dramatic differences: only 3% of the lecture participants were serving the unpopular foods while 32% of the discussion groups were serving them.

In 1956, Betty Bond conducted a more systematic examination of the Lewin hypothesis using longer time periods between treatment and observation (1956). She was interested in strategies for improving early detection of breast cancer. Two groups of women were studied using procedures similar to Lewin's: one group was subjected to a lecture while the other was involved in discussion and decision making. Follow-up interviews were conducted 7 and 13 months after the treatment. The discussion group reported more frequent self-examinations, were more likely to have visited a physician for a breast examination, and could better demonstrate the techniques of self-examination than the lecture group; further, the differences were more pronounced at 13 than at 7 months.

In 1948, Lester Coch and John French conducted a classic test of the Lewin hypothesis at the Harwood Manufacturing Corporation in Marion, Virginia. Coch and French were interested in determining if they (and management) could alter informal group norms regarding piece rate without the problems that typically occurred when such changes had been tried in the past. The factory produced pajama garments and employed women who, for the most part, were quite young (the ratio of women to men was approximately 5:1, and the average age of employees was 23). It was common in the late 1940s for women to seek employment only until they married and began a family. One can suspect that this accounts, at least in part, for the young average age of Harwood employees; if so, the participants in this study may not have felt a long-term career commitment to the organization.

Traditionally, change was introduced into this garment factory by lecture and fiat: the workers were told of the change, given a rationale, and told what the new piece rate would be. This approach had historically produced significant turnover in the workforce, extended periods of re-learning, confrontations with foremen, and low morale. Coch and French compared this approach with a more Lewinian strategy. Three work groups were used in their study. Two experimental groups discussed the proposed change. One of these groups selected members from their group to experiment with the new process and to establish piece rates; the other experimental group participated as a whole in the change decisions. The third group was subjected to the usual lecture and fiat.

The differences between discussion and lecture groups were striking. The control group exhibited the traditional patterns of low morale and productivity, and 17% left the company within the first 40 days following the change. By contrast, no workers in the experimental groups resigned. Productivity in the first experimental group (where group representatives made decisions) returned to its pre-change levels within 14 days and productivity was re-established in the second group (in which everyone participated in decisions) within just 2 days. Morale remained high in the experimental groups, and only one act of aggression toward management was exhibited.

A follow-up by John French of the study at the Harwood pajama factory that he and Lester Coch had conducted in 1948 revealed a chink in the closed perspective of the Human Relations movement. After the dramatic successes in that first study, French and some Scandinavian colleagues attempted to replicate it in a Norwegian shoe factory (French, Israel, & Aas, 1960). The participants in the original study with Coch had been, for the most part, young females, who apparently had short-term career interests (the average age of employees was 23). The Norwegian participants, by contrast, were male by almost a 4:1 ratio; French did not provide information about the average age of the Norwegian workers. Both the Harwood and the Norwegian participants were unionized; however, while French felt that this was a significant factor in his Norwegian study, Coch and French said almost nothing about union influence at the Harwood facility.

The replication failed. The members of French's experimental group were more likely to report enhanced control over change than were the members of the control group, and two of the four test groups did reach the standard faster than usual, but the feeling of control did not translate into greater productivity. The researchers attributed the failure to weaknesses in the experimental manipulation and in union-controlled productivity rates. This later point, however, gets at a broader issue that French and his colleagues missed. Change involves a number of social, structural, technological, and organizational factors. The social expectations imported from the environments of these two plants (women had short careers before marrying while men had life-long careers) undoubtedly influenced the outcomes, for example. The external impact of unionization was apparently different in the two studies. Organizational and structural differences likely played a role in the differing findings, as did gender and cultural differences. Despite the promising research into the Lewinian method by Human Relationists, change is not so simple as to yield to the manipulation of one or a few factors. As we shall see in subsequent chapters, change is the product of a complex mix of internal and external issues, many of which are beyond manipulation by organizational managers. Indeed, the whole infrastructure of Human Relations theory—the assumptions that effectiveness is the solitary goal of organization, the idea that effectiveness can be obtained through human relations strategies—was seriously challenged by this issue. To understand organizational behavior, theoreticians had to break out of their rather simple Closed Systems perspectives and view organizations as Open Systems with multiple goals within an environment of multiple forces.

Diary

- In your diary entry for this chapter, summarize your thoughts on the Roundtable discussions that were proposed.
- Given what you have learned in this chapter, what are some important functions of leadership? In what way does your answer change your previous answers to this question?
- The Hawthorne effect has long been an important consideration in research design. Advocates suggest that people who know they are part of an experiment will perform better because of the novelty of the situation. In medical research, this is called the placebo effect. Given the actual results of Mayo in the Hawthorne plant (novelty was not the first reason for improvement), is there an alternative interpretation of this phenomenon?
- Critique Mayo's research design, and his conclusions.

- You obviously are a motivated person; otherwise, you probably wouldn't be taking this class. What motivates you? Why do you want a higher degree or principal's certification. Use your answers to both support and critique Maslow's and McGregor's proposals.

- Are certain people disposed to be work-motivated while others are disposed to putting in their eight hours and getting on to more important things? Explain. Assume this is the case: are these different types of people generally attracted to different types of jobs? Explain. Should each be led differently? How so?

- Identify an informal group in your school. Describe its leadership and activities. Does it benefit or harm the organization? How does the school leader deal with it? What could a member of this group do to get ostracized? How would you deal with it if you were the administrator?

- Human Relations leaders focus on the importance of communication. Can there be too much communication in an organization? Explain. Under what conditions would you want to suppress the amount of communicating taking place?

Recommended Readings

The following recommendations are all original source documents or (in the case of the Trahair book) the next best thing to an original source. They are all classics of organizational theory and should be on the "must read" list of organizational theorists.

Coch, L., & French, J. R. P. (1948). Overcoming resistance to change. *Human Relations, 1,* 512–533.

This is the original article that so dramatically affirmed the potency of the Lewinian model of organizational change. Coch and French tried the Lewin method of involving workers in decisions regarding change and achieved highly significant improvement over a lecture control group in the learning curve, acceptance, and morale. If you read this article, however, you may also want to see the article on French's follow-up in a Norwegian factory that contradicted these findings. It can be found as French, J. R. P., Israel, J., & Aas, D. (1960). An experiment on participation in a Norwegian factory. *Human Relations, 13,* 3–19.

Maslow, A. (1943, July). A theory of human motivation. *Psychological Review,* 370–396.

Maslow's original article about the structure of human needs. His research was based upon observations of a large database of engineers and study of the lives of great people.

Trahair, R. C. S. (1984). *The humanist temper: The life and works of Elton Mayo.* New Brunswick NJ: Transaction Books.

Trahair provides a comprehensive biography of the life and research of Elton Mayo. The findings about the middling priority of novelty in the Hawthorne relay room study are discussed.

References

Alderfer, C. P. (1972). *Existence, relatedness, and growth.* New York: Free Press.

Asch, S. E. (1963). Effects of group pressure upon the modification and distortion of judgments. In H. Guetzkow (Ed.), *Groups, leadership, and men* (pp. 177–190). New York: Russell & Russell.

Bensman, J., & Gerver, I. (1963). Crime and punishment in the factory: The function of deviancy in maintaining the social system. *American Sociological Review, 28,* 587–598.

Blau, P. M. (1974). *On the nature of organizations.* New York: John Wiley & Sons, Inc.

Bond, B. W. (1956). The group-discussion-decision approach: An appraisal of its use in health education. *Dissertation Abstracts, 16,* 903–904.

Clark, P. M., & Wilson, J. Q. (1961). Incentive systems: A theory of organizations. *Administrative Science Quarterly, 6,* 129–166.

Coch, L., & French, J. R. P. (1948). Overcoming resistance to change. *Human Relations, 1,* 512–533.

Cole, S. (1969). Teachers' strikes: A study of the conversion of predisposition into action. *American Journal of Sociology, 74,* 506–520.

Etzioni, A. (1961). *A comparative analysis of complex organizations.* New York: Free Press of Glencoe.

French, J. R. P., Israel, J., & Aas, D. (1960). An experiment on participation in a Norwegian factory. *Human Relations, 13,* 3–19.

Greenberg, J., & Baron, R.A. (1993). *Behavior in organizations* (4th ed.). Boston: Allyn & Bacon.

Hackman, J. R., & Oldham, G. (1976). Motivation through the design of work: A test of a theory. *Organizational Behavior and Human Performance, 16*(2), 250–279.

Hackman, J. R., Oldham, G., Johnson, R., & Purdy, K. (1975). A new strategy for job enrichment. *California Management Review, 17*(4), 57–71.

Herzberg, F. (1966). *Work and the nature of man.* Cleveland, OH: The World Publishing Company.

Herzberg, F., Mausner, B., & Snyderman, B. (1959). *The motivation of work* (2nd ed.). New York: John Wiley & Sons, Inc.

Homans, G. C. (1950). *The human group.* New York: Harcourt, Brace & World.

Kahn, R. L. (1964). Field studies of power in organizations. In R. L. Kahn & E. Boulding (Eds.), *Power and conflict in organizations* (pp. 43–74). New York: Basic Books.

Kast, F., & Rosenzweig, J. (1970). *Organization and management.* New York: McGraw Hill Book Company.

Katz, D., & Kahn, R. L. (1966). *The social psychology of organizations.* New York: John Wiley & Sons, Inc.

Katz, D., Sarnoff, I., & McClintock, C. (1956). Ego-defense and attitude change. *Human Relations, 9,* 27–54.

Knowles, H. P., & Saxberg, B. O. (1967). Human relations and the nature of man. *Harvard Business Review,* 22-40ff.

Lewin, K. (1952). Group decision and social change. In G. E. Swanson, T. M. Newcomb, & E. L. Hartley (Eds.), *Readings in social psychology,* rev. ed. (pp. 459–473). New York: Holt.

Luthans, F. (1992). *Organizational behavior* (6th ed.). New York: McGraw-Hill, Inc.

Maslow, A. (1943). A theory of human motivation. *Psychological Review,* 370–396.

Maslow, A. (1968). Some fundamental questions that face the normative social psychologist. *Journal of Humanistic Psychology, 8,* 143–153.

Maslow, A. (1970). *Motivation and personality* (2nd ed.). New York: Harper & Row.

Mayo, E. (1945). *The social problems of an industrial civilization.* Boston: Graduate School of Business Administration, Harvard University.

McGregor, D. (1960). *The human side of enterprise.* New York: McGraw-Hill, Inc.

Roy, D. (1954). Efficiency and 'the fix': Informal intergroup relations in a piecework machine shop. *American Journal of Sociology, 60,* 255–266.

Sergiovanni, T. J. (1967). Factors which affect satisfaction and dissatisfaction of teachers. *Journal of Educational Administration, 5*(1), 66–87.

Sergiovanni, T. J. (1992). *Moral leadership: Getting to the heart of school improvement.* San Francisco: Jossey-Bass.

Shakeshaft, C., & Nowell, I. (1984). Research on theories, concepts, and models of organizational behavior: The influence of gender. *Issues in Education, 11*(3), 186–203.

Taylor's famous testimony before the special house committee (1924). *Bulletin of the Taylor Society, 11*(3-4), 95–196.

Trahair, R. C. S. (1984). *The humanist temper: The life and works of Elton Mayo.* New Brunswick, NJ: Transaction Books.

Van Zelst, R. H. (1952). Sociometrically selected work teams increase production. *Personnel Psychology, 5,* 175–185.

CHAPTER 4

Tasks Versus People

Structuralism, which emerged in the 1930s, sought to understand the interrelated impact of the task and the people dimensions of organizations. This movement proposed a tension between the rational, task-oriented, nature of organizations and their irrational people side. A number of interesting hypotheses were derived from this observation. Industrialist Chester Barnard, for example, proposed that leaders have a responsibility to establish a moral imperative among workers to achieve the formal goals of the organization. He argued that organizational success depends on the willingness of workers, and that it is management's role to build that willingness. Phillip Selznick contended that organizations should not be defined in terms of their formally stated goals; rather, they should be understood in terms of the compromises they have made with irrational forces. Talcott Parsons defined organization as a homeostatic equilibrium between rational and irrational forces. Others will define leadership style relative to task and people orientations.

This movement bridged the Closed Systems perspectives of Machine and Human Relations and the Open Systems theories to be discussed starting in the next chapter. Its advocates began to understand the significant importance of environment to organizational behavior, for example. They defined the relationship between people orientation and task orientation that will become so important in the 1960s and 1970s. They even provided an important foundation for Institutional and Critical theories, which will dominate the last decades of the 20th, and early decades of the 21st, centuries (more on that when we get to Chapters 11 and 12).

This chapter examines the thoughts of Barnard, Selznick, and others. It reviews leadership from the Closed Systems perspectives (Machine theory and Human Relations), then expands these perspectives into a Structuralist perspective, which merges task orientation (the Machine focus) and people orientation (the Human Relations focus) into a single model.

In this chapter, students will:

- Develop a research proposal based on Selznick's Institutional model.
- Examine trait theories of leadership, and engage in activities that illustrate how trait perspectives can result in inappropriate leadership decisions.
- Explore implications of Human Relations in educational leadership.
- Categorize different organizations according to their appropriate leadership style (task versus people orientation).
- Debate the appropriate mix of task and people orientation in education.
- Refine their definitions of the function of leadership in education.

LEADERSHIP AND CHESTER BARNARD'S COOPERATIVE SYSTEM

Chester I. Barnard, president of the New Jersey Bell Telephone Company, developed his perspectives on organization at about the same time that Mayo was winding up his work with the Western Electric plant in Cicero. Barnard was aware of, and receptive to, the findings of the Hawthorne studies and maintained close relationships with Mayo and his colleagues.

The result of Barnard's observations and executive experience with people and leadership was his famous book, *The Functions of the Executive* (1938). This book was to influence the work of a number of noted theorists, including Philip Selznick and Herbert Simon; it has even sparked renewed interest among Culture theorists in the latter years of the 20th century (particularly in Japan where Barnard Societies are active).

Barnard, like Mayo, adopted Spencer's organismic perspective of social behavior, arguing that organizations are cooperative systems that integrate the contributions of their individual participants. Formal organization, to Barnard, was a "kind of cooperation among men that is conscious, deliberate, purposeful" (1938, p. 4). He deduced two conclusions from this assumption: (1) organizations depend on the willingness of participants to make contributions (an irrational dynamic); and (2) participants must contribute toward a common purpose (rationality). Purposefulness requires a common belief among participants in the centrality and importance of organizational goals, and an important function of the executive is the nurturing of such a belief system.

His first observation (above) refers to a bottom-up phenomenon: willingness starts with workers themselves. The notion that authority resides with the manager is myth, he argued; rather, authority relies on the willingness of workers to comply with demands. Authority is not based on the legalistic position of the manager; rather, it is based on the legitimacy extended by those who obey authority. As Barnard put it, "the decision as to whether an order has authority or not lies with the persons to whom it is addressed, and does not reside in 'persons of authority' or those who issue these orders" (p. 163).

Workers must be oriented to a common purpose, however, and that common purpose comes from the top down. It is the role of management to create the goals that motivate the organization. This involves two important subfunctions. First, the manager must effectively communicate goals to the workers. "All communication relates to the formulation of purpose and the transmission of coordinating prescriptions for action and so rests upon the ability to communicate with those willing to cooperate" (p. 184). Second, the manager must create a moral imperative for the common purpose, to morally bind participants to the collective good.

> The distinguishing mark of the executive responsibility is that it requires not merely conformance to a complex code of morals but also the creation of moral codes for others. This is the process of inculcating points of view, fundamental attitudes, loyalties, to the organization or cooperative system, and to the system of objective authority, that will result in subordinating individual interest and the minor dictates of personal codes to the code of the cooperative whole. (p. 279)

Ultimately, however, the organization is shaped by a force even greater than the moral imperative: the need to survive. As Barnard said in his famous opus, "They [organizations] tend to perpetuate themselves; and in the effort to survive may change the reasons for existence" (p. 89). Later, in the 1940s, Philip Selznick will expand this, arguing that survival pressures motivate a system to make accommodating adjustments that compromise its original, rational intent.

PHILIP SELZNICK AND INSTITUTIONALISM

Philip Selznick was a student of bureaucracy theorist Robert Merton at Columbia, but his work was more heavily influenced by Chester Barnard and Structuralist theory. One can see Barnard's influence, for example, in Selznick's thoughts about an organization's goal orientation and the leader's role in formulating that orientation. Like Barnard, Mayo, and others, Selznick adopted Spencer's organismic, or cooperative, perspective of social systems, and recognized the importance of the informal group's influence on organizational dynamics.

Selznick, like Barnard, begins with Machine theory rationality—organizations are first and foremost goal-oriented systems—but he continues that organizations cannot attain the Closed System ideal of rationality because of nonrational pressures. The nonrational elements of a system are made up of

> (1) individuals, who participate in the organization as "wholes" and do not act merely in terms of their formal roles within the system; and (2) the fact that the formal structure is only one aspect of the concrete social structure that must adjust in various ways to the pressures of its institutional environment. . . . The organization strikes bargains with its environment that compromise present objectives and limit future possibilities. (Scott, 1987, p. 64)

Scott said the mix of rational and irrational leads to something akin to Alice's croquet game in Lewis Carroll's *Alice in Wonderland:*

> . . . if the organization as conceived by Weber operates like a smoothly functioning professional football team, Selznick's image corresponds more closely to Alice's efforts at croquet with equipment and competition provided by the Queen of Hearts. Alice swings her flamingo mallet but the bird may duck his head before the hedgehog ball is struck; just so, the manager issues his directives but they may be neither understood nor followed by his subordinates. (1964, p. 511)

The organization, according to Selznick, is an adaptive and social system rather than a mechanical one, and its adaptations are forged not only by its desire to achieve its goals, but also by the nonrational people and forces with which it must deal. A system is ultimately motivated by the need to survive (this was also Barnard's culminating conclusion), and will do whatever is needed to accomplish that end. If a system's nonrational elements are sufficiently compelling, it may even change its stated or professed goals in order to assure its survival.

Selznick wrote that "the most important thing about organizations is that, though they are tools, each nevertheless has a life of its own" (1949, p. 10), and that one learns about organizations by analyzing the frustrations these living entities experience with their nonrational elements—those needs "which cannot be fulfilled within approved avenues of expression" (1948, p. 32). Like psychologists who analyze frustrations that shape the human personality, sociologists should study the critical organizational decisions, the coping strategies, that shape a system's structure and give it a distinct personality. Selznick refers to the process by which an organization develops such personality as "institutionalization." He argued in 1957 that "An 'institution' . . . is . . . a natural product of social needs and pressures—a responsive, adaptive organism" (p. 5). Institutionalization is a process that occurs across time as an organization reacts to internal and external pressures and needs.

Selznick's most famous application of this idea was his study of the Tennessee Valley Authority (TVA) project that began in the United States in the 1930s (Selznick, 1949). The stated goals of the TVA were to build a series of dams to control flooding along the rivers in the Southern Appalachia region, to provide income for chronically poor people in this area, to provide hydroelectric power to the region, and to help conserve farmland and forests. Administrators were located in the affected regions themselves instead of in Washington to help assure decisions that met the needs of the people who would be most affected. To co-opt suspicious locals, area leaders were invited to serve on advisory boards for the project. In return for their cooperation, however, some of these representatives managed to subvert TVA goals: forests intended as watersheds were given to loggers, for example, and private developers obtained property that was meant to be public lands. By studying the evolutionary history of the TVA and how its features and functions changed over time, Selznick demonstrated that the system's operative goals, or practice, had become something different than its professed goals. The personality of an organization, he maintained, is in what it does (the operative goals) and not necessarily in what it professes to do.

RESEARCH TOPIC

Develop a research proposal based on Selznick's Institutionalism. Investigate a policy with which you are familiar, for example. Look at how formal expectations (goals) for that policy were compromised and altered to accommodate the needs and desires of clients, interested parties, and implementing personnel. Selznick used historical documents and collected case study data from interviews with informants familiar with the TVA's history. Similarly, you should identify the original stated goals, determine how (and why) those stated goals have changed, and trace the emergence of actual goals of the organization. Design an analysis, paying attention to the type of information that must be collected, how it will be collected, and from whom it will be collected.   ■

PERSPECTIVES OF LEADERSHIP

The role of leadership within a social system is surprisingly difficult to define. We all can recognize leadership when we see or experience it, but defining just what leadership does is an elusive exercise. Why? In part, it's because one's definition depends on one's perspective of an organization. Thus, Machine theorists will define leadership differently than Human Relations theorists. Further, as one's perception of organization becomes more complex (and organization will indeed become more complex for you as you work your way through this book), one's definition of the role of leadership will become more complex—perhaps even prohibitively so.

It helps to differentiate management from leadership, even though the distinction is somewhat contrived. Management involves seeing to the routine standardized operations of a system. As Mark Hanson (1996) put it, managers "see to the nuts and bolts of making the organization work, such as hiring, evaluating, distributing resources, and enforcing rules" (p. 155). Leadership is those activities that influence the goal-oriented dynamics of a system—a definition that is sufficiently general to apply across several perspectives of organization.

We discuss Machine and Human Relations perspectives of leadership here, instead of in the last chapter, so you can see them side by side and with the Structuralist perspective. This also allows us to review the first part of this book (Closed Systems).

Machine Theorists' Perspectives on Leadership

The Machine theorist defines the leader's role as one of formulating goals and seeing to their efficient accomplishment. To be successful in this, leaders must be intelligent, strong, articulate, and inventive; that is, they must possess certain traits. This is called Trait theory. Not all people possess appropriate characteristics nor can they develop them.

Prior to and during WWII, Ralph Stogdill analyzed the characteristics of 124 leaders. He summarized his findings in 1948 into six categories:

1. Capacity (intelligence, alertness, verbal facility, originality, judgment)
2. Achievement (scholarship, knowledge, athletic accomplishments)
3. Responsibility (dependability, initiative, persistence, aggressiveness, self-confidence, desire to excel)
4. Participation (activity, sociability, cooperation, adaptability, humor)
5. Status (socio-economic position, popularity)
6. Situation (mental level, status, skills, needs and interests of followers, objectives to be achieved). (p. 64).

Stogdill's work displays a problem that is all too common in social research, particularly that conducted by the neophyte researcher—it is tautological. "Tautology" refers to circular logic, and includes arguments in which outcomes or side issues are mistaken for causes. The clearest example of this in Stogdill's summary involves socio-economic status (SES). He implies that low SES persons need not apply for leadership positions; in reality, leaders may be high SES because they have become a highly paid leader rather than because they were high SES before assuming the leadership role. SES is not necessarily a prerequisite for leadership; it may be a result of it. Similarly, it is appropriate to ask whether intelligence or humor or judgment is required of effective leadership, or if personnel departments tend to hire people with those characteristics (or people with those characteristics tend to seek leadership positions in disproportionate numbers). There are plenty of examples to support the fact that one need not be intelligent or verbal or socially mature to lead. Almost everyone (unfortunately) knows administrators who couldn't think their way out of a paper bag, but who relate to people well enough to garner respect. Tautology is an easy trap to fall into when one attempts to describe characteristics associated with a given role; Stogdill is guilty in this line of his research.

McCall and Lombardo (1983) examined the traits of people who were "on a track to leadership," but who fell by the wayside before achieving their goals. They identified 10 reasons why they failed. In order, these are:

1. Insensitive to others: abrasive, intimidating, bullying style
2. Cold, aloof, arrogant
3. Betrayal of trust
4. Overly ambitious: thinking of next job, playing politics
5. Specific performance problems with the business
6. Overmanaging—unable to delegate or build a team
7. Unable to staff effectively
8. Unable to think strategically
9. Unable to adapt to boss with different style
10. Overdependent on advocate or mentor.

Similarly, Geier (1967) identified three traits that hinder one's ability to obtain a leadership position: the perception by others that the candidate is uninformed, is a nonparticipant, or is too rigid in behavior and expectations.

The research into leadership characteristics, however, has been unable to identify any characteristics that systematically predict leadership ability. This is not to say that certain characteristics may not help a person achieve a leadership position or be effective in that position. Tallness, for example, is thought to be associated with leadership ability, thus being tall gives one an advantage when seeking leadership positions (Governor Michael Dukakis, a U.S. Presidential candidate in 1988, demanded to be allowed to stand on a platform in his debates with George Bush so that his somewhat short stature wouldn't have a biasing impact on public opinion, for example). Height is not a cause of leadership ability, however. Similarly, other physical and psychological characteristics, while they may predict leadership roles, are not necessarily required of effective leadership nor are they associated with the capacity to lead.

Great Men and Other Issues This Machine theory perspective of leadership is related to the Great Man debate. This asks the question, are great leaders born or are they a product of circumstances? Is leadership genetic or can anyone be a leader if he or she is properly groomed and/or just happens to be in the right place at the right time? Do great leaders make great events or do great events make great leaders (did Hitler create the anti-Semitic movement in Germany or did anti-Semitism create Hitler)? I leave this to the student to debate. Consider Oskar Schindler (*Schindler's List*), who produced vast wealth and did heroic deeds during World War II, but was never able to reproduce his successes after the war. Was Horace Mann, the leader of the common schools movement in the United States, a product of the nationalistic and egalitarian fervor of the late 19th century or would he be a great educator even today? Could Dr. Martin Luther King, Jr. have been a great civil rights leader in the 1920s? What constitutes leadership anyhow? What do your answers say about the nature of leadership and about Closed Systems theory in general?

Triggers Almost everyone judges others based on certain traits. Evolutionists might argue that we are genetically programmed to respond to traits such as health, youthful vigor, and strength, although this explanation may be a bit too tautological for others (can you explain why?). Whatever the reason (if there is one), it's a very human characteristic. The traits by which we judge people can be called "triggers." A trigger is any trait that elicits a given emotional response in us. One may see a well-groomed person, for example, and assume that the person would make a good leader. The trait (grooming) triggered an emotional response that was manifested as perceptions of leadership.

ACTIVITY AND ROUNDTABLE

Imagine that you are on an air rescue mission in a flooded and rapidly deteriorating area. You spot a group of campers on a high piece of ground that has become surrounded by water, thus blocking escape by land. You land your helicopter to evacuate these stranded people. Your helicopter will hold only five people, however, and there are eight campers that need to be rescued. You fear that you may not be able to return in time to evacuate the three people who can't be taken out on the first flight, but you must make a decision. Whom will you rescue, and whom will you leave behind.

The eight people are:

The editor of the local newspaper, who is a fellow Rotarian.

A young graduate student.

An attractive female who works at the bank you use.

An obese male who had come camping for exercise.

A Middle Eastern immigrant carpenter.

A local high school football star.

A 60-year-old man whom you don't recognize.

A rather slovenly person whom you suspect is a drifter.

Make your choices individually, then share them, along with your rationale, in small groups. The intent of this exercise is to explore your biases or triggers. How do these triggers inappropriately influence attitudes and decisions about others, and what sort of response is elicited by given physical traits? If you are (or become) an administrator, how might such triggers affect your decisions about personnel hiring, selection for leadership roles, and other judgments? Share stories about how triggers sometime lead one to bad decisions. What do you need to do to help you avoid inappropriate judgments?   ■

Human Relationists' Perspectives on Leadership

Human Relations theorists approached leadership in terms of facilitating cooperative behavior, providing opportunity for personal growth, and dealing with human needs. Administrators were advised to communicate openly with workers, counsel those with personal problems, create a friendly comfortable work environment, be attentive to the human side of workers, project positive expectations about worker behavior, and deal effectively with informal groups. Hackman and Oldham (1976) identified five ways that leaders can build these positive work climates:

- Use more of [worker's] talents and skills.
- Engage in activities that allow them to see the whole and understand how their contributions fit into the overall purpose or mission.
- [Help teachers to] view their work as having a substantial and significant impact on the lives or work of other people.
- [Allow teachers to] experience discretion and independence in scheduling work and in deciding classroom arrangements and instructional procedures.
- Get firsthand, and from other sources, clear information about the effects of their performance (see Sergiovanni, 1992, p. 61).

 ROUNDTABLE

Marcus Buckingham and Curt Coffman (1999), working with the Gallup Organization, have summarized the results of a multi-year effort to find out what goes on in great workplaces ("great" was defined in terms of employee retention, customer satisfaction, productivity, and profitability). They identified 12 dimensions of great workplaces, which they summarize in the following statements:

1. I know what is expected of me at work.
2. I have the materials and equipment I need to do my work right.
3. At work, I have the opportunity to do what I do best every day.
4. In the last seven days, I have received recognition or praise for doing good work.
5. My supervisor, or someone at work, seems to care about me as a person.
6. There is someone at work who encourages my development.
7. At work, my opinions seem to count.
8. The mission/purpose of my company makes me feel my job is important.
9. My associates (fellow employees) are committed to doing quality work.
10. I have a best friend at work.
11. In the last six months, someone at work has talked to me about my progress.
12. This last year, I have had opportunities at work to learn and grow.

What implications for leadership activities are suggested by these statements? Evaluate an administrator with whom you are familiar against the list of activities you derive. As a leader, will (or do) you have problems implementing any of the activities suggested by the Gallup survey, and what can you do to overcome those problems (or should you correct them—that is, do you agree that the survey suggests an appropriate leadership model for you)? Can an organization exhibit these characteristics and still not be a "great" organization; alternatively, can they be a great organization and not possess some of these characteristics?

Structuralists' Perspective on Leadership

The Structuralist perspective on leadership emphasizes tension between organizational rationality and productivity on the one hand, and irrational social needs structures of workers on the other. Chester Barnard (1938) suggested that the leader should deal with irrationality by effectively communicating goals and by creating a moral imperative for those goals among workers. The intent of Barnard's recommendations is to make an organization's goals as much a part of the individual's goals as possible, thus reducing the tension between rational and irrational dimensions of the system.

Phillip Selznick developed a Structuralist definition of leadership behavior in his 1957 book, *Leadership in Administration*. Selznick's early work, such as his TVA study (1949),

> emphasized the cressive, unplanned, and unintended nature of institutional processes. . . . By contrast, in his later, more prescriptive writings [such as *Leadership in Administration*], following the lead of Barnard (1938), he embraced an "enacted" conception, emphasizing that effective leaders are able to define and defend the organization's institutional values—its distinctive mission. (Scott, 1987, p. 494)

Selznick identified four behaviors of effective institutional leadership:

1. The definition of institutional missions and role. Setting of goals is a creative task. Self-assessment to discover the true commitments of the organization, as set by effective internal and external demands. He must specify and recast the general aims of his organization so as to adapt them, without serious corruption, to the requirements of institutional survival.
2. The institutional embodiment of purpose. Must shape the character of the organization, sensitizing it to ways of thinking and responding so that increased reliability in the execution and elaboration of policy will be achieved.
3. The defense of institutional integrity. The leadership of any polity fails when it concentrates on sheer survival; institutional survival, properly understood, is a matter of maintaining values and distinctive identity.
4. The ordering of internal conflict. The struggle among competing interests always has a high claim on the attention of leadership. Direction of the enterprise as a whole may be seriously influenced by changes in the internal balance of power (Selznick, 1957, pp. 62–63).

"Nonetheless," according to Scott (1987), "Selznick's conception remains largely definitional rather than explanatory: he defined and described the process but did not explicitly account for it. His treatment of institutionalization informs us that values are instilled; not how this occurs" (p. 495).

Another tradition was emerging at about this same period of time. This tradition is attributed largely to the Ohio State Leadership Studies. It is stretching the point a bit to label these studies as Structuralist, for the Ohio studies, while they address the two dimensions of organization that are typically identified by Structuralists, do not deal with the ramifications of the tensions between them. Rather, the advocates of this leadership perspective suggest that leaders should adjust their behavior to accommodate the needs of the particular organization within which they function. This is more of a Contingency theory argument (which emerged in the 1960s; see Chapter 6) than a Structuralist one. However, these leadership studies straddled these two eras in organizational theory; thus, it is no surprise that they blended elements of both. By discussing the leadership studies here, we are able to see how Structuralism bridged the transition between Closed Systems theory and subsequent Open Systems theory (which we will develop in the next chapter), and how it influenced and shaped later arguments.

Stogdill, a faculty member at Ohio State University (the same Stogdill who gave us trait theory), began an extensive study of the functional dimensions of leadership in 1945. With the help of a staff of researchers such as Andrew Halpin and James Winer, he developed a leadership scale called the Leadership Behavioral Description Questionnaire (LBDQ). Over the next few decades, this index became almost synonymous with leadership; in education alone, over 30 studies using the LBDQ are reported in *Dissertations Abstracts* (Hanson, 1996).

Stogdill's team formulated over 1,800 questions that described leadership, and, along with Halpin and Winer, administered the scale to the crews of Air

Force commanders. A factor analysis was performed on the results (factor analysis is a statistical procedure for identifying commonalties among questionnaire items). Two factors emerged from the data: the first they labeled *initiating structures,* the second was called *consideration.* Halpin (1966) defined these as follows:

> Initiating structures refer to the leader's behavior in delineating the relationship between himself and members of the work group, and in endeavoring to establish well-defined patterns of organization, channels of communication, and methods of procedure. Consideration refers to behaviors indicative of friendship, mutual trust, respect, and warmth in the relationship between the leader and the members of his staff. (p. 86)

Items that were categorized as initiating included:

- The leader assigns group members to particular tasks.
- The leader asks the group members to follow standard rules and regulations.
- The leader tells group members what is expected of them.

Consideration items included the following:

- The leader finds time to listen to group members.
- The leader is willing to make changes.
- The leader is friendly and approachable.

This dichotomy is consistent with the earlier work of Structuralists. Initiating behavior is related to Barnard's rational goals, while consideration is related to his moral imperative leadership function, for example. Dorwin Cartwright and Alvin Zander (1960) created profiles of informal groups that likewise fell into rational/nonrational categories: groups that seek to achieve some specific goal or that seek to maintain and strengthen the group itself.

ROUNDTABLE

The two dimensions of leadership that Stogdill identified are often represented as a managerial grid, as depicted in Figure 4.1. This grid identifies four general leadership profiles. It is tempting to assume that cell II, high task/high people, represents the best leadership style, but, as we will see in Chapter 6, this is not necessarily true. You may want to debate the optimal style for educational leaders. Under what conditions might an administrator function more effectively using different combinations of initiating and consideration behaviors? Identify logical relationships between different organizational types and leadership style (manufacturing factories, nonprofit organizations, or research hospitals, for example). What are the limitations of this two-dimensional perspective of leadership? ▨

Management Styles of Effective Leaders   Rensis Likert (1961) examined patterns of management used by effective leaders. He found that "supervisors with the best records of performance focus their primary attention on the human aspects of their employees' problems and on endeavoring to build effective work groups with high performance goals" (p. 7). They tended to effectively communicate goals

Initiating Structures

	Low	High
High	I	II
Low	III	IV

Consideration
Structures

FIGURE 4.1 Managerial grid based on findings of the Ohio State Studies.

to employees and to give them the freedom to do the job. He called these managers *employee-centered*. By contrast, *job-centered* managers pressured production and closely supervised employees. Employee-centered managers were not uniformly successful, and job-centered managers weren't uniformly unsuccessful, but the pattern of successful employee-centered managers and unsuccessful job-centered managers was strong.

Likert identified four styles of leadership from this. The styles represent points on a continuum that runs from job-centered to employee-centered. Style 1, the job-centered administration, represents the manager who has no confidence in employees, doesn't involve them in decisions or goal-setting, and supervises closely using fear tactics. Informal groups frequently emerge to oppose this type of manager. Style 2 managers, whom Likert labeled "benevolent authorities," have condescending attitudes toward employees, reserve responsibility for most goals, and monitor those decisions that are delegated, and are somewhat punishment-oriented. Informal groups typically emerge under this management style, but don't always oppose management. Style 3 managers are labeled "consultative." For the most part, they express confidence in employees' abilities, and therefore delegate specific decisions (but keep broad policy and decision-making powers for themselves). Communication flows rather freely within the system, and motivation utilizes a mixture of punishment and involvement. Informal groups are mostly supportive but may, at times, be resistant to managerial directives. Finally, style 4, what Likert labeled the "participative" style, has complete confidence in employees, delegates decision- and policy-making extensively, fosters extensive flow of communication, and motivates through involvement. Social forces are supportive.

PUNCTUATION

By the 1950s, Structuralist theorists increasingly recognized the impact of environmental issues on the formal system. Selznick, for example, was concerned about the effect of environmental pressures on organizational psychology, and

Parsons wrote of an institutional level within a system that is responsible for relating the organization to the larger society. Further, they were aware that organizations must deal with more than rational goals, that social organizations must juggle and adjust to multiple social and environmental goals in order to survive. It had become evident that Closed Systems theory, with its emphasis on unitary rational goals and its self-contained perspective, was untenable, and a major shift in perspective was becoming inevitable.

Diary

- In your diary entry for this chapter, summarize your thoughts on one or more Roundtable discussions that were proposed. You are also encouraged to reflect on the following questions (and on any other thoughts that you may have struggled with as you read the chapter, of course).
- Given what you have learned in this chapter, what are some important functions of leadership? In what way does your answer change your previous answers to this question?
- Drawing from Selznick's work, what are some of the forces in your school that operate to "compromise" formal organizational goals?

Recommended Readings

Barnard, C. I. (1938). *The functions of the executive*. Cambridge, MA: Harvard University Press.

Chester Barnard's classic was the handbook of organizational theory for years. In it, Barnard develops his thesis that leadership is derived from followers, and that the leader's role is to inculcate organizational values in followers.

Buckingham, M., & Coffman, C. (1999). *First break all the rules: What the world's greatest managers do differently*. New York: Simon & Schuster.

This book is referred to in an earlier Roundtable. A useful, modern treatment of leadership from a Human Relations perspective, it is a good addition to your reading queue.

Selznick, P. (1949). *TVA and the grass roots*. Berkeley: University of California Press.

Students wanting to conduct an institutional research study should start by reading this book. It is not only a good study and useful theory, it is fascinating history as well.

References

Barnard, C. I. (1938). *The functions of the executive*. Cambridge, MA: Harvard University Press.

Buckingham, M., & Coffman, C. (1999). *First break all the rules: What the world's greatest managers do differently*. New York: Simon & Schuster.

Cartwright, D., & Zander, A. (Eds.). (1960). *Group dynamics: Research and theory* (2nd ed.). Evanston, IL: Row, Peterson & Co.

Geier, J. G. (1967, December). A trait approach to the study of leadership in small groups. *Journal of Communications,* 316–323.

Hackman, J. R., & Oldham, G. (1976). Motivation through the design of work: A test of a theory. *Organizational Behavior and Human Performance, 16*(2), 250–279.

Halpin, A. (1966). *Theory and research in administration.* New York: Macmillan.

Hanson, E. M. (1996). *Educational administration and organizational behavior* (4th ed.). Boston: Allyn & Bacon.

Likert, R. (1961). *New patterns of management.* New York: McGraw-Hill, Inc.

Likert, R. (1967). *The human organization.* New York: McGraw-Hill, Inc.

McCall, M. W., & Lombardo, M. M. (1983, February). What makes a top executive? *Psychology Today,* 26–31.

Scott, W. R. (1964). Theory of organizations. In R. E. L. Faris (Ed.), *Handbook of modern sociology* (pp. 485–529). Chicago: Rand McNally.

Scott, W. R. (1987). *Organizations: Rational, natural, and open systems* (2nd ed.). Englewood Cliffs, NJ: Prentice Hall, Inc.

Selznick, P. (1948). Foundations of the theory of organizations. *American Sociological Review, 13,* 25–35.

Selznick, P. (1949). *TVA and the grass roots.* Berkeley: University of California Press.

Selznick, P. (1957). *Leadership in administration.* New York: Harper & Row.

Sergiovanni, T. J. (1992). *Moral leadership: Getting to the heart of school improvement.* San Francisco: Jossey-Bass.

Stogdill, R. M. (1948). Personal factors associated with leadership: A survey of the literature. *Journal of Psychology, 25,* 35–71.

PART TWO

Prescriptive Open Systems Theory

T he history of organizational theories is never as uncluttered as textbooks (like this one) make it out to be. Our textbooks must sort through a confusion of events that make up the body of theory and practice, must understand their common assumptions, and must convey all this in a way that can be understood. That sometimes means we must categorize and simplify the chronology of events. But life, and the full story of organizations, is never so simple. My point is that there was more going on during the 1940s and 1950s besides Human Relations and Structuralism. All of it, however, was converging toward the general theoretical principles we will be discussing over the next two chapters—and really the rest of the book—Open Systems theory.

I will relate some of these other "goings on" with stories, for the tales are fascinating and instructive. The first is a story of how one of the precursors of Open Systems theory helped win World War II. This theory is called Operations Research (OR, for short). OR is a process in which the management scientist formulates a problem, constructs a mathematical model to represent the system under study, solves the mathematical model, tests the model, establishes controls over the process, and implements the solution (Kast & Rosenzweig, 1970). OR was important in solving a number of tactical problems during World War II. It was first used in England during the Battle of Great Britain to organize the English radar interceptor defense system into an integrated man-machine system. This allowed optimal utilization of that system, thus dramatically improving the effectiveness of Great Britain's air defense. OR was used in the United States to organize the deployment of merchant marine convoys and to improve tactics for tracking down enemy submarines.

After the war, the OR model was expanded. During the war years, its use had been limited to the management of massive resource networks that could be quantified. In the 1950s, it was expanded to describe even larger, less quantifiable systems. Consequently, OR took on more of a general systems perspective, one that analyzed the interactions of a number of different dynamics and events. This perspective became an important basis for Open Systems theory.

The second story I wish to tell begins back in the late 1800s. Darwinism posed a major puzzle to scientists of this era. Natural selection could explain how life evolved, but it could not explain what life is or where life came from. What makes the difference between an inert blob of protein and a living blob of protein? Is life merely a complex system of neurons and electro-chemical pulses, or is there something more, perhaps something irreducible and indefinable by scientists?

One school of thought on this issue believed that chemical laws cannot account for life, and argued instead that life comes from a force known as "élan vital," also called entelechy. This force is the rough equivalent of what religions refer to as the soul. Hans Driesch, a German biologist, conducted a series of brilliant experiments to test whether life comes from a life force or is chemical in nature. He hypothesized that, if life is chemical, a complete blueprint for an adult must physically reside within its embryo and thus can be disrupted or severed from the embryo. If life derives from some nonchemical life force, then it cannot be separated from the animal by science. Driesch tested his hypothesis by cutting a fertilized embryo in half. When the halves developed, they formed two complete adult animals. He then fused two fertilized eggs between glass plates, and got one, not two, adults. Driesch argued that the physical and chemical laws of nature fail to explain these results. If the blueprint for maturity existed within the original embryo, then cutting away half the blueprint should have left half an adult and two blueprints should have created two adults. He felt that some uncanny force was at play, a force that was supernaturally unaffected by his manipulation. This life force, the élan vital, was not physical, and it alone carried the blueprint of maturity.

Sixty years later, biologist Ludwig von Bertalanffy (1956) picked up the story. He felt that Driesch was mistaken in his assumption that the complete blueprint for a system's adult form is either physically complete in the embryo or attributable to a supernatural force. He argued instead that the embryo need only contain the rough outline of the animal's final form and that the rest of the picture comes as the system interacts and exchanges materials with its environment. He proposed that the environment's input is constant, so regardless of what the system starts with, the final form will be the same. Half an egg, two eggs, it doesn't matter; the environment gives the same thing regardless, and one adult will result.

Now all of this was debated before and about the same time that DNA was discovered by Crick and Watson. We now know that there is indeed a rather complete blueprint within the embryo, but that the blueprint exists in every cell. For Driesch to have surgically disrupted this blueprint, he would have needed procedures and patience that just weren't available to him. But whereas Driesch's experiments have been laid to rest, von Bertalanffy's proposals have not. His notions about the importance of environmental inputs in system development are important today, and constitute an important part of Open Systems theory.

Systems, he proposed, exist within an environment of resources. The system imports these resources, processes them, and returns a product to the environment. This exchange feeds the system, invigorates the environment, and changes both system and environment. Systems, he suggested, are products of their initial blueprints *and* their exchanges with the environment.

This is the essence of the theories to which we now turn. The old theories—Machine theory and Human Relations—portray the attitude that everything of importance lies within the organization. Those theorists, like their counterparts in Darwinian biology, felt that the determinants of organizational effectiveness and form lay within organizational walls. Thus, Taylor, Mayo, and the others largely ignored the environment or assumed that its effect could be readily controlled within the organization. Businesses were self-contained worlds.

The theories that emerged in the 1960s sought to understand how environment affects organizational structure, behavior, and productivity. The next chapter discusses Open Systems theory itself and uses it to explore worker motivation. The chapter after that examines Contingency theory, a derivative of Open Systems theory. This theory explores strategies for adapting to environmental and organizational contingencies. We will use that discussion as a platform for discussing leadership strategies.

Contingency theory and our discussion of Open Systems theory are "prescriptive;" that is, they are intended to provide prescriptions for organizational problems. Consequently, they assume a regular, law-like relationship between contingency and organizational outcome. Later theories (those to be developed in Part III of this textbook) contradict that assumption. Regardless, these later theories are based on the Open Systems assumption of environmental influence. Open Systems theory is a global concept that has, to varying extents, guided all theoretical development since about 1960. For that reason, Part II is titled Prescriptive Open Systems Theory, to help differentiate it from later nonprescriptive theories.

References

Kast, F., & Rosenzweig, J. (1970). *Organization and management.* New York: McGraw Hill Book Company.

von Bertalanffy, L. (1956). General systems theory. In L. von Bertalanffy & A. Rapoport (Eds.), *General systems: Yearbook of the society for the advancement of general systems theory* (Vol. 1, pp. 1–10).

CHAPTER 5

Motivation and Communication in Open Systems

Open Systems theory takes the next logical step in the evolution of organizational theory during the 20th century: it adds extra-organizational dynamics to the list of things that explain organization. This change dramatically upsets the neat little explanatory bundles that Closed Systems theorists had so carefully assembled during the first half of the century. It marks the beginning of the end to the notion that management and leadership is a science, with intuitive, one-size-fits-all prescriptions about efficiency or human relations. And in doing so, Open Systems theorists shed an illuminating light over some of the puzzles in Closed Systems theory. Frederick Taylor's difficulty with employee resistance to his efficiency efforts (the "soldiering" incident described in Chapter 2), for example, can now be explained not only as a social-psychological event (the explanation of Human Relationists), but as a product of external social, cultural, and technological forces as well. French's failure to replicate the famous change agent outcome of his pajama factory experiment can be understood relative to similar environmental forces (Coch & French, 1948; French, Israel, & Aas, 1960; see Chapter 3). Open Systems adds a level of reality to organization that was naively missing from earlier theories, and, in doing so, made it possible for administrators to improve their ability to lead.

One should not conclude, however, that the recommendations of earlier theorists can now be uniformly relegated to the circular file, for there is much that remains useful for us. Taylor's advice about efficiency is still important guidance for industry and education. Informal groups are still potent forces in social life and much of the research on this topic by Human Relations theorists is useful for understanding and dealing with them. Lewin's recommendations about change still work, although we should be conscious of complicating factors. Clearly, of course, some of the early administration prescriptions are bogus (no one can be serious about Mayo's organic equilibrium, for example). However, much of the advice from these early years can help modern leaders do better jobs, particularly if the advice is tempered by an understanding of the added complexity introduced by Open Systems theory.

Open Systems theory will be the template from which all the subsequent theories discussed in this book are, in one fashion or another, derived. Some modern students of organization have tended to retreat a bit toward a Closed Systems perspective—some motivational speakers, for example—but all the mainstream theories of the last half of the 20th century recognize the impact of environment on organizational behavior.

The basic principles of Open Systems theory are introduced in this chapter. We will analyze organizational dynamics with a general Open Systems model and with a variation of Open Systems known as the Getzels model. We will then focus the Open Systems model on the evaluation of employee motivation and organizational communication, and will explore strategies that can be applied to improving these organizational dynamics.

In this chapter, students will:

- Examine and critique models of open social systems.
- Use the Open Systems perspective to develop effective organizational change strategies.
- Apply an Open Systems model to evaluate organizational behavior.
- Apply the Open Systems model to understand, evaluate, and improve the motivation of organizational actors.
- Use Open Systems principles to evaluate organizational and personal communication patterns.
- Develop personal strategies for improving their response to communication overload.
- Refine their definitions of the function of leadership in education.

THE OPEN SYSTEMS PERSPECTIVE ON THINGS

Open Systems theory, which became popular in the 1960s, made the then-revolutionary claim that organizational structure and behavior are significantly influenced by their environments. Previous theories had told us that leaders were rational and that the sole focus of organization was the pursuit of productivity. Open Systems theorists argue that organizational dynamics are the product of complex causality and that organizations juggle multiple pressures.

Open Systems theory emerged during an interesting era, one that undoubtedly influenced its popularization. It was a period of social upheaval, a time in which baby boomers reached puberty and were exercising teenage rebelliousness, a time of liberal politics, a time in which our society was becoming increasingly concerned about the disenfranchised and the alienated.

In earlier years, theorists had tended to hold workers responsible for their behavior: if someone failed, it was because of his or her own shortcomings and not because of shortcomings in the system itself. Maslow, for example, focused on the dynamics of individual psychologies, suggesting that personal attitude, rather than external events, is the key to worker motivation. Similarly, in education student failure was considered a failure of the individual, and educational quality was attributed almost exclusively to funding levels and what money could buy (see Marion and Flanigan, 2001).

Open Systems theory, by contrast, seeks solutions to problems within a broad range of organizational and environmental dynamics. If a person fails, its advocates propose, it is because of failures in the system and only partially because of individual shortcomings. Similarly, the broader movement of the 1960s attributed crime to anomie and disenfranchisement, student failure to poverty and other environmental problems, and educational shortcomings to the failure of society in general. No one factor is responsible for problems and shortcomings; rather, they are a function of the interactions among a number of different structures and events.

Social expectations, laws, raw materials, technological sophistication, the behaviors of other systems, fiscal realities, competition, and buyers all shape and constrain organizational structure and behavior. Leaders act as they do because of what they were taught by their culture, because of the nature of the raw materials they process, because of the degree of volatility in the competitive environment, because of unions, and because of legal constraints. The tasks we perform in our organizations are determined by learned behavior, the state of technology, and by the nature of the raw material the organization processes. Systems do not act in a vacuum; they do not control their own destinies. They are products of their environments.

CHARACTERISTICS OF OPEN SYSTEMS

To the Open Systems theorist, organizations are holistic; that is, their capacity for action is greater than the summed capabilities of their parts. The system can comprehend more about its environment, can process vastly more information, has a broader repertoire of symbolic languages, has more advanced reproductive capabilities, possesses a more effective survival potential, and exerts greater control over its environment than do any of its parts individually. A system is a super-entity, and it is smarter and more potent than any mere mortals individually. One can readily understand this by mentally contrasting the effectiveness of 10 individuals acting alone with that of the same 10 people acting in concert.

Open systems are themselves made up of subsystems—structures or functions that perform specific tasks. These subsystems interact with one another and, if the system is fit, are stably related to one another; that is, they are "homeostatic." If one element of the system is perturbed or damaged by outside forces, all other subsystems feel the effect of that perturbation. They react by adjusting their own structures and behaviors, and by applying pressure on the originally perturbed element to make collateral changes. The net result is that the system finds a new stable relationship among its component parts.

FIGURE 5.1 Simplified representation of the Open Systems model.

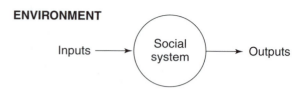

Systems theory visualizes systems floating in an environmental sea that is bombarding it with demands, or inputs (see Fig. 5.1). The system selectively absorbs those demands (it has a semi-permeable membrane), processes them, and returns some form of output into the environment. Open systems utilize feedback mechanisms to gauge the state of the environment and the environment's reaction to the system's output.

The forces that motivate a system lie in its environment; the environment is its source of energy, the medium that determines internal structure and function and that dictates change. A system that is not in sync with environmental demands is not optimally fit. Feedback mechanisms enable sync, or homeostasis, with the environment by providing information needed to adapt to external pressures and changes.

Mapping the Environment

Open systems "map" the information in an environment; that is, they have the ability to sense and imprint environmental stimuli and to react to those imprints at future times. Newly hatched ducklings, for example, imprint images of their mother (or whatever/whoever is present) and subsequently follow the lead of that mother figure. Because of this ability to map the environment for future reference, persistent relationships can evolve, or self-organize.

Mapping requires three abilities: (1) the ability to sense and assign meaning to symbolic information; (2) the ability to map or imprint parts of the environment, to take photos so to speak and to store the pictures; and (3) the ability to relate new stimuli to previous mappings.

Humans sense their environments with their eyes, ears, nose, touch, and taste. Organizations sense their environments with the eyes, ears, nose, touch, and taste of their employees. The complex system assigns meaning to a given stimulus by relating the stimulus to a pre-existing concept map. If it has no pre-existing map for defining a given bit of information, then that information may be either figuratively (if not actually) invisible to the system, or it may be mapped into an improper category (i.e., misinterpreted). If an administrator has no experience with a problem the organization is facing, he or she may just not perceive the problem or may draw incorrect conclusions based on other maps that are believed pertinent to the problem. If a principal has no map of school law, for example, he or she may not realize a law is being violated or may interpret matters in light of personal experiences.

The system's environmental map must match the current state of the environment, and the system constantly changes its map to maintain congruence. If the system's map is not tuned to its environment, the system must work to bring it up to date. It must alter portions of that map, rearrange connections between different parts of the map, or delete and replace certain sections. Feedback information is the mechanism by which this is accomplished.

Open Systems Theory: Feedback   One system is a source of feedback for others, and systems do work on each other's maps through the feedback of symbolic information. Feedback, according to Systems theory, is important to any system that requires internal adjustments in order to remain in step with the environment. A thermostat maintains a constant temperature by adjusting its internal state in response to fluctuations in air temperature. The thermostat has a goal, say, to achieve and maintain an air temperature of 68°F. By selectively turning on the furnace when the air temperature is below 68°F and turning it off (or activating an air coolant system) when the temperature exceeds 68°, it can achieve its goal. Feedback, in this example, is a goal-directing process that dampens deviation from a target goal.

Systems theorists argue that an organized complex system modifies its goals as it interacts with the environment, and that goals and environmental stimuli are dynamically intertwined. Thus, the system can change its goals "on the fly" in response to environmental fluctuations or demands; that is, it can adapt.

Negative Feedback   Feedback comes in two varieties: positive and negative. Negative feedback suggests that maturing systems eventually run out of steam. They reach a point in their development at which further effort provides negligible return, and they settle into an equilibrium state. The thermostat described above is a negative feedback system. Homeostasis, according to systems theory, occurs when deviations from a goal are dampened through negative feedback. Peer pressure suppresses behaviors that peers consider deviant and directs the deviant toward stable, acceptable behavior, just as feedback mechanisms on elevators suppress motion as a target floor is approached.

Diminishing returns—the economic equivalent of negative feedback—argue that market demand stabilizes as a need becomes saturated. The initial sales of a new car model stir up considerable market interest; subsequent sales generate increasingly less interest. At some point, the market for that car stabilizes. A glass of lemonade after a round of tennis on a hot day would be quite important to you, and you would probably be glad to pay a child at a lemonade stand, say, a dollar for it. The second glass is of less value to you, however, and the third even less so. This is diminishing returns.

Negative feedback and diminishing returns favor no time, person, or place. They allow no particular advantage except the advantage that accrues to excellence (the "free market" principle). Diminishing returns corral growth and prevent any given system from monopolizing environmental resources; thus, there is plenty of opportunity to go around. With hard work and intelligence, any child who is born a citizen of the United States can become president; any mom and pop outfit could become a megacorporation, and any town can become a Silicon Valley.

"School Choice," a popular political issue in the United States at the end of the 20th century, illustrates this. Choice would allow parents to decide which public school their children attend. Proponents assume that choice would force schools to compete for students, and that better schools would thrive while the less competent would have to improve to survive. Negative feedback favors only excellence, and deviations from excellence are either pulled to the norm or they don't survive. All schools, according to this free market assumption, have the same basic opportunity to pull themselves up. Opportunity for success is equally distributed across the "landscape" of schools; a school in the northern part of a district has the same opportunities as one in the south. The process is, to be sure, egalitarian.

Positive Feedback   Economists have only recently begun to accept the importance of positive return, or increasing returns, in explaining economic dynamics (Waldrop, 1992). Resistance, particularly in the United States, was in part attributable to the fact that it challenges the premises underlying free market philosophy (negative feedback, the preferred economic paradigm, is democratic to a fault). Positive feedback, or "increasing returns" in economic language, refers to the deceptively simple ideas that are epitomized by a rolling snowball or by microphone feedback: "Them that has, gets more," or speaking Biblically, "To them that hath shall be given" (the rich get richer and the poor get poorer—we could go on for a while here). Positive feedback is deviation-amplifying—feedback feeding on itself and its environment and pushing itself away from its current status. Unlike economists, systems theorists have flirted with these ideas from the early years of their movement. Magoroh Maruyama, writing in 1963, provided several examples. For example, he argued that the growth of a city on an agricultural plain begins when a farmer, for chance reasons, locates on that plain. His presence attracts other farmers, which, in turn, attracts farming-related industry, and so on.

Proponents of increasing returns derive different conclusions about school choice, discussed a bit earlier, than do proponents of diminishing returns. Increasing returns suggest that initially advantaged schools, those with a brighter class of students, a better football team, or better organized parents, will be able to capitalize on that advantage at the expense of other schools, and that school choice would only exacerbate differences. Given a choice, more parents—in particular, more parents who value education—would choose to have their children attend an advantaged school rather than a disadvantaged one. The advantaged school would benefit from an increasing population of concerned parents and disadvantaged schools would suffer from their loss. This handicaps the latter in its efforts to attract the type of parent that can help pull them out of their doldrums. Further, better teachers would seek employment at the advantaged school and tax money would flow to the better school because of its burgeoning enrollment. The disadvantaged school is locked in a vicious spiral of decreasing resources from which no amount of will power can save it. The advantaged school, by contrast, is locked in a spiral that feeds it ever-increasing resources. Egalitarian excellence is not enabled by choice; rather, effectiveness is polarized into the haves and the have nots. It's not free exchange and excellence that create Silicon Valleys and Japanese success and VHS video dominance, it is initial advantage. Minor differences become exaggerated differences, and the lucky, rather than the best, rise to the top.

MODELS OF OPEN SYSTEMS

Open Systems theorists derived a number of specific models of organization from the basic systems model. Harold Leavitt (1964), for example, described organizations as sociotechnical systems composed of four subsystems. A sociotechnical system, he argued, is a social entity dedicated to a certain technology. The four subsystems in his model are tasks, structure, technology, and humans. The task subsystem defines the processes that are performed within the system, the structure subsystem defines the way the system is organized and governed, the technological subsystem defines the type of equipment and knowledge a system must possess, and the human subsystem defines such things as the skills, attitudes, psychology, roles, and motivators of the people in the organization.

Daniel Katz and Robert Kahn (1966) focused more on the dynamics required to process environmental inputs than on the structures associated with processing (as Leavitt had done). They identified five general subsystems: the production or technical subsystems, managerial subsystems, supportive subsystems, maintenance subsystems, and adaptive subsystems. Production subsystems are concerned with the technology of production, thus they differ little from Leavitt's tasks and technologies subsystems. Managerial subsystems are concerned with organizing and governing organizational processes. The supportive subsystems interact with the environmental to insure a constant influx of energy (such as raw materials and new recruits). The maintenance subsystems maintain the boundaries of the subsystem; they represent the forces of stability and status quo. The adaptive subsystems provide checks and balances for the maintenance structures; they represent forces devoted to change in response to environmental pressures and environmental change.

John Seiler's (1967) description of systems is a bit more complex than either Leavitt's or Katz's and Kahn's models. He argued that organizations possess three broad, interdependent subsystems: internal inputs, actual behaviors, and internal outputs (see Fig. 5.2). Each of these internal functions is further segmented into its own set of sub-subsystems. Internal inputs are divided into humans, technologies, social systems, and organization. Human inputs refer to the skills, needs, motivations, and attitudes of participants. Technologies are the competencies required to perform organizational functions—education's principal technology, for example, is instruction. Social systems are the informal structures within organizations. Organizational subsystems are the structural and coordination patterns by which

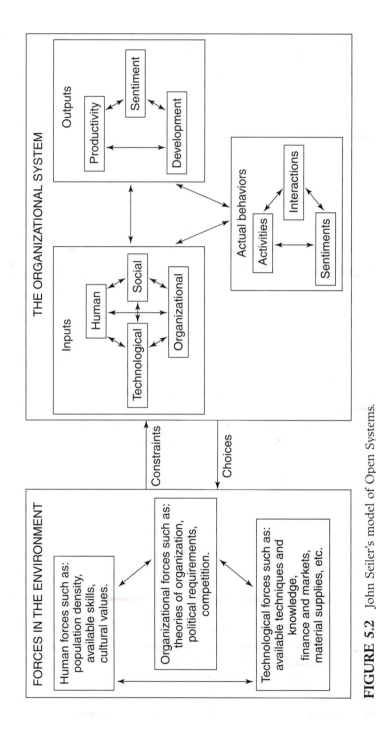

FIGURE 5.2 John Seiler's model of Open Systems.

From John A. Seiler, *Systems analysis in organizational behavior.* (Homewood, IL: Richard D. Irwin, Inc., and The Dorsey Press, 1967), p. 33. Copyright © 1967 by McGraw-Hill Companies. Adapted by permission.

the organization accomplishes its tasks. The internal behaviors of an organization refer to the activities, interactions, and sentiments of participants. Internal outputs include productivity, satisfaction, and development (individual growth or learning).

Seiler argues that a system's external environment is composed of three elements: human forces (population density, available skills, attitudes, cultural values, etc.); organizational forces (theories of organization, political requirements, competition, etc.); and technological forces (available techniques and knowledge, finances and markets, materials and supplies, etc.). These environmental factors influence the organization and provide the pool from which the organization selects its internal inputs. The organization's social structures are selected from, and influenced by, the social forces available in the environment, for example. The organization's human forces are selected from, and influenced by, the pool of human skills, attitudes, and motivations in the environment. This is not to say that internal inputs are representative of the environment, that the human pool is a mirror image of the human pool in the environment, or that an organization's technology is a microcosm of all technologies available to it. The organization selectively chooses from the environment; thus, schools try to avoid selecting teachers who don't like children or who have failed to demonstrate sufficient ability to obtain licensure.

ROUNDTABLE

Now that you have examined several generic Open Systems models and studied the dynamics of these systems, try constructing a model of an educational system (school, district, university, etc.). You will probably want to build on the functions identified by the theorists described above, but your model should be identifiably educational.   ■

Case Study on Change

We will now use a hybrid model of Open Systems using Seiler's environmental forces and Leavitt's sociotechnical system (Fig. 5.3) to illustrate how sensitivity to Open Systems interaction can improve the practice of educational change. Consider a school principal who is trying to change the way instruction is delivered in the classroom (instruction is a school's technological subsystem). The principal introduces change in the form of computer technology (for the sake of illustration, we will assume that the teachers in this school do not have experience with computers). The principal follows an all too familiar (if somewhat exaggerated) pattern of change: he or she purchases the equipment and software, rolls it into the teacher's classroom, provides a bit of training in the operation of the system, and leaves. He or she assumes that change has been wrought, and that great things will now occur.

In reality, a number of dynamics have been set into motion, and the principal's failure to deal with these dynamics may derail the change effort. The perturbation of the classroom's technology subsystem places strain on, and is mediated by, the skills, motivation, and attitudes of teachers (the human subsystem). It calls

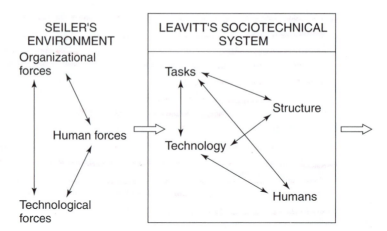

FIGURE 5.3   A hybrid model of Open Systems based on Seiler's (1967) environmental subsystems and Leavitt's (1964) organizational subsystems.

From John A. Seiler, *Systems analysis in organizational behavior.* (Homewood, IL: Richard D. Irwin, Inc., and The Dorsey Press, 1967), p. 33. Copyright © 1967 by the McGraw-Hill Companies. Also from H. Leavitt (1965). Applied organizational change in industry: Structural, technological, and humanistic approaches, in *Handbook of organization* (Chicago: Rand McNally & Co.), p. 1145. Copyright by James G. March. Adapted by permission.

for a reorganization of the way instruction is delivered, curriculum is structured, and classroom space is organized (all elements of the task subsystem). It demands changes in the way resources are allocated and will require revision of the school's policies to deal with issues such as software piracy or Internet access (structural subsystems). It also elicits a response from teachers' social groups (another element of the human subsystem). These other subsystems will seek ways to adapt to the original technological change, but will also attempt to alter the original change to suit their own needs and preferences (you should recognize elements of Selznick's Institutionalization theory in this).

As the subsystems work their way through this adjusting process, they must simultaneously accommodate environmental issues as well. Parental attitudes (a component of Seiler's human forces) will influence the internal process, and the internal process will, in turn, affect the attitudes of parents. The opinions and policies of the school board will play a role in the emerging dynamics (external organizational forces). Educators will look to the knowledge base in the environment (external organizational forces) for clues about how to best organize classroom resources. The sophistication of educational software, the state of data transmission capabilities, and other issues in the technological environment will either restrict or enable internal processes, and internal dynamics among the school's teachers will influence the development of technological solutions for educational issues.

A driving force in all this is the natural tendency of a system to seek homeostatic stability, a state in which the various internal and external forces are at rest relative to one another. If the principal fails to deal effectively with the interactive cascade set loose by the introduction of computers, the homeostatic state that the system achieves could be one in which the original change is isolated and neutralized, rather than one in which computers have become an active element of the instruction. To avoid such "scabbing over" of change, teachers should be shown how to organize classroom activities, how to integrate computers into existing curricula, how to manage classroom logistics, and how to make computers a part of the instructional flow. Budgetary line items should be dedicated to purchases and repair, network maintenance, and such. Buildings may need renovation: a classroom with two or three electrical outlets and a single 15-amp breaker, for example, is not going to support much technology. Teachers should be involved in decision making; they should have opportunities to attend conferences and workshops; their creativity should be encouraged. Parents should be sold on the change, and policy support of the school board should be sought. The effective principal will attempt to maneuver the numerous internal and external factors that influence the change launched within the school. These forces will not likely submit to control in the Machine theory sense, and they will throw unexpected developments into the mix. The school board, for example, may balk at allowing students access to the Internet because of generalized fears about the types of things they may be exposed to, or an informal group of "technologically challenged" teachers may rebel against changes in the way they teach. The principal prods, maneuvers, stimulates, and, at times, just goes with the flow. It's like herding chickens; you do the best you can, but if the chickens decide to go to the hen house instead of the yard, you pretend that was what you intended all along and you make the best of it. But you don't merely open the gate to the yard and then sit back and let the chickens do what they want.

 ## RESEARCH TOPIC

Select an organizational change episode with which you are familiar. If the change has run its course, your task is to explain why it was successful or unsuccessful. If the episode is just beginning, your task is to identify organizational features that will require adjustment in order for the change to succeed. Sketch the change diagrammatically, with the focal change in the middle of your diagram and affected subsystems floating around the change. Connect subsystems with one another and with the focal change using single- or double-headed arrows representing one- or two-way effects. For example, the availability of suitable textbooks would affect the implementation of a new curriculum, and the new curriculum may affect demand for textbook revisions (double-headed arrow). As you identify appropriate subsystems, consider not only dynamics that go on inside the school but outside as well; a curricular change in k-12 education, for example, may place demands on university teacher preparation programs—an external subsystem. Explain or predict based on your analysis of the change dynamics. What are the implications for educational change?

Holistic Analysis of World Dynamics

There is a problem with the holistic Open Systems perspective: it is not easily researched. The traditional reductionist approach in which phenomena are isolated for study violates the holistic principles that are key to Systems theory. One of the more credible analyses by a systems theorist is attributable to J.W. Forrester (1969, 1971), whose studies of world and urban dynamics were ambitious efforts to apply interactive principles and the power of computers to prediction. His findings led to some interesting debates and revelations about Open Systems theory.

Forrester identified what he considered to be major elements of urban or world dynamics, then mathematically modeled the interactions of those elements. In the world model, for example, he examined such things as population, standard of living, pollution, natural resources, capital investment, and percentage investment in agriculture (see Fig. 5.4). His models predicted a collapse of world markets by 2050 A.D. This, predictably, generated considerable public discussion and consternation when it hit the press.

A group of scientists from MIT, however, found that his model's formulas, when run in reverse to "predict" the past, produced some rather bizarre results (see B.P. Bloomfield's 1986 discussion). Population predictions, for example, began to grow exponentially in about 1895 and reached 3.9 billion by 1880 (remember, the model is running in reverse); this, of course, did not happen in reality. If the models fail to work in reverse, the scientists argued, how can one believe their predictions of the future? Forrester countered that the data on which the formulas depended (the initial conditions, or state of the variables at the beginning of the analysis) were improperly estimated. Forrester adjusted his initial population estimates to correct the 1880 anomaly, but the change caused strange results to emerge in other variables. He and his supporters suggested, among other things, that initial conditions are problematic and that difficulties with data hardly invalidated the importance of the models or of the general findings.

Forrester's defense got close to the truth when he focused on initial conditions; indeed, as we shall see in Chapter 13 when we examine Complexity theory, system trajectories are highly sensitive to their initial conditions. Forrester—and his critics—would have expected small initial differences to translate into small outcome differences, leading one to conclude that difficulty with reversal experiments is due to large initial errors (or inadequate models). Complexity theorists have demonstrated that the dynamics in interactive systems of the sort that Forrester investigated tend to diverge unpredictably, and that small errors in initial conditions can generate large, unpredictable errors in subsequent outcomes. In other words, even a small error in Forrester's initial conditions can produce futures (or pasts) that have nothing to do with reality. Forrester's model probably had little chance of accurately predicting the future.

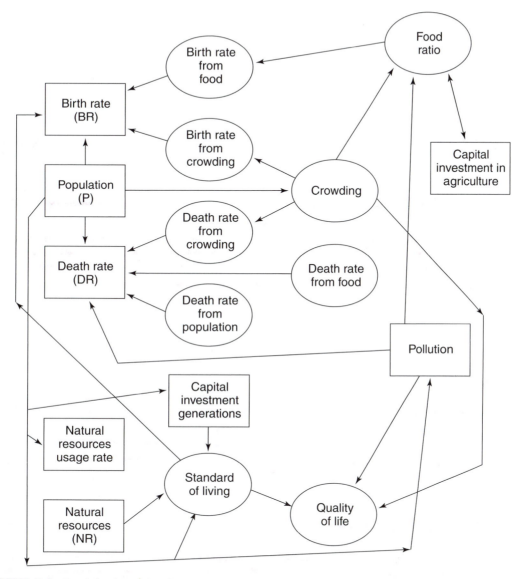

FIGURE 5.4 Partial schematic of Forrester's Worldview.

From J.W. Forrester, *World dynamics*. (Waltham, MA: Pegasus Communications, Inc., 1973), pp. 20–21. Copyright © 1973 by Pegasus Communications, Inc. Adapted by permission.

THE GETZELS-GUBA MODEL OF ORGANIZATION

Social psychologist Jacob Getzels, with the assistance of Egon Guba (one of Getzels' first doctoral students after he joined the faculty of the Education Department at the University of Chicago), has produced an Open Systems model that is still core to many organizational theory courses in school administration. Getzels, an émigré from Poland, served in the OSS, America's spy apparatus, during World War II, then earned his doctoral degree at Harvard University in 1951. In the 1960s, Getzels was an activist in America's civil rights movement and was present with Dr. Martin Luther King, Jr. at the famous voter registration march on Selma, Alabama, in 1965. But he is best known, at least among educational administration theorists, for his model of social behavior in educational organizations—the Getzels-Guba model.

Getzels and Guba argued that a model of organization must begin with social systems. Getzels and Guba wrote from the perspective of *social psychologists*. Social psychology is the study of people in social settings, particularly within formal organizational settings. It fused psychology with sociology. Social psychology bridged the Human Relations and Open Systems traditions both conceptually and chronologically, and was rather strongly influenced by the Structuralist movement. It included theorists such as Talcott Parsons, George Homans, Daniel Katz and Robert Kahn, and Harold Leavitt. You will see the various traditions represented by Open and Closed Systems, psychology and sociology, and Structuralism in Getzels' and Guba's conceptualizations of social systems. Their definition of social system, for example, assumes both psychological and sociological elements (what they call individuals and institutions), and their systems models clearly reflect the tension between rational and irrational that undergirds structuralism.

Getzels, Lipham, and Campbell define social system as "the interdependence of parts, their integration into some sort of whole, and the intrinsic presence of both individuals and institutions" (1968, p. 54). From this assumption they derive two dimensions of social activity, the nomothetic and idiographic dimensions (Getzels, 1958; Getzels & Guba, 1957). The terms "nomothetic" and "idiographic" correspond to sociological and psychological elements of social systems, respectively (or rational and irrational elements of Structuralist theory), but the terms carry deeper meaning. Nomothetic structures refer to things that have something in common; thus, their behavior can be generalized and described in terms of "laws." When researchers state that "socio-economic status accounts for 40 to 60 percent of variation in achievement test scores," or that "girls tend to develop more rapidly than boys during the early school years," they are making nomothetic arguments, generalizations that tend to be true across a wide variety of people. Hence, the nomothetic dimension is associated with sociology, or a set of generalized "rules" about human behavior. Idiographic describes phenomena that cannot be generalized, and that are locally defined and locally meaningful. If researchers argue that student achievement can be understood only by exploring a given school's policies, decisions, activities, and students, they are making

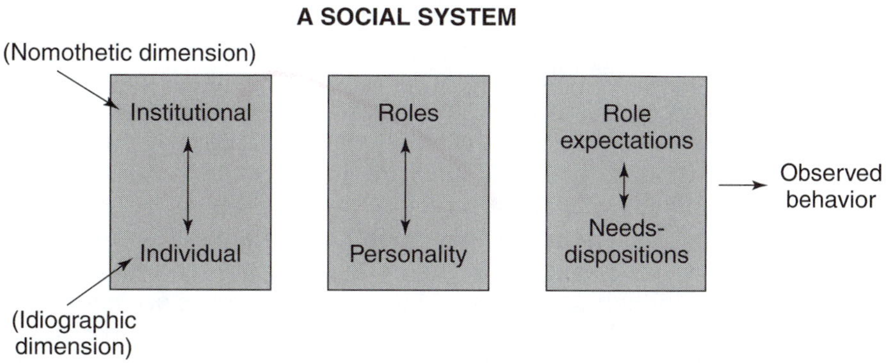

A SOCIAL SYSTEM

FIGURE 5.5 Getzels' and Guba's original (1957) model, nomothetic and idiographic dimensions are shaded.

From Jacob W. Getzels, (1957). Social behavior and the administrative process, *School Review 65,* p. 429. Copyright © 1957 by the University of Chicago Press. Adapted by permission.

an idiographic observation. Thus, the idiographic dimension of an organization is associated with individual, poorly generalizable psychologies or activities.

Getzels' and Guba's first model of social systems, published in 1957, is a Closed Systems model because it does not account for influences outside the system, such as culture or other general environmental factors (see Fig. 5.5). The model was developed at a time when the Open Systems perspective had not yet settled in the general theoretical mindset. This figure reflects their assumption that organizations are social systems with nomothetic (sociological) and idiographic (psychological) dimensions.

Following the nomothetic dimension (shaded) from left to right in Figure 5.5, social systems are composed of *institutions,* which are, in turn, composed of *roles,* which are composed of *role expectations*. Institutions, the first component of the nomothetic dimension, have five basic properties. Institutions are purposive (established to carry out goals), peopled (actors with functions to perform), structured (actors are organized by rules), normative (there are expected modes of behavior), and sanction-bearing (having the capability to enforce norms).

Together, the purposes, actors, structures, norms, and sanctions (i.e., institutions) produce a variety of organizational roles. A role is defined as expected, rather than actual, behavior. Any given individual (an idiographic unit) may choose to define his or her role differently from what is expected by the institution. As Getzels, Lipham, and Campbell (1968) put it, a judge may conduct him- or herself injudiciously or illegally—indeed all judges in a community may behave in an illegal manner—but "the role of judge as a structural and normative point of orientation within the legal institution would not thereby be altered to include behaving dishonestly" (p. 60). Indeed, they continue, it is the discrepancy between the expected and actual role that we use to evaluate the performance of judges—or anyone else.

Roles lead to role expectations, which are rights and duties associated with a given office or role. A person in a role acts in a certain way because of the expectations for that role. Teachers are expected to instruct children and physicians are expected to make us well. Role expectations, however, define not only the rights and duties of a person, but limit rights and duties as well. A teacher is not expected to prescribe medicine to sick children and is not held responsible for a child's bad teeth.

The personal, or idiographic, dimension of an organization is composed of *individuals, personalities,* and *needs-dispositions*. To understand an organization, it is not enough to understand its roles and role expectations; one must understand the individuals who occupy those roles and who carry out the role expectations. Individuals bring their own styles to the job, their own way of relating to people, of making decisions, and of managing responsibilities.

The idiographic dimension in Figure 5.5 is composed of individuals, personalities, and needs-dispositions. Individuals are distinguished by their personalities. Personality is the totality of one's behaviors, the way one reacts to stimuli, and the way others respond to the personality. Personality, in turn, drives needs-dispositions, forces within individuals that motivate them to be the way they are and to respond as they do.

The elements of the nomothetic dimension of an organization interact with the elements of the idiographic dimension. Individuals shape institutions and institutions shape individuals; roles affect one's personality (perhaps certain authority positions lend an element of arrogance to the personality, for example) and one's personality gives a distinctive twist to the role. Similarly, role expectations affect needs-dispositions and vice versa. The dynamics of these two dimensions, and the interactions between them, define observed behaviors in the organization.

In 1963, Getzels expanded the basic model to include culture—an environmental dimension; thus, the earlier Closed Systems model became an Open Systems model (see Fig. 5.6). Culture, he argued, is comprised of ethos, which is made up in turn of values. Culture inevitably affects the roles and role expectancies we define for our schools (the nomothetic dimension; a vocationally oriented culture, for example, is not likely to support the teaching of Latin), and it affects the people within an organization, as well as their needs and dispositions (idiographic dimension).

Over the following 10 years, Getzels came to the conclusion that his notion of "culture" was too monolithic; it implied that society is a single entity in terms of people's ideology, cultural identification, political orientation, and such. In 1978, he replaced culture with community (Fig. 5.7), and proposed that communities are composed of numerous interactive subcommunities. He identified six such subcommunities: local communities, administrative communities, social communities, instrumental or functional communities, ethnic communities, and ideological communities. Any one person can hold membership in several of these communities, and any one community category can be composed of a number of subcategories (there is no single "black community," for example). These communities were summarized in his 1978 model as "collective identities," and collective identities are composed of norms and values.

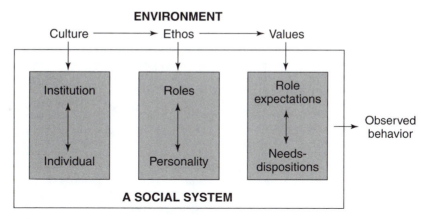

FIGURE 5.6   Getzels' 1963 model.

From J. Getzels, J. Lipham, & R. Campbell, *Education administration as a social process: theory, research & practice,* p. 106. (New York: Harper & Row). Copyright © 1968. Adapted by permission.

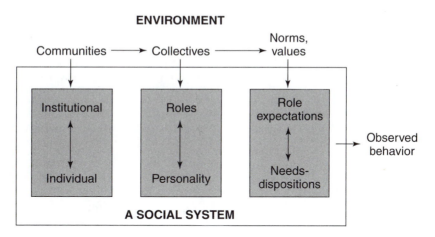

FIGURE 5.7   Getzels' community dimension model.

From Jacob W. Getzels, (1978). The communities of education, *Teacher College Record 79* (4), p. 673. Copyright © 1978 by Blackwell Publishers, Ltd. Adapted by permission.

Practical Application of the Getzels-Guba Model

Many training programs for school administrators have a course in school and community relationships, and all programs inevitably address issues of community relations in one context or another. One of the skills typically taught in such a course is how to assess community or group needs. By understanding those needs, administrators can better serve those constituencies. Variations of

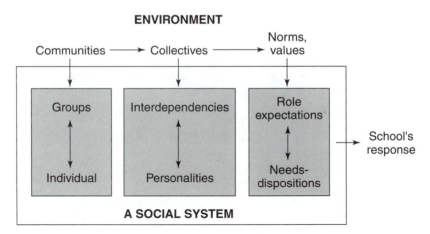

FIGURE 5.8 A model of community assessment derived from the Getzels-Guba model of social systems.

From Jacob W. Getzels, (1978). The communities of education, *Teacher College Record 79* (4), p. 673. Copyright © 1978 by Blackwell Publishers, Ltd. Adapted by permission.

the Getzels-Guba model can help focus such assessments. An example is presented in Figure 5.8.

This model suggests three levels of evaluation: community/cultural level, a more specific group (nomothetic) level, and an individual (idiographic) level. Let's say you are interested in understanding the needs and characteristics of a particular group of students in your school (or a group of parents, or probable contributors to your endowment program). The community level for your evaluation target is the general societal cultures or communities with which the group identifies. Cultural groups often are self-defined or obvious: examples include rednecks and preppies; ethnic groups such as African-Americans and Hispanics; and socio-economic groups such as middle class and blue collar. However, any given group will likely belong to several communities, so it may not be sufficient to understand only the dominant community with which the group is associated.

The group level refers to a specific group within a school. This group identifies with the broader cultures or communities to which it belongs, but inevitably possesses unique characteristics that must be evaluated separately from the broader culture. They are unique because, among other things, they may represent a particular subculture of the broader culture (high schools, for example, contain the teenage subculture of a broader culture), and because the particular mix of individual personalities within the system may add a unique twist. That is, it can only be assumed that the system-level group is influenced by the broader culture/community from which it is drawn, not that it is a clone of that community. The individual level refers to specific people within the school level group. These are the personalities, the idiosyncrasies, the unpredictable behaviors that give a group its "flavor."

Each of these dimensions is composed of three hierarchically related characteristics. The community level is composed of communities, collectives, and values. Communities are composed of collectives, or subgroups that are generally identified with one another because of their membership in the broader community. Each subgroup, in turn, is characterized by certain values; such values are interrelated across subgroups because of the common membership of those subgroups in the broader community.

A specific school group belongs to a broader community/culture. Groups, then, are influenced by the culture and community from which they are drawn, but their "group personalities" are also influenced by the setting in which they exist and the experiences they share within that setting. Groups are further divided into interdependencies and expectations. I use the term "interdependency" rather than subgroup to suggest that subgroups are shaped not only by the broader group, but also by their interactive relationships with one another and with their setting. The nature of such interaction is shaped by the group, which, in turn, is shaped by the community. All these dynamics together produce expectations—expectations about how the group should be treated, about the behavior of participants, and about how the actors relate to the other groups and cultures in the system.

Individuals within a given group can be defined in terms of personalities and needs-dispositions. The personalities and needs-dispositions of individuals are products of idiosyncratic forces that are only partially shaped by subgroup interactions or by broader community/cultural forces.

An assessment of these three levels, and their multiple complexities, is best accomplished by a combination of strategies, including survey questionnaires, focus groups, examination of documents, and interaction with the community. Of these, the last strategy, interacting with a community, is probably the most valuable of the possible choices. Just as you learn more by living with a person than by giving him or her a questionnaire, you learn more about a given community through your experiences with it over time than you do through surveys and focus groups.

 ## ROUNDTABLE

Select a group within a school or community and discuss ways you could develop an understanding of that group. Organize your discussion around the three levels developed above; include discussion of how one hierarchical level affects the next. ■

Criticism of the Getzels-Guba Model

Carol Shakeshaft and Irene Nowell (1984) argue that the Getzels-Guba model does not fully describe reality because it overlooks the feminine experience. "Getzels' and Guba's work on role and role conflict deals with the occupational roles occupied by men and the role conflicts they encounter on the job. Women are totally excluded from this problem formulation" (1984, p. 190). They observe that Getzels and Guba were heavily influenced by Talcott Parsons' definitions of social behavior, which exclude the family altogether.

> Parsons simply could not conceptualize women as occupational actors, but saw them as keepers of a "private realm" instead. Getzels' and Guba's conceptualization of the formal organization extends Parsons' work and, thus, defines it exclusively as a male sphere populated by males and given over to male concerns. (1984, pp. 190–191)

When Getzels and Guba do include females in analyses of conflicts between teachers' role expectations and their needs-dispositions, they fail to identify conflict based on gender. They did not, for example, see conflict between a teacher's role as mother and her responsibilities as teacher. As they argued in an article on role conflict and teaching:

> For women, teaching is a respected occupation often representing a top-level vocational goal. They can be more tolerant of the inconsistencies in expectations since it is not likely that they could do better professionally elsewhere, and in any case, many of the constraints represented by the expectations are already placed upon females qua females anyway. (Getzels and Guba, 1955, p. 39)

 ## ROUNDTABLE

The above quote is a "red flag" in modern society, and represents an attitude that would hardly be tolerated in today's organization, but the general society of the 1950s, when it was written, was likely not offended by the observations. Even so, it is hard to understand how Getzels and Guba could have come to this conclusion. If anything, the role conflict experienced by women in the 1950s may have been even stronger than today because of the significant emphasis then on the role of women as homemakers. The management model for schools in the 1950s (as it is today) was largely based on male expectations—teachers, for example, might have been judged "uncommitted" if they left teachers' meetings early because of family responsibilities. This model inevitably creates strain at the points where men and women differ in needs and outlooks.

Identify different ways that female teachers in the 1950s and today experience conflict among their various role expectations. Are there changes in cultural and community ethos and values that today have changed or even ameliorated role conflict for female teachers? What are some ways that the management model for education could be altered to reduce role conflicts among female teachers? ■

MOTIVATION AND OPEN SYSTEMS THEORY

Open Systems theorists base their perspective of organization on the assumption that organizational subsystems interact in complex ways with one another and with their environment. Similar assumptions underlie the Open Systems theory approach to motivation.

Closed Systems theories of motivation are called *content* theories because they describe characteristics (contents) of effectively motivated people (such as needs

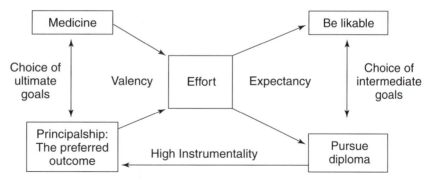

FIGURE 5.9   Application of Victor Vroom's expectancy model of work motivation. From Victor Vroom, *Work and motivation*. (New York: John Wiley, 1964), p. 26. Copyright © by Victor Vroom. Adapted by permission.

or personal characteristics). The Open Systems approach is called *process* theory because it examines the interactive processes that underlie motivation. These processes are influenced not only by the individual's psychology, but by organizational factors such as opportunity and role perception. That is, motivation is an open system.

Victor Vroom (1964) proposed one of the first Open Systems theories of motivation. Vroom felt that earlier content models were inadequate for explaining the true complexities of individual motivation. He argued that each person brings his or her own individual personality to the motivational table. People have different expectations and desires regarding work. It is not some hierarchy of needs that drives us; rather, we are driven by highly personalized desires and expectations, and these expectations are influenced by our experiences with events external to us.

Each of us envisions possible goals for our future. Perhaps our future possibilities include either medicine or school administration (see Fig. 5.9). We assign "valency" to each of those possible outcomes. Valence refers to one's belief regarding how readily attainable and desirable a given goal is. People who do poorly in science likely have negative valences about their ability to become physicians; they see such goals as having a low probability of occurrence and are unlikely to seek such status. If they faint at the sight of blood, the valency they attach to a career in medicine is even lower. People who see little utility in achieving some goal or who have little interest in the goal are unlikely to pursue it. Motivation begins with desire and with expectation that a goal can be achieved.

Valency and desire lead to some level of effort toward an intermediate goal. An intermediate goal is the vehicle by which an ultimate goal is achieved. Let's say a person assigns high valency to the principalship. There are a number of possible intermediate steps for becoming a school principal: one might, for example, seek to be likable; another might pursue a degree in leadership. The amount of effort invested in achieving a given intermediate goal depends on the person's belief that he or she can successfully achieve that goal and on perceptions of the instrumentality of given intermediate goals. A person may have a sour disposition and little desire to be likable, but may feel he or she has an aptitude for academics. In this case, there would be relatively little expectancy of being liked and little effort would be devoted to achieving that goal. There would be high expectancy, however, that one could obtain a degree in educational administration and that a degree is an instrumental path to administration; thus, a lot of effort might be devoted to that end. The choice to which the individual devotes effort is felt to be obtainable and useful.

Put simply, one's motivation is a product of what one wants most and feels is obtainable, whether one judges that he or she can do the things that must be done in order to obtain the goal, and whether he or she can do them well enough (or the ones he or she can do are sufficient) to obtain the ultimate prize.

ROUNDTABLE

How can an administrator influence this process in a manner that keeps worker motivation high? ▪

The Porter-Lawler Model

Lyman Porter and Edward Lawler (1968) have extended Vroom's model in several important ways (see Fig. 5.10). This model is more obviously open in nature than is Vroom's because of its claim that motivation is influenced significantly by events external to the actor. Porter and Lawler argue that valency, or goal desirability, is tempered by one's abilities and traits (such as personality, skills, and intelligence), and by role perceptions (congruence between self-perceptions and

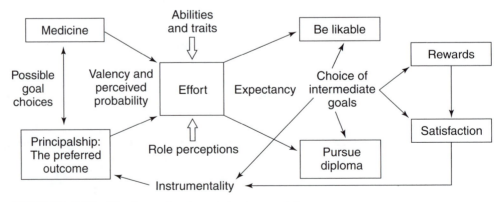

FIGURE 5.10 The Porter-Lawler motivation model.

From Lyman W. Porter and Edward E. Lawler III, *Managerial attitudes and performance.* (Homewood, IL: Irwin, 1968), p. 165. Copyright © by Lyman Porter. Adapted by permission.

reality; if one sees him- or herself as a leader but has a personality that garners disrespect, then role perceptions are incongruous). A problem here, of course, is that individuals are not always good at judging their own abilities; thus, they may have a level of desire, or valency, that cannot be achieved.

The instrumentality of intermediate outcomes is mediated in turn by perceptions of "equity," or the belief that one is appropriately rewarded or recognized for accomplishments. A feeling that one is not being justly rewarded for accomplishments will tend to extinguish desire and lead to reduced motivation and effort.

Equity means that the rewards or satisfaction one receives for efforts are directly related to the rewards received by a comparison group that he or she considers to be equally deserving (Adams, 1965). Inequity means that one receives less than he or she deems appropriate; it can also mean that one receives more than is appropriate. Inequity could motivate individuals to try harder to achieve a given reward but could also motivate them to reduce their efforts to the level that others in like circumstances exhibit. "I'm working my can off and I get the same pay as this person who does nothing, so why should I try?"

A person who is over-rewarded exhibits a different set of behaviors. As Jacques (1961) argued, "Over-equity payments . . . brings about disequilibrium in the form of an insecure non-reliance upon the continuance of earnings, provokes fear of rivalry in others who are not favoured, and stimulates an anxious and selfish desire further to improve the favoured position" (pp. 142–143). Over-rewarded persons may come to feel that their favored status is due them because they are "special" persons; it is an ego trip that associates reward with a general feeling that "I deserve it" and not with the level of their effort. It's what I call the "puppy dog syndrome"—a term I came up with years ago because of my experiences with certain students. People suffering this syndrome have been rewarded so often for doing nothing that they believe they are due special favor for who they are. People around them who perform the same task but are not rewarded at the same level will exhibit frustration and anger at the inequity, and may conclude that there is nothing to be gained by trying harder. Reward appears, to them, to have little relationship with effort, as demonstrated by the case of the over-rewarded individual.

CASE STUDY

I have a generalized friend and student who I will call Joe—I say "generalized" because Joe is actually a composite of a lot of imagination plus a little bit of different people I have known. Joe is bright; he does well in classes at the university and can master just about any subject he puts his mind to. Consequently, Joe enjoys going to school and is currently working on a post-master's degree in educational leadership. He has put a lot of money into his education, but it is personally rewarding and it's something he can do well. He also enjoys it because it's something that he accomplishes alone, which raises a key weakness: Joe is not good at working with people. His co-workers shy away from him because he has a rather sudden temper, he is inflexible about his attitudes ("it will be done my way or no way"), and he frequently gets heated over the smallest of issues. Joe wants to be liked, but he just can't seem to get past the shallowest of relationships with his co-workers. Joe realizes he is shunned and it hurts. The only way he knows how to respond is to get angry, and he always regrets it later. He just doesn't know how to deal with people.

Joe very much wants to become an administrator. He feels that leadership will give him the prestige he is lacking. It will give him an opportunity to finally shine because he knows he has good organizational skills—his success in leadership classes is proof of that. Deep down, he feels that, were he in charge, he could control those uncertain situations that make him so angry. If people respected him, then everything would be OK. These thoughts drive him forward; if need be, he will go on to a PhD, but one way or another, he will be an administrator.

Evaluate Joe's motivation using the Porter-Lawler model. What do you predict will eventually happen to Joe if things don't change? If you were Joe's administrator, how could you help him to maintain his level of motivation?

Leadership and MBO—Management by Objectives

Management by objective, commonly referred to as MBO, was developed in the 1960s and 1970s. It seeks to motivate by letting workers take ownership of their work goals. MBO is a cyclical process that starts with the setting of goals, followed by a period of goal implementation, then by evaluation of goal attainment. For example, a teacher and his or her principal would meet at the beginning of a school year and decide on a set of specific, definable goals for the teacher. A teacher might decide, for instance, to implement a new instructional technique or to submit some number of grant proposals. During the school year, the teacher works toward those goals, and at the end of the year the teacher and principal meet again to review progress. End-of-year evaluations are based on the degree of success in obtaining the goals, and the goals are modified, deleted, or added to for the next school year.

On the surface, MBO appears to be a Closed Systems procedure—there is no element of outside (environmental) influence in the model. It is labeled an Open Systems process, however, in part because it emerged out of the Open Systems literature, but primarily because it describes a cybernetic process in which a dynamic (goal implementation) is evaluated (provided with feedback) and modified based on the evaluations. MBO is still widely used by educational administrators, although the term, MBO, is itself rarely heard anymore.

COMMUNICATION AND OPEN SYSTEMS

Closed Systems perceptions of communication within the organization betray all the usual Closed Systems assumptions: assumptions of rationality, authority, unitary goal structure, and self-contained dynamics. One can readily see these assumptions in Chester Barnard's (1938) characteristics of effective communication:

- The channels of communication should be definitely known.
- There should be a definite formal channel of communication to every member of an organization.

- The line of communication should be direct and as short as possible.
- The complete formal line of communication should normally be used.
- The persons serving as communication centers should be competent.
- The line of communication should not be interrupted while the organization is functioning.
- Every communication should be authenticated (pp. 175–181).

Human Relations theorists defined communication in terms of the psychosocial system. They realized the tremendous importance of communication in organization, and advocated free and open interactions as the solution to many of the organization's problems. The Lewinian studies of change discussed in the last chapter illustrates that: change in these studies was premised on a democratic, open exchange of information.

Open Systems theorists propose a perspective of communication that accounts for complex internal and external forces. They define information more broadly than had previous theorists, equating it with the flow of energy into and through a system, energy that is used to perform work. Information is more than verbal or written communication; it includes such things as raw materials and products, influence, social pressure, fiscal resources, organizational or social action, and social ethos. Information is anything that carries usable energy.

Open Systems theorists reject the Human Relations emphasis on open, dynamic communication. They don't reject the value of communication and the important role information can play in social dynamics; rather, they see limits to the usefulness of open communication. Manipulative information, for example, can be substituted for productive behavior, as when a politician fosters an image that hides a failure to act (Katz & Kahn, 1966).

A bigger problem, however, is the fact that free, open communication is inefficient. Work cannot be accomplished unless communication flows are restricted and channeled. As Katz and Kahn (1966) observed, an unorganized group of 60 people communicating at random with one another can engage in $n(n-1)/2$ or 1,770 different interactive pairings. If work depended on patterns of communication such as this, very little could be accomplished. Were the same 60 people to be organized into 5 groups of 12 persons, with each group having a single voice, the number of communication channels would reduce to 10.

Organization, then, can be defined as the restriction of communication. Communication itself can be visualized as a continuum with free, open communication at one end and total, restricted communication on the other. A completely restricted state exists when the group communicates through one voice only (complete, undelegated authoritarianism). Actual organizations fall short of both poles, and the question arises whether one can identify criteria that determine, at least roughly, where along the continuum a given organization should fall. Are there contingencies, for example, that pressure one type of industry to adopt more open communication patterns and another to adopt more restrictive ones? There is a bit of foreshadowing here, for this question will be developed in the next chapter. For now, I challenge you to attempt to anticipate how Contingency theorists will address this issue.

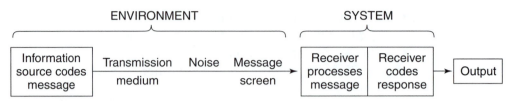

FIGURE 5.11 Open Systems perspective of information flow in a social system.

Information Flow

The flow of information among humans and organizations can be described with the Open Systems metaphor. Information is coded by an environmental agent, transmitted to some system that selectively interprets the message, processes it, codes a response, and sends that response back into the environment (see Fig. 5.11). There are numerous opportunities for error in this process. Messages can be ineffectively coded at the source; the transmission medium (voice, body language) can perform ineffectively; environmental distractions can distort the message; the receiver can screen out important parts of the message because of poor hearing, selective understanding, or bias; processing by the receiver can be defective; and the receiver can ineffectively code its output. When one human says something to another, he or she first codes the information in some medium (usually verbal, but coding could be written, kinesthetic [body language], or physical [striking or hugging] as well). The coder could mumble, pick the wrong words, use the wrong body language when speaking—the message can be miscoded in a number of ways. Environmental noise, such as traffic or a blocked line of sight, can garble the message. Receivers screen messages—some may pay more attention to messages from people they like than from people they dislike, for example. Receivers process information with whatever resources they have at hand, and these resources may be ill-suited to the task.

Finally, the receiver must code his or her response to the input, and that is often difficult. How does one convey the full range of one's emotions, for example, or the subtle undertones of social grace?

The points being made here can be related to the class game that elementary teachers sometimes play with their students. The teacher whispers something to the first child in a row, who whispers the message to the second child, and so forth. Each child can hear the message only once and can ask no questions. What shows up at the end of the line is rarely anything even remotely similar to the original message. The failure of this communication is attributable to potential problems with coding, medium (whisper), noise (room distraction), screening (preconceived notions), interpretation, and recoding.

In most communications among social systems, however, problems of misunderstanding are not as severe as this child's game suggests. The reason is simple feedback—the very dynamic that is missing in the whispering game. Social systems clarify messages by providing feedback on what is received. The transmitter responds to the degree of accuracy relayed by the feedback and the receiver tries again. Each cycle of transmission and feedback gets closer and closer to the meaning that the transmitter intended to convey. If a boy sees a girl across a crowded room and interprets her body language as an invitation to talk, he will likely do just that. If the young lady gives him a cold shoulder, it becomes evident that the original message was either mistransmitted or misinterpreted (or both). The feedback clarifies matters.

Similarly, miscues and miscommunication will plague a school administrator who hinders or limits information feedback within an organization. Principals, for example, who restrict communication from teachers run the risk of misunderstandings, both on the part of teachers and administration.

Katz and Kahn (1966) identified three types of communication: communication among and between peers (horizontal communication); from superior to subordinate (downward); and from subordinate to superior (upward). Downward communication, they argue, is the more common form of interaction in an organization: superiors pass information to subordinates about issues such as policy, expected and actual productivity, and change via memo, verbal presentation, and face-to-face encounter. Katz and Kahn argue that administrators are much better at telling (downward communication) than at listening. There is something of an ego investment in the leadership role for many managers, an investment that presumes leaders are smarter than subordinates and that leaders broker most of the information that is important to the organization. You should be able to corroborate this from your own experience: the structured channels for communication in many educational systems are far better developed for downward communication than for upward flow. Intercom systems, for example, have tended, until recent years, to be unidirectional from the principal's office to the classroom (in that teachers couldn't initiate a transmission), and even with more sophisticated two-way intercoms (allowing teacher-initiated transmission), only the principal can broadcast to all classes. Principals produce newsletters for teachers, but teachers rarely produce newsletters for administrators. Principals are more likely to be in charge of teacher meetings than are teachers themselves. Computer/Internet technology—e-mail and webpages—promises to improve the upward and interactive flow of communication, but authority will continue to exert its preeminence in information commerce.

Upward communication, the movement of information from subordinates to superiors, is often crucial for effective management. Supervisors need to have accurate and full information about what is going on in their schools, and they need this information from the "deep level" of the organization, the domains of teachers, secretaries, cafeteria workers, custodians, and students. Principals need to know what teachers are saying and doing, what problems they are experiencing with students, and how they, and other employees, feel about things. The principal who talks but doesn't listen is not going to obtain such information; those who revel in the downward flow of information but who don't foster upward channels of communication will have limited knowledge of their organizations.

The best way to get at that "deep level" is to "administer by walking around" (Snyder, 1988). This means, simply, that the leader devotes a block of time each day to roaming the hallways, going into classrooms or offices, speaking to faculty and students, and visiting with support staff. To be effective, this needs to become a ritual that is violated only by necessity, such as meetings at the central office or dean's office. When I was a school principal, I devoted two hours daily between 9 and 11 A.M. to walking around. My secretary knew to call me back to the office only for significant emergencies or calls from my wife or the superintendent. Others who wanted to talk with me quickly learned to call later in the day. An administrator who is "too busy" to get out into the school on a regular basis (barring certain emergencies or required events) simply has not prioritized that process.

Managers can cut themselves off from communication in any number of ways. The easiest way to do it, of course, is to ignore upward channels of communication. Another rather potent strategy is to use information from a subordinate to sanction or embarrass that subordinate. If a person knows that information will be used to punish or deride, he or she will not offer it. If people are asked for information under such conditions, they will likely attempt to lie, to sugarcoat it (thus misrepresenting the severity of the problem), or to shift responsibility to others.

Closely related to this is a strategy that usurps a subordinate's responsibility. It can be demeaning for a superior to solve a problem by bypassing the subordinate who presents it and who has ownership of that problem. It says to the subordinate, "You aren't capable of solving or dealing with this problem; rather, it requires my superior intellect and ability." It's easy to imagine how that goes over, and what it does to the communication process.

Administrators who pry *too* deeply can disrupt communication flow. Administrators need to get at the "deep level" of an organization, but there are limits to how deep they should go. Administrators can't, and shouldn't try to, be involved in every little aspect of the organization. The prying administrator, the one who is always there, who shows up at every meeting whether invited or not, who is constantly asking about every detail of organizational activities, is viewed with suspicion, and teachers will likely begin to find ways to hide from his or her prying eyes. Leaders don't need to know everything, and subordinates will "wonder" about a leader who forever seeks information about things that he or she doesn't really need to know.

Horizontal communication refers to interactions among peers, or workers at the same level of authority in an organization. Such interaction is important for social and emotional support and for task coordination. Unlimited, full horizontal patterns of communication can be counterproductive, as we discussed earlier, but a certain amount of peer interaction is important for effective organizational functioning. Further, peer interaction is going to occur, whether desired or not. This leads to two conclusions: (1) the administrator who attempts to squelch communication is due for frustration and resistance; and, more importantly, (2) "if there are no problems of task coordination left to the group of peers, the content of their communications can take forms which are irrelevant to or destructive of organizational functioning" (Katz and Kahn, 1966, p. 244). Point 2 states simply that if peers have nothing important to discuss, their interactions may, and often will, be counterproductive.

Information Overload

Information overload refers to those times in an administrator's work life when there are too many demands pressing on his or her time. For principals, first thing in the morning seems to be a ripe time for information overload. Busses are arriving bringing the inevitable discipline problems; parents are likely to show up with their share of problems; students are roaming the halls trying to get settled; teachers are trying to get issues resolved before class begins—and everything is happening at once. The beginning and ending of a school year, with all the reports, recognition programs, and last-minute problems are likewise hectic for school administrators. When new programs or legislative mandates must be enacted, when accreditation reports are due, when the school board demands reports, school administrators experience information overload.

J.G. Miller (1960) identifies seven typical responses to information overload. The first is *omission*, or the tendency to just not address certain pressing demands. The principal may simply ignore chaotic hallways and teacher demands during the morning rush in order to have time for discipline problems and parent complaints. The second typical response to information overload is *error*, or misinterpretation of information. When rushed, for example, principals may over- or underreact to reports of bus discipline problems in the morning because they mentally add or subtract meaning to information about the event. They do not take the time (or have the time) to hear the full story; rather, they get a skeletal outline of what occurred and fill in the blanks based on their prior experiences with the given student or situation and on their personal disposition or biases at that moment.

Both omission and error are dysfunctional reactions, and can prolong a problem beyond the time required had the administrator properly dealt with the issue. The principal who overreacts to bus discipline problems, for example, may have to deal with additional parent complaints and have to spend time rectifying mistakes. Problems that are ignored may snowball, thus creating even bigger problems (the chaos in the hallways during the morning rush, for example, may degenerate into a fight or may slow down the processing of absence excuses by attendance clerks). The administrator who regularly indulges in such strategies will likely be perceived as being unorganized, as losing his or her cool, or as ineffective. If nothing else, such managers can make life harder for themselves and for those with whom they work.

Miller's third categorization of response to information overload is *queuing*. In this strategy, the administrator handles problems in the order that they arise. If bus discipline gets his or her attention first in the morning, it is dealt with first; teacher demands may come short on the heels of discipline reports but are held in abeyance until the first problem is addressed. The difficulty with this approach is that important problems have no more precedence in the queue than unimportant ones; a parent, for example, may be left fuming in the hallway until the principal finishes a discipline report (this example is a bit extreme, of course, but it illustrates the problem). Barring this obvious drawback, however, queuing can be functional in that it delays certain decisions until there is a lull in the action, thus helping assure that decisions are properly processed.

Miller's fourth strategy is called *filtering*. Here the administrator uses some scheme or priority to selectively postpone certain demands, leaving more time to focus on other messages. This can be useful if the filtering process follows certain previously considered guidelines, or if priorities are established that are based on the needs of the organization. Filtering can be dysfunctional if the process is based on personal predisposition or bias. The administrator, for example, may simply skip over information not immediately understood, may ignore problems that are uncomfortable to deal with, or may use personal biases (such as lack of respect for the information carrier) to screen problems. These strategies can omit decisions that are important for organizational functioning, thus causing future (or even immediate) problems.

The fifth approach to overload is *approximation*. It is similar to filtering in that selected pieces of a given message are omitted. As with filtering, such omissions may be related to comfort level, bias, or understanding, and can cause additional problems for the administrator later on.

Other administrators may employ *multiple channels* to deal with information overload. Here the administrator solicits help from others to deal with certain decisions, or creates decentralized structures that can capture problems before they even reach the principal. In the morning rush example being used throughout this discussion, the secretary may be recruited to begin working on reports and to screen calls and visits; assistant principals may deal with discipline problems and some parental complaints; and teachers may be asked to deal with pedestrian traffic problems. The more effective strategy, however, is to decentralize responsibility for certain classes of problems. The principal who effectively decentralizes decision making has learned what issues are likely to crop up on a regular basis and has allocated responsibility for them before they occur (this is the simple essence of Learning theory, which will be discussed in Chapter 8).

Finally, Miller argues that some people seek to *escape* information overload. Escape means the principal arranges to be absent when problems are expected, or demands are simply ignored by whatever means available. Nominally this is a dysfunctional strategy for dealing with information overload, but it need not be so. Certain demands may, for example, be inappropriate or unrelated to the direct welfare of the principal's more important responsibilities. Central office personnel, for example, may demand reports (such as book counts) on the last day of school because it is convenient for them to receive them at that time. Most principals will have other, more important demands on that day, however, and may choose to ignore the deadline (the advisability of this presumes, of course, that the principal hasn't put off the task to the last minute, or that the timing of the report isn't crucial for, say, continued funding from external agencies). Similarly, principals may use their discretionary veto authority to protect teachers against information overload. If, for example, demands on teacher time during workdays are unreasonable (they must complete quarter grades yet a supervisor wants to schedule an all-day workshop), the principal may choose to intervene. It is occasionally prudent and appropriate to say "no" to demands when they limit more important projects or are inappropriately motivated. This, of course, represents a variation on prioritization.

One additional strategy for dealing with information overload (beyond the seven that Miller proposed) can be added to the list: some people are adept at *multitasking* problems. Multitasking is a computer term that refers to a strategy for utilizing processor time efficiently. Programmers in the 1950s and 1960s found that a computer's processor is not used continuously when evaluating a particular routine; it must pause intermittently while bits of information are stored, for example. Instead of letting this time pass unused, they programmed their control language to process commands from other routines during the slack time. Similarly, some administrators can deal with multiple demands simultaneously. They may talk on the phone with a parent while putting together a report, or may deal with a teacher's problem during interludes in hall duty (we've all seen people interrupt their conversation with another person to deal with a problem that flashes suddenly, then return to the discussion). The idea, in a sense, is to do more than one thing at a time. This doesn't work for people who must focus on one problem until it is completed (linear thinkers), but others are adept at it. A linear thinker who tries to solicit help from multitaskers, however, may find the experience rather frustrating. Further, multitasking may be inefficient when old ground must be re-covered when the user returns to a problem.

OPEN SYSTEMS THEORY AND SUBSEQUENT THEORETICAL DEBATES

Open Systems perspectives signaled the end of a period in which management specialists who proffered cookbooks for leadership were afforded academic credibility (I'm not saying these gurus don't still exist, of course). In a way, that is sad; there is something comforting about the simplistic assumption that one can effectively run an organization if he or she masters a set of scientific principles. I have had students read management training books from that era and lament the fact that we don't offer such guidelines in our administrative preparation programs anymore. The observations of such cookbooks can be useful if understood within a more complex, Open Systems ambiance, but the raw reality is that organizations are simply more complex than early theorists realized. Management aphorisms such as, "put first things first," "be proactive in your leadership style," or "managers plan, coordinate, and evaluate" offer only a false sense of control; actual control is far too complex for such simple witticisms.

Open Systems theory marked the beginning of new approaches to understanding and managing organizations. Contingency theory, which is the topic of the next chapter, is directly related to Open Systems theory. Contingency theory translates Open Systems theory into practical application and observation; in a sense, it is an Open Systems handbook for management. Open Systems, however, underscores the significant complexity implicit in organizational behavior, and later theories (Learning theory, Population Ecology, even Critical theory and Complexity) will pick up on this theme.

I have seen numerous leadership students struggle with just what Open Systems theory means for their actual leadership behavior, and indeed that answer is not immediately obvious from the traditional treatment of the subject. How, for example, does one translate Leavitt's observations about interaction among managerial and organizational subsystems into actual leadership behavior? I have attempted in this chapter to provide answers to such questions; we have discussed change within the context of interacting systems, for example, and have talked about strategies for dealing with information flow. However, a more complete answer lies in the theories that were spawned by Open Systems theory, for these theories have built on Open Systems premises to construct more complex perspectives of organization and leadership. One could say, then, that the rest of this book is about Open Systems theory.

Diary

- In your diary entry for this chapter, summarize your thoughts on one or more of the Roundtable discussions. You are also encouraged to reflect on the following questions (and on any other thoughts that you may have struggled with as you read the chapter, of course):
- Given what you have learned in this chapter, what are some important functions of leadership? In what way does your answer change your previous answers to this question?
- Redefine Weber's model of bureaucracy (see Hall's definition in Chapter 2) with an Open Systems component. How would this component help resolve some of the problems identified by Merton and Gouldner?
- Do you think that, in actual organizations, different subsystems are as sensitive to perturbations in each other as Open Systems theory suggests? Explain.
- Describe the environmental feedback mechanisms for your school. If they are not as effective as they should be, how can these mechanisms be improved? If you have had a school and community class in your graduate program, relate this discussion to the issues discussed in that class.
- Referring to Katz' and Kahn's model, what are the technical subsystems in your school? The managerial subsystems? Supportive subsystems? Maintenance subsystems? Adaptive subsystems? How do these subsystems interrelate and influence one another? Of what use is a maintenance subsystem?
- Any thoughts on why Forrester's world model failed to predict?
- Explain how your communities influence the idiographic and nomothetic dynamics of your school (the Getzels-Guba model).
- List some ways that you, as an administrator, could motivate those whom you supervise. How do the motivation models in this chapter influence your list?
- Why is horizontal communication an important element in public education? What can a leader do to improve the amount and quality of such com-

munication? If you were to have input into the construction of a new facility, what structural recommendations would you make that would help encourage horizontal communication among staff members?

- How do you respond to information overload? What can you do to make your response more effective?

Recommended Readings

Buckley, W. (1967). *Sociology and modern systems theory*. Englewood Cliffs, NJ: Prentice Hall, Inc.

Buckley's classic work on Open Systems theory includes a review of organizational theories of the previous 200 years. Though difficult to read, it provides an excellent sociological overview of the tenets of Open Systems theory.

Getzels, J.W., Lipham, J.M., & Campbell, R.F. (1968). *Educational administration as a social process: Theory, research, and practice*. New York: Harper & Row.

The book in which Getzels and his colleagues present their culture model of school systems. Includes chapters on school board relationships, staff relationships, and community relationships.

Seiler, J.A. (1967). *Systems analysis in organizational behavior*. Homewood, IL: Richard D. Irwin, Inc., and the Dorsey Press.

John Seiler develops a model of Open Social Systems that is applicable across disciplines. In this small, readable book, he provides a number of case study exercises and challenges the student to evaluate the organizational dynamics presented with his model of Open Systems.

References

Adams, J.S. (1965). Inequality in social exchange. In L. Berkowitz (Ed.), *Advances in experimental social psychology* (pp. 267–300). New York: Academic Press.

Barnard, C.I. (1938). *The functions of the executive*. Cambridge, MA: Harvard University Press.

Bazerman, M.H. (1990). *Judgment in managerial decision making* (2nd ed.). New York: Wiley.

Bloomfield, B.P. (1986). *Modeling the world: The social constructions of systems analysts*. Oxford, UK and New York: Basil Blackwell, Inc.

Coch, L., & French, J.R.P. (1948). Overcoming resistance to change. *Human Relations, 1,* 512–533.

Forrester, J.W. (1969). *Urban dynamics*. Cambridge, MA: MIT Press.

Forrester, J.W. (1971). *World dynamics*. Cambridge, MA: MIT Press.

French, J.R.P., Israel, J., & Aas, D. (1960). An experiment on participation in a Norwegian factory. *Human Relations, 13,* 3–19.

Getzels, J.W. (1958). Administration as a social process. In A.W. Halpin (Ed.), *Administrative theory in education* (pp. 150–165). Chicago: Midwest Administration Center, University of Chicago.

Getzels, J.W. (1978). The communities of education. *Teacher College Record, 79*(4), 659–682.

Getzels, J.W., & Guba, E.G. (1955). The structure of roles and role conflict in the teaching situation. *The Journal of Educational Sociology, 29,* 30–40.

Getzels, J.W., & Guba, E.G. (1957). Social behavior and the administrative process. *School Review, 65,* 423–441.

Getzels, J.W., Lipham, J.M., & Campbell, R.F. (1968). *Educational administration as a social process: Theory, research, and practice.* New York: Harper & Row.

Jacques, E. (1961). *Equitable payment.* New York: John Wiley & Sons, Inc.

Kahneman, D., & Tversky, A. (1972). Subjective probability: A judgment of representativeness. *Cognitive Psychology, 3,* 430–454.

Katz, D., & Kahn, R.L. (1966). *The social psychology of organizations.* New York: John Wiley & Sons, Inc.

Leavitt, H.J. (1964). *Managerial psychology.* Chicago: University of Chicago Press.

Luthans, F. (1992). *Organizational behavior* (6th ed.). New York: McGraw-Hill, Inc.

Marion, R., & Flanigan, J. (2001). Evolution and punctuation of theories of educational expenditure and student outcomes. *Journal of Education Finance, 26*(3), 239–257.

Maruyama, M. (1963). The second cybernetics: Deviation amplifying mutual causal processes. *American Scientist, 51,* 164–179.

Miller, J.G. (1960). Information input, overload, and psychopathology. *American Journal of Psychiatry, 116,* 695–704.

Mintzberg, H., Raisin-ghani, D., & Theoret, A. (1976). The structure of 'unstructured' decision processes. *Administrative Science Quarterly,* 246–275.

Porter, L.W., & Lawler, E.E., III. (1968). *Managerial attitudes and performance.* Homewood, IL: Irwin.

Seiler, J.A. (1967). *Systems analysis in organizational behavior.* Homewood, IL: Richard D. Irwin, Inc., and the Dorsey Press.

Shakeshaft, C., & Nowell, I. (1984). Research on theories, concepts, and models of organizational behavior: The influence of gender. *Issues in Education, 11*(3), 186–203.

Simon, H.A. (1957). *Administrative behavior* (2nd ed.). New York: Macmillan.

Synder, R.C. (1988). New frames for old: Changing the managerial culture of an aircraft factory. In M.O. Jones, M.D. Moore, & R.C. Snyder (Eds.), *Inside organizations: Understanding the human dimension* (pp. 191–208). Newbury Park, CA: Sage Publications.

The Taylor and other systems of shop management. House Resolution 90 (3 Vol), (1912). Hearings before a Special Committee of the House of Representatives.

Tversky, D., & Kahneman, A. (1973). Availability: A heuristic for judging frequency and probability. *Cognitive Psychology, 5,* 207–232.

Vroom, V. (1964). *Work and motivation.* New York: John Wiley & Sons, Inc.

Waldrop, M.M. (1992). *Complexity: The emerging science at the edge of order and chaos.* New York: Simon & Schuster.

CHAPTER 6

Prescriptions for Leadership

OVERVIEW AND CHAPTER OBJECTIVES

Contingency theory, the focus of this chapter, is constructed from the Structuralist and Open Systems building blocks of the last two chapters. Contingency theory explores how environmental and organizational variables affect organizations and seeks ways for leaders to respond to those variables—that is, it prescribes how leaders should behave in given situations. Contingency theory, then, is ultimately about how to lead. Consequently, the second half of this chapter examines Leadership Contingency theories—Stogdill and the Ohio State Studies, Fred Fiedler, House and Mitchell, and Hersey and Blanchard. The first half of the chapter examines what Contingency theorists generally have to say about contingencies and organizational behavior.

In this chapter, students will:

- Explore how educational institutions should be organized and led, given the contingencies they face.
- Explore the appropriate mix of people and task orientation in educational settings.
- Evaluate their own tendencies regarding task or people orientation, and develop a plan for molding their leadership dispositions to more appropriately meet the needs of education.
- Develop personal leadership styles based on the leadership models of Fiedler, House and Mitchell, and Hersey and Blanchard.
- Refine their definitions of the function of leadership in education.

THE PHILOSOPHY UNDERLYING CONTINGENCY THEORY

Contingency theory, like its predecessors in the 20th century (Machine theory, Human Relations theory, Structuralism), is positivistic. The Australian theorist Lex Donaldson (1996) defines positivism as follows:

1. It is *nomothetic,* meaning that the phenomena are analyzed using a general framework with factors that apply to all organizations. . . . General causal relationships in the form of law-like regularities are sought between contingency and structural factors.

2. The research associated with the theory is *methodologically positivist* in that there is much use of comparative empirical research, usually with the measurement of variables and statistical analysis of variables.

3. The theory explains organizational structure by *material factors* such as size, technology, and so on, rather than by ideationalist factors such as ideas, ideologies, perceptions, norms and the like.

4. The theory is *determinist* in that managers are seen as having to adopt the organizational structure that is required by the contingency factors in order to gain organizational effectiveness.

5. The theory is closely *informed by empirical research* rather than armchair speculation or extended theorizing prior to empirical data collection. It is built upon the data patterns and arguments of the pioneering works.

6. The theory is consciously scientific in style, with *the aim being to produce scientific knowledge of the type achieved in the natural sciences* (p. 3; italics in original).

Allow me to rephrase some of this, for the points are important. Contingency theory presumes that there are regular relationships between organizational contingencies and organizational structure or behavior, and that, if one can understand those relationships, one can make generalizations about most all organizations. In the medical field, scientists know that a diuretic will reduce blood pressure in most any patient and that individual differences (gender, race, SES, quality of physician, quality of medical facilities, mood swings in patient) don't alter that ability to any significant degree. That is, the drug's effectiveness isn't particularly dependent on individualistic conditions. Further, a lot of diuretic has a profound effect on one's body while a little diuretic has minimal effect—there is a regular relationship between cause and effect. Positivist theories, such as Contingency theory, make these sorts of assumptions.

In subsequent chapters, we will study the anti-positivists; they argue that there is no particularly compelling relationship between contingencies (such as environmental conditions) and structure or leadership style; thus, managers have considerable discretion in the way they structure their organizations. Anti-positivists reject the notion that social systems respond to treatments like the body responds to medicine. They argue that organizational structure exhibits no compelling pattern and any given structure can be understood only by examining the complex, individualistic conditions that characterize the given organization.

I recently attended an educational finance conference at which the impact of fiscal expenditures on student achievement was discussed. The consensus of the group of discussants at one particular session was that achievement is so intimately dependent on local conditions (the skills of a given teacher, the leadership style of the given principal, the motivation of the given student, local policy decisions about expenditures, and so on) that one cannot identify any systematic relationship between money and achievement. That is anti-positivism. Positivists would disagree, arguing that one can explain a fairly significant degree of variation in achievement across districts with generalizable input variables, including expenditure level and how money is spent. Contingency theory would agree with the latter camp and disagree with the former.

Following from this, Contingency theory proposes that there is a generalizable relationship between organizational and environmental contingencies and organizational structure and leadership. Organizational contingencies include size and task structure; environmental contingencies refer, generally, to the degree of environmental uncertainty experienced by an organization.

BASIC CONTINGENCY THEORY

Contingency theory emerged about the same time as Open Systems theory. Popular in the 1960s and 1970s, it argues that an effective organization is one that has been properly tuned to the "situation of the organization, including its environment" (Donaldson, 1996, p. 10). Contingent conditions include environmental pressures, the nature of the system's raw materials, and the system's size.

Contingency theorists maintain that a system is effective when it is in tune with its contingent conditions and that it is ineffective when it is out of tune with those contingencies. As an organization passes through its life cycles, the contingencies that impact it will change. The leader's job is to alter the organizational structure to keep the system in sync with those contingencies. As Donaldson (1996) put it:

> They [Contingency theorists] postulate a set of states of equilibrium in each of which the structure is appropriate to a particular value of the contingency variable—for example, in an uncertain environment an organic structure fits. The theories also posit a dynamic process whereby there is a shift in the contingency variable bringing the organization into disequilibrium or misfit with resulting reduced performance so then the structure is adjusted to a new value to regain fit and higher performance. Thus the structure is essentially chosen by the state of the contingencies. Also the management is reactive rather than proactive. (p. 17)

The contingency-structure relationship generally works like this: Other things being equal, if an environment is stable and predictable, leaders can put together a rather simple organizational structure, one run by a handful of straightforward rules and minimal supervision. If the environment is unstable, however, organizational structure must be more complex. Such environments demand greater organizational flexibility—leaders and workers adapt on-the-fly to unpredictable demands.

Volatile environments are too complex to be dealt with by a simple organizational structure; rather, environmental demands must be divided into smaller, more manageable tasks and responsibilities. Those tasks are assigned to different individuals or departments within the organization. An organization that produces only bolts for a low-competition, stable market can function with only a few departments representing a limited number of skills—perhaps manufacturing, marketing and delivery, and management. A computer electronics industry, on the other hand, operates in a highly competitive and rapidly changing environment, and must depend on many different departments representing many different skills. This is called *differentiation*.

In Chapter 5 we discussed environmental mapping, and that discussion helps illuminate what is going on here. Open, adaptive systems map their environment; that is, they develop mechanisms for sensing, remembering, and acting on stimuli from that environment. If the environment is complex, the system requires many different structures to map different parts of the environment, and the system as a whole coordinates these different maps. Thus, the ear maps the song of a bird and the eye recognizes its form; together these maps merge to form a single sense of "birdness." This differentiation allows the system to know a complex environment. Businesses do it (differentiate), governmental bureaucracies do it, and schools do it. Public education deals in knowledge, and knowledge is an extensive and complex environment. No one person could possibly master that environment as a whole, for there is just too much to understand. The educational industry responds to educational complexities by dividing the environment into disciplines; thus, certain people are assigned responsibility for math, some take language arts, some social studies, and so on. Occasionally the educational environment increases in complexity and the school must respond in kind. In the last few decades, for example, we have seen significant expansion and differentiation in exceptional children's programs because of complexities in laws and policies governing identification and treatment. Each subgroup in a school is responsible for appropriate mastery, or mapping, of its specialized part of the environment.

When an organization splits into subdepartments with different responsibilities, the people in these subroles tend to develop differing perceptions of need, task relevance, status, priorities, goals, time, and responsibility. It is easy to understand why this happens; people's egos are tied up in their own roles and they tend to feel that what they are doing is more important than what others are doing. Individuals in different parts of an organization are exposed to different pieces of the environment; thus, they develop differing views of reality. A math department within a high school, for example, deals with the math portion of the academic environment as well as outside agencies (such as the National Council of Math Teachers) that define standards for their discipline. The English department relates to a different scholarship, and its sense of propriety in education is influenced by different professional agencies. Each of these areas will have different ideas about what the school's goals are, what knowledge is important for students to learn, who is in charge of what, how funds should be allocated, how status is allocated, and what roles the organization plays within its niche.

As differentiation increases, then, conflicts and miscommunications increase. The system needs some mechanism for coordination, or *integration*. There are two broad categories of mechanisms for integrating the various subsystems of an organization. A system can be coordinated either by *plan* (rules, goals, standardized procedures or outputs) or by *feedback* (decentralized communication and adaptation). If environmental demands are relatively stable, if outcomes can be predicted, then coordination by plan will suffice. Such environments demand little differentiation and the resulting simple set of subsystems can be fairly easily coordinated with standardized procedures. Imagine a school in which children only needed to know a set of 100 vocabulary words and how to add 1- and 2-digit numbers. Instructional procedures would be straightforward and simple, one person or department could master all that was required for production, children could be moved rather quickly through the process, and the school's activities and behaviors could be reduced to a set of simple rules and regulations.

By contrast, volatile environments require highly differentiated organizations, and such organizations must be coordinated by feedback. When the environment is unstable, when contingencies and ambiguity would rip any plan or standardized procedures to shreds, coordination must occur more spontaneously. Leaders and teachers who are close to the action must be able to respond uniquely to unique problems; they must interact directly with the environmental conditions that create problems; and they must have the knowledge and the authority to make decisions that solve problems. Imagine schools in which the tasks to be performed are complex, production methods (pedagogy) can be standardized only in their most general features, raw materials (students) come with non-standardized learning profiles, and external, unpredictable contingencies (such as child abuse, poverty, anti-educational prejudice) constantly intrude on and disrupt the learning process (perhaps you don't have to work very hard at imagining this). Such a system defies standardization under the banner of a few rules and regulations; rather, teachers and principals must have the latitude to respond uniquely to the unique problems they face daily. The system must be coordinated with feedback mechanisms.

This basic outline of Contingency theory is grounded in large part on the 1967 research of two faculty members at the Harvard Business School, Paul Lawrence and Jay Lorsch. Lawrence and Lorsch examined three industries: a rapidly changing and highly competitive plastics industry, a packaging industry experiencing moderate change and competition, and a stable container industry. They found that the plastics industry was the most differentiated of the three, followed in order by the packaging industry, then the container industry. These variations in organizational characteristics correspond to variations in the respective environments of those organizations (turbulent, moderately changing, and stable).

Lawrence and Lorsch found that the most productive companies were also the most conflictive of the organizations studied. It would seem logical that just the opposite would occur, that effectiveness would be related to low levels of conflict. Indeed,

Closed Systems theories, which had dominated organizational theory in the decades before Contingency theory, preached that organizations were composed of harmoniously fitted pieces and conflict was more a matter of deviance than of functional behavior. Conflict in well-oiled, effective organizations was indicative of poor management and was not considered a natural side effect of effective management.

Given the whole situation, however, the conflict made sense to Lawrence and Lorsch. Dynamic environments offer great reward, hence the greater returns, but success and effectiveness amidst ambiguity require that organizations differentiate to divide that environment's demands into manageable pieces. It is quite reasonable to expect that individuals occupying the different roles this creates would assume different environmental perspectives and would consequently have different priorities. When people working under the same roof have different priorities, conflict is inevitable, and the more highly differentiated they are, the more conflictive they will be.

ROUNDTABLE

All this raises several important questions for the student of organizational theory and educational systems. Given that the environment and function of the educational institution is complex, for example, how can leaders best organize their schools? Interaction among faculty, staff, and between administration and subordinates is key to effectively dealing with such environments. How then can schools be structured and organized to promote such interaction? Of what use are rules and regulations in a complex structure such as education? What leadership style best serves the complex structure? How can the numerous subsystems in the educational organization be effectively organized? ▧

Generalists and Specialists

There are two broad categories of workers in the Contingency theory scheme of things. The first is the *specialist* worker. Specialists perform roles that can be largely isolated from other roles because job activities can be clearly defined, and each specialist has the expert knowledge needed to perform his or her delegated task. Jobs that require specialists include school bus driver trainers, computer network administrators, and bulk mail preparation personnel. The second type of worker is the *generalist*. Generalists have broad knowledge about many things and they wear many hats; they include teachers, school administrators, and nurses. Teachers, for example, must have general knowledge of human growth and development, instructional procedures, curriculum development, student discipline, and subject matter. Teachers are parents to their students, they are instructors, they are nurses, they coach, they deal with public relations, they are academics, they are policy-makers, and they are disciplinarians. Their responsibilities cannot be clearly isolated and defined, and each must be competent at many things.

Whether a particular role requires a specialist or a generalist depends on the nature of the environment with which the role deals. Complex and ambiguous environments breed complex and ambiguous tasks that require generalists; stable and predictable environments foster stable and predictable tasks that are best served by specialists.

Environment

According to the Open Systems perspective, environments provide inputs for systems; among other things, these inputs take the form of raw materials, knowledge, and organizational expectations. Generalists are more effective when the raw materials that the system processes are unstable and when knowledge about those raw materials is complex, inexact, and generalized. Specialists can be utilized when raw materials are stable and when knowledge of those materials is exact and clearly defined (generalist knowledge is inevitably complex but specialist knowledge can be complex or simple).

Contingency Theorist Charles Perrow (1970) defined organizational environment as raw materials. He pictured this basic notion with a two-by-two table (such tables are called, appropriately, contingency tables). The columns of his table represent the nature of an organization's raw material, whether uniform and stable or nonuniform and unstable (see Fig. 6.1). Uniformity and nonuniformity refer to the degree of variety in the problems presented to the system by the raw material. Sometimes, quoting from Perrow, "The variety [in a raw material] is great and every task seems to be a new one demanding the institution of search behavior of some magnitude [efforts to find ways to process the raw material]." Perrow continues, "Sometimes stimuli are not very varied and the individual is confronted chiefly with familiar situations and few novel ones" (1970, p. 77).

The rows of Perrow's contingency table represent the state of knowledge about how to transform the system's raw materials into target products. "If a good deal is known that is relevant to the transformation process, search can be quite routine and analyzable," according to Perrow (p. 76). Ambiguous knowledge, by contrast, demands the ability to reference a broad scope of possible production

		RAW MATERIALS ARE	
		Uniform and stable	Nonuniform and unstable
RAW MATERIALS ARE	Not well understood	Craft 1	Nonroutine 2
	Well understood	Routine 3	Engineering 4

FIGURE 6.1 Perrow's raw materials contingency table.

Adapted from *Organizational analysis-06B5600,* 1st Edition, by C. Perrow (Belmont, CA: Wadsworth). Copyright © 1970.

solutions, for what works for one situation may not work in another. One size does not fit all, so to speak.

> If you perceive a delinquent as simply lacking in respect for adults because he has never been made to obey adult rules, your is clear. The raw material is simple and known, and the techniques are readily available from military or prison history, if nothing else. If you perceive the delinquent as complicated, self-activating, unique individual about whom not a great deal is known, search is unanalyzable and must rely upon vague processes, such as empathy, understanding, or interpreting early childhood experiences. (Perrow, 1970, pp. 76–77)

The cells formed by the table in Figure 6.1 represent different organizational types. Cell 1 includes craft institutions that produce customized products (the craftsman cannot predetermine what the customer will demand, thus demand is not well understood), yet much is known about how to transform the demand into a product (glass-blowing is a science, for example). Cell 2 organizations are nonroutine in that neither the environmental contingency nor the transformation process is well understood. The work of nuclear fuel systems, according to Perrow, is "highly nonroutine, combining nonanalyzable problems with great variability of problems" (1970, p. 78).

Cell 3 systems are industries whose raw material is well understood and stable; this typology includes mills that weave fabric or smelt metal. Cell 4 systems process stable raw materials but transformation processes are not well understood. Perrow places engineering design firms in this category because they "must continually modify designs and introduce modifications to meet the customers' needs" (p. 77).

ROUNDTABLE

Perrow identified supervisory behaviors appropriate for each organizational type in his contingency model. Such leadership behaviors were categorized according to:

- discretion (high discretion exists when the supervisor must make customized decisions for each transformation),
- most effective coordination structures (plan or feedback), and
- overall structure (decentralized decision making, flexible structure but centralized decision making, flexible structure with multiple levels of centralization, or formal control and centralized decision making). ◼

Add a fourth category to this list: type of worker needed, whether specialist or generalist.

Using these categories, identify the appropriate organizational or worker type in each cell of Perrow's table, then place four different people-processing systems (schools, psychiatric hospitals, programmed learning schools, and custodial institutions such as prisons) into the appropriate cell. A template for this activity is provided in Figure 6.2. Perrow's categorizations of these behaviors and organizational types are provided at the end of this chapter (along with suggested placement of

	Uniform and stable	Nonuniform and unstable
Not well understood	Discretion: Coordination: Structure: Worker: Example:	Discretion: Coordination: Structure: Worker: Example:
Well understood	Discretion: Coordination: Structure: Worker: Example:	Discretion: Coordination: Structure: Worker: Example:

FIGURE 6.2   Activity template for Perrow's contingency table.

From *Organizational analysis-06B5600, 1ˢᵗ Edition*, by C. Perrow. Copyright © 1970, p. 81. Reprinted with permission of Wadsworth, an imprint of Wadsworth Learning, a division of Thompson Learning. FAX 800-730-2215.

worker type). Compare your categorizations with those of Perrow. Do you agree with Perrow's categorization of public schools? Could schools fit better in a cell other than the one Perrow identified? Why? What implications does your categorization of education have for administrative behavior?

Differentiation in Organization

We noted earlier that organizations differentiate their structure to deal with complex environments. Organizations can differentiate horizontally, vertically, and spatially (Hall, 1991). Horizontal differentiation refers to the extent that, and manner in which, tasks are subdivided; vertical differentiation refers to the number of hierarchies in an organization; spatial differentiation refers to the geographical dispersion of an organization.

Horizontal Differentiation   Horizontal differentiation per se is a fairly straightforward notion; it refers to the degree of differentiation that exists among workers at the same level of authority, or the number of subtasks required to process the raw material. Contingency theorists have studied relationships between contingent variables and number of divisions (departments, work groups, etc.) in an organization. In education, for example, one might ask, "How many different specialties are needed in a public high school to achieve society's goals for educating teenagers?"

One would think that defining the organizational division is a simple matter—use an organizational chart. The problem is that organizational charts often fail to reflect actual work groups. A work division is a set of interdependent individuals, all of whom are working interdependently on a given task. A given department may have several work groups, or two or more divisions on the chart may actually be difficult to differentiate in reality. An organizational chart for a hospital may differentiate doctors and nurses, but doctors and nurses who work together in the operating room or in emergency rooms work as a team and cannot be cleanly differentiated in reality. The nurses and doctors in a division are unified in an interdependent network dedicated to a given task, and there are likely several such teams where the formal organizational chart designates only an emergency ward or a pediatrics ward.

Similarly, a school's organizational chart may designate such divisions as grade levels, teams, or departments, when in reality a team may be better defined at the classroom level (teacher and aide), or perhaps as subdivisions within a given department. It may be natural for literature teachers in a high school English department to group together in one interdependent unit and for grammar teachers to form another, for example. Divisions may be a function of social dynamics (the "informal group" discussed in our chapter on Human Relations theory). They may be defined by the nature of the tasks to be performed; it may be useful to divide a given task into subtasks and to assign different subtasks to different groups of workers. The chemistry department of a university may assign freshman chemistry (which typically is a general college requirement) to one division of professors and other chemistry classes to another division, for example.

The issue of interdependence has been examined by a number of Contingency theorists. In 1972 Jerald Hage and Michael Aiken looked at interdependence and participation in decision making. They found that interdependent tasks encourage participatory decision making, and that participation in decision making was negatively related to routinization and coordination by rules. In 1976, Andrew Van De Ven led a study in which he found that horizontal communications increased with task uncertainty.

We return now to the question that started all this: how many divisions are needed? For Contingency theorists, the answer relates to the nature of the environment (it is also a function of size and of economy of scales, as we shall see shortly). That was what Lawrence and Lorsch found in their 1967 study of different industries discussed earlier. The plastics industry in this study existed in an ambiguous environment and had more divisions than did the container factories they examined that existed in a stable environment. How many divisions does a school need? Certainly knowledge is a complex issue and demands numerous divisions. Other environmental factors, such as legal or policy requirements, demand further divisions, as we discussed earlier with exceptional children's programs.

Vertical Differentiation Vertical differentiation refers to the number of authority levels in an organization. Vertical differentiation can be represented on a continuum that ranges from flat to steeply hierarchical. The simplest way to calculate the degree of vertical differentiation in an organization is to count the number of authority levels between the CEO and the lowest worker. This doesn't always work, however, because organizations may be divided into divisions with different degrees of verticalness. One solution is to count the number of authority levels in each division and calculate an average for the entire organization. This approach generally works, although it raises questions about whether divisions that have dramatically different structures, such as R&D and manufacturing, should be averaged together.

Both vertical and horizontal differentiation have characteristics in common. Both are related to ambiguity in the environment, for example—but for different reasons. Horizontal differentiation exists to break tasks into manageable pieces, while vertical differentiation results from a need to coordinate the different roles required to deal with the environment.

Spatial Differentiation   An organization that is spatially differentiated has divisions or departments at different geographical locations. The reasons why an organization might disperse its operation are varied. If the needs of the clientele are so varied or ambiguous that service must be customized, then those services might best be placed close to the clientele. A state department of education operates in a complex environment and coordination of the diverse needs of schools and their students may be better served by regional offices than by a centralized office. Alternatively, an organization whose raw materials are costly to transport may locate refining factories at diverse geographic locations that are closer to the sources of raw material. An industry whose market is unstable or dwindling might diversify by purchasing different manufacturing operations at different geographical sites. An organization might spread out simply to take advantage of different taxing opportunities, or to place certain parts of its operations near populations that contain high percentages of workers with particular skills or near finance centers such as New York. An R&D operation may want to locate near a university, for example, while manufacturing could best be placed in low-tax areas, and corporate offices would best be served near large cities with ample money markets. Finally, an organization may differentiate spatially simply because it has grown too big to be coordinated at one site.

ROUNDTABLE

Discuss the nature and form of differentiation within schools and within school districts. How does such differentiation cause conflict (give examples from your own experience)? What control procedures are in place to reduce conflict among different divisions within schools? What is the relationship between differentiation and rules? Does your school have too many or too few rules given its level of differentiation? If so, is effectiveness affected (how)? How would you improve effectiveness in that situation (be specific about the role of rules in educational systems)?   ■

Differentiated Differentiation   As we have already observed, different divisions within an organization are responsible for different parts of the environment. It follows logically that degree of involvement with the environment will vary from division to division. Thus, an organization's sales division will be more intimately related to the environment than manufacturing, and research will respond to a different set of contingencies than will management. In 1960, Talcott Parsons devised a typology for illustrating the general relationships of different organizational structures with the environment. He argued that there are three generic systems in a complex organization: the *technical system,* the *organizational system,* and the *institutional system.* The technical system is where actual production occurs; the institutional system mediates the organization's relationship with the environment and is composed primarily of higher level management; and the organizational system interprets issues identified in the institutional system for the technical core, and is usually composed of middle management.

Thomas Petit (1967) conceptualized Parsons' typology of an organization as a set of imbedded systems. This can be pictured as a set of concentric rings, like a bullseye, floating in an environmental sea. The institutional system lies at the outer ring of the bullseye, thus suggesting its close relationship with the environment and suggesting that this system represents an "open system" in the fullest sense of the term. Actors who operate in this system include school superintendents and college presidents. Much of the workload for these actors involves interaction with the environment. The institutional system is primarily concerned with environmental demands and how they can be maneuvered to best serve the organization. The technical core lies at the center of the bullseye, suggesting that it is protected to a significant extent from environmental influence—that is, it is more nearly a closed system than are the other two systems. Actors in this system include teachers and support staff; it is their job to process the organization's raw material. The organizational system lies in the ring between the technical core and the outer institutional system. This middle layer of the organization is responsible for coordinating the activities of the technical core and for translating messages that pass between the outer and inner systems. In education, it includes school principals, deans, and department heads.

ROUNDTABLE

Does Petit's model accurately represent the realities of public education? What type of organization does Petit's model best represent? Draw a representation that more adequately illustrates public education. What roles in public education are represented by the three general subsystems? ▪

How Size Affects Structure

Contingency theory examines not only relationships between environmental contingencies and organizational structure, it examines the effects of a number of internal contingencies on structure as well. These internal contingencies include organizational size, formalization, and centralization of authority.

In 1971, Peter Blau and Richard Schoenherr looked at the relationship between size and number of organizational divisions among 52 public personnel agencies in Canada. They found that the number of organizational divisions (positions, hierarchical levels, sections per level, etc.) increases as the size of organizations increase, but that the rate of differentiation tapers off as size increases, rather than expanding at a constant rate as one might think it would. Managers in large organizations supervise larger departments than do their counterparts in smaller organizations; thus, larger systems have a smaller percentage of sections than do smaller ones. Blau and Schoenherr explained this by arguing that large organizations accrue a certain economy of scale that allows them to function with less administrative intensity and with larger departments than their smaller counterparts.

This conclusion, however, isn't entirely satisfactory. If, as Contingency theorists also claim, increasing size creates increasing problems of coordination, there would seem to be a practical limit to how large a division can get in the name of scale economy. This fact does not seem to be supported by Blau and Schoenherr's data, however (see Fig. 6.3), and the problem is not addressed in the Contingency theory literature. It may simply have been that Blau and Schoenherr did not include organizations that were of sufficient size to produce unwieldy departments. If they had, the regression line in Figure 6.3 might have turned upwards at a steeper angle at its upper end.

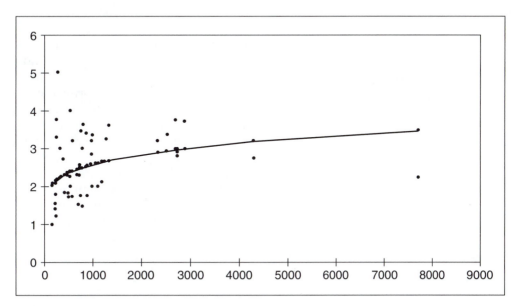

FIGURE 6.3   Plot of Peter Blau and Richard Schoenherr data on organizational size (x-axis) and number of organizational sections (y-axis) among 52 public personnel agencies in Canada. Solid line represents best fit to data.

From P. M. Blau & R. A. Schoenherr. (1971). *The Structure of Organizations.* (New York: Basic Books, Inc.). p. 72. Copyright © 1971 by Basic Books, Member of Perseus Books Group. Reprinted by permission of Basic Books, a member of Perseus Books, L.L.C.

Formalization and Integration

Formalization is the degree to which rules and procedures are imposed on an organization. If a delivery service standardizes its delivery procedures to the point of gauging the precise time at which a pickup is made and specifying the amount of time allowed for that pickup, that organization is formalized. Formalization in education is evident when written rules regulate the activities of teachers, when arrival and departure times are specified and enforced, for example, or when teachers consult curriculum manuals for detailed instructions about lesson plans. Research has shown that formalization is high when environmental or task uncertainty is low, and vice versa (Hage & Aiken, 1972). This raises the obvious questions: Why are some public schools so highly formalized, and do teachers function better in an environment of rules or in a more decentralized environment? Tackle this as a Roundtable discussion with other classmates.

Centralization of Authority   The degree to which organizational control is centralized at the upper levels of the hierarchy is a function of uncertainty (less uncertainty, more centralization). In a study of social welfare agencies, for example, Hage and Aiken (1972) found that routine work is related to the centralization of decisions, formalized procedures, and a less professional staff.

Hage and Aiken also looked for a relationship between uncertainty and the number of rules that an organization creates (formalization). It seemed an obvious conclusion that organizations in stable environments would run their organizations via rules. Their results surprised them: they found only a weak link between uncertainty and the number of rules. Similarly, the important study of public personnel agencies by Blau and Schoenherr (Blau, 1970; Blau & Schoenherr, 1971) found only a weak relationship between formalization (rules regarding personnel regulations) and centralization of authority.

Blau and Schoenherr did not consider this contradictory, however. They observed that, in organizations where procedures foster development of merit-based leadership, a highly trained cadre of leaders will emerge who are capable of decentralized decision making. This, Blau argued, accounts for the presence of decentralization among the formalized organizations in his study, and explains the weak relationships he found between formalization and centralization. As he said in his 1971 study, "Rigidity in some cases may breed flexibility in others" (p. 160).

LEADERSHIP

A number of leadership theories emerged from the Contingency theory worldview, and we will loosely lump them together under the rubric of Leadership Contingency theory. Such theories are easy to recognize: they postulate that leadership behaviors will vary with environmental and internal conditions. We will examine several such micro-theories and try to understand how they influence actual administrative behavior in the educational environment.

Managerial Grids

We discussed the leadership behavior studies of Stogdill, Halpin, Winer, and others at Ohio State University in Chapter 4. Stogdill and his colleagues sought to profile leadership behaviors. Their research identified two categories of such behavior: *initiating structure* (which they roughly defined as management-oriented behavior) and *consideration* (roughly defined as warm and trusting relationships with employees). These early studies suggested that different situations call for different mixes of initiating and consideration behaviors, and that implication gets at the heart of the Contingency theory assumption.

The managerial grid typically associated with the Ohio State studies is reproduced in Figure 6.4. This model depicts four cells representing the two dimensions of leadership behaviors identified in the Ohio State studies (initiating and consideration). A number of other researchers have confirmed and even expanded this basic model. Researchers at Michigan State University, for example, conducted similar analyses of leadership behavior and identified two similar clusters: employee orientation and production orientation. Employee orientation was associated with a democratic style of leadership, while production orientation was associated with an authoritarian style.

Robert Blake and Jane Mouton (1964) expanded the managerial grid to include five quadrants (still using the same two dimensions). The fifth cell was carved out of the center of the grid and represents what Blake and Mouton called middle-of-the-road behavior (see Fig. 6.5). In describing this behavior, they argued that "adequate organization performance is possible through balancing the necessity to get out the work while maintaining morale of people at a satisfactory level" (p. 136). They labeled the low task, low people cell as "impoverished" leadership behavior in which there is the "exertion of minimum effort to get required work done" (p. 136). High people, low task is "country club" behavior, or "thoughtful attention to needs of people for satisfying relationships [which] leads to a comfortable, friendly organization atmosphere and work tempo" (p. 136).

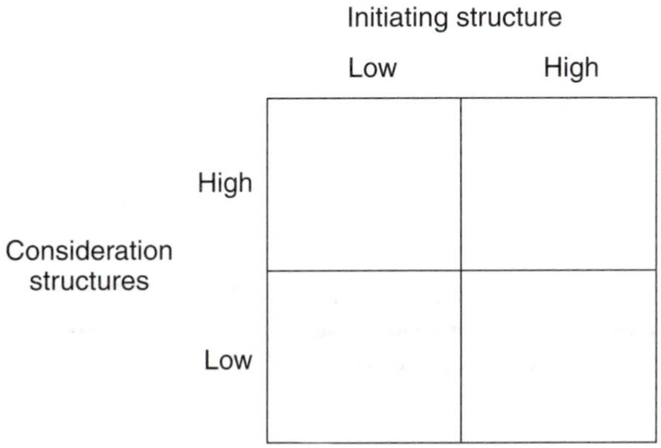

Initiating structure

Low   High

Consideration
structures

High

Low

FIGURE 6.4 Managerial grid based on findings in the Ohio State Studies.

FIGURE 6.5   Blake's and Mouton's managerial grid based on findings of the Ohio State Studies.
From Robert A. Blake and Jane S. Mouton, *The managerial grid III: a new look at the classics.* (Houston: Gulf, 1985), p. 12. Copyright © Grid International, Inc. Adapted by permission.

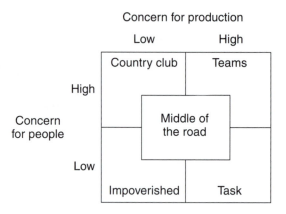

They labeled the high task, low people profile as "task," in which "efficiency in operation results from arranging conditions of work in such a way that human elements interfere to a minimum degree" (p. 136). Finally, high people, high task is labeled "team," and refers to a situation in which "work accomplishment is from committed people; interdependence through a 'common stake' in organizational purpose leads to relationships of trust and respect" (p. 136).

ROUNDTABLE

Where, on the Blake and Mouton grid, do you think the effective educational leader lies? Defend your answer. Are there circumstances in which the effective leader would exhibit a different profile? What sort of contingencies might impact the mix of task- and people-oriented behaviors of a leader? ■

Fiedler's Contingency Theory

Fred Fiedler is generally considered the father of Leadership Contingency theory because of his pioneering and influential work in this area. Fiedler was clearly influenced, however, by the leadership behavior studies of Ralph Stogdill, Andrew Halpin, James Winer, and others at Ohio State University in the 1960s (see, for example, Halpin, 1966), and by the many related studies that grew out of the Ohio State research.

Fiedler (1973) identified three contingencies that determine appropriate leadership behavior. The first is *leader-member relations,* or the nature of the interpersonal relationship between leaders and followers. Leader-member relations could be relatively poor in a large factory or mill and relatively good in a small elementary school. It can be influenced by such things as labor unions. The second contingency in

Fiedler's model is *task structure,* or the degree of structure or specificity in work tasks. The task structure of millwork is quite high, while that in an experimental research lab can be relatively low. The final contingency is *position power,* or the degree of power and authority invested in the leader's position. Position power in a formal bureaucracy is high, while that in a volunteer organization is rather low.

Fiedler argued that certain combinations of these contingencies create a *favorable situation* for leadership; he defined a favorable situation as "the degree to which the situation enables the leader to exert his influence over his group" (1967, p. 13). The most favorable situation is one in which there are good leader-member relations, high position power, and well-specified task structures. Other combinations create an *unfavorable situation* for leadership. The least favorable situation is one in which leader-member relations are poor, task structures are unspecified, and position power is low to nonexistent.

There are eight possible combinations of Fiedler's three contingencies (see Fig. 6.6). These range from favorable combinations to unfavorable combinations. Fiedler argued that the particular mix of contingencies in an organization determines the nature of effective leadership behavior, whether task-oriented, relationship-oriented, or a compromise between task and relationship orientation (labeled "moderate" in Fig. 6.6; these leadership behaviors are, of course, derived from the managerial grids of Stogdill and others). The more favorable combinations of these

	ORGANIZATIONAL CONTINGENCIES			APPROPRIATE LEADERSHIP BEHAVIOR	
	Leader–member relations	Task structure	Leader–position power	Task–motivated behavior	Relationship–motivated behavior
Favorable conditions	Good	High	Strong	HI	LOW
	Good	High	Weak	HI	LOW
	Good	Low	Strong	BOTH MODERATE	
→	Good	Low	Weak	LOW	HI
	Poor	High	Strong	LOW	HI
	Poor	High	Weak	BOTH MODERATE	
	Poor	Low	Strong	HI	LOW
Unfavorable conditions	Poor	Low	Weak	HI	LOW

FIGURE 6.6   Fiedler's Contingency Theory of Leadership.

From Fred E. Fiedler, (1974), The contingency model: New directions for leadership utilization. *Journal of Contemporary Business, 3,* p. 71. Copyright © 1974 by the Business School of the University of Washington at Seattle. Adapted by permission.

contingencies are conducive to task-motivated leadership behavior. Leaders in these environments can count on the "followership" of workers (good leader-member relations), know clearly what needs to be accomplished (high task structure), and are supported by clearly delineated authority (position power). He or she can, consequently, focus on "getting the job done;" that is, leadership styles can and should be task-oriented. A well-liked bus maintenance supervisor (good leader-member relations, high task structure, high position power), for example, should exhibit task-oriented behavior.

Leaders in the least favorable situations (poor relationships, low structure, and weak power) can count on none of these benefits: followers are not supportive, the leader has no particular authority to act, and the task at hand is ambiguous. Such individuals can most effectively serve their organization, and build their reputation in the process, with task-oriented behavior—thus, both favorable and unfavorable conditions favor the same leadership style. A leader of a contentious volunteer parent-teacher organization, for example, needs to focus on accomplishing the goals of the organization because no amount of public relations savvy will salvage a poor performance in this case.

Relations-motivated leadership behavior lies in the middle of the favorableness continuum. The work environment here exhibits a moderate amount of ambiguity. Leaders can best serve this organization by drawing on the creativity and cooperation of organizational members and by nurturing worker growth. Like cell 2 of Perrow's model discussed earlier (unstable raw materials and unclear procedures; see Fig. 6.1), this situation demands a relations-oriented leadership style. Problems facing the organization require high engagement and creative problem-solving, and if the leader cannot stimulate such worker behavior, the organization will be ineffective.

ROUNDTABLE

Where along Fiedler's continuum would you place k-12 schools? Research universities? Community colleges? Why? Locate the following on the model and explain why you feel each fits where it does: routine factory production, genetic research lab, custodial institute, nonprofit organization, rapidly changing electronics industry, religious organizations, a poorly disciplined middle school classroom taught by a substitute teacher. In each case, explain why the particular mix of task and people orientation recommended by Fiedler is appropriate. Compare Fiedler's model to the managerial grid proposals discussed earlier. In what manner does Fiedler modify these grids? Is there correspondence between where you placed schools on Fiedler's continuum and where you would place them on the managerial grid? ■

Path-Goal Contingency Model

Robert House and Terrence Mitchell (House, 1971; House & Mitchell, 1974) produced an important variation on Fiedler's Contingency model. House did much of his leadership research at Ohio State with Stogdill and his colleagues, and was nat-

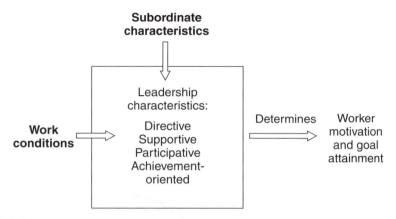

FIGURE 6.7   House's and Mitchell's path-goal contingency model of leadership.

urally influenced by their work. House and Mitchell were also influenced by expectancy theories of motivation. Expectancy theories presume that people will strive to achieve if they believe that their efforts will lead to desired rewards (e.g., "If I show a capacity to deal effectively with curricular issues, I will become a principal;" refer to the discussion of motivation in Chapter 5). This suggests that effective leaders are sensitive to the goals of their followers and motivate their performances by enabling their goals. It could also suggest that leaders should help subordinates define or modify goals, that they should provide coaching or direction to help subordinates achieve their goal, and that they should remove barriers and frustrations.

House and Mitchell identified two categories of contingent factors that determine effective, motivating leadership behaviors (see Fig. 6.7). The first category is subordinate characteristics. Some workers, for example, prefer to work in an authoritarian environment or, conversely, exhibit a need to control their own behaviors. The second category of contingencies in House's and Mitchell's model is the work environment. This refers to the nature of the pressures with which subordinates must deal. Is the task highly or loosely structured? Is there a formal authoritarian system or is the control system decentralized?

Effective leaders adjust their leadership to fit these contingency pressures and to motivate subordinates. If workers are most comfortable in an authoritarian structure and if tasks are highly structured, then effective leaders might adopt a directive leadership style, for example.

House and Mitchell identified four leadership styles that leaders might use in different situations. The first is the *directive* style, in which followers are told what is expected of them. The second is the *supportive* style, in which the leader is friendly and demonstrates genuine concern for subordinates. The third is the *participative* style, in which leaders invite participation in decision making but reserve veto power. The last is the *achievement-oriented* style, in which leaders seek to challenge subordinates and demonstrate confidence that followers will achieve their goals.

Leaders help subordinates achieve their expectations by providing the leadership needed in a given situation. If, for example, working conditions are unstructured but the situation, or contingency, calls for a structured environment, effective leaders will provide that structure. This, of course, is contingent on whether worker characteristics are receptive to structured leadership. A new principal who replaces a laissez-faire leader may find that student discipline is out of control and teachers are not receiving resources they need to teach effectively. That principal might best motivate teachers and increase their job satisfaction by introducing structure into discipline and budgeting. Teachers themselves may resist structuring of their own activities, however, so this principal might adopt an achievement-oriented style of relating to the staff.

House and Mitchell propose that, all things being equal, when tasks are unstructured (a contingency factor), job satisfaction is enhanced by leaders who are more directive than supportive. Unstructured tasks are inherently challenging and satisfying; thus, the leader need not focus on supportive relationships with workers. This leader can best serve the organization and the worker by providing direction—reducing uncertainty and structuring resources and decisions wherever possible. By contrast, structured tasks call for low direction and high support. House and Mitchell argue that structured tasks are inherently less satisfying, and more boring, than unstructured tasks. Leaders can reduce dissatisfaction by being supportive of workers. Further, since the workers' tasks are routine, there is little need for leader direction.

ROUNDTABLE

Consider what House's and Mitchell's model says for educational leadership. What is the state of the contingencies with which the educational leader in your school must deal? What is the nature of the work environment? The people? What leadership behaviors does the particular mix of contingencies in your school suggest? Are contingencies and leadership behavior in your organization appropriately matched? If not, does this impact job satisfaction, acceptance of leadership, and worker motivation? Under what conditions might your school leader be directive? Supportive? Achievement-oriented? Participative? Should leadership behaviors vary from individual situation to situation, or are leader behaviors more generalizable (e.g., must each budgetary or curricular issue be approached differently, or can the leader treat most all budgetary issues with one style and most all curricular issues with another)? Illustrate your responses. ∎

Hersey's and Blanchard's Tri-Dimensional Leader Effectiveness Model

Paul Hersey and Kenneth Blanchard developed a Contingency theory model of leadership that they called a "situational model" (1993). Like the other Leadership Contingency theories we have examined, their model is grounded in the managerial grid that evolved out of the Ohio State studies. They added, however,

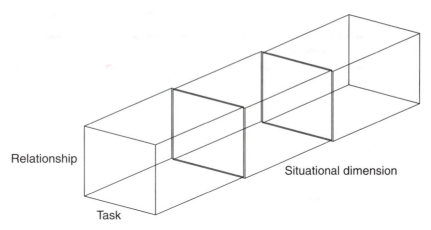

FIGURE 6.8   Hersey's and Blanchard's effectiveness dimensions.

From P. Hersey and K. Blanchard, *Management of organizational behavior: utilizing human resources,* 6th ed., p. 131. (Upper Saddle River, NJ: Prentice Hall, Inc.). Copyright © 1993. Copyrighted material adapted by permission of the Center for Leadership Studies, Escondito, CA, 92025. All rights reserved.

a situational dimension, thus converting the two-dimensional managerial grid into a three-dimensional model (see Fig. 6.8). The two-dimensional managerial grid, they argue, suggests a one-best style of leadership, typically high task, high consideration. In reality, however, effectiveness or ineffectiveness depends on the given situation faced by the leader; thus, appropriate leadership behavior, whether task-oriented or people-oriented, is a function of situation. Hersey and Blanchard label this third dimension *effectiveness,* but this is somewhat confusing. It is more consistent with their argument to label it *situation.* Effectiveness is not a dimension; rather, it is the result of an appropriate match between situation and leadership behavior. Their model, then, defines effectiveness as a proper match between leadership behavior and leadership situation. We will discuss each of these (effectiveness, behavior, and situation) in turn.

Leadership Effectiveness   According to Hersey and Blanchard, effective leaders act in the best interest of the organization. To illustrate, they distinguish between "getting a job done" (success-oriented leadership) and "impacting the disposition of followers" (effective leadership). Leaders sometimes focus on rapid accomplishment of goals but fail to develop a foundation on which productivity becomes a permanent element of organizational culture. Success-oriented leaders focus on short-term goals, often at the expense of long-term organizational health. Hersey and Blanchard compare these leaders to sports coaches who play only their seniors in order to maximize the immediate win-loss ratio, but fail to develop their freshmen and sophomores to help assure future strength, or to school superintendents who implement a number of radical changes to make themselves look good in the immediate job market but who sacrifice future morale and organizational effectiveness in the process. Effective leaders, by contrast, are less interested in immediate productivity and more concerned about the long-term health of an organization. This leadership style produces enduring, stable results while shortsighted, success-oriented leaders lay the groundwork for future disaster. The coach in the above illustration creates conditions that will likely lead to poor seasons over the ensuing few years. Similarly, the success-oriented superintendent previously mentioned is setting the stage for follower backlash in the form of sabotage, absenteeism, low morale, and turnover. An effective coach or superintendent will sacrifice short-term gain if needed for long-term, stable productivity.

Leadership Behavior   As stated above, Hersey and Blanchard premised their model on the two dimensions of leadership behavior from the Ohio State leadership studies, task behavior and relationship behavior (the Ohio State researchers called these the initiating structures and the consideration structures). Hersey and Blanchard define these dimensions as follows:

- Task behavior is the extent to which the leader engages in spelling out the duties and responsibilities of an individual or group. These behaviors include telling people what to do, how to do it, when to do it, where to do it, and whom to do it to.
- Relationship behavior is the extent to which the leader engages in two-way or multi-way communication. The behaviors include listening, facilitating, and supportive behaviors (1985, p. 19).

Unlike the Michigan State researchers, Hersey and Blanchard did not define task behavior in terms of authoritarianism with all the normative baggage that term carries. If a person gives directions on how to get to some destination, he or she isn't necessarily being authoritarian or overbearing. A person who seeks such direction probably is not looking to bond or to gain emotional support, he or she merely needs the directions. Similarly, task-oriented leadership behavior is first and foremost geared toward enabling a task that needs to be done. Certain situations call for nothing more than task-oriented behaviors, and giving directions on how to get somewhere is one of them.

Similarly, relationship behavior is more than just being friendly or collegial, for task-oriented behavior can be delivered in a friendly manner as well. Relationship orientation means nurturing, supporting, and encouraging. It's what one does to help subordinates gain confidence or to motivate them. A worker who is uncomfortable about a change needs supportive behaviors from a leader, as does a worker who must develop new skills in order to perform a given task.

Leadership Situation   The situations in which leadership performs are defined by a number of factors, including followers, supervisors, key associates, organization, job demands, and decision time (Hersey & Blanchard, 1993). The key element of situation, however, is followership. "The relationship between leaders and followers is the critical variable in the leadership situation" (1993, p. 189).

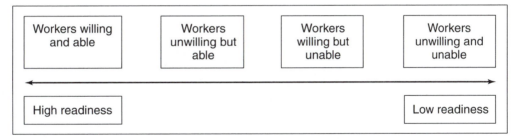

FIGURE 6.9 Hersey's and Blanchard's readiness continuum.

From P. Hersey and K. Blanchard, *Management of organizational behavior: utilizing human resources,* 6th ed., p. 186. (Upper Saddle River, NJ: Prentice Hall, Inc.). Copyright © 1993. Copyrighted material adapted by permission of the Center for Leadership Studies, Escondito, CA, 92025. All rights reserved.

Thus, in Hersey's and Blanchard's model, followership, or more specifically, *follower readiness,* becomes the "situation dimension" in Figure 6.8.

Readiness is related to (1) workers' ability to perform (able or unable, referring to whether they have the necessary knowledge and skills for a task); and (2) their willingness to perform (willing or unwilling, referring to confidence and commitment). By combining these two categorical dimensions, Hersey and Blanchard identified four points on a continuum from low to high readiness (Fig. 6.9). At the two ends of this continuum, low readiness is defined as being neither able nor willing, while high readiness is defined as both able and willing. Workers who are unable but willing are one notch above low readiness; they have desire but do not have the required skills. Workers who are unwilling but capable of a task are next highest on the continuum. Hersey and Blanchard argue that the difference between moderately low readiness (willing but unable) and moderately high readiness (unwilling but able) has to do with the fact that the first is leader-directed and the second is follower-directed. Workers become increasingly responsible for tasks as they move up the readiness scale. Previously willing persons may become somewhat unwilling when faced with the anxiety of self-direction. A faculty member may be entirely competent to direct a committee but unwilling to do so because of feelings of anxiety about the task or because of time constraints, for example. They are willing and secure when someone else takes responsibility for the task, but when told they are sufficiently competent to take over the responsibility, they may become less secure or willing.

Effective leaders are able to correctly diagnose worker readiness and to adapt their leadership styles (task behavior and relationship behavior) accordingly. This idea is summarized in Figure 6.10. The first cell on the left, which corresponds to a low worker readiness state (unable and unwilling), requires high task and low relationship leadership behavior in which the leader provides specific instructions and close supervision. The leader tells the worker what to do, hence Hersey and Blanchard label this *telling* behavior. The focus is on getting the job done; it is leader-directed behavior. The next cell (willing but unable) is likewise

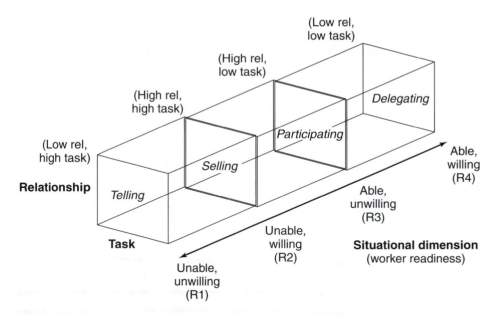

FIGURE 6.10 Hersey's and Blanchard's Situational Leadership Model.

From P. Hersey and K. Blanchard, *Management of organizational behavior: utilizing human resources,* 6th ed., p. 186. (Upper Saddle River, NJ: Prentice Hall, Inc.). Copyright © 1993. Copyrighted material adapted by permission of the Center for Leadership Studies, Escondito, CA, 92025. All rights reserved.

focused on task accomplishment, but the leader is focused on relationships with workers as well (high task, high relationships). Here, the leader explains decisions and provides opportunities for clarification. Hersey and Blanchard call this *selling* behavior.

The third cell from the left (able but unwilling) assumes a greater degree of worker responsibility for a task than did the first two cells. Accordingly, leadership behavior is high relationship, low task-oriented; this involves the sharing of ideas and facilitating in decision making. This is labeled *participating* behavior. In the last cell (workers are able and willing), the leader turns over responsibility for decisions and implementation to workers; this is called *delegating* behavior. Here, leadership behavior is low task and low relationship.

To summarize, the first two cells from the left define worker readiness states that call for leader-directed behavior, and the last two cells define readiness states that call for worker-directed behavior. Accordingly, the lowest level of readiness, unable and unwilling, is associated with Telling behavior; the next level is associated with Selling behavior, the third level is associated with Participating behavior, and the highest level of readiness is associated with Delegating behavior. Put simply, as worker readiness increases, leaders function in a manner that helps workers accept increasingly greater responsibility.

CASE STUDIES

Hersey and Blanchard provide a number of illustrations of how their situational model can be applied in an educational setting. Hersey and two colleagues in Brazil, for example, compared classrooms that were taught by traditional methods (mostly lecture with some discussion and audiovisual components) with classes in which instruction was guided by situational principles (students were given increasing responsibility for their learning as their readiness increased). They found that students in the situational-directed classroom performed higher on class tests than did students in the other class and had higher levels of enthusiasm, morale, and motivation.

Hersey and Blanchard further cite evidence that boards of trustees for colleges and universities should be led as unable but willing systems: trustees should be involved in decision making but the tasks should be leader-directed (selling behavior). They explain that trustees have little time or experience for board work; consequently, the effective college president will provide significant structure and direction. The same principles apply to public school boards as well.   ■

ROUNDTABLE

Hersey and Blanchard also discuss effective administrator/faculty relationships in public schools, but I leave this as an exercise for you (once you have formed your opinions about how educational leaders should work with faculty; refer to Hersey's and Blanchard's discussion in their 1993 book, p. 212). Evaluate the readiness of faculty in your school for the tasks they perform (consider their experience, knowledge, willingness to take responsibility, and motivation), then identify the optimal leadership behavior for their readiness profile. Does the leader in your school exhibit these behaviors? If not, does this lack of congruence compromise organizational effectiveness, as defined earlier? How so? When and under what circumstances might the leader in your school alter his or her leadership behavior?   ■

CRITICISMS OF CONTINGENCY THEORY

Anna Grandori (1987) has provided a useful summary of the criticisms that have been leveled against Contingency theory, but we will need to expand on her work a bit in order to grasp the full impact of what she is saying and to understand more fully the premise of the next theory we will examine. Grandori's summary offers four critiques. First, Contingency theory suggests a one-to-one correspondence between organizational structure and environment that, according to its detractors, cannot be supported (see, for example, Crozier & Friedberg, 1977). They argue instead that there are a number of equally effective ways to deal with a given environmental contingency. This is particularly true where the environment is forgiving—where there are ample resources on which organizations can draw, for example—or where competition is low.

Second, organizations sometimes resist environmental adaptation because of inertia or because of costs associated with change. Contingency theory is criticized because it does not explain what happens if an organization fails to adapt under such circumstances.

Third, Contingency theory assumes that causation is essentially one-way, that environment drives organizational structure rather than the alternative, that organizations may affect environment. In fact, organizations control their environments by strategies such as direct influence—attempting to control suppliers, clients, etc.—or by selecting less problematic environments through diversification. Organizations may even select the environment in which they choose to operate, or they may choose to perceive only certain parts of the environment and ignore others—that is, they create their environment.

The notion that organizations might select their environments leads us to the fourth criticism found in the organizational theory literature: environment is not an absolute, given entity. Two organizations may define the same market differently, approach it with different strategies, and have each be successful. One firm, for example, may choose to build its fortunes on a quality, dependable product, while another builds a reputation for innovation. Such choices imply different approaches to the same environment or different perceptions of environmental problems.

The essence of these arguments is that organizations and environments are sufficiently "loose" to allow significant administrative discretion. There is not a tight relationship between administrative behavior and organizational outcome, or the environment is not so demanding that it is intolerant to a number of organizational solutions to given problems. This empowers the leader to behave in a number of different ways. This perspective defies generalizations about the effectiveness of one structure or leadership style over another.

I can illustrate with an observation of recent events from my own university. In 1994, our president and board of trustees decided to reorganize the university. Nine colleges were collapsed into four, the departmental structure was significantly realigned, middle and top management positions were drastically cut, the budgetary structure was reformulated, and several university support services were privatized. Whether university leaders understood it or not, these rather draconian changes were premised on the assumption that the administration has significant discretion in how an organization is structured. They, then, would agree with the critics of Contingency theory. Contingency theorists would counter that various contingencies—the size of the university, the nature of its tasks, the nature of demands from its environment, the disposition of its employees—limit its structural choices. Who is right?

Interestingly, events of the intervening years provide a possible answer, one that supports Contingency theorists. Within a year of reorganization, a fifth college was created; four colleges were simply too unwieldy to manage—unwieldy in terms of size and diversity of function (Education and Business Management, which had been combined in the reorganization, were simply too different, and the resulting college too big). Within the next year, the alumni and faculty of another college successfully lobbied for the creation of a semi-autonomous "school" within its college. Meanwhile, it was becoming apparent that the drastic cuts in middle management placed significant strain on remaining personnel (some of the responsibilities were even shifted to faculty, thus detracting from teaching and research), and the deleted positions began to reappear. In 1999, the trustees agreed to the creation of yet another "school," primarily because the college from which the school was carved was too diverse and difficult to manage. Within five years, then, the university had expanded to five colleges and two schools, and much of the original middle management has been reinstated; we are looking much like we did before reorganization. It would seem that the administrators did not have quite the degree of discretion presumed, and that various university contingencies pretty well shape the structure of the organization.

RESEARCH TOPIC

Identify a rather significant organizational change with which you are familiar (reorganization, program implementation, new leadership, etc.), one that seems to violate one or more of the premises underlying Contingency theory. Alternatively, you might examine a situation of misfit between Contingencies and structure that is not particularly related to dramatic change, such as a college in which departments are too large to be adequately integrated.

Discuss organizational effectiveness relative to the nature and degree of misfit between contingency and structure or leadership. Is there pressure within the organization to return to the fit relationship, or does the administrator in this situation have unbridled discretion in the nature of leadership or organizational behavior? Explain. How would you design data collection for a study of this type? What sort of data would be needed, where would you get the data, and how would you obtain them? How would you analyze the data once obtained? ▪

ACTIVITY

In the discussion on Charles Perrow, you were asked to complete a contingency table (Fig. 6.2) by identifying certain appropriate structural features (discretion, coordination, structure, type of worker) for the four environmental contingencies that define the table. Further, you were given four organizational types and asked to categorize them. Following are Perrow's categorizations (Figure 6.11). If you disagree with any of them, make an argument for your interpretation. ▪

The observations of Contingency theorists can be summarized as the following relationships:

- Appropriate relationships between organizational size and degree of formalization or level of differentiation;
- Appropriate relationship between the nature of the work task and the type of worker (generalist or specialist);

	Uniform and stable	Nonuniform and unstable

Not well understood	*Discretion:* High
	Coordination: Feedback
	Structure: Decentralized
	Worker: Generalist
	Example: School
		Discretion: High
		Coordination: Feedback
		Structure: Flexible with
		      multiple levels
		      of centralization
		Worker: Generalist
		Example: Psychiatric
		      hospital

Well understood	*Discretion:* Low
	Coordination: Plan
	Structure: Formal and
	      centralized
	Worker: Specialist
	Example: Custodial
	      institution
		Discretion: Low
		Coordination: Plan
		Structure: Flexible but
		      centralized
		Worker: Specialist
		Example: Programmed
		      learning school

FIGURE 6.11   Perrow's contingency table with certain structural features categorized. Perrow's raw materials contingency table.

From *Organizational analysis-06B5600, 1ˢᵗ Edition,* by C. Perrow. Copyright © 1970, p. 81. Reprinted with permission of Wadsworth, an imprint of Wadsworth Learning, a division of Thompson Learning. FAX 800-730-2215.

- Appropriate relationship between the nature of the raw material and differentiation, coordination, formalization, and decision-making discretion;
- Appropriate relationship between leadership style (telling, selling, participating, delegating) and worker readiness;
- Appropriate relationship between task, power, and relationship environments (Fiedler's Contingency model) and leadership behaviors (people or task orientation);
- Appropriate relationship between worker and task characteristics (House's and Mitchell's model) and leadership behaviors (directiveness, supportiveness, achievement orientation, participative).

Diary

In your diary for this chapter, summarize your thoughts on one or more of the Roundtable discussions. You are also encouraged to reflect on the following questions (and on any other thoughts that you may have struggled with as you read the chapter, of course):

- Given what you have learned in this chapter, what are some important functions of leadership? How does your answer change your previous responses to this question?
- Why is Contingency theory considered a subset of Open Systems theory?

- Describe how schools map their environment. The amount of diversification in public education has increased significantly over the past 30 years. Identify how diversification has increased, and try to explain why (in Contingency theory terms).
- Identify some school-related conflictive episodes with which you are familiar. How can these conflicts be explained relative to diversification? How should an administrator handle these conflicts? Should the conflicts be suppressed?
- Are highly formalized relationships between educational leaders and faculty (rules and regulations) appropriate in a school environment? What effect does formalization have on educators? Are faculty more generalist or specialist? Does this influence your conclusions about formalization? Does school size have anything to do with this discussion?
- According to Hersey and Blanchard, a leader whose leadership style is incongruent with worker readiness is less effective than when there is congruence between the two. Explain, with illustrations.

Recommended Readings

Donaldson, L. (1996). *For positivist organization theory: Proving the hard core.* London: Sage Publications.

Contingency theory has fallen into disfavor among organizational theorists in recent years—the currently favored models are anti-positivist in nature. Donaldson argues that Contingency theory warrants reevaluation. He presents well-reasoned evidence that administrators have less discretion over issues of leadership and organization than the anti-positivist would have us believe. Instead, contingencies exert significant influence over how organizations are structured and how leadership behaves. This book is valuable not only for its discussion of the positivist/anti-positivist matter, but for its development of the assumptions underlying major current theories.

Hersey, P., & Blanchard, K.H. (1993). *Management of organizational behavior: Utilizing human resources* (6th ed.). Englewood Cliffs, NJ: Prentice Hall.

A "must read" book for all educational leaders. Hersey and Blanchard develop their important Situational theory of organizational management in this text. The authors provide a number of educational applications.

Perrow, C. (1970). *Organizational analysis: A sociological view.* Belmont, CA: Wadsworth Publishing Company, Inc.

One of the fascinating aspects of organizational theory is its stories, and Charles Perrow is one of its better storytellers. In this book, he develops the raw materials contingency table that is discussed in this chapter. He illustrates with a number of stories—about the use of pigeons during World War II as homing devices in bombs and an experiment to use pigeons to inspect for product defects on assembly lines, or how the bureaucratic structure constructed for the assembly of Model T cars almost did in the Ford Motor Company when it came time to produce a different design.

References

Blake, R.A., & Mouton, J.S. (1964). *The managerial grid.* Houston: Gulf.

Blau, P.M. (1970). Decentralization in bureaucracies. In M.N. Zald (Ed.), *Power in orga- nizations.* Nashville, TN: Vanderbilt University Press.

Blau, P.M., & Schoenherr, R.A. (1971). *The structure of organizations.* New York: Basic Books, Inc.

Crozier, M., & Friedberg, E. (1977). *L'acteur et le système.* Paris: Editions due Seuil.

Donaldson, L. (1996). *For positivist organization theory: Proving the hard core.* London: Sage.

Fiedler, F. (1967). *A theory of leadership effectiveness.* New York: McGraw-Hill, Inc.

Fiedler, F. (1973). The contingency theory and the dynamics of leadership process. *Ad- vances in Experimental Social Psychology, 11,* 60–112.

Fiedler, F. (1974). The contingency model: New directions for leadership utilization, *Jour- nal of Contemporary Business, 3,* 65–79.

Grandori, A. (1987). *Perspectives on organizational theory.* Cambridge, MA: Ballinger.

Hage, J., & Aiken, M. (1972). Routine technology, social structure, and organization goals. In R.H. Hall (Ed.), *The formal organization* (pp. 55–72). New York: Basic Books, Inc.

Hall, R.H. (1991). *Organizations: Structures, processes, and outcomes* (5th ed.). Englewood Cliffs, NJ: Prentice Hall.

Halpin, A. (1966). *Theory and research in administration.* New York: Macmillan.

Hersey, P. (1985). *Situational selling.* Escondito, CA: Center for Leadership Studies.

Hersey, P., & Blanchard, K.H. (1993). *Management of organizational behavior: Utilizing hu- man resources* (6th ed.). Englewood Cliffs, NJ: Prentice Hall.

House, R.J. (1971). A path-goal model of leader effectiveness. *Administrative Science Quar- terly, 16*(3), 321–338.

House, R.J., & Mitchell, T. (1974). A path-goal theory of leader effectiveness. *Journal of Contemporary Business, 3,* 81–97.

Lawrence, P.R., & Lorsch, J.W. (1967). *Organization and environment.* Cambridge, MA: Har- vard University Press.

Marion, R. (1999). *The edge of organization: Chaos and complexity theories of formal social or- ganization.* Newbury Park, CA: Sage.

Parsons, T. (1960). *Structure and process in modern society.* Glencoe, NY: The Free Press.

Perrow, C. (1970). *Organizational analysis: A sociological view.* Belmont, CA: Wadsworth Publishing Company, Inc.

Petit, T.A. (1967). A behavioral theory of management. *Academy of Management Journal, 10*(4), 341–350.

Van De Ven, A., Delbecq, A., & Koenig, R. (1976). Determinants of coordination modes within organizations. *Administrative Science Quarterly, 41*(2), 322–338.

CHAPTER 7

Conflict

This chapter is about conflict in organizations; it is also an interlude for reviewing select elements of the first two parts of this textbook and segues into the last part. To this point, we have examined Social Darwinism, Closed Systems theory, and positivistic Open Systems theory. Social Darwinism defined parameters of sociological debates that lingered long into the 20th century, debates over whether organizations are cooperative or conflictive. For the most part, the theories we have discussed have adopted Spencer's cooperative perspective, but this will change in the last half of the 20th century when theorists will be challenged by conflict/Marxian perspectives (as we shall see, this debate began with the Structuralists).

Five major organizational theories have been examined in the first two parts of this book. Machine theory took a rather heavy-handed approach to management, one that tended to generate hostility among workers. Human Relations theory attempted to humanize management but accomplish the same productivity goals sought by Machine theorists (sans the hostility). Structuralists sought to understand the tension between formal productivity goals and human irrationality in organizations. Open Systems theory recognized that productivity is influenced by multiple, uncontrollable environmental pressures, and Contingency theory sought laws for adapting to those external contingencies.

We now look at how these perspectives influence different microtheories of conflict. Spencer's organic (conflict) model is clearly reflected in the first microtheory we will examine. It is called, appropriately, Conflict theory. The second theory will reflect a Structuralist, cooperative perspective of organization. We will then look at a model that is grounded in Contingency theory's hypotheses about task and people orientations. The last model we will examine will define conflict from the Conflict theory perspective, but will otherwise relate to a theory in the next part of this book called loose coupling.

In this chapter, students will:

- Review the first two parts of the textbook and preview the final part.
- Develop strategies for dealing with different types of conflict in organizations.
- Analyze a case study on conflict and propose strategies for dealing with the issues posed in the study.
- Develop the outline of an analysis of teacher union conflict.
- Refine their understanding of the role of leadership in education.

CONFLICT THEORY

An important perspective of conflict during the middle decades of the 20th century was closely related to Spencer's organic view of society. The perspective assumed that social behavior was conflictive, a dog-eat-dog world. Perhaps the most important spokesperson for this view was the German sociologist, Ralf Dahrendorf (1959). Dahrendorf defined conflict as an episodic and instrumental struggle between collective adversaries over scarce resources. Conflict, he argued, has a manifest stage, in which conflict is directly expressed, and a latent stage, in which conflict seethes quietly beneath the surface of social interaction. Thus, conflict is a perpetual presence in society, even though it is not always visible. Dahrendorf felt that conflict runs in cycles, latent to manifest and back to latent. Conflict is instrumental because it serves the goals of a conflict group. It exists because society never has sufficient resources (such as money, prestige, and power) to satisfy everybody's needs.

Dahrendorf identified five conditions that must exist for conflict to become manifest. First, groups with common identities or needs must exist. These groups must have differential access to society's resources—one group may have access to more power than the other, for example. Second, certain instrumental conditions must exist. For example, the deprived group must have leadership and must feel that the group suffers deprivation based on the common identity of its members. African-Americans, for example, feel deprivation based on their common identity as a race.

A group will sometimes try to manufacture perception of deprivation in order to create conflict. In the 1950s, the ultra-conservative John Birch Society placed unauthorized cards in stores warning against the purchase of goods manufactured in communist countries. Their goal was to manufacture an issue and create media coverage—even if the coverage was negative—that would, in turn, bring converts to their cause. Cities found that the best way to deal with this problem was to quietly remove the cards and otherwise ignore it.

Third, deprived groups must feel that conflict will lead to satisfaction of their needs. President Ronald Reagan's forceful reaction to the strike of flight controllers in the early 1980s sent a powerful message that labor unrest would not be tolerated; consequently, there were relatively few labor strikes in the United States during the 1980s. The political atmosphere simply was not conducive to conflict. Fourth, the deprived group must have access to a clearly defined adversary. In the 1960s, blacks in the United States rebelled against Southern white hegemony—a clearly defined adversary. The adversaries of labor unions are corporate owners. Part of the John Birch Society's objective in the previous story was to manufacture an adversary. This is called the "them-us" phenomenon.

Fifth, there will typically be some sort of triggering event that sets off conflict. The conflict that followed the jury's decision in the Rodney King affair in Los Angeles in 1992 was triggered by the decision and by an attempted arrest on a traffic violation in a Black community of that city. The tension preceding the verdict set the stage for conflict, but the verdict and the subsequent attempted arrest were the actual triggers.

Sociologist James Geschwender (1964) identified several types of deprivation, among which are status inconsistency (one group feels its status in society is less than that of some other group); rising expectations (expectations of social, status, or monetary gain exceed actual gains, as when a market boom fosters unrealized expectations of teacher salary increases), and rise and drop deprivation (a period of improvement is followed by sharp reversals, as when legislative promises of increased support for education are reversed). James Gamson (1966) argued that conflict does not occur while a group is suffering severe deprivation; rather, it occurs when conditions begin to improve, giving the group hope of better times ahead. He called this the "J curve" hypothesis—a plot of deprivation level (y-axis) against time which looks like a "J," in which the worst deprivation is experienced at the bottom of the J but conflict occurs when the curve begins to rise again.

Lewis Coser (1956) differentiates between major conflict and minor conflict. Minor conflicts, he argued, serve an important function in society. They permit mutual accommodation among competing needs, and foster cross-cutting ties among different factions of society. Minor conflict allows people to express their differences and work out their hostilities. It encourages a social fabric of coalitions, accommodations, and compromises that weave different factions together into a social whole. If minor conflicts are suppressed, then differences are not resolved and coalitions are not created. Such societies may experience extended periods of peace, but when conflict does erupt, it easily polarizes people into major factions (because there are no cross-cutting accommodations to resist it) and threatens the survival of that society.

RESEARCH TOPIC

You could produce an interesting term paper out of an analysis of the dynamics of labor unrest in your state (assuming you live in a state that has teacher unions). A number of different research questions are suggested by the preceding discussion of conflict. One could look for the five precursors of conflict that Dahrendorf identified. Geschwender's and

Gamson's hypotheses could guide analysis of events in your state. A particularly interesting study could use Coser's proposals to examine the problems and benefits of political conflicts between policy-makers and teacher unions. Do these hypotheses about conflict suggest strategies for controlling conflict in your state or district?

CONFLICT AND THE STRUCTURALIST PERSPECTIVE

Structuralist theorists tended to make a somewhat controversial assumption: they assumed that structure is a product of necessity, that things happen because they are needed. This may seem an innocent, even common-sense assumption, but it is grounded in deep philosophical controversy. The assumption is called "teleology," or "final causation." Teleological logic states that structures organize as they do because the given form best serves the predetermined needs of people. A tumbler is round because round fits comfortably in the hand, a dog has a tail to swat flies, and schools are divided by subject matter because that is the best way to present academic content. The opposite of this is called "efficient causation," in which structure is a product of forces unrelated to outcome. By this logic, tumblers are round because that's the shape molten glass assumes when spun, dogs developed tails and then found they were useful for swatting flies, and schools assumed departmentalized structures because that was the popular thing to do when their structures coalesced at the turn of the 20th century.

Tension arises when needs are unfulfilled, and when there is discrepancy between needs and reality. Deviancy, defined as failure by certain persons or groups to conform to social norms, can create a sense of discrepancy in a social group. Incompatible structural forms can generate social discrepancy, as when the needs of one group frustrate the needs of another. Discrepancy exists when needs are unmet by existing social systems.

Conflict arises from such discrepancy, from a disjuncture between what should be and what is. Because discrepancy is a function of "what should be," it is referred to as Normative theory.

In education, discrepancy can be observed between the needs of a professional faculty and the reality of a bureaucratic organizational structure. Such professional-bureaucratic discrepancy creates conditions in which conflict and anomie can flourish. According to sociologist Robert Merton (1971), discrepancies lead to conflict when (1) the discrepancy is perceived by some group, (2) the discrepancy exerts a proximal and dramatic influence on the group (discrepancies with roots in China, for example, are not likely to breed conflict in England), and (3) the affected group believes its actions can resolve the discrepancy.

The Structuralist approach to conflict differs from the Conflict theories of Dahrendorf, Gamson, and others in several important ways. The assumptions underlying Conflict theory are certainly different from those of Structuralists: Conflict theories attribute struggle to efficient, rather than final, causation, for example. In Conflict theory, hostilities emerge because of existing physical conditions (scarce resources) and not because of functional needs. Consequently,

Conflict theory is not normative, while Structuralist theory sees conflict as a struggle over what is good for society.

These differences mean that what the two theoretical perspectives perceive to be conflict may differ. To the Structuralist, a football game is not conflictive because it is accepted behavior (nondeviant) and only involves discrepancy between needed and actual states in a rather shallow sort of way. To the Conflict theorist, football is a struggle over scarce resources such as prestige, money, and alumni support. Similarly, legislative wrangling is normal to the Structural theorist and a struggle over scarce resources is normal to the Conflict theorist. Football games and legislatures are part of the cooperative social fabric to the Structuralists but part of a dog-eat-dog struggle to Conflict theorists.

A number of researchers have studied the effects of discrepancies on social anomie and conflict. Sorensen and Sorensen (1974) found that professional-bureaucratic discrepancy caused job dissatisfaction among CPAs. George Miller (1967) observed alienation among scientists and engineers who experienced professional-bureaucratic discrepancy. Pearlin (1975) investigated marital stress associated with status inequality between mates. Marion (1976) found that professional-bureaucratic discrepancy was associated with perceptions among teachers of conflict with school administrators. Ronald Corwin, in a massive study of educational conflict (1966), found that professionals in bureaucratic settings were more likely to be conflictive than were professionals in professional settings or bureaucrats in bureaucratic settings. He further observed that professional teachers react contentiously to standardization of procedures and other such strategies of bureaucratic organization.

CONFLICT AND LEADERSHIP PRESCRIPTIONS

Some researchers have argued that organizational conflict can be delineated along task and relationship axes that are similar to those that Contingency theorists such as Stogdill, Halpin, and Winer have used in leadership studies (Jehn & Werner, 1992, 1997; Pinkley, 1990). Task-related conflict refers to struggles over processes or goals, and relationship-related conflict refers to interpersonal disagreements that are not directly related to tasks. Similarly, Lewis Coser refers to goal-oriented conflict, or disagreements over the outcomes of a social system, and emotional conflict, which refers to personal frustration and interpersonal problems (Coser, 1956).

Empirical research indicates that relationship conflict has a negative impact on group performance and satisfaction (Evan, 1965; Gladstein, 1984; Wall & Nolan, 1986). Such conflict distracts participants, reduces cooperation, and creates resentment. Task conflict, by contrast, can improve group performance by forcing participants to look at different points of view and to deal with constructive criticism (see Fig. 7.1).

Jehn (1997) argues that these two categories of conflict may interact with one another. Task conflict, for example, may degenerate into relationship conflict when participants personalize criticism. To explore this possibility, she conducted

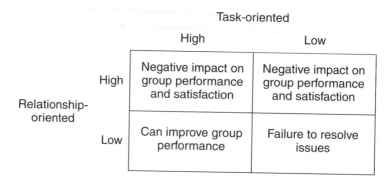

FIGURE 7.1   The impact of task and relationship conflict on organizational effectiveness.

a qualitative examination of conflict in six industrial work groups. Jehn's findings revealed a third category of conflict, which she called process conflict. This refers to conflicts over how tasks are to be performed, which was often manifested as who would perform given tasks.

Jehn also identified four dimensions of conflicts, dimensions that tended to influence the impact that conflict had on work groups: emotionality, importance, acceptability norm, and resolution potential. Emotionality refers to the nature of feelings in a conflictive episode; importance refers to the size and scope of the conflict; acceptability refers to group norms about conflict, whether disagreement is expected and tolerated; and resolution potential refers to the degree to which disagreements are perceived as resolvable.

Negative emotionality includes rage, anger, annoyance, frustration, and resentment. Negative emotionality can characterize all three types of conflict, although it is most common in relationship conflict. Interestingly, emotional outbursts can exist in task and process conflict without arousing personal animosity. Jehn (1997) illustrated this with quotes such as, "It's not you, I'm just frustrated that I can't express myself clearly" (p. 544). Emotionality tended to depress group performance wherever it manifested for all three categories of conflict (relationship, task, and process).

Importance must be understood in terms of group perceptions—participants might say, for example, "it (the disagreement) is a big deal," or otherwise distinguish between a big fight and a little tiff. This judgment is related more to the perceived outcome of the conflict than on whether the conflict is constructive or destructive. Importance had a generally positive impact on performance in task conflicts and a generally negative impact on performance in relationship conflicts.

Positive acceptability norms usually mean that group members openly discuss their differences and display feelings. With negative acceptability, members suppress expression and feelings. Acceptability norms vary by type of conflict:

open expression might be acceptable in task or process conflicts but not in relationship conflicts, for example. Positive acceptance tends to increase group performance in task and process conflict, but negative acceptance tends to be better for group performance when conflict involves personalities.

Resolution potential focuses on whether a group feels that a given conflict can be resolved. Factors that influence this perception include history of animosity, status differences, potential costs, and uncertainty. Conflicts judged low in importance or low in emotionality are more likely judged resolvable than are high importance or high emotion conflicts. Conflicts perceived as resolvable typically are indeed resolved and members are more motivated to deal with conflicts that are so perceived. Resolvability has a positive impact on performance and satisfaction across conflict types.

CONFLICT AND ALLIANCES

The discussion of conflict that follows is related to Dahrendorf's Conflict theory, particularly in the way it defines conflict. It is more closely aligned with two of the anti-positivistic theories to be discussed in subsequent chapters, however: loose coupling theory and network theory. Thus, this discussion serves not only to summarize the preceding half of this book, it serves to introduce the second half of the book as well. It is about conflict alliances.

Conflict begins with incompatible preferences, when the needs or wants of one person or group are contrary to the needs or wants of another. Two people competing for the same position in an organization have incompatible preferences—they both want the same thing but only one can have it. Incompatible preferences exist when two departments compete for scarce resources, when prestige is allotted to one person but not another, or when one person's ego needs are deterred by someone else's actions. The incompatibility of preferences need not be real in order to cause conflict; incompatibility need only be perceived as real. Conflict can erupt over the belief, whether true or not, that one's desires or needs have been thwarted. This conflict is a zero-sum game (remember Prisoner's Dilemma?).

Conflict requires that the parties in a dispute be coupled; it is difficult to deprive the needs of, and wage hostilities against, someone with whom you have no relationship. Further, the relationship should be fairly tight; otherwise, the actions of one party will have limited, if any, impact on the other.

Relationships can be either affirming or tense. Affirming relationships are supportive and mutually beneficial; tense relationships are nonsupportive and hostile. Consequently, a relationship can be strong and tense, weak and affirming, or any other such combination. Obviously a conflictive relationship is tense; according to our earlier argument; it is likely also to be rather tight.

It is characteristic of conflicting parties that they seek allies. Consider three tightly linked school personnel, A, B, and C. If A and B become conflictive toward one another, the link between them changes from affirming to tense (see Fig. 7.2).

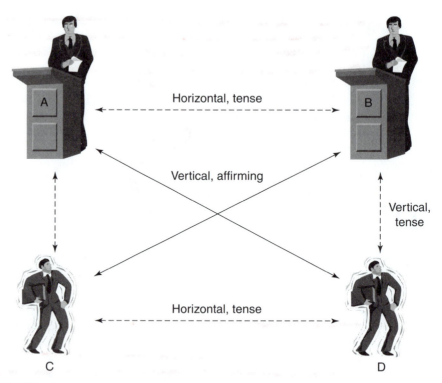

FIGURE 7.2 Congruent conflict groups involving horizontal and vertical divisions (A and B are administrators, C and D are subordinates). Dashed lines refer to tense couplings, solid lines are affirmative couplings. Note that if the link from, say, C to D was affirming, triangulation would be incongruent.

One or both of them will inevitably seek to recruit C, who is tightly and affirmatively linked to both, into his or her camp. Let's say that person B manages to recruit the support of C. This strengthens B's position and weakens that of person A. The link between B and C remains affirming, but now link A-C is tense. All the links remain tight, however; thus, any one actor can affect any other. Cartwright and Harary (1956) and Heider (1958) refer to this as a congruent triad. An incongruent triad exists if C attempts to maintain an affirming relationship with both A and B, thus putting C itself in a difficult position.

Person A, who is isolated in the above congruent triangle, may seek to correct the imbalance with an alliance of his or her own. If successful, two warring camps emerge. A mix of affirming and tense relationships (Fig. 7.2) couples the parties in the conflict. As for coupling strength, the camps may actually seek to increase the degree of tightness between themselves, for by doing so they can increase the damage done to one another. They can frustrate the efforts of one another by meddling in each other's affairs. They will withhold cooperation from one another. And they will likely attempt to recruit still others into their respective camps.

Conflictive splits (tense relationships), according to Kenwyn Smith (1989), are horizontal when they involve groups at the same level of authority. Combatants may also seek to involve participants at higher or lower authority levels. If recruits come from a higher level of authority, the combatants enhance their relative positions of power. If recruits are at lower levels of authority, then combatants extend their power base and may be able to enact their agenda among subordinates over the objection of, or to the detriment of, their "enemies." This is called vertical division. Assume that A and B are administrators and C and D are faculty subordinates. Figure 7.2 now represents congruent triangulation with a combination of horizontal and vertical conflicts.

CASE STUDY

Smith (1989) describes a conflict story that is all too familiar in education: A school board split by ideological differences. This school board from the New England region of the United States had nine members; one was chair, four considered themselves fiscal conservatives, and four considered themselves educational progressives. Many of their votes were 4–4, which put the chair, a lawyer, in the uncomfortable position of casting the tie-breaking vote and, consequently, of alienating clients of his law firm. The chair often tried to avoid this by calling for public input into decisions. The public itself, however, was split along similar ideological lines, thus these forums typically degenerated into public attacks on board members from the "other" camp and rarely resolved anything.

At other times the board would turn its acrimony, and that of the public, onto one or more school administrators. This allowed them to deflect their battles onto someone else, thus masking the fact that they themselves were the source of the conflict.

Smith relates an incident that began with the board deadlocked over where to place the district's ninth grade. There were compelling educational reasons to place the ninth grade in the middle school and compelling fiscal reasons to leave it in the high school. The battles were deflected onto the high school principal, who came under such severe attack from the public that he had a heart attack and died.

The board selected one of the two existing assistant principals as interim principal (the other refused the position); he was subsequently confirmed as permanent principal. There now was an open slot for assistant principal. The educational progressives proposed to increase the number of assistants at the high school to three. They argued that there was too much work for just two assistants, as witnessed by the recent death of the original principal. The fiscal conservatives, of course, opposed this, and the stage was set again for the usual 4–4 board split.

As this debate heated up, each school board coalition sought to recruit the existing high school administrators into its respective camp. The progressives did this by arguing that an extra assistant would make the administrative task of the high school easier; the conservatives argued that the salary for an extra principal would force cuts in important curricular programs. If one group could have recruited the support of both existing administrators (principal and assistant), it would have significantly strengthened its bargaining power. If each recruited one of the administrators, the relative power of the two groups would have remained in balance but the stage would be set for horizontal and vertical splits or tenseness. There would be vertical tenseness between each administrator and the board coalition he or she did not support. Horizontal splitting already existed at the board level and, if the administrators split their allegiance, tense horizontal relationships would exist at the school level. This is the scenario represented by Figure 7.2. Failure to inject tenseness among the administrators would have compromised the board's battle lines, for they needed strong allies and they needed others fighting their battles.

The chairman intervened, however, by saying that he would not support the motion for the third assistant, and that proposal collapsed—but the story continues. A committee of school personnel was then chosen to screen applications to fill the vacant assistant principal's position. The committee eventually settled on four candidates, all of whom were employees of the school district. Their top candidate was a good politician; it was felt that he could deal effectively with the community. The fourth-ranked candidate was a strong disciplinarian and had good support from the faculty and students of the high school. The second- and third-ranked candidates were ignored in the ensuing debate over whom to hire.

The community split over its preference for the first- and fourth-ranked candidates and barraged the members of the selection committee with phone calls in support of their respective choices. The selection committee held firm and refused to buckle under the pressure. Community members then appealed to the school board, which, predictably, split on the issue—the progressives supported the fourth-ranked disciplinarian and the conservatives supported the politician.

The matter got even stranger. It then occurred to the fiscal conservative members of the board, who had originally opposed hiring a third assistant principal, that they could solve the impasse on which candidate to hire by reversing their position on a third assistant. Then, in an even stranger twist of events, the progressives who had originally supported hiring a third assistant were now insulted by this blatant political move and vowed to oppose it! Yet another 4–4 split was imminent, but the battle lines were just the reverse of what they had been a short time earlier. The chair, working behind the scenes, managed to breach the differences and the board agreed to hire two new assistant principals.

Board members assumed that each could now get the assistant principal they wanted—the conservatives would get the politically savvy candidate and the progressives would get the popular disciplinarian. They failed to account for the preferences of the selection committee, which stuck by its decision to advance the names of its first and second candidates instead of the first and fourth ones.

The board progressives reacted by trying to subvert the selection committee on the issue. They did this by threatening the superintendent. They made it clear that the superintendent could hire the number one candidate (the choice of the fiscal conservatives), but that they would reject any other candidates brought before them until their choice showed up. Further, if the superintendent refused to bring forth their candidate, he could expect his contract to be terminated when the contract period ended and they would advance his assistant superintendent into the superintendency (an inelegant attempt to introduce tension in the coupling patterns of the superintendent's office).

The patterns of alignment and tension had become quite complex. There were a number of horizontal and vertical splits involving board and community, the selection committee, the superintendent's administrative staff, and the administrative staff of the high school.

In order for the school board combatants to strengthen their respective power bases, they sought not only to recruit allies from the ranks of subordinates (vertical splits), but to create horizontal splits among school groups as well. The focus had long since ceased to be on education, and the single goal was to "win the war." The board was insensitive to the casualties strewn along its path (casualties that even included a death) or to the morale and functional problems associated with the spread of hostilities among peers.

The superintendent eventually capitulated and the two groups got their respective candidates. However, this spun off two opposing factions in the high school administrative staff. The two new assistants were, perhaps predictably, at odds with one another; the politically savvy assistant felt the disciplinarian left him with all the paperwork, while the disciplinarian felt the savvy assistant shirked his responsibility with teachers and students. Respective camps of the school board sided with one or the other assistant. Repeated efforts were made to reconcile the differences without success.   ■

Kenwyn Smith (1989), the author of this case study, interpreted the conflicts in the school district in terms of triangulation and splitting. We will further interpret events relative to coupling patterns.

Each of the various actors in this story—the two board factions, the two community factions, the selection committee, the superintendent's administrative staff, and high school administrative staff—represent different divisions that are coupled together with links that vary in strength and nature. The linkages in the horizontal conflicts were rather strong and tense. The two factions of the school board, for example, each strongly and negatively influenced the preferences of the other. Had the relationship between the two been asymmetrical— had one held a numerical majority—the coupling strength would have likewise been asymmetrical. The majority group would have had greater influence over the minority (their link to the minority would have been strong). The minority, however, would have had lesser influence over the majority (their link to the majority would have been moderate to weak). The overt conflict would have been correspondingly less intense unless the minority group could have found allies to bolster its position. Each group, then, fought for asymmetrical dominance and fought to avoid asymmetrical subservience.

To create asymmetrical dominance over each other, the two board groups recruited allies. For example, they manipulated the dependence of the high school administrative staff in the struggle over two versus three assistants by tantalizing them with reduced workload or by threatening them with program cuts. In both cases, the factions offered to manipulate resources desired by the administrators in return for their support; that is, they attempted to link the preferences of the administrators to their own preferences.

The board sought to use its power to interject tenseness into horizontal relationships, while at the same time strengthening their interdependence, among subordinates (the two ingredients needed for successful conflict). The school board's actions in hiring the two assistant principals, one for each camp, interjected inevitable tenseness between these two subordinates. Simultaneously, they strengthened the interdependence between the assistants by providing each with a "big dog" (the sponsoring board faction) to back them. Each assistant may not have been able to directly influence the preferences of the other, but was able to indirectly influence the other's behavior through his supporting board faction. The threat that they held over each other was not in what they themselves would do, but what their supporters on the board would do.

One group in a conflictive relationship can gain advantage over the other by weakening the other's affirming links to potential or to real allies. When the progressives threatened the superintendent over the hiring of their fourth-ranked candidate, they not only exerted their own control over him, they assailed the relationship of the superintendent with the conservative board faction as well. They did this by indirection: they said in effect that, even if the other faction supported his reappointment, their strong opposition to him would leave him in an uncomfortable, if not untenable, position. The fight over his contract would have inevitably spilt over into the community, and the resulting acrimony would have likely forced him to seek employment elsewhere. They were saying that the other faction could not protect him from this; thus, his linkage to that faction was essentially weakened.

The patterns of weak and tight relationships, vertical and horizontal groups, and tense and affirming relationships can be reduced to a few simple dynamics. Each board faction engaged in four basic strategies:

- Weaken the impact that its adversary had upon it;
- Create affirming, tight relationships with different subordinate groups;
- Create tense, tight relationships between subordinates that supported, and those that opposed, their positions; and
- Weaken the relationships between adversaries and their allies.

Unfortunately, the board factions were quite good at these strategies, but they left quite a bit of damage in their wake.

 ## RESEARCH TOPIC

Social conflict always makes for an interesting research topic. Select a conflictive episode with which you are familiar and analyze the events in terms of triangulation, splitting, horizontal and vertical relationships, the strength of relationships, and the nature of relationships. How might you, as administrator, have effectively intervened in the conflict you are studying? How might the superintendent in the story of the New England school board have intervened to head off, or reduce the damage from, the conflicts in that district?   ■

This chapter reviewed Closed Systems and Positivistic Open Systems theories with discussions of how these various worldviews affect how we understand organizational conflict. Conflict can be defined as a dog-eat-dog struggle over scarce resources (the conflict theory perspective) or an effort to return homeostatic (cooperative) balance to organization (the structuralist perspective). Conflict was dichotomized in terms of Contingency theory's task- and people-orientation dimensions, and recent research has added a third dimension: process conflict. These different dimensions of conflict were then correlated with four contingencies: emotionality, importance, acceptability norm, and resolution potential. Finally, we looked at conflict and alliance-building, and argued that successful conflict is related to the nature of coupling among combatants and allies. Combatants will seek to increase the strength of their relationship with one another in order to increase the damage they inflict on one another. They will seek to create strong bonds with allies and to weaken the bonds between enemies and their allies. Last, they seek to foster conflict between their allies and the allies of their enemies.

Diary

- Given what you have learned in this chapter, what are some important functions of leadership? In what way does your answer change your previous answers to this question?

- We had a rather extensive discussion of conflict in this chapter. That discussion suggested that networks and alliances are key to understanding the nature and emergence of conflict. Could network analysis also help us understand how to deal with conflict? What strategies could a leader implement to head off, neutralize, or channel conflict?

- How would you deal with relationship conflict? Task conflict? Process conflict?

Recommended Readings

Coser, L. (1956). *The functions of social conflict*. New York: The Free Press.

This is a small book, but it is packed full of interesting insights about the nature of conflict in society. Coser makes the counter-intuitive argument that internal conflict serves, rather than harms, society. It helps us work out differences, to create crosscutting ties that bind us in a strong social fabric, and it helps us deal with small problems before they erupt into something big. Coser also argues that externally derived conflict can help unify a group; when outside enemies threaten a people, they drop their differences and unify in opposition to the common threat.

Smith, K. (1989). The movement of conflict in organizations: The joint dynamics of splitting and triangulation. *Administrative Science Quarterly, 34,* 1–20.

This is the full story of the New England school board that was discussed in the case study in this chapter. It is fascinating reading, and unfortunately the basic dynamics are not all that uncommon.

References

Cartwright, D., & Harary, F. (1956). Structural balance: A generalization of Heider's theory. *Psychological Review, 63,* 277–293.

Corwin, R. G. (1966). *Staff conflicts in the public schools* (Cooperative Research Project No. 2637). Washington, DC: US Office of Education.

Coser, L. (1956). *The functions of social conflict.* New York: The Free Press.

Dahrendorf, R. (1959). *Class and class conflict in industrial society.* Stanford, CA: Stanford University Press.

Evan, W. (1965). Conflict and performance in R&D organizations. *Industrial Management Review, 7,* 37–46.

Gamson, W.A. (1966). Rankorous conflict in community politics. *American Sociological Review, 31*(1), 71–81.

Geschwender, J.A. (1964). Social structure and the Negro revolt: An examination of some hypotheses. *Social Forces, 43,* 253–255.

Gladstein, D. (1984). A model of task group effectiveness. *Administrative Science Quarterly, 29,* 499–517.

Hannan, M.H., & Freeman, J. (1977). The population ecology of organizations. *American Journal of Sociology, 82,* 926–964.

Heider, F. (1958). *The psychology of interpersonal relationships.* New York: John Wiley & Sons, Inc.

Jehn, K.A. (1997). A qualitative analysis of conflict types and dimensions in organizational groups. *Administrative Science Quarterly, 42,* 530–557.

Jehn, K.A., & Werner, O. (1992). Theory, a thesaurus, and word frequency. *Cultural Anthropology Method, 5,* 8–10.

Marion, R. (1976). *Job satisfaction and conflict among high school teachers.* Unpublished Dissertation, University of North Carolina at Chapel Hill.

Merton, R.K. (1971). Social problems and sociological theory. In R.K. Merton (Ed.), *Contemporary social problems.* New York: Harcourt Brace Jovanovich.

Miller, G.A. (1967). Professionals in bureaucracy: Alienation among the industrial scientists and engineers. *American Sociological Review, 32,* 762–766.

Pearlin, L.I. (1975). Status inequality and stress in marriage. *American Sociological Review, 40,* 344–357.

Pinkley, R.L. (1990). Dimensions of conflict frame: Disputant interpretations of conflict. *Journal of Applied Psychology, 75,* 117–126.

Smith, K. (1989). The movement of conflict in organizations: The joint dynamics of splitting and triangulation. *Administrative Science Quarterly, 34,* 1–20.

Sorensen, J.E., & Sorensen, T.L. (1974). The conflict of professionals in bureaucratic organizations. *Administrative Science Quarterly, 19,* 98–106.

Wall, V., & Nolan, L. (1986). Perceptions of inequality, satisfaction, and conflict in task-oriented groups. *Human Relations, 39,* 1033–1052.

PART THREE

Anti-Positivistic Theory

One of the hottest arguments today in organizational and leadership theory has to do with choice versus determinism. There is actually nothing new about this argument. Religious scholars have debated it for centuries (free will versus predestination). Albert Einstein claimed that God does not play dice with the universe; Nobel prize winner Ilya Prigogene claimed God did. Even the ancient Greeks took sides on the question: The philosopher Epicurus said, for example, that "it would have been better to remain attached to the beliefs in gods rather than being slaves to the fates of physicists . . . [for] the latter . . . brings with it inviolable necessity." He was referring to the scientific assumption that everything in nature is ultimately predetermined. In other words, it's an old argument for philosophers and scientists, but it's a relatively new one for organizational theorists and for educators.

For most of the 20th century, we assumed there was a "science" to education or a "science" to leadership. Theorists sought principles that would describe the right way to teach or the right way to lead. Taylor certainly thought he had the answers on how to lead, but, then, so did Maslow. In education, the effective schools movement of the 1980s purported

163

to hold the keys to productive classroom instruction. Contingency theory likewise is a deterministic science of leadership and organization. Like physical scientists and philosophers, it asks how changing contingencies affect outcomes if every effect has its cause, every cause is functionally related to its effect, and (exaggerating the point a bit) every organization can be logically traced back to some organizational "big bang." It presumes law-like, continuous relationships between structure or leadership and certain variable contingencies. It poses science-like questions such as, "How does one best lead the worker who is unmotivated and unskilled as opposed to workers who are motivated and skilled?" "How should one structure a school when discipline is poor and the general environment is volatile?" "What is the relationship between type of raw materials and organizational structure?"

At the end of Chapter 6, we looked at a story of change at a university and asked, "Do leaders have significant discretion over how an organization is structured?" That story introduces the theories to which we now turn. Unlike Contingency theories, these theories assume that leaders have considerable latitude in how organizations are structured and managed, that leaders are not constrained by scientific determinism. They assume that there are relatively few general principles of leadership, that there is only a limited, direct relationship between leadership cause and organizational effect, and that organizations can be understood only within the organization's unique context. Contingency theorists would argue that the president in the case study that ended the last chapter was constrained by organizational and environmental contingencies. The theories that we now examine propose that he was not particularly constrained and could organize the institution more or less as he liked.

The assumptions underlying the theories we will be examining in the next few chapters are "anti-positivistic," a term borrowed from Lex Donaldson (1996). Other terms one might use include postpositive, postmodern, non-prescriptive, and natural. I choose to adopt Donaldson's term not for any personal bias, but simply because I want to keep the positivistic/anti-positivistic debate in the forefront. Some will disagree, arguing that positivism is no longer germane or that postmodernists have moved beyond this debate. This latter statement may be true (though the former may be hard to support), but moving beyond the debate is not consistent with the intent of this book, which is to present all theoretical perspectives fairly and not to subtly dismiss a whole class of theories with terminology. Ironically, to do otherwise is to violate the premises of postmodern thought itself, which has argued vigorously against linguistic bias. Professors using this text will, of course, make their own arguments, as well they should.

Contingency theory was introduced in the last chapter with a definition of positivism. Anti-positivism is the opposite of that definition. Following is a six-point definition of anti-positivism; if you compare it to the definition of positivism in the last chapter, you will see that the two parallel one another in diametrically opposite ways.

1. Anti-positivism is idiographic, meaning that organizations are understood within the context of their individual, unique situations. Every organization has a unique set of needs.
2. The research methodology is often nonpositivist and qualitative, although empirical methods have been used effectively by these theorists (Donaldson, 1996).
3. The theory explains organizational structure by non-material factors such as ideas, ideologies, perceptions, and norms.

4. The theory is nondeterminist in that managers are seen as having considerable discretion regarding structure and management style (this is the freedom of choice issue).

5. Theory is closely informed by qualitative research and armchair speculation; there is limited, if any, hypothesizing prior to data collection. It is not necessarily built on data patterns and arguments of earlier works.

6. The theory is consciously nonscientific; the aim is to understand local conditions rather than to make generalizations.

Anti-positivism, as we've stated, gives administrators considerable latitude, and, its proponents argue, that's a good thing. Such latitude is consistent with the human way of doing things and with the inherent complexity of social behavior. We don't always make rational decisions, and the social systems with which we must deal are too complex for rationality anyhow. We bring many different preferences to the decision-making table—power preferences, ego preferences, growth preferences—and such preferences frequently usurp rational, effectiveness-oriented decision making. We make mistakes as administrators; we overlook things; we bring our personal agendas to the job; we are human.

Anti-positivism represents a third major shift in organizational thought in the 20th and 21st centuries. The first major "paradigm" was Closed Systems theory, and the second was Open Systems and Contingency theory. Both of the earlier theories were positivistic. Anti-positivism accepts the Open Systems assumption of environmental influence, but is otherwise dramatically different from any theories we examined thus far. In many ways, it requires a new way of thinking about organization. There are few rules of leadership; indeed, the first of the theories we will examine argues that leadership behavior is often only weakly related to organizational behavior. It will turn your notions of leadership upside down, and leave you wondering whether principals and superintendents and deans and department heads have any influence over their organizations whatsoever. But bear with it; there are important lessons to be learned about leadership in the chapters that follow.

In the first chapter of this anti-positivism unit, we examine a macro theory called Strategic Choice theory. In subsequent chapters, we will examine other variations on anti-positivism, including Population Ecology, Culture theory, Critical theory, Institutionalism, and Complexity theory. They all have in common the presumption that organizational structure and behavior is a rather fickle affair that is better described by our humanness, beliefs, culture, and philosophies than by a science of organization.

OVERVIEW AND STRUCTURE

The anti-positivistic theories will seem to be a hodgepodge of perspectives whose only common ground is their anti-positivistic philosophy. To help you bring some sense to this jumble, I propose a unifying model—realizing that it is subject to academic critique. At the core of this model is the anti-positivistic assumption that much of organizational structure and behavior can be explained in terms of idiosyncratic, irrational preferences. Of the anti-positivistic theories, Strategic Choice, which argues that contingency and outcome are loosely related in organizations, best represents this generalized perspective. Just as Open Systems theory represents the core thesis underlying theories since the mid-1900s,

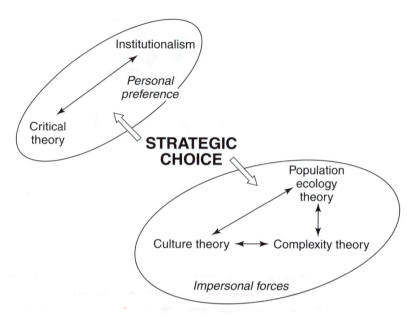

FIGURE III.1 Unifying model for anti-positivistic theories.

Strategic Choice represents the core thesis of anti-positivistic theory. This centrality is represented by the positioning of Strategic Choice in Figure III.1.

Two of the theories examined in this unit explore the idiosyncratic nature of specific human preferences. They propose, essentially, that organizations and organizational activity are shaped by personal wants and needs. The first of these theories, Critical theory, examines control and power preference of managers; the second, Institutionalism, explores legitimacy preference. These two theories are grouped as a class and as a specific derivative of Strategic Choice theory. You will see when you examine these chapters that they have much in common—Institutionalists, for example, at times define control as a legitimacy pressure.

The remaining anti-positivistic theories in this unit deal with broad forces that are beyond the control of individuals. The first, Culture theory, deals with social cultural needs. One could argue, of course, that there is a certain amount of overlap between personal needs and socio-cultural preferences. Still, its stronger kinship is with impersonal social pressures. Population Ecology deals with the random forces of natural selection, and Complexity theory is about (not quite so random) forces associated with network interaction. These three anti-positivistic theories are grouped and labeled "impersonal force theories."

And again, the common root for all of this is Strategic Choice theory.

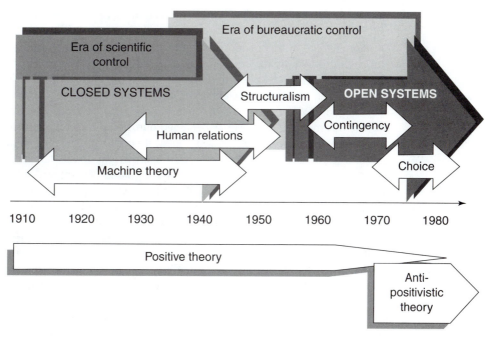

FIGURE III.2   Timeline of theories and ideas to this point in our study of organizations.

ORIENTATION

Before proceeding with Part III, let's take a quick look at where we are. A number of ideas and theories are beginning to swirl around, and it's easy to get lost in all the confusion. Figure III.2 is a timeline that summarizes these ideas. The timeline orients us in history, but beginning and ending dates are not to be taken as exact. Rather, they reflect the approximate period in which the respective theory was dominant. This figure shows the theories we have discussed against a backdrop of guiding philosophies. Three major philosophies are represented: philosophies of control, philosophies regarding the nature of organizations (whether open or closed), and philosophies of theory itself (positivistic or anti-positivistic).

There were two major philosophies of control by 1980: Scientific control and bureaucratic control. Scientific control refers to the period dominated by scientific management, in which control structures were oriented toward efficiency. This period replaced the late 1800s philosophy of the brave and heroic magnate who was firmly in control of his domain. With the emergence of Scientific Management came control structures that were based on assumptions that workers were simple extensions of machines and that both should be guided by principles of scientific efficiency. Workers were slaves to the stopwatch and to production quotas. Management procedures were structured to maintain production efficiency (review Taylor's notions of foremanship in Chapter 2).

Somewhere in this period of scientific management, the bureaucratic model of control began to take hold. Americans didn't see the seminal works of Max Weber until the late 1940s, but the ideas had migrated from Europe long before. This control philosophy shifted the emphasis from scientific efficiency to rules and regulations, impartiality, and specialization. Weber claimed that, once launched, bureaucracy would be irreversible, and indeed, this model of control has pervaded our thought up to, and including, the time of the theories in the next chapter. Subsequent theories will challenge this model, as we shall see, and it appears that Weber may have been wrong about bureaucracy's irreversibility.

A second major set of concepts that have guided perceptions of organizational structure and leadership is the notion of Closed and Open systems. The Closed systems perspective is that organizational dynamics are self-contained and subject to internal controls in much the same way that a chemical reaction is determined by the behaviors of chemicals in a (self-contained) beaker. This perception was usually associated with rather simplistic concepts of causality: one can achieve maximum productivity if he or she could only master a few simple rules of efficiency, for example. Structuralism signaled a transition from the closed system to the open system perspective. By the 1960s, theorists were arguing that organizations are not self-contained and that decisions cannot be optimized. Rather, there is a host of external pressures and demands that must be accommodated if organizations are to be effective. We have argued that this transition represents the second paradigm shift in organizational theory in the 20th century (the shift away from the era of magnates and Social Darwinism was the first).

The third major philosophy influencing theory has to do with the nature of theory itself, whether positivistic or anti-positivistic. The next chapter discusses the first of the anti-positivistic theories, the third major shift of organizational thought in the 20th century. This shift still influences our thinking as we enter the 21st century; indeed, its hold over organizational theory has increased significantly.

References

Donaldson, L. (1996). *For positivist organization theory: Proving the hard core.* London: Sage Publications.

Prigogine, I. (1997). *The end of certainty.* New York: The Free Press.

CHAPTER 8

Decision Making, Learning, and Loose Coupling

A theory appeared in the organizational behavior literature in the early 1970s that introduced a perspective of organization that prevails to this day. This perspective is called anti-positivism; it is characterized by its argument that organizational contingencies and organizational outcomes are, contrary to Contingency theory, only loosely related. The theory that started it all is called Strategic Choice theory; it is largely about decision making and organizational learning.

Strategic Choice theory and anti-positivism assume that administrators have significant latitude, or choice, about how to structure and run organizations. Of the anti-positivistic theories we will examine, Strategic Choice theory is most overtly free will; that is, it is less likely than the others to say that organizational behaviors are determined by contingencies. Actually, Strategic Choice theorists tend to fall into one of two camps on this issue. On one side are those (such as Wittington, 1989) who largely reject determinism and argue that managers have virtual free reign in how they shape their organizations (the university president in the story from Chapter 6 is, wittingly or unwittingly, in this camp). The other side argues that there is some determinism within organizations, but that leaders nonetheless have considerable discretion (Bourgeois, 1984; Child, 1972). This more moderate of these camps is probably the more widely accepted (Donaldson, 1996); it is difficult to exclude determinism and contingency from organizational description completely. Even so, the moderates focus more on the nondeterministic side of organization than on its science.

In this chapter, we will examine how organizational structure and behavior can be described as the products of idiosyncratic and nonrational activity. This thesis will then be applied to decision making. By the time we finish with the discussion of decision making, it will seem to you that an organization is an uncontrollable entity, and, to an extent, Strategic Choice theory does propose this. Actually, however, this theory is more a call to abandon the typical human assumption that an organization can be produced only by rational pre-planning, that organizational activities are deliberate and outcomes are controlled. It argues, instead, that we achieve not because we are brave sea captains courageously steering our ships to safe harbor, but because we interact with our environments and learn, on the fly, how to survive and thrive in them. Organizational futures are less what is envisioned in five-year plans and more the intelligent adaptation to experiences and opportunities encountered across time.

In this chapter, students will:

- Examine the nature of coupling patterns among organizational units and explore the implications of loose and moderate coupling for organizational structure and behavior.
- Look at how loose coupling affects change and innovation.
- Explore strategies for leading in loosely coupled organizations.
- Examine the irrational nature of decision making in organizations.
- Explore how they should capitalize on the irrational nature of decision making to improve their decision-making capacity.
- Understand how learning supplants rationality, and explore strategies for improving leadership in learning organizations.
- Refine their definitions of leadership in education.

LOOSE COUPLING

Loose Coupling theory proposes that different parts of an organization are loosely related to one another. This can be understood from two points of view. First, it can be interpreted to say that different divisions of an organization are loosely coupled with one another—activities in the math department, for example, are loosely coupled to those in the English department. That is, activities in one department have a minimal impact, or take a long time to show up, in the other. Second, loose coupling can be taken to mean that there's a lot of "play" in a system. Like a mushy steering wheel, the leader can muck about a lot without compromising the organization's performance. This, of course, is the anti-positivist perspective. For now, we will focus on the first of these interpretations.

In 1976, Karl Weick published an article in which he discussed loose coupling in educational organizations. In that article, he argued that there are seven pros and corresponding cons of loose coupling (Table 8.1). First, loose coupling allows parts of an organization to evolve independently of one another. Change, he argued, occurs more readily when the organization develops small, relatively independent divisions that are not forced to coordinate. Change can be enacted

TABLE 8.1   Summary of Karl Weick's seven pros and cons of loosely coupled systems.

Pro	Con
1. Allows sections of an organization to persist and evolve independently of one another	Units aren't pressured to discontinue nonproductive practices
2. Small, loosely coupled units are more sensitive to environmental demands	This may subject the system to the whim of energy-draining fads
3. Allows local adaptation to local environmental conditions	May hinder the diffusion of local changes that could benefit the entire system
4. Isolated units can experiment with novelty without committing the entire system to those innovations	Looseness may inhibit the diffusion of experiments that are productive
5. Allows the organization to isolate problems or breakdowns	Isolated units may receive little help from the rest of the organization
6. Loosely coupled units are self-sufficient, thus encouraging more flexible response to uncertain environments	Self-sufficiency means that units may be on their own in hostile situations
7. It may be cheaper to run a loosely coupled system than to provide the expensive coordinating structures needed for a tight system	The trade-off is loss of control

one division at a time in such a system. The alternative is to try to coordinate everything simultaneously—a daunting task. The down side of this, he continued, is that units in a loosely coupled system aren't pressured to discontinue nonproductive practices. Second, small, loosely coupled units are more sensitive to environmental demands than are large, tightly coupled systems; however, this may subject the system to the whim of energy-draining fads.

Third, loose coupling allows local adaptation to local environmental conditions, but it may hinder the diffusion of local changes that could benefit the entire system. Fourth, isolated units can experiment with novel structures or activities without committing the entire system to those innovations, but loose coupling inhibits the diffusion of productive experiments. Fifth, loose coupling allows the organization to isolate problems, but the troubled units may receive little help from the rest of the organization. Sixth, loosely coupled units are self-sufficient, thus allowing more flexible response to uncertain environments. However, this also means that units may be on their own in hostile situations. Finally, it may be cheaper to run a loosely coupled system than to provide the expensive coordinating structures needed for a tight system; however, the trade-off is loss of control.

Coupling and Stability

The literature on Loose Coupling theory is a bit unclear about the nature of tightly coupled structures. Jeffrey Pfeffer and Gerald Salancik (1978), authors of *The External Control of Organizations,* argue that, "The greater the level of system connectedness, the more uncertain and unstable the environment for given organizations" (p. 69). The implication, of course, is that, in tightly coupled organizations, perturbations have easy access to the entire system. Problems can sweep through the organization like wildfire; thus, the tightly coupled organization is unstable.

At other points in their book, however, Pfeffer and Salancik argue that highly connected systems throw up constraints to change. Karl Weick (1976) adds that tightly coupled structures are less adaptive than loosely coupled ones, thus implying that tightly coupled organizations resist change. So which is the case? Do tightly coupled structures resist change or are they sensitive to it?

Actually, they do both. Change can indeed decimate the tightly coupled structure because its different departments are so highly interdependent. Change in one department directly and quickly affects another, which impacts yet a third department, and so forth. Changes in the curriculum of the math department of a high school, for example, will have significant impact on the science department if the science curriculum intimately depends on the way its students learn math. Because of this, tightly coupled organizations tend to resist change. A high school will avoid changing its math curriculum when those changes have a widespread, devastating impact on the curricula of other departments. Tightly coupled structures resist change precisely because they are so sensitive to it.

Loosely coupled organizations, on the other hand, can embrace change because its impact is limited. The math department above can change with impunity if no other departments are affected by its changes. Because the loosely coupled organization as a whole isolates and neutralizes perturbation, however, it tends to change only sluggishly. External and internal influences are absorbed by this "mushy" organizational structure. Change agents must conduct "guerrilla warfare;" their attack must proceed department by department, person by person. The individual departments are not themselves typically difficult to change; rather, the problem lies in getting the entire organization to change, in diffusing the change across the network.

Leadership and Change

Loose Coupling theorists maintain that most organizations are loosely structured; I have proposed elsewhere that they tend to be more moderately coupled (arguing, among other things, that moderate coupling allows stability while enhancing the ability to change; Marion, 1999). Whichever is the case, these coupling patterns pose problems for leaders who want to change their organizations. Loose or moderately coupled systems will tend to simply absorb the change agent's efforts.

Pfeffer and Salancik (1978) were well aware of this problem of change in loosely coupled systems. They argued that administrators can get around it by finding ways to tighten the coupling patterns in their organizations, such as reorganization and stabilization of exchange relationships. The idea is to reduce internal and external variability in the system so that it can be more easily controlled.

ROUNDTABLE

How might an administrator tighten coupling patterns in a school to enable change? What unintended consequences could result? The board of trustees in the story of the university from the last chapter tried to implement change in just such a manner, by tightening coupling patterns. They did so by reducing the number of colleges, by giving deans a broader scope of control, and by reducing the number of staff administrative levels. As we noted in the original telling of the story, the university has largely returned to its original structure. How does this shed light on leadership and change from the loose coupling perspective?   ▪

Change and Dissemination

"Dissemination" refers to the movement of innovation and change through a system. Paul Mort was one of the earliest and most influential dissemination theorists. Mort focused on dissemination in public education. In the late 1950s, he reported that invention initially spreads very slowly in education and that, in all, it takes about 20 years to diffuse throughout the American educational system (Mort, 1958). The *NEA Bulletin* reported in 1969 that, at that time, kindergartens were offered in only 46% of the school districts in America—94 years after their introduction to this country. Education, at least in the United States, is slow to adopt new ideas.

Other institutions do better jobs at disseminating change than we do. Agricultural systems, which include land grant universities, agricultural experimentation stations, agricultural extension programs, and farmers, are able to spread innovation much more rapidly than are educational networks. Education can, at times, do better also. An innovative physics curriculum developed by J. R. Zacharias of MIT in 1956 was rather thoroughly disseminated among public high schools in the nation within 10 years of the date he introduced it. Zacharias was able to accomplish this with a prepackaged program and aggressive training initiatives. He was further helped by the national obsession with math and science studies that followed Russia's launch of the Sputnik satellite.

The rate at which change and innovation spread through a system is related to the nature of its network. We've already observed that both tightly and loosely coupled organizations resist change. Education in the United States is a loosely coupled system, which can account for the fact that innovation spreads so sluggishly through it. Typically, the U.S. system is composed of independent school districts that are loosely associated under a state government. State governments do have plenary power over local districts, but they usually give their districts significant autonomy in decision- and policy-making. This structure can slow the spread of innovation because districts must be sold on new ideas one at a time.

Tightly coupled systems, on the other hand, resist change precisely because they are so sensitive to it. The former Soviet Union suffered from just this sort of problem (Kauffman, 1995). It was so tightly centralized and controlled that it had difficulty adapting to changing conditions, a fact that helps account for its demise in 1989.

Because of this, the optimal structure for disseminating innovation and change is probably the moderately coupled systems (Marion, 1999). Moderately coupled systems are sufficiently loose to experiment with innovation without engulfing the entire system, but sufficiently tight to allow the efficient dissemination of change. The agricultural system described earlier is neither tight, like the old Soviet system, nor loose, like the American educational system. Its coupling pattern is somewhere in between these extremes. Agricultural stations and universities within this network can experiment with change without involving the rest of the system; but when they discover something that would be helpful to farmers, they have ready access to that system through its extension agency network. Farmers who don't want to implement innovations can refuse to do so, or can delay doing so, without freezing the entire system, but all have access to the innovation within a reasonably short period of time.

ROUNDTABLE

Assuming moderate coupling is the answer to facilitating the spread of innovation and change, what sort of things could a state superintendent and state board of education do to make their state system more amenable to the spread of creative ideas? ∎

DECISION MAKING

As we have noted, Strategic Choice theorists argue that cause is loosely related to outcome, but they also argue that human behavior and decisions are often irrational anyhow. So it's a good thing that cause and effect are loosely related; otherwise, irrationality would make a mess of anything we tried to do.

In 1957, Nobel prize winner Herbert Simon identified three phases of decision making: he called them the *intelligence phase* (a period of data collection), *design phase* (when possible decisions are drafted), and a *choice phase* (during which a course of action is selected). You should see similarities between this and Dewey's decision-making model that was discussed in Chapter 2. Henry Mintzberg, Duru Raisin-ghani, and André Theoret analyzed Simon's three phases of decision making in 1976. They found that people may gather decision-making data when problems are mild, but are not likely to do so when they are severe. They discovered that decision making is more a trial-and-error process than a systematic search for alternatives. Finally, they found that the choices people make usually are more the result of intuition or political compromise than rationality.

This exposes a key problem with Closed Systems theory: decision making is not a rational process and decisions are not "optimized." As Simon put it, rationality is bounded and decision makers merely "satisfice." Administrators rarely have complete information about a problem, they must deal with numerous conflicting and often illogical forces during the decision-making process, they rarely have time to explore alternatives, and they rarely have a good grasp of cause-and-effect relationships (what the outcomes of their decisions will be). Decisions are subject to nonrational complexities; thus, administrators tend to find solutions that are only "good enough."

Katz and Kahn (1966) observed that decision making in open systems is hampered in a number of ways:

- A person's social space affects his or her knowledge, experience, attitudes, and judgments. We define reality in terms of the people and communities we associate with, the problems and tasks we deal with, and the attitudes we grew up with. As Peter Drucker (1946) said,

  > The executive of a big business . . . lives in an artificial environment and [is] almost as isolated as if he were in a monastery. . . . His contacts of people outside of business tend to be limited to people of the same set. . . . Hence, executive life not only breeds a parochialism of the imagination . . . but places a considerable premium on it. (p. 81)

  Therefore, we understand the problems of others in terms of our own social references. We make decisions about curriculum based on our middle-class upbringing or push students to achieve without understanding that some children who live in different worlds than we do may be ostracized in their home community if they make good grades.

- Identification with outside reference groups. People tend to relate to others at their own level of authority or slightly above, and to give more weight to input from these peers than from peers at lower levels. This biases our decisions in favor of those reference groups.

- Projection of attitudes and values. We sometimes assume that others see the world as we do and blithely toot along without looking about to make sure we are in touch with the rest of the world. It's the attitude that says, in effect, "I like lima beans and there must be something wrong with you if you don't." Administrators may be particularly subject to such self-delusions because subordinates are hesitant to disagree with them openly. Consequently, decisions may not be grounded in actual conditions or in the conditions experienced by others but, rather, are jaded by personal perceptions and attitudes.

- Global and undifferentiated thinking. Humans sometime base decisions on simplified perceptions of reality, thus leading to the loss of important information in the decision-making process. Perhaps, for example, we assume that people in other cultures all share similar motivations and characteristics, that leadership is functionally related to grooming and clothes, or that subordinates will respond positively to reprimand memos.

- Dichotomized thinking—viewing the world in terms of opposing categories. This person sees things in black and white—their decisions are global and undifferentiated.

- Cognitive nearsightedness. Administrators may make decisions based on the immediate and visible, and neglect elements of a problem that are more remote in time and space. Everyone knows administrators for whom a problem is framed by the first person to get to them, for example, or who make shortsighted decisions that address the immediate problem, but ignore or even create a long-term problem.

- Oversimplified notions of causality. We tend to believe that outcomes are the product of simple, immediate causes; however, social events are more likely the product of complex causes that occur some time before the event. We assume a one-way chain of causation when, in reality, causation is typically circular and complex. Over-simplification of causation can lead to gross miscalculation in decision making, and social phenomena are rarely as simple as we would like to make them out to be.

ACTIVITY

In the early 1970s Kahneman and Tversky (1972; see also Tversky & Kahneman, 1973) identified three categories of decision-making limitations: the *availability heuristic* (the tendency to assess the frequency or likelihood of an event occurring by how readily a given solution is remembered); the *representative heuristic* (the likelihood that judgments are based on stereotypes of similar occurrences); and the *anchoring* or *adjustment heuristic* (the possibility that judgment is biased by an initial, ungrounded value or anchor—by the way a problem is presented, for example). Before proceeding to an explanation of these factors, you should answer the questions in the activity exercise below. Your answers will help you understand these three points.

1. Are there more words in the English language that (a) begin with the letter "r" or (b) have "r" as the third letter?

2. On one day in a large metropolitan hospital, eight births were recorded by gender in the order of their arrival. Which of the following orders of birth (B = boy, G = girl) was the most likely?

   a. BBBBBBBB   b. BBBBGGGG   c. BGBBGGGB

3. A newly hired engineer for a computer firm in the Boston metropolitan area has four years of experience and good all-around qualifications. When asked to estimate the starting salary for this employee, a secretary (knowing very little about the profession or the industry) guessed an annual starting salary of $36,000. What is your estimate? (Tversky, 1973, as adapted by Luthans, 1992)

If your answer to the first question in this exercise was (a), there are more words that begin with "r," you are wrong. If you think about it a moment, letters that begin with "r" constitute only those words in the "r" section of a dictionary while words with "r" in third place are scattered extensively throughout the dictionary. According to Max Bazerman (1990), people make this mistake because they can more readily think of words that begin with "r" than of words with "r" in third place. This is the availability heuristic error.

For the second question, most people will answer (c) because they assume that birth order will be randomly distributed by gender. Given the small sample size, however, any of the three patterns is equally likely. This error illustrates the representative heuristic, or stereotypical assumptions regarding likelihood.

In question 3, many people's estimate of the computer engineer's salary will be adjusted from the starting point provided by the secretary's estimate. The $36,000 figure biases or anchors our thinking, although the question clearly stated that the secretary didn't know anything about engineers' salaries. This is the anchoring and adjustment heuristic error. The answer one gives may also be related to one's own frame of reference or experiential anchor. Educators reading this book will relate to the $36,000 figure because it is a good salary for a teacher with a few years of experience. Basing decisions on experience is a useful and often accurate strategy, but can lead to error when, as in this case, experience is stretched to cover questions that are outside one's frame of reference. ■

The upshot of all this is that social systems are too complex for optimal decision making and humans are irrational decision makers anyhow. We make decisions based on personal prejudices and desires. We take credit for successes we, in reality, often have no control over, and we try to shift responsibility for failures over which, again, we often have little control. We give meaning to, and attribute causation to, events after they have occurred. We come up with solutions, then find problems on which to use them. Humans are, simply put, irrational decision makers.

The problem isn't entirely one of personal limitations, however; our cultural upbringing has a lot to do with it as well. Deep within our cultural genes is an assumption that events are the product of simple causes, that most every "B" is preceded by some "A." We have been taught this by Aristotle and Newton and Einstein and, well, just about everybody. Strategic Choice theorists argue that this simply isn't true. Karl Weick said that managers make things difficult for themselves because they "continue to believe there are such things as unilateral causation, independent and dependent variables, origins, and terminations." Weick continues, "Examples [of this assumption] are everywhere: leadership style affects productivity, parents socialize children, stimuli affect responses, ends affect means, desires affect actions" (1979, p. 86).

In the real world, there are few simple causes of human behavior, however. Punishment *sometimes* causes student behavior to improve, but its effect on behavior is often idiosyncratic and complex. Inspirational speeches make teachers feel good for a short while, but morale is the product of too many convoluted dynamics to be substantively influenced by a little entertainment. Students' drug problems are just as likely driven underground by a get-tough policy as solved by it. While parents do socialize their children, children also affect the behaviors of parents; and while leadership style may affect productivity, productivity also affects leadership style. Nearly all social activities involve a complex of causes and effects. So not only do humans make decisions in an irrational way, our culture imposes insupportable expectations on social causation.

Decisions in a Garbage Can

Karl Weick began a 1976 article on decision making in educational organizations with what has become a rather famous metaphor for organizational behavior:

> Imagine that you're either the referee, coach, or spectator at an unconventional soccer match: the field for the game is round; there are several goals scattered haphazardly around the circular field; people can enter and leave the game whenever they want to; they can say "that's my goal" whenever they want to, for as many goals as they want to; the entire game takes place on a sloped field; and the game is played as if it makes sense. (p. 1)

Soccer games, of course, are not played in this manner, but, Weick argued, organizational 'games' very often are. We impose on sporting events the rationality we believe exists in organizations. In reality, organizational participants wander on and off the decision-making field, rules change on a whim, players fabricate opportunities to 'make goals' and even, at times, fabricate opponents, and everyone is convinced that it all makes sense. This Alice in Wonderland-like perception of social organization is at the heart of the 'Garbage Can Model of Decision Making.'

Michael Cohen, James March, and Johan Olsen defined organizational garbage cans with the following well-known quotation from their 1972 article:

> Organizations can be viewed for some purposes as collections of choices looking for problems, issues and feelings looking for decisions in which they might be aired, solutions looking for issues to which there might be answers, and decision makers looking for work. (p. 1)

Four streams swirl within this organizational garbage can: fluid participants, choice opportunities, problems, and solutions (Fig. 8.1). "Fluid participation"

FIGURE 8.1 The four elements swirling in Cohen, March, and Olsen's (1972) decision making garbage can.

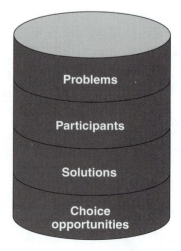

refers to random participation in the decision-making process. Decision making often entangles accidental or unsuspecting participants in its web. Have you ever walked unsuspectingly into an administrator's office and found yourself caught up in his or her problem of the day? Perhaps the administrator was thinking about implementing a new program and you showed up. Maybe he or she used you to think through a decision that had to be made. Whatever, the decision maker reached into the organizational garbage can and pulled out a participant (you) who just happened to have swirled to the top of the can at that moment.

"Choice opportunities" are situations in which choices must or can be made. Different organizational participants have differing access to decisions. Supervisors have access to different problems and decisions than do teachers, for example. Further, choice opportunities, like participants, swirl in and out of the decision maker's focus in an arbitrary fashion. This is due largely to the arbitrary way in which the environment generates problems, and in part to the decision maker's definition of environment. Humans tend to select their environments (their view of reality) based on personal preferences, biases, and knowledge. The problems we make decisions about are shaped by those perceptions. Junior high principals tend to make decisions about different sets of problems than do middle school principals. University deans who define their environment in terms of students will deal with different problems than do those who define it in terms of alumni.

Solutions and problems also move in and out of a decision maker's field of vision in an arbitrary manner, and the two are often unrelated to one another until someone links them. Decision makers have at their disposal a set of solutions and a set of problems, and neither necessarily precedes the other. People pick up solutions without having problems to which they can be applied; they do so in anticipation of an applicable problem or simply because the solution is attractive to them. This allows any of several possible scenarios in decision-making situations. When problems do arise, we might sort through our available solutions until one is found that seems appropriate (if we have time, the search may approximate rationality, limited only by the scope of available solutions). Alternatively, we may reach into our garbage can and grab the solution that is most accessible to us at the moment; like participants, solutions are often linked to problems because they just happened to be available. Or the solutions we have at our disposal may define the problems we focus on and may even lead us to create problems in order to have a forum for our solutions.

All this is seemingly counterproductive, but it need not be; we just need to look at things differently. The notion of a disjuncture between solutions and problems suggests that administrators should maintain a full and dynamic supply of solutions. We need to pick them up everywhere we go, and we need to seek situations that provide a fresh supply of solutions—the more the merrier. One can improve decision making by collecting many different solutions from which to choose in a decision-making situation. Attractive solutions encourage us to try new things or to identify problems that were not perceived before.

ROUNDTABLE

Brainstorm on possible sources of solutions that would be useful to an educational administrator.

ORGANIZATIONAL LEARNING

By now it should seem to you that Strategic Choice theorists have almost completely debunked the notion that leaders are rational and in control of organizations. So what does this mean for leadership and human involvement in organizational effectiveness? Do individuals have any influence over organizational effectiveness or are they mere flotsam in a social river? The answer is that they *do* influence organizational effectiveness, but to understand how, we must look at individual influence, at leadership, differently from the way we are conditioned to look at it.

People typically make somewhat Biblical assumptions about human control, believing that they can dominate the world and the animals therein. Strategic Choice theorists suggest that we don't "dominate" our environments, but learn to exist within them and to use them for our needs. The lion doesn't manipulate and control the jungle; rather, it learns to survive and get what it needs from the jungle. Similarly, people learn to survive in their "jungles" and to get what they need from them. This perspective is called Learning theory.

Learning occurs on two levels: there is learning by individuals and learning by organizations. Neither type, individual or organizational, is necessarily deliberate. Humans do learn by studying (deliberative behavior), of course, but we also learn from experience, from failure, from adaptation, from interacting—basically from just about anything we do.

Organizational learning is on a higher level of generality than individual learning. It remains with the organization long after the individuals who introduced it have left, becoming part of the organization's collective memory. It typically has greater potency than is accounted for by the summed abilities of individuals, and organizations may possess knowledge that transcends individual understanding. At one time, employees of IBM were expected to wear business suits while at work (and may still be required to do so, for all I know). For men, this meant a dark suit, white long-sleeve shirt, and conservative tie. For women, it meant suit, conservative blouse and shoes, and at most a small handbag. The practice was born somewhere in IBM's past, but employees I have talked to could only guess at why the practice existed. It was part of what the organization had learned. If workers are even conscious of such learned traits, they likely dismiss them as "the way we have always done things." They are done as matter of fact without much concern about why. Perhaps we call this tradition, but it is better referred to as learned organizational patterns for dealing with our environments.

Huber (1996) divides organizational learning into four dynamics: acquisition of knowledge; distribution of information; interpretation of information; and

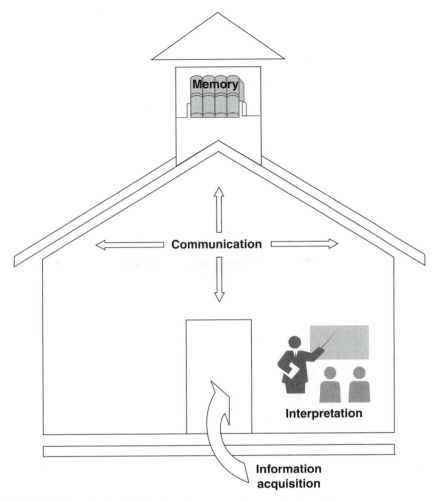

FIGURE 8.2   Huber's (1996) four elements of organizational learning.

organization memory (Fig. 8.2). We will use these categories to organize the next few sections of this chapter.

Knowledge Acquisition

Knowledge is acquired in several ways (Fig. 8.3). It is implanted by the organization's founders who, in turn, were influenced by the theories and philosophies of their time. This is called the "founder effect." Organizations acquire knowledge by experimenting with different ways of doing things. They learn from self-appraisal, from mimicking other programs, from new personnel who might be hired, and from experience.

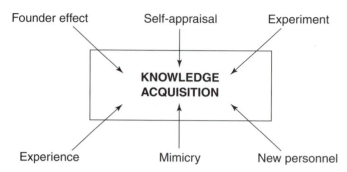

FIGURE 8.3   Summary of ways organizations acquire knowledge.

Experimentation is a common approach to learning—schools experiment with such things as new curricula, restructuring, and privatization. Often, however, such experiments are implemented in an all-or-nothing fashion; that is, the entire system is embroiled in the change rather than conducting the experiment on a small scale. Little or no time is devoted to testing the experimental change and working out the bugs prior to full implementation. Change of this sort is somewhat like myopic people jumping from one platform to another; they cannot be quite sure of what they're landing on. If the new platform is better than the old one, a good choice was made; if the destination is worse than the old one, obviously a bad choice was made. If the new platform is about the same as where the person started, he or she went through a lot of trouble for nothing. If you could check out the new platform before jumping, you would know whether it's OK to leap; if not, you take what you get. Total commitment to a change, like myopic platform jumping, can be a chancy thing because we can't always see clearly what our destination will bring us, but lots of educational organizations do it.

Organizations acquire knowledge through self-appraisal. Accreditation evaluations, such as SACS (Southern Association of Colleges and Schools) or NCATE (National Council for Accreditation of Teacher Education) accreditation are formalized self-appraisal experiences to which schools periodically subject themselves. Self-appraisal is a common element of a school's planning process (such as strategic planning). Such plans typically include a set of objectives and a set of benchmarks by which success or failure can be gauged. Schools then periodically appraise their progress against these benchmarks.

Experiential learning comes from the day-to-day successes and failures of organizational life. Humans aren't always very good at learning from their experiences, however. We all know people who judge a person's competence based on some nonpertinent physical characteristic such as dress or grooming. Unfortunately, such people rarely learn from the mistakes that inevitably arise from such practice, and they seem doomed to make the same errors of judgment over and over. Anna Grandori labels this the "human judgment bias" (1987, p. 99).

She attributes it to overconfidence, self-serving bias, insensitivity to negative evidence, illusory correlation, and narrow-minded conclusions about causality.

Organizations often imitate one another's successes—that is, they learn vicariously. Legislators seem particularly adept at this; it's almost a sure bet that if one state passes a unique piece of educational legislation, others will at least consider it for their states as well. Schools likewise imitate one another's successes—we go to conferences and visit other systems to find out what others are doing and to glean ideas for our own schools. It doesn't necessarily follow that imitation produces better ideas; it would be more accurate to say instead that imitation produces *new* ideas. As we observed earlier, people typically don't make optimal choices: they simply don't have the resources or the capacity for doing so. Similarly, imitation doesn't always directly improve an organization, but it can help it be dynamic and excited, and that in itself may make imitation worth the effort. In garbage can terms, it helps us fill our garbage cans, thus expanding our range of choices and solutions.

Organizations learn from the infusion of new personnel. It's not unusual for school districts to have an "unspoken" policy about hiring from the outside instead of promoting from within. Universities typically do not hire their own Ph. D. graduates into faculty ranks, for example. The rationale behind such policies has to do with the infusion of new ideas, or what Huber calls "grafting." Grafting is particularly evident when a system hires a person specifically for the knowledge he or she can bring to the organization. A school district or a university may hire a person, for instance, because he or she has been trained in Reading Readiness (an intensive, individualized reading program for at-risk children). The organization hires the person with the expectation that his or her expertise will spread to other faculty; that is, the new person helps the organization acquire new knowledge.

ROUNDTABLE

Do new people change organizations or do organizations change new people? When a new person comes on board, the process of acculturation automatically kicks into gear. New folks are "taken under the wing" of older, wiser incumbents. They are frequently told, "Let me show you how we do that around here." They are given a handbook that outlines rules and regulations on how things are done. Informal groups recruit them into "their way of thinking." There may even be formal initiation ceremonies that inculcate the individual into the existing culture. So, do organizations really get an infusion of new blood from recruits, or are new people the ones who get the infusion? Illustrate your position on this.   ▦

Communication, or Information Distribution

Information distribution, as used here, is not about the dissemination of innovation. It's not that a discussion of innovation wouldn't fit here, it is simply that I wish to focus on another dimension of this issue now. The question we need to address here is, how do organizations effectively access information, innovative or otherwise, they already possess?

As was noted earlier, learned information resides both within people and within the organizational culture, but the focus here is on the former. Individuals learn tricks of the trade, the quirks of their raw material, the idiosyncrasies of their clients. They learn what to pay attention to and what to ignore. They know whom to approach for information and they know how to approach them. They know what has been done, what needs to be done, and what shouldn't be done. They know what actions cause trouble and have learned to avoid those actions. They have acquired expertise, be it through training or experience, about their responsibilities. They have learned the shortcuts, they know the ropes, they have learned how to be effective at their job. This is knowledge that resides within individuals (re-read this definition and interpret it in relation to your knowledge about your own job or about a job you may have had at one time).

Now, the question before us is, "How does an organization effectively access the information possessed by individuals?" Organizations aren't always particularly effective at sharing such knowledge. As Huber (1996) put it, "organizations often do not know what they know" (p. 141), and, I would add, they don't have mechanisms for finding out what they know. We don't always have mechanisms whereby new employees can tap into the knowledge of their predecessors. Administrators aren't always good at understanding the responsibilities of employees. Finally, organizations often have only rudimentary structures for sharing information across different divisions or among individuals.

When incumbents in given positions move on, they take with them all their accumulated knowledge about those positions. They take with them knowledge of program nuances, participants, limitations, and opportunities. An assistant principal for discipline, for example, who moves on to a principalship takes with him or her an intimate knowledge of the students with which he or she has worked. That person knows which parents are cooperative and which are not: they know what has worked with a given student and what hasn't; they know which students have pushed the envelope of misbehavior and which are only occasional offenders. They know the rules and regulations and they know what the students know about those rules and regulations. A new person in this position will have to develop much of this knowledge from scratch unless there are mechanisms in place for passing along the knowledge.

 ## ROUNDTABLE

If you were an administrator, what mechanisms could you put in place that would help a new person come up to speed quickly?

Superiors are not always effective at tapping into the knowledge of subordinates for a number of reasons. We talked about some of these reasons in the discussion of communication in the Systems theory chapter. We noted that administrators are better at telling than at listening. We discussed the fact that such behavior tends to deprive the administrator of important information about his or her responsibilities. We're talking about the same thing here: poor listening skills deprive the administrator of knowledge that subordinates have learned from their experiences and their training.

Administrators may fail to listen because of ego investment in their jobs. This type of person feels that what he or she has to say is much more important than what subordinates have to say. Administrators may be embarrassed to solicit information from subordinates, thinking that it would put them somewhat at the mercy of subordinate expertise. Administrators may simply fail to comprehend that subordinates might know something important that they don't know. This latter problem is not necessarily because of arrogance or any such intentional behavior; rather, it is just human nature. We tend to make simplified judgments about the performance of tasks we know relatively little about. After all, how hard can it be as assistant principal in charge of discipline to put kids into ISS (in-school suspension) when they misbehave? Bourdieu (1977) argued that the difference between perceived and actual practice is like making a trip on the ground and seeing a trip's route from the air. The view from the air fails to observe the numerous experiences, problems, adventures, detours, spontaneous stops, and revised plans that the ground traveler experiences. We tend to assume that the job experiences of others can be adequately summarized by what we see from the air, and we fail to see the true complexities of the task. This could be called the "simplification error;" it refers to any situation in which an individual fails to appreciate or perceive the complexities inherent in a given function. Simplification errors lead, in turn, to failure to receive important information about a task.

 ## ROUNDTABLE

As an educational administrator, how could you capture the deeper nuances of individual knowledge? What sort of knowledge would be important to you, and what would not? What strategies could you implement that would help convert important individual knowledge into organizational knowledge?

Knowledge in one sector of an organization isn't always passed effectively to other sectors that may need it. A potentially devastating example of this has to do with student violence or student suicide. Students themselves very often receive advanced clues or even direct knowledge of such events hours or days before they occur. Students who are contemplating suicide will often talk about killing themselves with their fellow students and may even start to give away possessions. Teenagers likely will misunderstand the serious importance of such information; they are too naïve and too uninformed to interpret it for what it is. However, even when teens have direct knowledge of an impending problem, such as a fight, they may still fail to inform adults about it. This, of course, is attributable largely to peer pressure.

Employees may fail to communicate important information for a number of reasons. Failure may occur when the person who possesses knowledge needed by others has too much to do. They may not communicate when there are potential sanctions associated with the information. They may have had unfortunate experiences with the person or persons who need the information. It may simply not occur to them that someone else may need their information or, like the teenagers above, they may fail to appreciate the importance of a certain piece of information.

Finally, information may not be transmitted because the person who needs it either doesn't know where to find it or doesn't realize that it exists. A new employee, for example, may not realize that other employees have previously struggled with the very problem he or she is facing. Even established employees may not realize that others in the organization have dealt with, and have pertinent information about, issues they themselves are trying to address.

Individuals are likely to share information with people whom they have successfully communicated with in the past. They will communicate when they are provided opportunities to do so. They are more likely to communicate in non-intimidating atmospheres than in intimidating ones. They will communicate when there are rewards for doing so. They will communicate when they understand the timeliness and importance of given information. They will communicate when their messages are respected and when they respect the person with whom they communicate (see Huber, 1982, for a review).

ROUNDTABLE

How could an administrator manipulate the schedules, atmosphere, and organization of a school in a way that encourages communication? ◼

Information Interpretation

Environmental mapping was introduced in the chapter on Open Systems theory and was further developed in the chapter on Contingency theory. Mapping involves the ability to sense environmental stimuli, to store those maps in memory, and to use those remembered maps to make sense of future stimuli. In the Contingency theory chapter, we argued that systems—organizations—assign responsibility for different segments of the environment to different organizational divisions. Each division is responsible for mapping its particular part of the environment. Divisions should be linked together so that pertinent elements of what a given division learns can be shared with other divisions (as noted above, this mechanism isn't always very strong). Mapping is not unlike what we're discussing here. The sensing stage in mapping corresponds to Learning theory's knowledge acquisitions stage, and the sharing of mapped information corresponds to information distribution across networks. Information interpretation, the topic of this current section, occurs when systems interpret new stimuli using existing maps. Finally, imprinting, or the retention of maps, corresponds to the next topic of discussion, organizational memory.

Different divisions within a coupled system will often interpret a given stimulus differently; this may launch a process that eventually leads to common organizational learning. Let's say a principal is told by the school board that teachers should emphasize more basic skills. The principal will interpret the demand and condense it for distribution to teachers. The condensation will leave out nongermane details of the board's discussions about this issue, but may also add the principal's interpretation of the information. Each department in the school will then interpret the information relative to its own frame of reference. The math department might conclude that it is already teaching the basics and see no need to alter what it is doing. The English department, on the other hand, might see the board's concern as a call to de-emphasize the study of literature and devote more time to grammar. It might then respond to this interpretation by restructuring its strategic plan and curricular objectives. The revisions would certainly call for increased funding for grammar-related resources. It may also call for the math department to restructure its emphasis on word problems; thus, the math department is dragged into the process whether it wanted to be or not.

From a broader perspective, the system we just described is coming to terms with different interpretations of a stimulus. The respective responses of each department place demands, sometimes conflicting demands, on one another. The way math structures its curriculum, for example, may play minor havoc with the curriculum in the physics department. One department may demand that other departments comply with its needs, as was the case with the English and math departments above. Eventually, the different departments will come to some sort of common understanding about how the school board's demands will play out in their various curricula. They may not like some of the compromises they have had to make, but they will eventually learn to live with them.

Dramatic (media rich) information is more likely to be uniformly interpreted across an organization than is less dramatic information; it is also more likely to affect the behaviors of the receiving system (Huber, 1996). Drama is a function of (among other things) the respect or authority accorded the sender, the sanctions associated with complying or failing to comply, the media used to transmit the message, the proximity of the message source (a train crash in India has less impact on Americans than does a train crash in Indiana, for example), the novelty of the message, and the degree to which a message affects one personally.

 ROUNDTABLE

Huber (1996) raises an interesting question that I will turn over to you to debate in light of the above illustration: Does more learning occur when a message is uniformly understood from the beginning or when different divisions understand the message differently?   ■

Sometimes, to learn something new, people must unlearn old ways of doing things. Old knowledge may conflict with new knowledge, or it could influence the interpretation of new learning—the old way of doing things may get in the way of the new. When a school moves from a traditional six-period scheduling pattern with 50-minute classes to an A-B scheduling pattern with 90-minute periods, teachers must unlearn their old instructional patterns and learn new ones. Filling 90-minute periods typically requires greater variety in the way one teaches. It is difficult to keep students' attention in 90-minute lectures, thus teachers need to include more activity and discussion than they may be used to doing. Their life experiences have been organized around 50-minute periods, and the transition to 90 minutes can be somewhat difficult. Without proper unlearning and re-learning, some teachers will inevitably attempt to overlay their old patterns of instruction on top of the new organizational structure. They may, for example, continue to teach for 50 minutes to an hour as before, and let students do busy work or homework for the remainder of the 90-minute period. Nearly all teachers will experience some difficulty with such a transition if they are not helped to unlearn old behaviors and learn new ones.

Unlearning is not an inconsequential task. Much of one's learned behavior is not the property of the individual alone, it is instead the property of some larger group with which the individual interacts. Elementary teachers don't ability group for reading because of idiosyncratic preferences, they do so because that is the way they were taught, and because that is the way their peers and their administrators expect them to teach reading. Ability grouping is further encouraged by the way reading textbooks are organized, by parent and community expectations, and by the history of the profession. Elementary schools have invested in resource material to support the ability group structure, teachers have kidney-shaped tables for teaching small groups, and they have sophisticated systems of learning stations that provide for students not participating in group work. Ability groups are the products of organizational learning, and the different elements of the organization (teachers, resources, structure, parents, etc.) are interdependently related in a way that strongly supports that structure. We discussed this when we talked about interdependencies in the chapter on Systems theory; as we pointed out then, and reiterate now, there is a lot to untangle when you embark on change.

One way to help an organization unlearn existing behavior is to import new blood. We discussed this several paragraphs ago. The problem is, it may be the new blood that goes through the unlearning process rather than the organization itself. The organization may make some adjustments because of new personnel, but new people will be expected to make a lot of adjustments to conform to the existing way of doing things.

Organizational leaders can also facilitate the unlearning process by getting rid of existing people. This usually involves a "hatchet man" (or woman), a person hired into the system to turn it upside down and shake it out. To be successful, however, this may involve a real massacre, and that could be a public relations fiasco. Further, the costs associated with firing existing personnel (particularly if they are tenured), and of hiring new people and bringing them up to speed, could be quite high. Change of this magnitude would exact its pound of flesh.

A less painful way of doing this is to replace the leader of a school, under the assumption that the expectations of new leaders will trickle down through the school itself. National leaders, presidents, prime ministers, and the like typically attempt to gain control of their governmental bureaucracies in this manner, by putting their own people into office to lead these bureaucracies. They quickly find, however, that this does not work; bureaucracies have a life of their own that is largely immune to the meddling of leaders. Franklin Roosevelt attempted to bypass this problem by creating new bureaucracies. This worked for him, but left an even greater problem for future presidents (more intractable bureaucracies).

Schools are not as unmovable as are monolithic governmental bureaucracies, but they do possess some of the same capacity to resist change. Consequently, replacing leadership may or may not be successful. The key to change is not so much newness as it is the ability to help people unlearn old ways of doing things.

ROUNDTABLE

Earlier we talked about dramatic messages (media richness) and their capacity for getting a message across. Given our discussion of unlearning, it would seem that even drama would have a tough time evoking change. What do you think? Is media richness an effective strategy for helping people unlearn? What are some other strategies that you might use to help people unlearn old behaviors? ∎

Organizational Memory

Organizations and people do not have perfect memories. Information is lost when people leave an organization and it is lost because of failure to record new learning. It is likewise unavailable if people fail to retrieve it—because it doesn't occur to them to look for it, they don't know it exists, or they don't know where to find it.

A common and effective way to insert learning into organizational memory is to convert it into rules and regulations, a process normally associated with bureaucracy. Martin Shulz (1998) argues that "organizational rules are repositories of organizational experiences" (p. 845). He continues:

> Organizations learn by encoding inferences from their past experiences in rules. From this perspective bureaucratization appears as an outcome of organizational learning. Organizations create rules when they encounter new problems that do not seem to be covered by existing rules and when these problems are fairly recurrent, consequential, or salient. (p. 845)

As bureaucracy increases, however, the number of new situations from which an organization can learn should decrease. As more and more of its problems are standardized as rules, the organization experiences fewer and fewer novel situations with which to expand its knowledge base. Further, each new rule restricts the range of possible choices an organization can make in the future. If, for example, a school creates a rule specifying that students are automatically expelled from their bus after three incident reports, then it has left itself without options for dealing with problems more creatively. Consequently, according to Shulz, the number of rules in an organization does not increase exponentially as Weber argued; rather, the number increases rapidly early in the learning process and tapers off later on. Such plateaus are interrupted only when the environment changes or the organization's responsibilities are otherwise redesigned. Thus, if Shulz is correct, over time an organization becomes somewhat stodgy, or set in its ways. It becomes increasingly routinized and less open to change and creativity. Learning can lead to the paradoxical situation in which learning is actually inhibited.

RESEARCH TOPIC

I argue, however, that this may not be entirely the case in educational organizations. It might be argued that education's environment changes too often and radically to allow learning to plateau. Further, much of the learning that is processed by an educational organization is quite diverse and complicated, and we're not always good about maintaining records of what we have learned or of using those records when they are recorded. Committees may keep records of their minutes, but those minutes may be filed away and forgotten. University faculty grievance committees and other pseudo-judicial committees tend not to build case law; that is, they don't base judgments on prior findings as the American judicial system does. Instead, cases are determined on the basis of their immediate merit and on recent experiences of the given committee. Faculty senates usually maintain formal records of their proceedings, but with the massive periodic turnover of senators characteristic of such bodies, succeeding senates don't always encumber themselves with past decisions. Decisions that are made in faculty or committee meetings are not always cast in stone anyhow; we tend to expect them to serve only our immediate needs. In other words, educational organizations simply do not routinize or memorize everything they learn. This may itself reflect organizational learning; perhaps we subconsciously or collectively realize that failure to do so keeps us vibrant and creative. Such failures of our collective memories help us avoid those stodgy plateaus.

I make this assertion without data to support it, however, and suggest that it would be an interesting research topic. ■

Problem-Solving Versus Problem-Finding

McPherson, Crowson, and Pitner (1986) observe that some school administrators are "problem-solvers" and others are "problem-finders." Experienced school leaders should have an intuitive sense of just what they meant by this. New administrators typically spend a lot of time rushing from one fire to another. They seem unable to settle into a routine because so many surprise problems pop up for them to solve. These principals are problem-solvers: they deal with problems as they arise. As they mature into the job, however, many find that they can structure their activities to neutralize a number of these problems before they occur. They may do this with rules and regulations; they may do it by learning to anticipate problems before they occur; they may do it by establishing certain expectations of subordinates and by nurturing dependable behavior in themselves. These administrators become problem-finders and their lives become much calmer as a result. If they thought about it, they may not be able to pin down just what they are doing differently. They just remember that things were a madhouse when they first started out but that things are much calmer now. As they matured, they learned how to deal with their organization. Their organization also learned how to deal with them, and both leader and organization became increasingly effective as a result.

Diary

- Given what you have learned in this chapter, what are some important functions of leadership? In what way does your answer change your previous answers to this question?
- Based on what you now know about the nature of organizations, how would you go about implementing change in an organization in which you were leader?
- Identify things that make some people poor decision makers and make others good decision makers. Illustrate your answers from your experiences (without names, of course). What does your reflection suggest regarding improving your own decision-making capabilities?
- Learning theorists argue that organizational knowledge is innate, "the way we do things around here." How can a leader influence this innate learning?

Recommended Readings

Cohen, M. D., March, J. G., & Olsen, J. P. (1972). A garbage can model of organizational choice. *Administrative Science Quarterly, 17,* 1–25.

This is the classic article in which Cohen, March, and Olsen outline the elements of their garbage can model of decision making. They frame the issue of decision making in this article with their famous quote: "Organizations can be viewed for some purposes as collections of choices looking for problems, issues and feelings looking for decisions in which they might be aired, solutions looking for issues to which they might be answered, and decision makers looking for work." (p. 1)

Cohen, M. D., & March, J. G. (1974). *Leadership and ambiguity: The American college president.* New York: McGraw-Hill.

Cohen and March apply their garbage can model of decision making to the higher education environment in this book. They conclude that colleges and universities are characterized by problematic goals or preferences, unclear technology, and fluid participation in decisions. That is, they are organized anarchies, and the decision-making process in these organizations reflects this turbulence.

Weick, K. (1976). Educational organizations as loosely coupled systems. *Administrative Science Quarterly, 21,* 1–19.

In this article, Karl Weick, one of the early advocates of Strategic Choice theory, makes his often-quoted comparison between organizational life and an unorthodox soccer game played on a fluid field. The core of the article, however, is his discussion of the seven pros and cons of loosely coupled structures (previously summarized in Table 8.1).

References

Bazerman, M. H. (1990). *Judgment in manegerial decision-making* (2nd ed.). New York: John Wiley & Sons, Inc.

Bourdieu, P. (1977). *Outline of a theory of practice* (R. Nice, Trans.). Cambridge, MA: Cambridge University Press.

Bourgeois, L. J., III. (1984). Strategic management and determinism. *Academy of Management Review, 9*(4), 586–596.

Child, J. (1972). Organizational structure, environment and performance: The role of strategic choice. *Sociology, 6,* 1–22.

Cohen, M. D., March, J. G., & Olsen, J. P. (1972). A garbage can model of organizational choice. *Administrative Science Quarterly, 17,* 1–25.

Donaldson, L. (1996). *For positivist organization theory: Proving the hard core.* London: Sage Publications.

Drucker, P. F. (1946). *Concept of the corporation.* New York: The John Day Co.

Grandori, A. (1987). *Perspectives on organizational theory.* Cambridge, MA: Ballinger.

Huber, G. P. (1982). Organizational information systems: Determinants of their performance and behavior. *Management Science, 28,* 135–155.

Huber, G. P. (1996). Organizational learning: The contributing processes and the literatures. In M. D. Cohen & L. S. Sproull (Eds.), *Organizational learning* (pp. 124–162). Thousand Oaks, CA: Sage Publications.

Kahneman, D., & Tversky, A. (1972). Subjective probability: A judgment of representativeness. *Cognitive Psychology, 3,* 430–454.

Katz, D., & Kahn, R. L. (1966). *The social psychology of organizations.* New York: John Wiley & Sons, Inc.

Kauffman, S. A. (1995). *At home in the universe: The search for the laws of self-organization and complexity.* New York: Oxford University Press.

Kindergarten education, 1957–68. (1969). *NEA Research Bulletin, 47*(1), 10.

Marion, R. (1999). *The edge of organization: Chaos and complexity theories of formal social organization.* Newbury Park, CA: Sage.

McPherson, R. B., Crowson, R. L., & Pitner, N. J. (1986). *Managing uncertainty: Administrative theory and practice in education.* Columbus, OH: Charles E. Merrill.

Mintzberg, H., Raisin-ghani, D., & Theoret, A. (1976). The structure of 'unstructured' decision processes. *Administrative Science Quarterly, 21*(2), 246–275.

Mort, P. (1958). Educational adaptability. In D. H. Ross (Ed.), *Administration for Adaptability* (pp. 32–33). New York: Metropolitan School Study Council.

Pfeffer, J., & Salancik, G. R. (1978). *The external control of organizations: A resource dependence perspective*. New York: Harper & Row.

Schulz, M. (1998). Limits to bureaucratic growth: The density dependence of organizational rules births. *Administrative Science Quarterly, 43*(4), 845–876.

Simon, H. A. (1957). *Administrative behavior* (2nd ed.). New York: Macmillan.

Tversky, D., & Kahneman, A. (1973). Availability: A heuristic for judging frequency and probability. *Cognitive Psychology, 5,* 207–232.

Weick, K. (1976). Educational organizations as loosely coupled systems. *Administrative Science Quarterly, 21,* 1–19.

Weick, K. E. (1979). *The social psychology of organizing*. Reading, MA: Addison Wesley.

Wittington, R. (1989). *Corporate strategies in recession and recovery: Social structure and strategic choice*. London: Unwin Hyman.

CHAPTER 9

Evolution of Organizational Species: Schools as Professional Bureaucracies

With an eloquence to which his readers were unaccustomed, Herbert Spencer wrote in 1851 that "Progress . . . is not an accident, but a necessity. Instead of civilization being artificial, it is a part of nature; all of a piece with the development of the embryo or the unfolding of a flower." Thus Spencer launched the movement known as "Social Darwinism," which claimed that social systems are a part of nature and subject to its laws of evolution and natural selection. Spencer attributed social and industrial progress to social mutations, improvements in human adaptability, and to forces that selected the best of these mutations. He argued that society, left to its own design, will naturally adapt to its environment because of these forces, thus enabling its survival and effectiveness. Spencer coined that famous catchphrase of Darwinian logic, "survival of the fittest," to describe this dynamic.

In Chapter 1, we observed that Spencerian theorists made the mistake of assuming that natural selection produces ever-improving social species, that fitness is hierarchical, with man (particularly Caucasians) at the top of the heap. This notion proved to be difficult to support; after all, who's to say that a shark is less fit than a monkey, at least for the environment it occupies, or that our mortal enemy, the virus, is less fit than humans?

But this might be academic were it not for the moral legacy. The assumption that natural selection leads to improvement fed the belief that some of us are better than others. The rich are better than the poor, the captain of industry is better than workers, white people are better than black people, and Aryans are better than Jews. When this superiority thesis became politicized the results were devastating. This was never more evident than in Nazi Germany.

Frederick Taylor's Scientific Management crowded Social Darwinism out of organizational sociology in the early years of the 20th century, although it was kept alive in politics by racists and Fascists through the first half of the 20th century. In 1950, the sociologist Amos Hawley was responsible for a brief revival of Social Darwinism, but this time without its superiority complex. Hawley's brand of Social Darwinism was discovered again in the 1980s by anti-positivists, and relabeled Population Ecology theory.

Stripped of its rhetoric and politics, Darwinian theory is neutral on the issue of progression; it merely states that natural selection will favor organisms that are better able to survive in a given environment. Darwin himself vacillated on the issue. He did write in his book, *On the Origins of Nature,* that "natural selection works solely by and for the good of each being, all corporeal and mental endowments will tend to progress toward perfection." However, later in his life he told an American friend, Alpheus Hiatt, that, "After long reflection I cannot avoid the conviction that no innate tendency to progressive evolution exists." Had he been more attuned to these latter instincts earlier in his life, he might have saved the world a lot of trouble. Or maybe not; people do hear what they want to hear.

In this chapter, we will look at how adaptation to environment shapes the structure of organizations. Population Ecologists argue that selection favors the emergence of a limited number of organizational genres, much as it does in biology. The genre to which education belongs is called the Professional Bureaucracy, and we will explore the nature of this organizational type in some detail. Finally, we will look at what Population Ecologists say about leadership, and will explore the question of how organizations, movements, and ideas fail.

In this chapter, students will:

- Define the nature of organizational environments and examine how different environments affect organizational structure and activity.

- Understand the characteristics of professional bureaucracies (the class of organizations to which education belongs), and describe strategies for encouraging change and improvement in professional bureaucracies.

- Discuss the pros and cons of organizational stability (inertia), and explore how leaders might best respond to inertia.

- Understand why organizations, movements, and ideas fail.

- Describe the functions of leadership from a Population Ecology perspective.

- Refine their definitions of the function of leadership in education.

POPULATION ECOLOGY

Population Ecologists argue a relationship between environment and organization, and in this regard the theory is similar to Contingency theory (Chapter 6). The two theories differ, however, in that Population Ecologists envision a limited number of stable solutions to environmental demands, while Contingency theorists envision a continuum of such solutions. Contingency theory is based on a model derived from physics in which outcome Y is directly proportional to input X; thus, it sees leadership style changing in direct relationship to changes in follower readiness (Hersey & Blanchard, 1993) and worker motivation changing with shifting valency and expectancy (Vroom, 1964).

In Population Ecology, perceptions of change are based on a notion from biology called "punctuated equilibrium." Darwin thought that species changed gradually in response to changes in the environment—like the Contingency theory perspective. The evidence from paleontology, however, suggests that plants and animals experience long periods of stasis (averaging 5 to 6 million years), punctuated by brief periods of dramatic change. The periods of stasis represent stable, relatively unchanging accommodation to a broad range of environments. Similarly, Population Ecologists hypothesize that organizational structures are largely unaffected by gradual environmental changes; they call this "inertia." Further, they maintain that, within a given industry (one might call them organizational species), there is typically only one, or at most a few, structural solutions to environmental demands. That is, organizations in a given industry are largely "isomorphic"—they look alike. Hence, airline providers are structured essentially in the same way, as are most public high schools, elementary schools, and universities. Some even carry this a step further and claim that there are only a few generalized structures across all organizations; Henry Mintzberg (1979), for example, identifies five basic structures (we will discuss them later in this chapter).

Population Ecology is labeled as anti-positivist in part because of this tendency to lump organizational types into a few broad categories (Donaldson, 1996). Such broad categorization of forms does not accommodate gradual transitions based on environmental nuances; thus, Population Ecologists do not seek law-like functional relationships between contingencies and outcomes.

Population Ecology is further anti-positivistic because of its argument that organizations may pursue more than just the goal of effective production. They may, for example, pursue goals of growth, as when an organization increases its size in order to extend its control over a market. An organization may even have goals that exist at the expense of effectiveness or efficiency. Unionized businesses that do not turn a profit, for example, may find themselves unable to shut down because of pressure from that union. In this case, the union's goal of providing jobs takes precedence over the goal of profit. Edgar Schein (1992) has suggested several latent goals of education in addition to the goal of instruction. These include

> "(1) to keep children off the street and out of the labor market until there is room for them and they have some relevant skills, (2) to sort and group the next generation into talent and skill categories according to the need of the society, and (3) to enable the various occupations associated with the school system to survive and maintain their professional autonomy." (p. 54)

 ROUNDTABLE

Education clearly must juggle multiple goals in addition to the goal of instruction. Identify some of these goals and debate the degree to which, and manner in which, these non-instructional goals degrade education's central goal of instruction. ∎

Otherwise, Population Ecology theory is somewhat positivistic in nature. It is largely "nomothetic," which means it examines structural and behavioral characteristics that can be generalized across a large set of similar organizations. Organizational structure and behavior are explained by material factors such as market demand and environmental stability. This theory is deterministic to the extent that it suggests leaders adapt their organizational structures to general environmental demands. Finally, Population Ecology is scientific in style; its goal is to produce scientific knowledge in much the same way that biologists seek to produce scientific knowledge.

One of the strengths of Population Ecology theory is that it provides a comprehensive analysis of the organizational environment. It argues that environmental forces represent variation, and without variation organizations would have no incentive to elaborate and improve. Organizations adapt, and environmental forces, such as financial markets, choose the best of these organizational adaptations to survive. Once the adaptive process matures, organizational structure and behavior stabilize for an extended period of time, resisting minor or even moderate fluctuations in environmental forces. Eventually, however, the environment changes to such an extent that it will no longer support existing structural solutions. This forces massive changes, what Population Ecologists call quantum jumps, in the structures and behaviors of organizational systems.

ENVIRONMENT

The core idea behind both Darwinian theory and its organizational offspring, Population Ecology theory, is that the fit will survive in a dangerous and unforgiving environment and the unfit will be weeded out. Environment determines structure and behavior in nature and in social systems. Contingency theory is also sensitive to the importance of environment, but its focus is more on how leaders can deal with those environments than on the nature and eminence of environment itself. Environment, whether stable or unstable, is a given in Contingency theory, and leadership that is attuned to the given environment is the driving force in an organization. Population Ecology reverses the emphasis: it is the environment, more than leadership, that determines the shape of organizations. As I summarized it in an earlier book (Marion, 1999), "environment isn't merely a rough sea to be navigated by a wise ship's captain, environment is the captain" (p. 180).

An organization's environment contains an assortment of resources, and organizations develop strategies for exploiting those resources. Organizations with strategies that supply sufficient resources to meet their needs will survive and those that don't, won't. The nature and criticalness of an organization's survival strategies depend on how readily the environment yields its resources. Rich environments are easy to exploit and an organization within such an environment can have sloppy exploitation strategies and survive just fine. Lean environments are difficult to exploit and organizations in such environments cannot afford strategic errors.

ROUNDTABLE

Develop a list of environmental resources needed by educational institutions (the next few paragraphs will help you with this list). What are some of the strategies educators have developed to exploit those resources? One might argue that public educational institutions have their needs provided for them by a benevolent government and, consequently, do not exist in a survival-of-the-fittest world. Can you argue otherwise? Decide the degree to which the environment for public education is rich or lean, and whether the exploitation strategies in your district are appropriate for that environment. ▪

People are the most important resource that organizations exploit. People serve as an organization's labor force. They provide tangible resources (such as monetary donations), and intangible resources such as allegiance and defense (as when the organization is threatened by budget cuts). People purchase an organization's products and, in education, provide it with raw materials. Supporters can help an organization deal with its environment (by helping assure favorable legislation, for example), and can imbue it with prestige.

Money is, of course, an important resource in education, a resource that is typically in short supply. This resource is particularly difficult to exploit because people are so sensitive about taxes. Requests by school districts to increase taxes for education can generate a significant amount of acrimony in a school district. Fiscal conservatives will resist increases, arguing that schools should make better use of the resources they have. They will often point to a district's rather substantial reserve fund as evidence that more money is not needed (this is a rather cheap shot, however, for it is fiscally necessary for a district to keep 5 to 10% of its budget in reserve). Retirees and others without school-aged children (or whose children are in private schools) will resist tax increases, arguing that they should not have to educate other people's children. Still others resist taxation because of political opposition to big government. The result of these environmental dynamics is often a compromise that may leave school programs underfunded and school facilities in poor repair.

Schools are victims not only of fiscal conservatism but also of the public's tendency to blame them for many of society's ills, such as low standardized test scores and teen violence. Further, social demands on schools tend to drain needed fiscal resources from the classroom; increasing concern about student violence forces us to invest in expensive security measures, for example, and spiraling legal challenges to school programs or activities drain money into enforcement programs or judgment payments (the multiple-goal problem discussed earlier). We, as educators, are partly to blame for fiscal problems, however. We aren't always effective at exploiting our fiscal environment. Some districts tend to invest too much money in administrative overhead and fiscal conservatives are fond of pointing this out (research, incidentally, is fairly clear that educational returns come from classroom rather than administrative investment; see Childs & Shakeshaft, 1986; Ferguson, 1991; Flanigan, Marion, & Richardson, 1996; Hanushek, 1986; Perl, 1973; Stern, 1989; Winkler, 1975). We aren't always effective at public relations and sometimes we do shoot ourselves in the foot with poorly conceived programs, poor management, or by making publicly visible mistakes.

ROUNDTABLE

Identify other ways that education contributes to its own fiscal woes. ■

You have been asked in several of the Roundtables in this chapter to discuss various aspects of education's environment. The question is complicated by the fact that education does not exist in the traditional market environment; it doesn't have to buy and sell goods in order to survive. Rather, education exists in a political and a public relations environment, but it survives whether its relationship with those environments is good or not. In a very real sense, education exists in a benevolent environment; social sensibilities and public law require that children be educated, so support will flow regardless.

Education's environment can be hostile, however. School boards, parents, and general taxpayers can be unhappy about what is happening in their schools and can retaliate with a variety of sanctions, including cuts in financial support, retributory legislation, and angry confrontations at school board meetings. These can threaten the autonomy, work responsibilities, and even the jobs of educators. Education itself will survive such hostile environments (although it may change), but educators may not. Survival of the fittest in education, then, refers in part to the survival of educators and their behaviors. Educators who do things that the environment approves of will survive and those who don't will be sanctioned or even fired.

Further, education must compete with other demands for a limited pool of government money. Other government agencies, including other schools, compete for funding. At yet another level, schools compete with taxpayers who want to keep their money for themselves. Education and its competitors exist within shifting environments, however; what is a successful strategy one year may be a losing one the next. From this perspective, education doesn't improve as it evolves, it simply keeps pace with its environment.

SOCIAL EVOLUTION

Aldrich (1979) identified three stages through which evolution passes—variation, selection, and retention. Variation provides the energy for change; it is the fuel that drives selection. Selection is the process by which useful structures are separated from useless ones. Retention enables structures to stabilize and to maintain themselves.

Variation

Variation is the root of evolution. In a world where everything is the same and nothing ever changes, there would be no reason to evolve and there would be little to adapt to. If all students were essentially identical, if educational funding were consistent and uncontested, if all teachers were equally competent and equally valued, and if the demands on student skills in adulthood were predictable and constant, there would be little evolution or change in education. Colleges and business would have a uniform pool from which to select, all students could be controlled in the same manner, and instructional procedures would be stable and their effects well understood. This, of course, may be the foundation on which Utopian tales are spun, but such conditions do not exist in reality.

 ## ROUNDTABLE

Even so, some educational environments are more stable than others. Some schools have relatively uniform ethnic and socioeconomic student bodies, while others have broadly diverse student bodies, for example. One could argue that the former breeds instructional excellence because it permits educators the luxury of developing effective strategies. Another might counter, however, that such stability leads to rigidity. It does not encourage experimentation and creativity as would the latter environment, and creativity, rather than stability, breeds excellence. The counter-counter argument is that volatile educational environments force teachers to jump from one experiment to another, never allowing sufficient experience with any one strategy for teachers to become effective. Debate the merits of these respective arguments. Is there common ground?

Variety can come from anywhere and can take just about any form. It can come in the form of mistakes, political preferences, administrative decisions, caprice, personality changes—anything. Variety could be categorized as either deliberate or accidental. The deliberate variety refers to human actions that are deliberately intended to mold future outcomes, as when a university decides to implement policies that crack down on student alcohol consumption. Accidental variety is simply any activity that is not deliberate or crafted to influence the future. Granted, there is a fuzzy line between these two categories, but the intent is not to operationally define these categories; rather, it is to make the point that evolutionary forces are indiscriminate about what they act on. They act equally on our deliberate attempts to control environment, on actions that are not intended to control the future, and even on actions that we hope won't influence our future. The random forces of natural selection are in the driver's seat; leaders may influence the path taken by an organization, but they are, nonetheless, in the back seat and are subject to the whims of natural selection. Stated yet another way, leaders don't so much determine what will be successful or unsuccessful as they seek to fathom, and implement, strategies the environment will deem successful.

RESEARCH TOPIC

Open classrooms were a popular fad among curriculum specialists in the late 1960s and '70s. This organizational strategy was built around large, open classrooms (50 to 60 students typically). Each class would have two to three teachers and one or more teacher aides. The idea was to foster team planning and teaching, and to better meet the needs of students. Although widely implemented (one can still see the legacy in schools built during these years: the classrooms are large and have been retrofitted with partitions to divide them into smaller classrooms), the movement died after only a few years. One could argue that the movement failed because it was judged unacceptable by an impersonal environment. It was a case in which leaders attempted to dictate to the environment what was to be successful, but the environment showed just who was in control. Identify other such failed educational movements, then choose one to develop into a paper. Try to explain why the given movement failed. Alternatively, you might select a movement that succeeded and try to explain why it was successful. We will examine failure in more detail further on in this chapter, so look at that material as well when you formulate your position.   ■

Aldrich (1979) identifies three types of variation: that which exists between organizations; variation within an organization; and variation over time. Variation between organizations refers to structural and behavioral differences among organizations. Internal variation refers to such things as organizational modification, leadership turnover, and changes in the way an organization processes its raw material. Time-related variation refers to changes in the structure and behavior of organizations over time.

Between-Group Variation   Between-group variation is a source of selection pressure if differing organizations affect one another's well-being. Two unrelated organizations do not exert selection pressure on one another—the quality of Starbuck's® coffee does not affect school curriculum, for example (although the wag might argue otherwise). That is, variations in production strategies between the coffee industry and education or between education and any unrelated industry do not typically constitute selection pressure for education. The home schooling industry, by contrast, *is* related to the well-being of public education, so changes in that industry can place pressure on education to change. Such interdependent relationships can lead to what biologists have labeled the "Red Queen Effect" after the character in Lewis Carroll's classic, *Through the Looking Glass,* who had to run furiously just to stay in one place. Changes in one system spark changes in another; that, in turn, provokes response by the original system, and so forth. There are limits to the competitive ability of any given system, however; thus, this process must end at some point. It may conclude with the destruction of one or the other of the systems, but it more likely ends with a co-existing truce.

Within-Group Variation   Within-group variation refers to changes within a given organization itself, changes that add to or detract from an organization's competitiveness. Such variations include faculty turnover, innovations in curriculum, changes in organizational structure, and changes in instructional strategies. Within-group changes can be considered at two levels. At a more general level, within-group variation enhances or inhibits an organization's between-group competitiveness. Innovation, for example, is a within-group change that affects between-group competition. At a more localized level, within-group variation can refer to changes in a given element of the organization that bring pressure to bear on other elements. If the math department in a school adopts a new instructional approach, that change may alter its competitive relationship with other departments (it may attract increased funding, for example).

Innovations are an important source of within-group variation. Teachers who implement innovative instruction in their classrooms are a source of variation. High schools that adopt block scheduling in a school district interject within-group variation.

Leadership turnover is a form of within-group variation that raises an interesting question. If Population Ecology theory is correct, individuals better suited for leadership should rise to the top (survival of the fittest) and those poorly suited should be weeded out. Yet everyone knows people in authority positions who are poor leaders and yet those leaders are there to stay. Any of several dynamics may be at work here. First, selection forces aren't particularly strong in some situations. Natural selection functions best in highly competitive conditions, but not all leadership positions are particularly demanding. In 1969, Arthur Stinchcombe and Robert Harris studied this leadership phenomenon in a steel-producing industry. They found that effective leadership is more prevalent in hot processing units than in cold processing units. Hot processing units, not surprisingly, process steel while it is hot. If anything goes wrong along the hot processing line, the work must start over again at the stage when the metal is initially heated—hot metal cannot just be stockpiled until problems are worked out. Leaders in these units must know what they are doing in order to keep things moving, and ineffectiveness is separated out by what could be termed market forces (fail to turn a profit and you're gone). In cold processing units, metal can be stockpiled when the process breaks down; thus, leadership effectiveness is not as much a premium.

A second dynamic that may explain why poor leaders survive has to do with the definition of effectiveness. We assume that effectiveness refers to one's expertise, to the ability to perform effectively, or to the ability to get the most out of subordinates. In some jobs, effectiveness may mean political savvy, the ability to project a favorable image, or to impress the boss. In these conditions, functional aptitude may be secondary to three-piece suits. *Esse quam videre,* North Carolina's state motto meaning "to be rather than to seem," can be reversed to describe this situation—*Videre quam esse,* to seem rather than to be (I am not picking on North Carolina; the phenomenon is universal). Natural selection still applies, however; fitness is simply defined as image rather than effectiveness, and the selected leader is still a better fit for the demands of the system.

ROUNDTABLE

Continue this discussion. Consider the case of a poor leader in your experience who was able to stay in a position for an extended period of time. Why was this person able to survive for so long? Obviously, tenure laws may have something to do with the answer, but selection pressures, such as public disfavor, can overcome hesitancy to deal with such problems. ■

Variation over Time Variation over time is called "random drift." Aldrich argues that drift occurs because tasks are not performed exactly the same from one situation to the next, thus random changes are accumulated and the organization drifts into altered behaviors. Random drift, then, usually refers to unintended changes, although drift can be introduced intentionally through innovation or through attempts to imitate behaviors in other organizations.

Learning as a Source of Variation Learning is society's way of passing information from one generation to another; it's the social equivalent of genetic transmission in biology. According to Aldrich (1979), learning is not always a source of variation; rather, it is often variation reducing. Aldrich equates learning with standardization: educated people learn the "right" way to do something rather than new ways to act. We have seen this in Thomas Kuhn's (1970) notion of paradigms; paradigms, you will remember, dictate how we interpret phenomena.

Even so, an educated mind is usually capable of understanding events from more perspectives, and of being more flexible, than an uneducated one. As the old putdown goes, "He not only doesn't know anything, he doesn't even suspect anything." If you don't know about architectural engineering, it's difficult to come up with novel ways to support a roof. If you haven't studied instruction, it's difficult to find new ways to teach children. One could, of course, make an argument for unbiased minds and creativity, but I suspect it would be difficult to defend. New knowledge tends to spring from old knowledge rather than from ignorance. Learning may focus our attention at the expense of alternatives, but it is still the best tool for creativity that we have.

Aldrich's observation can be interpreted from another angle. There are people whose way of doing things is so ingrained that they wouldn't be any less flexible if knowledge were encoded on a DNA molecule and tattooed on their chests. We're not talking just about narrow-minded people, however. For example, some primitive societies have strong prohibitions against nonnormative behavior, prohibitions that are powerful and unquestioned. This is, in a sense, variation reducing, learned behavior. Such stable cultures do not provide the sort of variation on which selection can act. Aldrich argues that natural selection is biased against such invariant behavior. We cannot automatically define stability of this sort as maladaptive, however. In stable environments, stable behavior is an element of a functional equilibrium between the culture and its environment. Given the number of thriving, unchanging cultures in our world, one could hardly agrue otherwise.

Selection

The second law of classical thermodynamics states that energy is entropic—it runs down, dissipates. Thus, heat seeps out of a glass of warm water, messages deteriorate when they are transmitted, and the universe will eventually run out of steam. Life does just the opposite: it increases in energy, or decreases its entropy. The engine of this negentropy, according to evolutionists, is natural selection. Natural selection is a sieve that sorts order from disorder or randomness. Natural selection sorts useful structures from useless ones and sorts the fit from the unfit. In nature and in organizations, natural selection causes ordered, fit systems to emerge and to evolve.

Natural selection is a force that is largely independent of the system on which it operates; that is, it is beyond the control of participants and decision makers within an organization. Population Ecologists do not suggest that administrators are powerless; the shark is not powerless against the octopus, the wolf is not powerless against the cougar, and the leader is hardly powerless in his or her domain. Leaders do manipulate their organizations and their environments. However, natural selection sits quietly in the environment and rewards organizational actions, including leadership activities, deemed useful and sanctions actions and activities deemed useless. It may not fully reveal its criteria for making such decisions, although there is no reason why the administrator couldn't improve his or her odds of positive judgments by intelligently evaluating the environment. Even so, natural selection often acts in capricious ways. At any rate, it acts on more than just administrative behavior, it acts on just about anything, including unintended behaviors such as mistakes and incidental decisions and intended behaviors that were thought to be neutral.

Selection, natural selection, is an irresistible force where variation is present, thus, evolution cannot be avoided. Evolutionists argue that selection is driven by accident; thus, biological and social forces, rather than God, are the driving force behind evolution. Selection acts with indifference to class or position, thus rich and poor, famous and obscure, large and small alike have access to success. Natural selection depends on competition, and this is the root of the free market philosophy in Western capitalism. Natural selection favors only those who are better at acquiring resources. It does not necessarily favor "the best;" modern Darwinian philosophy now sidesteps the hazards of a science of superiority.

Retention

Evolving systems tend to experience long periods of stability interspersed by brief periods of rapid change—the punctuated equilibrium discussed earlier. This pattern would seem odd at first blush, particularly in cases when the environment of a system is changing (which is just about always). Why would a system stabilize for long periods of time, not adjusting to the environment or attempting to improve the effectiveness of its process in any significant way?

There are four broad issues that need to be discussed in answering this question. First, organizations experience stasis because it is to their disadvantage not to. Second, stasis contributes to organizational fitness. Third, stasis enables natural selection to build structure effectively and efficiently. Fourth, the downside of stasis is its inertial characteristics; this point focuses on the potential detriment associated with change resistance.

Instability Is Expensive   The first issue has to do with the necessity of stasis. Organizations stabilize for extended periods of time because of the costs associated with change. Organizations invest significant time, money, and effort into an existing strategy, and at least some, if not most, of such investments must be scrapped to make way for a new strategy. Existing equipment may have to be abandoned in favor of new technology. Existing expertise may not apply to the new strategy. Organizational structures and supporting networks that evolved around the old strategy may have to be dismantled.

In the earlier chapter on Open Systems theory, you were asked to consider the different systems that support educational activities such as instruction. Reading instruction in many elementary schools, for example, is supported by textbook publishers, the reading curriculum in teacher preparation programs, parental expectation, classroom structure and resources, and so on. This is what causes inertia and why it is costly to change inertial states. Many different support structures must be dismantled to accommodate change. A change in public education from reading groups to individualized instruction would require realignment of relationships with textbook publishers, teacher training programs—all these support structures. This is an expensive and somewhat prohibitive task.

Change may not only be expensive or complex, it may compromise production effectiveness as well. Workers will initially be unable to perform new tasks at the same level of proficiency as they performed the old ones. There will likely be some level of resistance to learning a new way of doing things, but at any rate a learning curve can be expected when new strategies are adopted. Embryonic support networks for the new strategy will be less effective or efficient than the old as well.

It may cost more for a while to process raw material with a new strategy. In business, the cost associated with new or low-volume production is high compared to that for mature production of similar technologies—a video player for 8-mm tape, for example, costs about three times the price of a VHS player. This is due in large part to the fact that cost drops as the number of units produced increases, and production runs of new technologies are smaller than are those for mature technologies. Additionally, workers may take longer to produce a unit and may do so less effectively than with an earlier strategy, production procedures may be relatively immature and inefficient, and the tools for production may be somewhat less than effective.

A new product may, for a while, be of lesser quality than the old, and may appeal to people more on its novelty than its usefulness. The first microcomputer could do little more than flash a few lights, but many of us wanted one. It was "cool," but if you needed to get something done, you still used pencil, paper, and a hand calculator. Similarly, a new curriculum doesn't have all the bugs worked out and is less refined than it will be once teachers have had some time to work with it.

Consequently, organizations resist adopting new behaviors, sticking instead with their old way of doing things. They find it too expensive and inefficient to switch to new production strategies, and as long as the old strategy serves them reasonably well, the incentive of newness isn't sufficient to overcome these barriers.

RESEARCH TOPIC

It is human nature to second-guess things, to ask "Why don't they just do it this way?" or to criticize others who are not adopting improved strategies for performing tasks. So we question why the government doesn't just go to a flat tax rate for everyone, why education officials don't give parents the option of choosing what school their children will attend, or why graduate programs in education don't embrace distance learning in order to better meet the needs of their working clientele? Identify just such an issue and attempt to explain why a preferred change isn't implemented. Alternatively, identify an instance of change with which you are familiar and describe the costs associated with that change. ■

Stability Is Good for Fitness   The second general point to be made about retention is that stability enhances an organization's fitness. This claim follows naturally from the first point just discussed: new strategy is less fit and more expensive than mature strategy. Over time, organizational actors build expertise with a given strategy; thus, they are able to perform effectively. Perhaps more importantly, organizations build networks of support around a given strategy over time and such networks are a major source of an organization's fitness (Marion & Bacon, 1999).

Stability Permits Complexity   The third general point is that stasis allows natural selection to build structure effectively and efficiently. Aldrich (1979) illustrates with a story of two watchmakers that he called Hora and Tempus. Hora built watches one piece at a time, with each new piece adding to the total product. Hora was unable to build complex watches, however, because after a while the accumulation of pieces became too much to juggle. Tempus, by contrast, built modules and then assembled the modules into even larger modules, and then into a completed watch. Each module was composed of a few individual pieces; thus, the modules were easy to handle. Tempus was able to build highly complex watches as a result. Organizations grow in similar fashion, by building and stabilizing structural modules, then assembling the modules into even more complex forms.

Organizational Inertia   The fourth general issue of retention, organizational inertia, is one of the more widely discussed issues in Population Ecology theory. It is used to help explain organizational failure, organizational weakness, and resistance to needed change, among other things.

Aldrich (1979), drawing from the work of Donald Campbell (1969), distinguished between internal and external selection forces. External selection refers to differences among different organizations and to variations in the general environment. Internal selectors are forces that act on the internal structures of an individual organization. Aldrich claims further that there are two types of internal selectors, those favoring internal stability, and those favoring past history—both of which are inertial. Internal stability exists because people prefer consistent work experiences, because they desire nondisruptive working conditions, and because incompatibility and instability are seen as counterproductive. Regarding past history, organizations may be stuck in the way they did things in past adjustments to long-gone environments. In a sense, past environments are the selection criteria that determine present structure. This is called the "founder effect." Internal selectors may have little or nothing in common with external conditions; they may, for example, resist change when change is desperately needed. Consequently, they could very well reduce the overall fitness of the organization.

Earlier, the issue of poor leadership was discussed. Poor leaders can persist because of inertia. The individual may have important allies that maintain him or her in the position and support the status quo. The poor leader may be approaching retirement and people are just waiting it out. He or she may have an exemplary past record and the system is showing respect for that record by overlooking the present malaise. Or, interestingly, the poor leader may be an important part of an accommodation among networks that would be disrupted by his or her removal. The leader's weakness, for example, may have allowed decentralization of decision making; subordinates in this case may resist losing the administrator because the loss could threaten their authority. Such an accommodation may even be quite effective and a stronger leader could damage overall productivity. Thus, we have a seemingly contradictory situation in which a weak leader could actually be favored by internal natural selection forces.

TYPES OF ORGANIZATIONS

In an earlier section, we observed that Population Ecology theorists group organizations into categories or forms. McKelvey (1982) argued that such typologies can be based on what he called "comps," or similarities in underlying technology. Henry Mintzberg (1979) created a typology that is based on organizational functions. He identified five organization types (Fig. 9.1). The first is the Simple Structure, or organizations characterized by direct supervision and centralized decision making. Young, small, technical businesses fall into this category. The second type of organization in Mintzberg's typology is the Machine Bureaucracy. These organizations are characterized by standardized work processes and organizational structures that are formalized, specialized, and vertically centralized but horizontally decentralized. Mintzberg's third functional type is the Professional Bureaucracy; this includes public education and will be discussed in detail later in this section. The fourth is the Divisionalized Form, characterized by standardized outputs, limited vertical decentralization, and market orientation. It includes large, old organizations in diversified markets. Mintzberg's final form is the Adhocracy. This type of organization is coordinated by mutual adjustments among actors, is structured organically, and is largely decentralized. It is useful

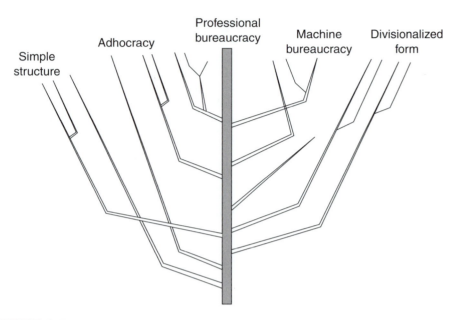

FIGURE 9.1   Mintzberg's (1979) five organizational types depicted as a family tree to suggest evolutionary dynamics.

for dealing with complex, technical tasks, and is represented by agencies such as NASA and similar high-tech research organizations.

Professional Bureaucracies have decentralized organizational structures that perform relatively routine tasks. Their technologies are sufficiently stable to allow standardization of procedures (most surgeries, for example, are routine, as are the strategies used in elementary schools to teach reading), but their tasks are so complex that they must be controlled directly by the operators who perform them. Professional Bureaucracies are common in universities, school systems, general hospitals, and social work agencies, each of which depends on the skills and knowledge of professional employees, but which produces standardized services.

Mintzberg identifies five characteristics of Professional Bureaucracies (see Fig. 9.2). First, the Professional Bureaucracy does not depend on rules to control and standardize its procedures, rather it depends on *extensive but standardized training* and indoctrination by training programs. School principals, for example, are taught in their university training programs how to apply a uniform legal code to issues of student rights, are indoctrinated in the importance of enforcing the legal rights of students, and, consequently, can be expected to reliably enforce these laws. By contrast, Machine Bureaucracies likewise operate with standardized procedures, but they enforce standardization with centralized, organizationally based rules and procedural specifications.

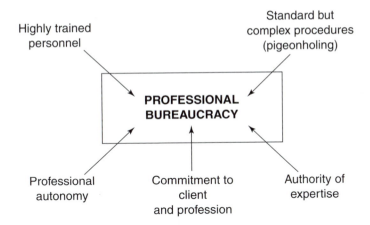

FIGURE 9.2   Mintzberg's (1979) five characteristics of a professional bureaucracy.

Second, Professional Bureaucracies function by *pigeonholing* their tasks; that is, professionals develop repertoires of standard solutions to client problems. Schools, for example, diagnose learning problems as learning disabled (LD), trainable mental handicap (TMH), and so on. Classroom teachers ability group for reading. By pigeonholing, professionals are able to gain some control over the significant complexities of the problems they face. "People are categorized and placed into pigeonholes because it would take enormous resources to treat every case as unique and requiring thorough analysis. Like stereotypes, categories allow us to move through the world without making continuous decisions at every moment" (Perrow, 1970, p. 58). Even so, pigeonholing requires sophisticated diagnostic abilities and, despite categorizations, clients within a given pigeonhole express sufficient diversity to test the flexibility and competence of the professional.

Because Professional Bureaucracies depend on the expertise of their employees, they must allow those employees significant *autonomy* in carrying out their responsibilities. Autonomy, however, poses problems of coordination, problems that are resolved by the nature of standardization within the Professional Bureaucracy. Mintzberg argues, quoting Bidwell, that, "Teacher autonomy is reflected in the structure of school systems, resulting in what may be called their structural looseness. The teacher works alone within the classroom, relatively hidden from colleagues and superiors, so that he has a broad discretionary jurisdiction within the boundaries of the classroom" (Bidwell, 1965, pp. 975–976). Autonomy is critical to the effective operation of the Professional Bureaucracy, and it all works and is coordinated because everyone operates from a common knowledge base. All members of a surgical team know exactly what needs to be done at any given point, and operations can proceed in relative silence. Each member's responsibilities are highly complex, but everyone on the team understands those responsibilities and can coordinate accordingly. Such standardization of behavior among otherwise autonomous professionals is attributable to common training and indoctrination.

The relative disassociation of professionals from the organization and the autonomy that they enjoy permit a close relationship between professional and client, and breed a *loyalty to client and to profession* that supersedes loyalty to organization. Professionals are indoctrinated with a service- and profession-orientation by their training programs and this indoctrination is reinforced by their interaction with colleagues. Because of this, and because the professional's responsibilities are so complex that the organization is unable to demand accountability to organizational control (as do Machine Bureaucracies), the professional's commitment leans more to those he or she serves and to the profession than to the organization itself.

Finally, standardized procedures, as we've noted, are too complex to be coordinated by a central control structure. Thus, while the Machine Bureaucracy can rely on the authority of position, the Professional Bureaucracy relies on the *authority of expertise.* Consequently, the professional has a significant amount of power within the organization. In most universities, for example, considerable governing authority is vested in faculty bodies such as faculty senates and peer review committees.

Leadership in Professional Bureaucracies

From the traditional perspective of leadership and management, there is little left for an administration structure to coordinate in the Professional Bureaucracy. Analysis, assignment, treatment decisions, and allocation of effort and time are the responsibility of the line worker—the professional. Consequently, the subordinate-to-supervisor ratio in a Professional Bureaucracy is typically quite large; it is not uncommon for university administrators to be responsible for departments of 50 or more professors, and school principals may manage up to 30 teachers and 600 students without an assistant.

This does not mean that administrators in a Professional Bureaucracy are powerless—quite the contrary. A key characteristic of Professional Bureaucracies is complexity and uncertainty, and considerable power is to be found at the nexus between these dynamics. Administrators, for example, are power brokers in disputes over turf, as when two departments disagree over which is responsible for a given course.

Perhaps more importantly, the simple fact is that, in order for professionals to have the resources needed to function, certain administrative tasks must be performed, and these tasks inevitably are a source of power. Budgets must be generated and managed, grants must be administered, alumni and legislators must be dealt with, purchases must be made, resources must be allocated, and buildings must be maintained. Most professionals prefer to spend their time practicing their profession—physicians prefer to doctor, social workers prefer to counsel, and teachers prefer to teach and do research. But someone must organize the support services. If the professional performs them, keeping the power associated with such decision-making authority for him- or herself, then time is taken away from the pursuit of preferences. To protect their time, professionals willingly delegate administrative responsibilities to others.

Managerial tasks, such as purchasing and accounting, are usually delegated to nonprofessionals (nonprofessional in that they are not drawn from the pool of professionals). This typically gives rise to a Machine Bureaucratic structure within the larger Professional Bureaucracy. Such dualism often leads to conflict over control, for professionals desire that management processes be responsible and answerable to the professional function, while Machine Bureaucrats feel answerable to standardized rules and regulations. Professionals fume, for example, when a secretary limits access to resources such as copy paper or photocopying. In this case, the secretary is responding to, and deriving power from, centralized rules. The professional is responding to, and deriving power from, the need to function effectively.

Leadership functions, however, are reserved for a subgroup of professionals themselves. To perform effectively in complex environments, professionals must answer to professionals and not to machine bureaucrats. Decisions about promotion and tenure, for example, must be made by professionals who are competent to evaluate a colleague's ability to deal with the complex tasks of the organization. Consequently, principals, superintendents, deans, and department heads are selected from the ranks of the professionals they represent. These administrators are given significant discretion and power over decisions that affect the professionals they administer.

Professionals who are chosen for leadership positions must be willing to give up most, if not all, of their professional responsibilities to devote time to administering. University deans have little if any time for teaching and research, and social service directors have little time for counseling. They derive significant power from their sacrifice, however. University administrators participate significantly in tenure and promotion decisions and in allocation of resource decisions. School principals are even more critical to tenure and resource allocation. The power isn't necessarily preemptive, however. Administrators who fail to provide the resources that professionals need could find their careers in jeopardy, for professionals do retain considerable power for themselves. University presidents have resigned because of votes of no confidence from faculty senates, and principals have been reassigned because of faculty complaints.

Shortcomings in the Professional Model

The Professional Bureaucracy organizational form is well-suited to the tasks it performs, but it is not without problems. There are problems associated with coordination within the Professional Bureaucracy, for example. Coordination between professionals and Machine Bureaucratic management functions within the same organization can be difficult and conflictive. Coordination among professionals themselves can also be problematic. Professionals will tend to assume that their particular expertise is highly valuable and deserving of more resources than are other services. If a particular client cannot be cleanly pigeonholed, battles over jurisdiction may erupt. Tenure and promotion decisions in universities sometimes hinge on whether peer review members feel that a candidate's specialty threatens their own, or the degree to which its value compares to the value of their own specialty. This can breed hard feelings and turf wars.

Incompetence is difficult to deal with in the Professional Bureaucracy. Clients might assume that most professionals are more or less equally competent, or at least possess a fundamental level of competence that will serve most clients' needs. Professors are equally smart and competent because they all have doctoral degrees; physicians are extensively trained and are likewise generally all competent. Unfortunately, this just isn't so; there are incompetent people in all professions. Clients will probably come to realize incompetence after a period of experience with an incompetent professional; parents and students eventually see through incompetent teachers, and patients come face-to-face with incompetent physicians when diagnoses or treatments are botched. Clients do not typically have the knowledge or data needed to judge incompetence before committing to a relationship with a professional, however, and may not even sense incompetence during a relationship.

Professionals themselves are responsible for sanctioning incompetence but are often loath to do so. Tenure procedures in public schools and in universities are pretty good at screening incompetence among tenure track candidates, but it is difficult to deal with tenured incompetence. Tenure laws, of course, place significant barriers in the way of firing teachers. Professionals themselves are hesitant about committing the significant effort, time, and emotion required to pursue sanctioning—time that they would prefer to devote to pursuing the practice of their profession. It is often difficult to prove incompetence when it is difficult to define one's product; how does one define effective instruction, for example?

 ROUNDTABLE

Let's pursue this further. Tenure laws do make it difficult to get rid of incompetent faculty (they also, of course, protect competent faculty and academic freedom). But professionals seem to exhibit a reluctance to sanction colleagues that goes beyond the difficulties associated with tenure regulations. Why do you think this might be so?   ■

Some professionals, particularly those who fail to develop their skills, have a one-size-fits-all mentality about their services. They feel proficient in a limited focus and presume that most clients, regardless of their diversity, should be treated with that limited focus. Certain teachers, for example, may feel that all units should be taught in 50-minute blocks using a lecture approach to instruction.

Some administrators may feel that discipline problems should be automatically referred to in-school suspension (ISS), regardless of the facts of the discipline infraction or the needs structure of the misbehaving student. Some professors have developed knowledge on a few given topics (say, motivational speaking or Open Systems theory) and somehow all their classes seem to revolve around those topics.

The autonomy and client/professional orientation characteristic of Professional Bureaucracies may lead incumbents to ignore the needs of the organization with which they are associated. Schools and universities need volunteers to serve on committees and to work on projects. It is far too easy to become absorbed in one's professional activities and to neglect those needs.

Professional Bureaucracies may not be particularly receptive to innovation. Professionals tend to be individualists; they may collaborate on a given task such as a research project or developing a new course, but resist the large, often cross-disciplinary efforts required of innovation (Mintzberg, 1979). Further, innovation usually requires that professionals reconsider their pigeonholes, and they tend to resist this. Many elementary school teachers would resist giving up their reading groups in favor of individualized, competency-based instruction, and high school teachers would resist giving up their departmentalized structures in favor of team-teaching. Autonomy and the democratic decision-making structures characteristic of Professional Bureaucracies exacerbate this problem. When Machine Bureaucracies resist change, administrators can make a decision to innovate and then force their decision down the chain of command. In the autonomous Professional Bureaucracy, everybody must be persuaded to accept the innovation one at a time.

This can be frustrating to outsiders such as parents, school boards, and legislators. They don't appreciate the strengths associated with the Professional Bureaucratic structure, nor do they understand the dynamics that resist change in these organizations. Mintzberg (1979) argued that these external groups tend to believe that the professional's resistance can be cured by external controls. "Specifically, they try to use direct supervision, standardization of work processes, or standardization of outputs" (p. 376).

Direct supervision translates into closer oversight of work activity (such as requiring administrators to increase the number of faculty evaluations per year), more detailed specifications of workflow (time-on-task regulations, for example), or more intense reporting requirements (such as requiring teachers to submit daily lesson plans). Such activity typically increases the punitive workload of professionals without significantly impacting actual work dynamics. Teachers may have to turn in daily lesson plans to the principal, but they are going to teach their three reading groups using the lesson plans in their teacher's manuals with or without the submitted lesson plans. They may have to devote hours in committee work to implement their state's accountability program and even more hours completing the associated paperwork, but the way they teach biology and literature will probably be about the way they taught it before the accountability program. When it comes right down to it, teachers have a lot of autonomy when they shut their classroom door, and getting them to change the way they practice their profession can be a daunting task. External controls are more likely to affect morale and increase resistance than to create the positive changes that the implementers envisioned.

The standardization of work processes and the standardization of outputs have a similar effect. Standardization of work processes and outputs refers to efforts to mandate Machine Bureaucratic-like behavior. Mintzberg (1979) illustrated this with a story of an East German official who once bragged to him that, on any given date at any given time, all teachers in his province would be teaching from the same page of the textbook. Other governments at times do the same thing in less dramatic ways. School boards who mandate 30 minutes of phonics education every morning in the primary grades are attempting to mandate standardized work processes. Superintendents who mandate a "three strikes, you're out" bus discipline policy are essentially doing the same thing to principals. Legislators who mandate standardized testing programs are attempting to standardize educational output. By reducing the professional's discretion and flexibility, however, the policy-maker runs the real risk of reducing, rather than improving, organizational effectiveness. Professionals are hired because of their extensive training; Professional Bureaucracies are structured as they are to allow professionals to use that expertise in dealing with the complex and diverse problems they encounter. As we've observed before, education, medicine, counseling, and other such professions involve dynamics that are far too complex to be legislated, but that is exactly what's happened when procedures and outputs are standardized.

 ROUNDTABLE

The discussion about changing Professional Bureaucracies in the past few paragraphs should have been familiar to you. The education profession has experienced numerous similar attempts by school boards, central office administrators, and legislators to control and channel its activities. The research literature, however, reports little evidence that such attempts succeed. Mintzberg (1979) summarizes and recommends alternative strategies for improving education.

> Change in the Professional Bureaucracy does not seep in from new administrators taking office to announce major reforms, nor from government technostructures intent on bringing the professionals under control. Rather, change seeps in, by the slow process of changing the professionals—changing who can enter the profession, what they learn in its professional schools (ideals as well as skills and knowledge), and thereafter how willing they are to upgrade their skills. Where such changes are resisted, society may be best off to call on the professionals' sense of responsibility to serve the public, or, failing that, to bring pressures on the professional associations rather than on the Professional Bureaucracies. (p. 379)

Flesh this out and add to it; how do you think society can improve the delivery of education?

THE FAILURE OF ORGANIZATIONS, MOVEMENTS, AND IDEAS

Organizational decline and failure is one of the many interests of Population Ecologists. However, public schools rarely fail in the sense that they are closed down, and when they do, it is typically because of a community decline. Public schools do not fail as market-driven organizations do. Schools do decline, though, in the sense that they fail to meet the needs of their environments. Educational movements and ideas, such as new math and open classrooms, can and do fail. Furthermore, private schools are entrepreneurial and thus subject to market forces. It is appropriate, then, to examine the literature on organizational decline and failure in relation to educational institutions. As we shall see, a discussion of organizational failure will also give us some hints about the role of leadership in the Population Ecology scheme of things.

There are three categories of organizational failure (see Fig. 9.3). The first examines the vulnerability of new organizations, what Stinchcombe (1965) has called the "liability of newness." The second examines failure due to technological or catastrophic shock or similar changes, such as the shift from 8-bit to 16-bit microprocessor technology that occurred when IBM entered the microcomputer market in the early 1980s (see, for example, Anderson, 1995; Anderson & Tushman, 1990). The third focuses on the failure of mature organizations that cannot be attributed to sudden environmental change.

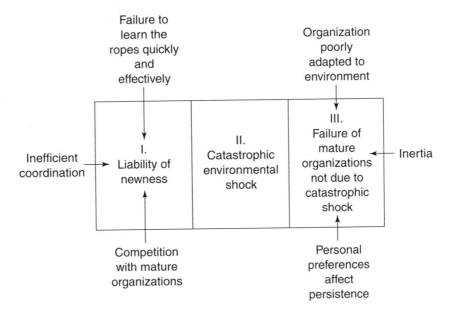

FIGURE 9.3 Three types of organizational failure and hypothesized causes.

New organizations or organizational initiatives experience failure at a much higher rate than mature systems—that's the liability of newness. Singh and Lumsden (1990) identified three reasons for failure among new organizations. First, young organizations or endeavors must learn to survive in their new niche. They (or rather their people) must learn how to create their product effectively, how to exploit resources in the environment, how to attract supporters, and how to compete against rivals for their market. When open classrooms (a rather classic educational failure) were tried in the 1960s in the United States, educators needed to learn to work effectively in the larger classrooms and leaders needed to learn how to win over reluctant teachers and parents, and gain the support of policymakers. We failed to learn and the movement failed.

Second, new organizations are hampered by the considerable amount of time that must be devoted to coordination. Stable relationships among organizational roles evolve over time and require significant energy to establish. A new organization is less viable than mature systems until these stable relationships are formed.

Third, the new organizations must often compete with established organizations that have already learned the ropes of survival in the environment. Mature organizations have strong networks of interdependency and support that new organizations do not have. By interdependent relationships, I mean the extended network of related organizations, including, but not limited to, direct suppliers and clients that support a system's production. A new mom-and-pop store likely has not built a relationship with a shipping firm to handle its products, has not generated connections that would help feed its customers, and has not worked out relationships with suppliers. Similarly, a new educational idea (like open classrooms discussed above) does not have a network of supporters, it may not have industries that can provide it with teaching resources (because the ideas it espouses are so new), and may not have long-term political support.

Because mature organizations have worked out the learning and coordination bugs and have built strong, supporting networks, they are typically able to offer products more cheaply than new organizations. Further, mature organizations have developed clientele bases that are familiar with their services and products, and new organizations will find it difficult to make inroads into this clientele base. Imagine trying to go up against Microsoft Windows® in the operating systems market, or trying to open an independent drug store in a small town that already has a long-established, locally run drug store. Imagine trying to introduce a new approach to reading in an elementary school dominated by a history of instruction with ability-based small reading groups.

The second major category of organizational decline and failure involves catastrophic change of some sort. Changes, such as reorganization, revolutionary technological changes, or change in leadership can reintroduce liability of newness risks into otherwise mature organizations (Carroll, 1984; Pfeffer, 1997). Existing roles and procedures become obsolete and must be redeveloped, and existing networks are disrupted, requiring that new ones be created.

The third major category involves failure in mature organizations that is not due to catastrophe. Such failure has been attributed to three categories of causes

(Meyer & Zucker, 1989). The first set of causes comes from Contingency theory, which hypothesizes a direct relationship between organizational structure and survival. Organizations whose structures and activities are out of tune with environmental demands are at risk for decline and failure. Population Ecologists argue, however, that the relationship between environment and organizational structure often is not all that crucial—that is, there's a lot of play in the relationship (the anti-positivistic perspective). Consequently, organizations can pursue other goals, such as power or growth, without compromising overall effectiveness. In other words, organizational decline is not necessarily related to efficient production. Thus, schools can tolerate poor leadership, ill-advised projects, and inadequate budgets without suffering significant decline.

The second subcategory of decline in mature organizations has to do with organizational inertia, or lack of change (Hannan & Freeman, 1984; Miller & Chen, 1994; Sastry, 1997). Organizations tolerate inertia quite well actually. Inertial behavior emerges naturally in organizations, in part because of a human affinity for stability. More importantly, it is a source of strength and competitive advantage because stability permits efficient and effective production. Change is expensive and somewhat dangerous—the liability of newness problem. Stable organizations have learned the ropes of production, have established cost-effective production strategies, and have built networks of support. They are good at what they do, and change agents often do them a disservice in their zeal to "improve" matters.

However, inertia has its down side as well: it is notoriously hard to dislodge when change is needed, and the longer an inertial state is in place, the harder it is to change. Inertial behavior is good for a while, but eventually the world is going to move on (so to speak). If, when this happens, the stable organization fails to break out of its inertia, it may fail. Organizations need long periods of inertial stasis to survive, but occasionally its stasis needs to be punctuated with periods of change.

Finally, Meyer and Zucker (1989) argue that persistence in mature systems may be affected by the personal preferences of organizational actors. Managers and owners, for example, typically prefer profits; other actors, such as workers and clients, desire continuity or service. Such diverse preferences can lead to ironic situations in which organizations persist even when they lack proper survival skills. Thus, when profits (efficiency) decline, continuity preferences may force the organization to persist despite poor productivity. Parents may block the closing of a small, inefficient school because of nostalgic desires to keep the facility, for example. In a way, this problem is related to the issue of inertia: people tend to grow fond of the way things are and will resist giving up "the old ways."

RESEARCH TOPIC

Just about everyone knows of good inventions that just don't seem to get off the ground (betamax tape format, for example), and we know of bad inventions that inexplicably become very popular (mood rings from the 1970s come to mind, but this may be a matter of taste). The same is often true of educational ideas—sometime good ideas just don't seem to go anywhere, while bad ideas catch everybody's imagination. Judgments about what is good or what is bad are somewhat subjective, of course, although it may be a bit easier to agree on what ideas are good than it is to agree on what is bad. Most everyone would agree, for example, that using computers in education is a good idea; similarly, most would agree that desegregation, preschool education, after-school programs, and drug awareness are good ideas. However, there are potentially good ideas, such as team teaching in high school, the school-within-a-school structure in large schools, and inter-disciplinary cooperation in higher education, that just don't seem to develop a significant following. Pick such an idea and try to explain why it doesn't catch on. Apply the themes previously discussed, such as inertia, the liability of newness, and learning. Use case study research strategies if possible to collect data.   ■

LEADERSHIP

Population Ecology examines issues that are critically important to organizational success or failure but over which leaders have little control, issues such as age, natural selection, and level of environmental competition (Pfeffer, 1997). As Anna Grandori (1987) put it, "adaptation becomes a game of chance in which a firm chooses a strategy . . . and environment chooses an outcome (say by flipping a coin)" (p. 110). It would seem, then, that leaders are mere flotsam in a raging social river. Indeed, Population Ecologists don't often speak of leadership in a deterministic sense, and the question of whether leadership even makes a difference in the big picture of things is an important one in Population Ecology.

The impact of leadership is limited by selection forces and by inherent organizational constraints. Such constraints assure that there is little variability in the qualifications and the behaviors of leaders selected for a given organization. That is, selection forces tend to mold uniform expectations of leadership behavior and leader personality, they favor leaders who are prepared in relatively uniform university professional preparation programs, and they even influence our beliefs about the physical characteristics associated with leadership. School principals, for example, all come from rather uniform university backgrounds and tend to approach problems in roughly similar fashion (there may not be a lot of variability in how we feel discipline should be applied, for example). Without significant variability in leadership behavior, there will be little variability in outcomes across different organizations, at least not differences that can be attributed to leadership.

But even if there were pertinent differences among leaders, the relationship between competence and organizational resources would blur or neutralize any impact they might have. An organization that is resource poor and low performing is unlikely to attract highly competent leadership, while those with abundant resources are unlikely to accept an incompetent leader. Even in public education, principals that we think are effective often get assigned to the better schools. In like manner, sports programs are limited in the choices of coaches they can recruit by the quality of their programs, and good instructional programs tend to attract the better teachers. Given this, one must ask whether better coaches make the difference in a team's performance or is it better athletes and more resources? Similarly, do better principals explain the differences among schools or are differences due to better students and more resources.

When program quality is accounted for in statistical analyses, leadership effect tends to disappear, suggesting that it is the program rather than the leader that makes the difference (Pfeffer, 1997). Lieberson and O'Connor (1972) examined the effects of organizational and leadership characteristics on productivity in 167 large industries, and found that organizational features, not leadership, dominated the outcome variable. Salancik and Pfeffer (1977) conducted a similar analysis of the effects of mayors on city budgets, and again found little effect attributable to leadership. Weiner and Mahoney (1981) conducted a somewhat more sophisticated analysis of 193 businesses over a 19-year period and found a substantially larger leadership effect than what had existed in these previous studies; even so, the effect of leadership on productivity was relatively small when compared to other effects. More recent studies using better measures of outcome and of leadership, however, have been somewhat promising. Lieberman, Lau, and Williams (1990), for example, found a significant leadership effect on productivity in the automobile industry over a 40-year period.

 ## RESEARCH TOPIC

This issue begs analysis in educational studies. Educational administration programs in universities throughout Western society are premised on the assumption that educational leaders *can* make a difference, thus we need to better understand this question. Researchers who tackle this question will need to carefully formulate measures of leadership and of educational outcomes, include environmental and organizational factors in their prediction equations, and use sophisticated quantitative and qualitative research design structures. ∎

Population Ecologists continue to state that we have over-romanticized leadership in our culture (Pfeffer, 1997). So much of an organization's productivity is determined by other factors—economic conditions, available resources, legal restraints, and such—that little is left for leadership to influence. But when organizations do well or when they do poorly, we credit (or blame) leaders, not conditions. Meindl, Ehrlich, and Dukerich argue that

> . . . it appears that the concept of leadership is a permanently entrenched part of the socially constructed reality that we bring to bear in our analysis of organizations. And there is every sign that the obsession with and celebration of it will persist. . . . Such realities emphasize leadership, and the concept has thereby gained the brilliance that exceeds the limits of normal scientific inquiry. (1985, p. 78)

Meindl and his colleagues support this radical claim by observing that the number of doctoral dissertations on leadership increases when the economy declines; that is, in bad times, we look to leadership for salvation. They analyzed stories in the *Wall Street Journal* and found a pervasive tendency to assume that organization effectiveness is related to leadership behavior. In a series of related studies, they found a statistical tendency to attribute performance to some human agent. They argued that the data on leadership simply do not support this sort of optimism about leadership effect, but our culture persists in believing that leaders are the key to organizational effectiveness.

RESEARCH TOPIC

Pfeffer (1997) identified two areas in which research on the romanticization of leadership is needed. First, he suggests that it may be interesting to investigate this question across different cultures. Eastern cultures, for example, may attribute less potency to leadership than do Western cultures, or there may be differences within a given national or cultural boundary. Second, it may be useful to understand conditions under which leadership attribution is most likely or least likely to occur. Is an unpopular administrator more likely to be blamed for organizational failure than a popular one, for example? Is failure likely to be attributed to a leader who replaces a popular leader, despite his or her actual performance?

In practice, however, these questions may be somewhat moot. The question might better be asked, what effect would *lack* of leadership have on an organization? From this perspective, it is apparent that someone must make decisions and initiate activities, regardless of whether those decisions and activities positively influence organizational effectiveness, for failure to make them would undoubtedly have a negative impact on the system. We must continue to ask, what do effective leaders do? Leaders do make decisions and engage in activities that affect the future of their organizations, and it is possible to make generalizations about appropriate leadership behavior that are consistent with Population Ecology theory.

Anjali Sastry (1997) suggests one answer to the question of what effective leaders do. She argued that natural selection breeds inertia for the simple reason that inertial organizations are both reliable and, usually, effective. As Hannan and Freeman (1984) argued, "In modern societies organizational forms that have high levels of reliability and accountability are favored by selection processes." Inertia enables organizational actors to benefit from experience and learning, and this enhances effectiveness and positive selection. Thus, inertia is not necessarily a bad thing. However, as Sastry noted, "When inertia is high enough, organizational managers are less able to recognize and respond to the need for a change" (p. 244). Thus, signals of poor performance in a developed, inertial organization must be stronger than in a young organization in order to force managers to make change decisions, and because of this, managers may wait until it is too late before trying to do something. Selection favors effectiveness and effectiveness comes from inertia, but inertia can mask and resist needed change.

Here is where good leadership may play a role. Good leaders know when it is time to change and when it is not; when inertia should be left alone and when it should be challenged. Organizations should change when performance is inconsistent with environmental demand and when evidence suggests that the costs associated with change are less expensive than the costs associated with not changing. Costs associated with change include conversion costs for new technology, re-training costs, risks associated with depressed effectiveness during the learning curve, and losses associated with scrapping existing resources that will no longer be needed. Effective leaders can total these balance sheets, perceive that change is genuinely needed, and can lead their organizations through the change process. Such skills can mean the difference between organizational success and failure.

Effective leaders may be particularly potent when an organization is young, for they can help guide the organization through the learning process and can help it develop the networks it needs to grow. Leaders can likewise help an organization weather transitions, or those times of change when an organization is faced with challenges similar to those it faced when it was young. Effective leadership is crucial when the organization experiences environmental shock, for those organizations that recover rapidly and adapt effectively to new conditions will be more likely to survive than those who don't.

 ## ROUNDTABLE

Describe other functions of leadership consistent with the Population Ecology perspective. ■

Population Ecologists perceive organizations as pawns in the mass movements of social dynamics. Organizational structure, organizational success and failure, leadership behaviors, and organizational activities are all products of impartial selection processes, a "flip of the coin," as Grandori (1987) put it. This would seem to leave little for leaders to do; but, as we have discussed, if they understand the system, leaders can "play" with nature. They can read the signals that indicate that organizational stability should end and can spark change (they may not know which changes nature will judge as "good," but they can perhaps know when continued stasis will be judged "bad"). They can help new organizations "learn the ropes" of their trade and can help them develop networks of support. They can mobilize an organization faced with environmental shock.

Population Ecologists further argue that organizations can be described in terms of a set of stable organizational types, or "species." Mintzberg described education as a professional bureaucracy, or a system in which highly complex activities have been standardized. This standardization is not the type that lends itself to rules and regulations, for the functions it performs are too complex; rather, it is a standardization of general procedures. It is standardization that permits professionals to "pigeonhole" clients for more efficient service. It reduces, but hardly eliminates, complexities. Professional bureaucracy is an efficient way to deliver complex services, but its nature resists change. A challenge for our society is to find ways to encourage these bureaucracies to change without sacrificing their ability to serve us effectively.

Diary

- Given what you have learned in this chapter, what are some important functions of leadership? In what way does your answer change your previous answers to this question?
- When leaders take over a new position, change is often at the top of their agenda. One almost expects it to happen: new leadership means strategic planning or reorganization or downsizing. In this chapter, we have discussed pros and cons of change and stability. Population Ecology suggests that a knee-jerk change agenda for one in a new leadership position may be inappropriate. Or it may be appropriate. How would you decide between change and stability if you assumed a new leadership position? Debate whether the downsides are sufficiently compelling that change should be avoided during the first year or so of a new leader's tenure, until he or she has properly evaluated conditions, or whether it should be tackled during the leader's "honeymoon" period with the new system.
- If leadership does not make the difference we think it does (as was argued in the last section of this chapter), then what *does* make the difference between effectiveness and noneffectiveness in educational organizations? Can the leader influence any of these factors, and if so, how?

Recommended Readings

Carroll, G. R., & Hannan, M. T. (Eds.). (1995). *Organizations in industry.* New York: Oxford University Press.

This book provides a number of case studies in Population Ecology, including Anderson's study of the microcomputer industry (which was referred to in this chapter), an article on the microbrewing industry, and an article on home food services at the turn of the century (an industry that failed to catch on).

Mintzberg, H. (1979). *The structuring of organizations: A synthesis of the research.* Englewood Cliffs, NJ: Prentice Hall, Inc.

Mintzberg's discussion of professional bureaucracies is fascinating. I could, obviously, only hit the high points of his discussion in this chapter; he expands on these topics and adds much that wasn't covered here. It is well worth your effort to read at least the sections of his book that deal with the education profession.

Sastry, M. A. (1997). Problems and paradoxes in a model of punctuated organizational change. *Administrative Science Quarterly, 42*(2), 237–275.

Sastry develops her thesis of stasis and change.

References

Aldrich, H. E. (1979). *Organizations and environment.* Englewood Cliffs, NJ: Prentice Hall.

Anderson, P. (1995). Microcomputer manufacturers. In G. R. Carroll & M. T. Hannan (Eds.), *Organizations in industry* (pp. 37–58). New York: Oxford University Press.

Anderson, P., & Tushman, M. L. (1990). Technological discontinuities and dominant designs: A cyclical model of technological change. *Administrative Science Quarterly, 35*(4), 604–633.

Bidwell, C. (1965). The school as a formal organization. In J. G. March (Ed.), *The handbook of organizations* (Chapter 23). Chicago: Rand McNally.

Campbell, D. T. (1969). Variation and selective retention in sociocultural evolution. *General Systems, 14,* 69–85.

Carroll, G. R. (1984). Dynamics of publisher succession in newspaper organizations. *Administrative Science Quarterly, 29,* 93–113.

Childs, T. S., & Shakeshaft, C. (1986). A meta-analysis of research on the relationship between educational expenditures and student achievement. *Journal of Educational Finance, 12,* 249–263.

Donaldson, L. (1996). *For positivist organization theory: Proving the hard core.* London: Sage Publications.

Ferguson, R. F. (1991). Paying for public education: New evidence on how and why money matters. *Harvard Journal on Legislation, 28,* 465–498.

Flanigan, J. L., Marion, R. A., & Richardson, M. D. (1996). Causal and temporal analyses of increased funding on student achievement. *Journal of Research and Development in Education, 30,* 222–247.

Grandori, A. (1987). *Perspectives on organizational theory.* Cambridge, MA: Ballinger.

Hannan, M. Y., & Freeman, J. (1984). Structural inertia and organizational change. *American Sociological Review, 49,* 149–164.

Hanushek, E. A. (1986). The economics of schooling: Production and efficiency in public schools. *Journal of Economic Literature, 24,* 1141–1177.

Hawley, A. (1950). *Human ecology.* New York: The Ronald Press Company.

Hersey, P., & Blanchard, K. H. (1993). *Management of organizational behavior: Utilizing human resources* (6th ed.). Englewood Cliffs, NJ: Prentice Hall.

Kuhn, T. S. (1970). *The structure of scientific revolutions* (2nd ed.). Chicago: The University of Chicago Press.

Lieberman, M. B., Lau, L. J., & Williams, M. D. (1990). Firm-level productivity and management influence: A comparison of U. S. and Japanese automobile producers. *Management Science, 36,* 1193–1215.

Lieberson, S., & O'Connor, J. F. (1972). Leadership and organizational performance: A study of large corporations. *American Sociological Review, 37,* 117–130.

Marion, R. (1999). *The edge of organization: Chaos and complexity theories of formal social organization.* Newbury Park, CA: Sage.

Marion, R., & Bacon, J. (1999). Organizational extinction and complex systems. *Emergence: A Journal of Complexity Issues in Organizations and Management, 1*(4), 71–96.

McKelvey, B. (1982). *Organizational systematics.* Berkeley, CA: University of California Press.

Meindl, J. R., Ehrlich, S. B., & Dukerich, J. M. (1985). The romance of leadership. *Administrative Science Quarterly, 30,* 78–102.

Meyer, M. W., & Zucker, L. G. (1989). *Permanently failing organizations.* Newbury Park, CA: Sage Publications.

Miller, D., & Chen, M. J. (1994). Sources and consequences of competitive inertia: A study of the U. S. airline industry. *Administrative Science Quarterly, 39,* 1–23.

Mintzberg, H. (1979). *The structuring of organizations: A synthesis of the research.* Englewood Cliffs, NJ: Prentice Hall.

Perl, L. J. (1973). Family background, secondary school expenditure, and student ability. *The Journal of Human Resources, 8*(2), 156–180.

Perrow, C. (1970). *Organizational analysis: A sociological view.* Belmont, CA: Wadsworth Publishing Company, Inc.

Pfeffer, J. (1997). *New directions for organization theory: Problems and prospects.* New York: Oxford University Press.

Salancik, G. R., & Pfeffer, J. (1977). Constraints on administrator discretion: The limited influence of mayors on city budgets. *Urban Affairs Quarterly, 12,* 475–498.

Sastry, M. A. (1997). Problems and paradoxes in a model of punctuated organizational change. *Administrative Science Quarterly, 42*(2), 237–275.

Schein, E. H. (1992). *Organizational culture and leadership* (2nd ed.). San Francisco: Jossey-Bass.

Singh, J. V., & Lumsden, C. J. (1990). Theory and research in organizational ecology. *Annual Review of Sociology, 16,* 161–195.

Stern, D. (1989). Educational cost factors and student achievement in grades 3 and 6: Some new evidence. *Economics of Educational Review, 8*(2), 149–158.

Stinchcombe, A. L. (1965). Social structure and organizations. In J. G. March (Ed.), *Handbook of organizations* (pp. 142–193). Chicago: Rand McNally.

Stinchcombe, A. L., & Harris, T. R. (1969). Interdependence and inequality: A specification of the Davis-Moore theory. *Sociometry, 32*(1), 13–23.

Vroom, V. (1964). *Work and motivation.* New York: John Wiley & Sons, Inc.

Weiner, N., & Mahoney, T. A. (1981). A model of corporate performance as a function of environmental, organizational, and leadership influences. *Academy of Management Journal, 24,* 453–470.

Winkler, D. R. (1975). Educational achievement and school peer group composition. *The Journal of Human Resources, 10*(2), 189–204.

CHAPTER 10

Schools as Cultures

Nearly everyone has had the experience of driving down a long expressway in the middle of nowhere and seeing a tight bunch of cars approaching rapidly in the rearview mirror. This cluster of drivers will likely be exceeding the speed limit by 10 or more miles per hour and each car will be jockeying for position relative to other cars in the group. Within a few minutes the cluster catches up with you and you may feel the urge to join this mad dash. If you resist, the cluster will pass on by as if you weren't there. If you join in, you find yourself increasingly obsessed with getting ahead, with maintaining or increasing your speed so the persons pressing from behind don't pass you, and with preserving your status as a group member. You interact with the members of the cluster, influencing their behavior and being influenced in return.

I have heard these referred to as "rat packs" or as "pods." Once in a pod, it is difficult to get out. By interacting with other drivers in the group, your respective behaviors become coordinated. You are no longer in sole control of your activities; rather, you have become a part of something bigger. To break out, you must forcefully take hold yourself and say, "This is stupid; I'm not going to do this." Eventually, a rat pack will break up on its own (or via a policeman's blue light), but for a short period of time, participants experience a crude example of the interactive, mutual-influencing dynamics that underlie culture.

O'Reilly and Chatman (1996) define culture as a "system of shared values (that define what is important) and norms that define appropriate attitudes and behaviors for organizational members (how to feel and behave)" (p. 160). Culture is not just ethnic or national, it is any stable order that emerges from interactive, social dynamics. When people interact, they influence one another's beliefs, understandings, behaviors, and perceptions of reality (Fig. 10.1). Newlyweds spend the first year or so

225

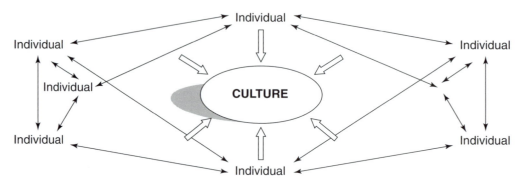

FIGURE 10.1 Individual interaction generates culture.

of marriage working out differences about money, personal habits, politics, beliefs, perceptions of what is important and what is not, children, family, chores, and such. They don't give up their individuality, but each person does modify his or her individuality to accommodate the other. The result is often a reasonably common understanding about important (and even unimportant) issues, and this commonality will increase over time. The two people become a family culture.

Something similar happens in schools. When teachers come together in a long-term work relationship, they experience interaction and interdependency of their individual natures. Stable and enduring relationships based on correlated outlooks emerge as teachers seek accommodation among themselves and between the school and its environment. As Schein (1992) put it, "[Culture is] a pattern of shared basic assumptions that the group learned as it solved its problems of external adaptation and internal integration" (p. 12).

Culture theory has lurked within modern organizational thought since at least the 1920s when Elton Mayo conducted his famous experiments at the Western Electric plant in Hawthorne, Illinois. In these experiments, he found that the level of lighting in a work room—any level, high or low—improved the productivity of workers. That was counterintuitive for social scientists of that day; increased lighting, they argued, should encourage productivity and low lighting should discourage it. Mayo's major conclusion from these studies was that human attitudes and perceptions—elements of culture—are more powerful determinants of organizational behavior than are externally manipulated variables.

Other noted theorists have addressed elements of culture over the years, although they usually did so within the context of the "harder" sciences of decision making, management strategies, and such. In the 1930s, Chester Barnard (1938) defined culture as a social fiction that gives meaning to work and life. In the 1940s, Phillip Selznick (1949) defined institution relative to meaning, solidarity, and commitment. George Homans (1950) explored the nature of informal groups in the 1950s. In the 1960s, Andrew Halpin and Don Croft (1962) popularized the notion of organizational climate. Culture, however, is more than just human relations, climate, or commitment; it is a phenomenon that encompasses every element of organizational life.

In this chapter, we examine the nature of culture and explore ways in which leaders can capitalize on this phenomenon to improve organizational productivity. We examine general characteristics and functions of culture, then look at Ouchi's (1981) Theory Z, at Burns' (1978) Transactional Leadership, at Sergiovanni's Lifeworld 2000, and at Deming's Total Quality Management. We will look at how culture leadership is supplanting bureaucracy as an organizing paradigm in business and education. We will see how the physical characteristics of a school or business can affect culture, and, finally, will examine some of the pitfalls and shortcomings of culture theory.

In this chapter, students will:

- Define schools as cultures composed of subcultures.
- Explore ways to build cultures that contribute to educational productivity.
- Propose what they would do during the first 100 days of an administrative assignment to build positive culture.
- Critique culture theory.
- Refine their definitions of the function of leadership.

THE ELEMENTS OF ORGANIZATIONAL CULTURE

Culture theory has the same holistic nature as Open Systems theory. Thus, the elements of open systems, as defined by Open Systems theorists such as Katz and Kahn (1966), Harold Leavitt (1964), and John Seiler (1967), are useful in defining the elements of culture. These elements are:

- Social systems, or groups of people who interact for such things as companionship, interaction, and conversation.
- Psychological systems, or personalities, needs, and drives.
- Management systems, or the structures used to control the organization; includes rules and regulations.
- Technical systems refer to the competencies required to transform a raw material; in education, such competencies include instruction and classroom management.
- Organizational systems refer to structures for processing raw material; many high schools, for example, adopt a departmentalized organizational structure.
- Environmental systems refer to structures that are considered external to the organization, but that influence the organization's activities; parents, for example, are part of the environmental system for public schools.

An important point here is that human behavior and culture are the product of more than just social activity and psychological personality. "Pop culture" writers treat culture as if it were nothing more than a human relations issue or an issue of psychological motivation. Human relations and psychology are important elements of culture, but motivational speeches and "win-win" will not remedy outmoded equipment or poor management strategies. Culture is influenced by the totality of the organizational experience; thus, the physical layout of a school plant is an important determinant of culture, as is the way the school day is divided into periods and the nature of instruction that goes on in a classroom. Sergiovanni (1992) echoed this when he said that "focusing on leadership separate from such issues as school governance, finance, parental involvement, curriculum reform, labor relations, diversity, teaching and learning, and assessment may cover up problems and provide symptomatic relief that makes us feel good but changes little that matters" (p. xi). Culture is people and processes and tools, and cultural leaders must tend the total creature.

THE CHARACTERISTICS OF CULTURE

What are the functional traits of a culture? What happens in an interactive group of people that causes them to become the culture? How does a culture behave; what are its characteristics? Cultural behaviors could be categorized in any number of different ways, although all would say essentially the same thing: cultures develop their own language, perceptions, rituals, norms and values, and feel (or climate). Edgar Schein's (1992) 10 characteristics of a culture summarize these activities nicely. They are:

- Observed behavioral regularities when people interact
- Group norms
- Espoused values
- Formal philosophy
- Rules of the game
- Climate
- Embedded skills
- Habits of thinking
- Shared meanings
- Root metaphors

We will use these categories to organize our discussions over the next few pages.

Observed Behavioral Regularities when People Interact

Members of a culture have standardized ways of interacting with one another. You might think of these as the "social graces" that evolve in a culture. We develop language conventions, for example. Teachers are addressed using their title (Mr., Mrs., Ms., Dr.), and the "boys'" soccer team in high school becomes the "men's" soccer team in college. We develop conventions about eye contact; some cultures greet one another with a handshake, while others greet with a kiss on the cheek. There are conventions about proper elevator conduct, about eating, and about dating. A given organizational culture will develop conventions that are specific to its particular group; thus, it may be convention for students in a particular school to walk on the right side of a hallway or for seniors to break into the front of the lunch line.

Such conventions serve to help us live peacefully with one another. We have conventions about driving, for example (many of which are codified as laws), that help assure automobile safety and prevent road rage. Social conventions are intended to foster respect and, in some cases, deference; thus, teachers are referred to by title and seniors get preferences not accorded freshmen. Conventions serve to maintain social class structure (a function that is somewhat frowned on in Western culture). They add predictability to our interactions.

ROUNDTABLE

In small groups, identify and discuss conventions common to education and conventions that are specific to your school district, school, or university. What purposes are served by these conventions?

Group Norms

Group norms are values or beliefs that are commonly considered proper and correct; violation of such norms is considered improper or even immoral. Norms often are subconscious expectations—everybody just understands them. For example, it may be a norm in a particular elementary school that teachers in one grade will develop students to a given skill level and that teachers in the next grade will take over at that point. It may be normative expectation that teachers maintain classroom discipline or are adequately prepared for daily instruction. The way instruction is conducted is norm-based. Teacher and student dress is subject to normative expectation. Educational norms label cheating as inappropriate behavior and reward students who study hard and achieve good grades.

There is a broader notion underlying this: members of a given culture have a somewhat common perception of reality. Actually, these perceptions are, for them, reality itself, which suggests that reality is more a perceived than a concrete state. Reality, like beauty, is in the eye of the beholder. Members of a culture define for one another what is true or false, real or unreal, important or unimportant, beautiful or ugly, proper or improper, just or unjust. The culture of the 1950s did not label sexual bias as unjust and beauty was not necessarily defined as lean and muscular, as is the case at the turn of the millennium. Western societies today tend to define corporal punishment as bad, while earlier Western culture used it routinely. Norms about appropriate and inappropriate language also have changed over the last 30 years. Each of these examples represents perceptions of reality that are more a product of cultural projection and interaction than of objective reality. Culture has a powerful influence over what its members believe and think.

Espoused Values

Espoused values are "the articulated, publicly announced principles and values that the group claims to be trying to achieve" (Schein, 1992, p.9). These values are often codified in a school's "mission statement." They typically deal with such issues as improved test scores, safe environments, and winning sports programs. Like norms, they are often heavily influenced by what the culture feels is good and proper.

Formal Philosophy

A formal philosophy is a broad statement of policies, ideology, or principle that is intended to guide a group's actions and influence perceptions of clients and other environmental actors. Philosophies may be coded as organizational mottos such as "Where learning is everything," or "Home of a winning attitude." The formal philosophy represents an attempt by culture to summarize its perception of itself.

Rules of the Game

This is commonly referred to as "the way we do things around here." "We only take as much construction paper as we need and we don't stockpile it." "Discipline problems are sent to Mr. Jones because Mr. Smith is too easy on students." "Leave the white board clean for the next teacher." Newcomers in particular are taught these rules as the appropriate way to act and to respond.

Climate

Climate is "the feeling that is conveyed in a group by the physical layout and the way in which members of the organization interact with each other, with customers, or with other outsiders" (Schein, 1992, p. 9). A school that is surrounded by an eight-foot wire fence and has signs everywhere telling visitors to check in at the administrator's office projects a besieged climate, regardless of what actually goes on within the building. An administrative office in which the principal works behind closed doors all day long conveys something of an aloof or uninterested persona, regardless of his or her real personality. A school with plants in the foyer and pictures on the walls is warm and inviting; if the pictures are children's work, it feels child-oriented.

Renato Tagiuri (1968) defines an organization's climate as its *ecology* (the physical elements of the facility), *milieu* (the social dimension of the organization, including its demographic makeup, morale, and motivation), *social system* (organizational and administrative structure), and *culture* (values, beliefs, norms, etc.). His inclusion of culture within this definition reveals his perception that culture is an element of climate. Culture theorists, of course, argue just the opposite—climate is an element of culture. Tagiuri's other three elements of climate underscore the fact that climate is a perception one obtains from the interactions among physical, human, and organizational features. It is not merely a function of how happy or friendly or busy the people in an organization are. Leaders can influence the climate of their organizations, but they must do more than just put pictures on the wall or give an inspiring speech at the beginning of the school year: they must effectively juggle the multiple features that comprise climate.

Embedded Skills

Embedded skills are the "special competencies group members display in accomplishing certain tasks, the ability to make certain things that gets passed on from generation to generation without necessarily being articulated in writing (Schein, 1992, p. 9)." This might be considered the "craft" that defines the organization. All educational organizations share a core of embedded skills, such as instructional practices and organizational patterns. Some schools may possess skills that identify them as somewhat unique. A given preparation program for school administrators, for example, might be known for its expertise in school law; a public school might be known for its ability to work with discipline problems.

Habits of Thinking

This refers to the mental models and the language structures that members of a culture construct around their perceptions of reality. These mental models and words shape perceptions, thought, and beliefs, and are taught to new members in their early socialization process. Noted postmodernist Michel Foucault (1980) has argued that reality is an artificial construct of our language; that is, the words we use determine our mental models of the world. Thus, we refer to certain exceptional children as impaired rather than handicapped; the latter term carries implications of inferiority that the former does not, and influences our perceptions of such children in subtle, negative ways. Some would even prefer the term *challenged,* to avoid any sense that the exceptional student is not normal.

Shared Meaning

Cultures have a common understanding about certain things. Commonly understood meanings for words and concepts tend to evolve within a given culture; often the culture even develops new words that have meaning within the group but which are not understood outside of it. A "boot" in England can refer to the storage compartment in an automobile; in the United States, it refers to footwear or to kicking. Schools develop commonly understood acronyms that have meaning only within the school culture. I once knew a teacher who encouraged her students to say "bingo" whenever they heard a grammatical mistake. Teenagers are notorious for developing terms that nonteens don't understand. Words represent our common experiences and label our cultures.

ROUNDTABLE

Let me tell a joke: How do you know if an elephant has been in the room? You smell peanut breath.

You didn't find it funny? In the 1960s, it would have had my students popping their buttons, so why is it not funny now, and what does this have to do with culture and shared meaning?

Root Metaphors

Root metaphors are

> the ideas, feelings, and images groups develop to characterize themselves, that may or may not be appreciated consciously but that become embodied in buildings, office layout, and other material artifacts of the group. This level of the culture reflects group members' emotional and aesthetic responses as contrasted with their cognitive or evaluative responses. (Schein, 1992, p. 10)

Root metaphors are commonly expressed as beliefs, rituals, and myths (Pettigrew, 1979). Rituals are those things we do to commemorate a special event and to celebrate our common experiences. Rituals mark transitions of individuals in their relationship to the culture. They are used to acculturate new members, for example, or to "decommission" retiring members. Some cultures have rituals to celebrate the transition from childhood to adulthood. We have rituals that celebrate the opening or closing of a school year. We use rituals to celebrate common experiences such as holidays or other meaningful events. Rituals define our perceptions of culture, they reinforce our common beliefs, and they label us as a group with something in common.

Myths likewise symbolize and express our cultural identities. Myths are stories about events that define who we are—the principal who refused to allow central office supervisors to preempt home visitation time needed by kindergarten teachers with inservice programs, the teacher who built a reputation of his or her academic expectations, or the university president who walked the campus periodically to talk with students. Myths tend to be morality tales about who we perceive ourselves to be or who we want to be as a culture. They are almost always rooted in fact, but it is not all that unusual for fact to be stretched a bit. With myths, factuality is subservient to meaning and reality is defined by the latter.

Rumors are related to myths because they also interpret cultural meaning, fear, and beliefs. Like myths, they are typically founded in factual events, but their importance lies not in fact but in the interpretation of fact. Urban legends illustrate this concept. A recently popular example is about a gang that requires initiates to drive at night with their headlights off; the initiate must shoot at the first person who flashes a signaling light at them. The story is not true, but it represents cultural alarm about gang behavior and cautions us against exposing ourselves to cultural outsiders. Standard rumors (as opposed to urban legends) also interpret cultural angst. The late 1990s saw the proliferation of rumors about school violence. These rumors were born from actual events, but they were more representative of our fears than of actual danger.

THE FUNCTIONS OF CULTURAL BEHAVIOR

Cultural behavior performs a number of important functions for a society. Culture serves to control aggression by distributing and legitimizing power and status. In some cultures, such as the caste system in India, relative power and position are so firmly ingrained in the cultural psyche that social stability is all but absolute. In any culture, the rituals, myths, behavioral regularities, norms, values, rules of the game, and shared meanings all contribute to stable power relationships. The terms used to categorize participants, for example, are often subtle reminders of one's place within the culture. The term "student" implies a subordinate relationship to teachers (who in some cultures are referred to with the even more obvious term, master). Principals often refer to their teachers by their first name while teachers use formal titles to refer to their principals. Myths reinforce the eminence of certain people or roles. Norms specify and control the distribution of resources. All this reduces the need to struggle over scarce power and resources, hence reducing tension and conflict.

Culture defines and enforces norms of relationship, such as those that involve intimacy and love. Culture frowns on adultery, thus protecting family stability, reducing social tension, and freeing mates to pursue activities without fear of infidelity when separated. While cultural norms are often seen to provide the elites in a society with subtle control mechanisms over the less powerful, it may do just the opposite as well. The intimacy prohibition, for example, gives subordinate classes some measure of protection against, and even control over, their superiors. Cultural prohibitions against sexual harassment, for instance, limit a superior's range of control options by forcing one to be circumspect in one's treatment of the opposite (or same) gender.

Culture serves to bring people together for the accomplishment of tasks. A lone wolf cannot bring down a large animal, but a pack of wolves can. A single basketball player cannot play the game, but five players can. A single teacher is not able to produce the broadly educated individuals needed by today's society. A single administrator cannot run a large school district. Culture provides the glue that binds individuals together to perform complex or daunting tasks.

Cultural norms, rules, behavioral regularities, root metaphors, shared meanings, and myths provide and institutionalize mechanisms of control that facilitate coordinated behavior. It defines roles, behaviors, and structural protocols that enhance group productivity and efficiency. Imagine the chaos if every teacher in a school were responsible for every task that had to be performed and nobody (or nothing) was available to coordinate activities. Each teacher would have to teach every subject, everyone would have to attend principal's meetings, each would have to be involved in budget control and purchasing, drive school buses, participate in every decision, answer the phones, and perform other clerical tasks. On top of that, imagine that each person's activities and decisions were independent of everyone else's. Each person created a school budget or class schedule without coordinating with anyone else, for example. Some of you may joke that this does describe your work, and teachers are indeed involved to some extent in many of these tasks, but, for the most part, we do divide up the responsibilities for educating children and we do coordinate our efforts. We do this by allocating different roles and responsibilities within our cultures, and by institutionalizing these roles and responsibilities with normative structures, myths, and such. If we didn't, we couldn't make decisions effectively (imagine trying to get everyone to come to a consensus on how to spend money) and jobs would just simply be overwhelming.

Organizational memory and dependability are possible because of the nature of culture. Memory is only possible when there is stability of the sort provided by cultural norms and activities. Chaotic systems, like the stock market, are unable to retain information. The Dow Jones Index for today tells us little or nothing about what the index will be a year from now—long-term prediction is impossible. The present index has no predictable impact on the future, and, conversely, it has no memory of its past. Culture, however, provides stability that enables long-term memory and dependability.

Cultures retain knowledge by coding it as stable norms, myths, rituals, standardized behaviors, root metaphors, and common understanding. Such knowledge is passed from generation to generation within a culture. Each generation adds its own experiences to that knowledge; that is, the culture learns from its mistakes and its successes—it is typically vibrant. Culture can, of course, be too stable, and thus unable to incorporate new knowledge, and this can be nearly as debilitating as chaos. A school that is so steeped in tradition that it refuses to embrace technological advances (such as computer education) does a disservice to the future of its students. A football coach who knows only to run up the middle on third and long likely will not win many games. A university educational administration preparation program that caters only to the traditional full-time student may experience catastrophic decline in enrollment. Effective culture balances itself between chaos and stodginess.

 ## RESEARCH TOPIC

Politicians and their audiences revel in labeling education as broken and in need of change. One might argue, however, that frequent change hampers effective education rather than helping it. That is, we don't stay with a strategy long enough to build it into an effective program before jumping to something new. Choose an example from your school or state system and explore the hypothesis that the strategy was abandoned before it could have an effect. ▮

Cultural structures help a society manage conflicting constraints. Conflicting constraints were introduced in Chapter 2 in the discussion of Bureaucracy. The idea is this: When too many demands must be satisfied, the probability of finding good solutions that serve the needs of the whole system is low. Where you have many "prima donnas," each making selfish demands on resources, any decision will leave a lot of unhappy people. When there are numerous conflicting needs within a system, satisfying compromises will be virtually impossible to find. Cultural clustering tends to reduce the number of demands within a system, thus increasing the probability of finding solutions that are productive for the whole. If a principal in a 30-teacher school had to juggle 30 independent sets of demands, he or she would have to make compromises that satisfied no one's needs. If those 30 teachers clustered into three groups with only three sets of needs, then good compromises are likely. Similarly, cultural clustering serves a system by simplifying its network of needs, reducing its number of conflicting constraints, and increasing the likelihood that decisions can emerge that satisfactorily (as opposed to optimally—decisions are still compromises) serve the needs of the system.

RESEARCH TOPIC

Social class structures, cliques, and such are somewhat maligned in Western culture, in part because of excesses like elitism and prejudice. Such clustering, or the formation of subcultures, is a common dynamic in cultural behavior, however; thus leading one to suspect that it serves some important function or functions. Develop a paper that explores this issue. ■

DYSFUNCTIONAL CULTURES

Pfeffer (1997) observed that "not all empirical studies have found a relationship between strong cultures and performance . . . , and even those that have uncovered an effect have noted the relationship is often complex" (p. 122). Thus, Pfeffer continued, Kotter and Heskett (1992) found that, in order to enhance performance, culture needed to be matched to the firm's strategy, and even then, "strategically appropriate cultures will not promote excellent performance over long periods unless they contain norms and values that help firms adapt to a changing environment" (p. 142).

Pfeffer is making the simple point that a strong sense of culture does not necessarily enhance productivity. One can imagine, and maybe even identify, schools with a strong sense of cohesion and commonality, but in which instruction is only mediocre. Perhaps the school has failed to introduce productive technological changes, or clings to outmoded instructional strategies. Some schools are just too comfortable with the way things are for their own good. Effective organizations must develop cultures that enhance their productivity, but some develop cultures that, instead, enhance only community and tradition.

Dysfunctionality can assume other guises as well. Cultures may focus on secondary goals at the expense of primary goals. For example, a school might be focused on its sports program to such an extent that it prioritizes sports involvement over classroom involvement, teachers are pressured to give undeserved grades to athletes, and money is diverted from instruction. A culture might focus on productivity at the expense of social and belonging needs, thus creating a climate of dissatisfaction that actually hurts, rather than aids, productivity. A culture may be so wedded to a given technology that it ignores other potentially useful technologies; teachers may be so committed to, say, phonics reading instruction that they overlook other ways of teaching reading, for example. Culture can be marked by fear of authority; it can be dominated by imperious faculty or hampered by weak leadership; it can be besieged by student discipline problems; or it could be so ethnically diverse that allegiance is dispersed and uncoordinated.

Productivity is not the only criterion for judging the functionality of cultures, however. It should, for instance, be judged for what it does to participants. Does a given culture enhance or damage the dignity and growth of any individual or group? Is a school so focused on college-bound students that it overlooks the needs of students who will not attend college? Is it oriented toward one ethnic group at the expense of others, or does it reflect a gender bias that is uncomfortable for the opposite gender?

THEORY Z

William Ouchi (1981) offers a perspective of organizational culture that is based on his observations of Japanese management practices. He has labeled the Japanese model "Theory Z" and relates it to McGregor's Theory X and Theory Y. Theory X, you will remember, refers to an organizational atmosphere in which people are assumed to be lazy, indolent, and motivated only by reward and punishment. Theory Y describes organizational environments in which workers are assumed to be self-motivated, desirous of positive work experiences, and cooperative. Theory Z describes a work environment that is characterized by trust, subtlety, and intimacy (see Fig. 10.2).

Theory Z, according to Ouchi, "suggests that involved workers are the key to increased productivity" (1981, p. 4). Trust, subtlety, and intimacy are central to such involvement. An atmosphere of distrust between workers and management hinders productivity. Ouchi points to the distrust among union, government, and management in Great Britain during the 20th century, and the resultant paralysis of the economy in that nation, as evidence. A sense of trust must exist before people will make sacrifices that contribute to productivity. In baseball, batters may hit "sacrifice" fly balls to bring in a runner. They make such sacrifices because they trust their action will be judged for its broader contribution and not for its proximate failure. In education, a school principal may allow teachers to take the limelight for a given success because he or she trusts that

FIGURE 10.2 Trust, subtlety, and intimacy are key to Theory Z organization.

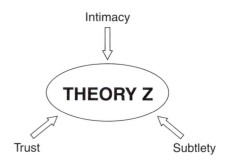

the "sacrifice" will be respected. Coaches will take risks in the current season in order to develop younger players for future seasons if they can trust their fans to be patient.

Subtlety means to base decisions on an understanding of the subtle complexities of a situation rather than on restrictive rules and regulations. In the discussion of learning theory in Chapter 8, it was observed that organizational roles are often defined by subtle nuances that can be mastered only through training and experience. Bureaucracy typically fails to respect such subtlety and imposes general rules that reduce subtleties to gross generalizations. A school rule that three disciplinary infractions automatically lead to suspension leaves no room for a principal to respond to the subtleties sometimes associated with problems. Children may act up at school because of trauma they are experiencing at home; an inflexible three-strikes regulation would only exacerbate such a situation. Subtleties, according to Ouchi, "can never be captured explicitly, and any bureaucratic rule will do violence to them" (1981, p. 7).

Intimacy is an atmosphere of caring and support that comes from close social relationships. Intimate organizational cultures foster social interaction among workers in which members seek each other's company, both inside and outside the organization. They have opportunities to interact socially during the work day, they often plan social events such as parties, they celebrate each other's milestones and mourn each other's losses, they are on a first-name basis and know each other's families, and they do things together outside of work. Intimacy fosters trust and knowledge of interpersonal subtleties. It enables the evolution of norms and shared understanding; that is, intimacy breeds culture.

Ouchi argues that American organizations differ from Japanese organizations on several important dimensions.

Large, profitable Japanese firms offer lifetime employment, and it is a mark of honor to receive such an appointment. These organizations recruit young, entry-level employees; anyone who has had other jobs need not apply. One is fired from such a job only for a major or criminal infraction and being fired is highly shameful. Life-long commitments enable workers to develop a high level of proficiency in the intricate subtleties and nuances of their jobs. Such proficiency is further encouraged by the slow evaluation and promotion system in Japanese industries. An employee might work 10 years at a task before being considered for promotion, and such promotions are decided on merit rather than tenure or personality.

Such practice fosters several characteristics that are useful to effective organizational culture. Life-long employment and slow promotion practices enable mastery of task subtleties. The long association with a stable set of colleagues and tasks promotes intimacy. Long-term relationships breed trust. Uncooperative or devious behavior is discouraged by, if nothing else, awareness that there is plenty of time for such behavior to come back and haunt you.

Life-long employment and slow promotion practices enable workers to develop broad, as opposed to specialized, skills. Employees have time to sample widely from the range of work opportunities available to them. Because of intimate interrelationships, they are exposed to the jobs of others. When promoted, this broad experiential base permits assignment to any number of different roles, thus enabling even broader skills development. Employees of a Theory Z organization typically are knowledgeable about, and empathetic to, nearly all elements of the production process, from its initial stages to the final product.

American organizations, by contrast, have four to eight times the turnover rate of Japanese organizations. According to Ouchi (1981), such "rapid employee turnover necessitates speedy evaluation and promotion. A constant need to replace managers places new employees not yet attuned to the subtleties of the organization in influential positions. This process of rapid evaluation and promotion often creates a hysterical attitude among managers who feel that three years without a significant promotion means they have failed" (pp. 58–59). Rapid evaluation and promotion, along with high rates of turnover, encourage the evolution of highly specialized jobs that can be learned quickly. Both jobs and relationships are reduced to a simplified set of standards that are often codified as explicit bureaucratic rules. This masks subtle nuances and inhibits intimacy, both of which are crucial in Theory Z organizations.

In contrast to the explicit control mechanisms characteristic of American firms (or what Ouchi called the "Theory A" organization), Theory Z organizations are more likely to depend on implicit control mechanisms. Implicit mechanisms are more subjective, qualitative, and nonrational than are explicit mechanisms. They draw more on the wisdom, experience, and subtle knowledge of decision makers, although in practice these organizations tend to forge a balance between implicit and explicit considerations. Explicit control mechanisms are grounded in quantitative data, rationality, efficiency-oriented reflection, bureaucratic rules, and objective evaluation.

Organizational life in Theory Z systems is marked by interdependence and interreliance. It is also characterized by a certain amount of ambiguity. Such ambiguity reflects an awareness and appreciation of subtle and complex nuances in production activities. Decisions are not merely a matter of the "bottom line," as they often are in Theory A organizations, and even if they were, that bottom line is recognized as the product of complex interactions. Instead, Theory Z organizations base decisions on projections of both short- and long-term impact, on the effect that decisions will have on organizational actors and the organization's reputation, and on awareness of the subtle personality and task interdependency behaviors of the given organization and its people. The complexity of decision making requires input and involvement by a number of persons. In contrast to Theory A organizations, where decisions are often made without consulting those most directly affected, Theory Z organizations seek broad counsel. This type of decision making requires a wide dissemination of information, which further reinforces the generalized skills base characteristic of Theory Z organizations.

Collective decision making leads to collective responsibility for such decisions. In Theory A systems, a single decision maker bears responsibility; if he or she makes a bad decision, then blame is squarely on that person's shoulders. Further, the decision maker tends to be alone in yet another way: one can often count on only lukewarm support from those excluded from the process, and may even find oneself embroiled in active opposition to the decision. With collective decision making, support for a decision is more probable and blame or praise is spread across a broader population.

Finally,

> . . . type Z companies generally show broad concern for the welfare of subordinates and of co-workers as a natural part of the working relationship. Relationships between people tend to be informal and to emphasize that whole people deal with one another at work, rather than just managers with workers and clerks with machinists. This wholistic [SIC] orientation, a central feature of the organization, inevitably maintains a strong egalitarian atmosphere that is a feature of all Type Z organizations. (Ouchi, 1981, p. 79)

DECLINE OF THE IRON CAGE

Theory Z underscores a significant transition in organizational behavior. Weber's "iron cage," which he argued was invincible, is not invincible: it is crumbling. Control structures based on impartial rules and regulations are being replaced by participatory, group-based decisions, control is being vested in workers, and hierarchy is being flattened. The transition is not universal, nor is it typically complete in any given organization, but participatory management has become a growing trend in the last decades of the 20th century. This trend is logically related to the emergence of anti-positivism, which deflected the focus of organizational theorists away from efficiency and effectiveness, and has refocused it on other preferences. Such refocusing has encouraged theorists to conceptualize organizations in terms of, among other things, cultural needs and behaviors. And bureaucracy is not particularly conducive to cultural enhancement.

ACTIVITY

Critics argue that efficiency, effectiveness, and even control drive the growing interest in decentralized decision making and worker empowerment. The next section of this chapter discusses transactional versus transformational leadership. As you study this material, watch for implicit and explicit understanding that transformational behavior, moral leadership, and lifeworlds serve to enhance productivity and, more importantly, increase managerial control. ■

LEADERSHIP AND IMPACTING CULTURE

Edgar Schein (1992) has argued that "the only thing of real importance that leaders do is to create and manage culture and that the unique talent of leaders is their ability to understand and work with culture" (p. 5). Schein suggests that effective leaders seek to understand and maneuver culture, to build a culture that best meets the needs of the organization. Like Open Systems theory, Culture theory calls for a holistic, as opposed to a reductionist, orientation to organizational behavior, and an effective leader seeks to build an effective whole.

Cultural leadership devalues the need for bureaucratic control structures and shifts the burden of control instead to work groups (Kunda, 1992, p. 218). Externally imposed controls tend to foster resistance. We resent restrictions of our freedom, and bureaucratic control can be a rather intrusive example of such constraint. Ironically, as Pfeffer (1997) observed, such resentment can create rebellious behaviors that make further control even more necessary. Cultural leadership overcomes this problem by emphasizing the internalization of values and by increasing reliance on peer control. In essence, leadership overcomes resistance and increases productivity by taking advantage of the "rat pack" mentality.

O'Reilly and Chatman (1996) identify four approaches to creating effective cultures. The first is *participatory decision making*. This increases commitment by creating a feeling that participants are making decisions that contribute significantly to organizational functioning. The idea is to help personnel "buy into" the goals and activities of the organization. Second, leaders build culture with the *signals* that their actions convey—what they spend time on, talk about, ask questions about, and do. The school principal whose only comment after visiting a classroom is that there is paper on the floor may be saying to the teacher that cleanliness is more important than instruction. The new principal who begins his or her tenure by spending limited resources on expensive office furniture sends a message about priorities. The leader who cancels a speaking engagement with a small neighborhood community club in order to speak before a more prestigious group has done irreparable symbolic damage.

ROUNDTABLE

New administrators should carefully craft the symbolic messages they send during their first few weeks of tenure. Identify a few symbolic acts that you would perform if you were appointed to a new leadership position. What sort of meaning would you intend to convey through these actions? ■

Third, cultures are influenced by *shared social information*. People work out their common understandings, the norms of behaviors, and their expectations by interacting and communicating with one another. Cultural leaders can influence this by maneuvering the language of interaction. Teacher lounges with overstuffed chairs and a soda machine, for instance, may encourage little more than gossip, while work rooms with supplies, copy machines, and idea books encourage work-related interaction. One might foster a language of student achievement by asking teachers to compose a mission statement about test scores. Stories about past accomplishments can create myths that reinforce such accomplishments in the present.

Fourth, organizations shape behavior through *reward systems* such as recognition, prestige, and advancement. Such rewards reinforce appropriate cultural behavior. However, "underlying all these forms of cultural control is always the implicit threat that those who don't fit in will be expelled from the organization, and this fear of social ostracism is also a strong factor promoting conformity to the organization's core values and decision premises" (Pfeffer, 1997, p. 126).

Several other leadership behaviors can be added to this list. First, leaders can influence culture with *rituals*. Like myths, rituals serve to bond cultures and to reinforce beliefs and actions. An annual faculty-student game day, particularly one in which the leader is an active participant, can build camaraderie and makes a statement about the relationship among faculty, between faculty and students, and between the leader and everyone. A yearly school-community celebration can build positive community culture. Harmless senior-year "pranks" reinforce nostalgic memories (and alumni support) of one's school.

Cultural leaders *articulate* the philosophy and values of an organization. They codify those values as mission statements, they exemplify them in their behaviors, they represent them to the community, and they defend them when they are challenged. If a school's culture values instruction, the school's leader will defend teachers against encroachment on instructional time by outside interests. If a culture espouses the importance of parent involvement in a child's schooling, the principal might annually make this the keynote topic of the school's first open house. If the culture believes in a comfortable, home-like environment for students, the principal will try to know students by name.

Cultural leadership might include the administration by *walking around*. This allows the leader to tap into the deep level of the organization where culture is embedded. During these times "on the floor," the administrator would have an opportunity to represent, verbally and through actions, values that are important to the organization. He or she might identify and reinforce teacher or student behaviors that are important to cultural norms. Cultural norms could be reinforced by what one attends to or doesn't attend to (one might focus on instruction and ignore minor messiness, for example). One could model effective communication if that were important.

The culture leader is, according to Deal and Peterson (1991), *a healer*. By that they meant that such leaders help their cultures mourn losses (as when tragedy strikes), weather transitions, and reconcile differences. This latter role can be difficult, for often animosities have deep roots and involve unforgettable wrongs (or perceived wrongs). Transitions are changes that cultures periodically experience, as when a school moves from a building that was home to several generations of students, when a long-time employee retires, or when students graduate. Ceremonies that celebrate the old life and embrace the new help people make these transitions. Deal tells a story of a school that was merged with another. The students and faculty of the school that was to be abandoned held a "farewell" ceremony at the old school before ceremoniously marching to the new one (with a band and fire trucks) where they were met by their new colleagues and classmates. The principal of the old school then symbolically passed his authority to the principal at the new school. They mourned their loss, then celebrated a new beginning.

ROUNDTABLE

Let's expand the last Roundtable. It asked you to consider the symbolic messages you would send early in your tenure as an administrator. Expand that to a discussion of what you would do overall to craft culture in an organization during your first 100 days in a new position. ■

Transactional and Transformational Leadership

James Burns (1978) has made a rather interesting and useful distinction between what he called "transactional" leadership and "transformational" leadership. He defined transactional leadership as "the exchange of rewards, such as security, tenure, and positive ratings, for performance (support or operation compliance)." The transformational leader, by contrast,

> . . . looks for potential motives in followers, seeks to satisfy higher needs, and engages the full person of the follower. The result of transforming leadership is a relationship of mutual stimulation and evaluation that converts followers into leaders and may convert leaders into moral agents. (p. 4)

William Bennis and Burt Nanus (1985) add that, "The new leader . . . is one who commits people to action, who converts followers into leaders, and who may convert leaders into agents of change" (p. 3). Transformational leadership, they continue, "is collective, there is a symbiotic relationship between leaders and followers, and what makes it collective is the subtle interplay between the followers' needs and wants and the leader's capacity to understand, one way or another, these collective aspirations" (p. 217).

Thomas Sergiovanni has probably done more to apply this distinction in the educational arena than any other organizational writer. Sergiovanni equated transformational and transactional leadership to sociologist Jürgen Habermas' (1987) notions of "lifeworld" and "systemsworld." The systemsworld is "a world of instrumentalities usually experienced in schools as management systems. These systems are supposed to help schools effectively and efficiently achieve their goals and objectives" (Sergiovanni, 2000, p. 4). Lifeworld, by contrast, reflects the culture and meanings of an organization. It embodies the "expression of needs, purposes, and desires of people;" it is about "the sources of deep satisfaction in the form of meaning and significance" (p. 5).

Sergiovanni argues that both these dimensions of social organization are important and that they complement one another. He uses the family social system to illustrate:

> Families are concerned with purposes, norms, and traditions; they focus on the protection, growth, and development of their members; and they seek to enhance the

meaning and significance that members experience, allowing them to lead a more satisfying life. Families also budget, save for college, plan vacations, have schedules, keep calendars, manage tax records, and worry about operating costs. With proper balancing, the systemsworld and lifeworld of the family enhance each other. (pp. 5–6)

Sergiovanni then adds, "For this relationship to be mutually beneficial in enterprises like families and schools, however, the lifeworld must be generative. It must be the force that drives the systemsworld" (p. 6). Either systemsworld will dominate the lifeworld or the lifeworld will dominate the systemsworld. Habermas calls this "colonization." Systems are culturally functional when lifeworld colonizes the systemsworld; they are dysfunctional when the reverse is true.

Systemsworld is a world of goals, objectives, efficiency, and effectiveness. It is structured by rules and regulations and it is enforced by transactions. Rules specify the nature and form of transactions, or exchanges in which participants trade one thing for another. Leaders, for example, provide monetary rewards, prestige, recognition, needs achievement, positive evaluations, and friendship in return for efficient and effective productivity—hence, the term "transactional." Much of organizational theory functions in the transactional realm: you should recognize the systemsworld notion in Maslow's lower order needs and Herzberg's motivators, for example. Systemsworld and transactional leadership deal in control mechanisms, whether benign or oppressive, subtle or obvious. According to Habermas, organizational and other social systems that are colonized by the transactional world of rules, efficiency, and objectives are out of balance.

This is not to say that rules, efficiency, and objectives are to be avoided. Rather, these systemsworld activities should be guided by, or functions of, the lifeworld. They should be mechanisms by which the culture achieves the "expression of needs, purposes, and desires of people" (Sergiovanni, 2000, p. 5). Married couples operate under unspoken rules about interaction with friends of the opposite sex. The limitations imposed by these rules serve the broader needs of the family culture. They serve the satisfaction and security of participants in the family and they foster the unity needed to provide a healthy atmosphere for children. This systemsworld rule serves the need of the lifeworld. If one spouse is unusually jealous, however, this rule will eventually grow to dominate the family culture in unhealthy ways—the systemsworld will colonize the lifeworld. Similarly, schools may have rules about student dress. These rules are intended to provide a wholesome and nonintimidating atmosphere for learning—they serve the needs of the academic lifeworld. If, however, the faculty becomes so slavish about dress codes that they measure skirt length, then the culture has become colonized by that systemsworld rule.

A colleague and I are tracking the school-level impact of our state's Principal Accountability Act with yearly surveys of school principals (Flanigan & Marion, 1999). We are finding that the principal evaluation process in our state is exhibiting retrenchment. For example, a former practice in a number of school districts of involving students and teachers in principal evaluations is disappearing. Evaluation has become almost exclusively the responsibility of district administrators. It appears that the accountability law, a systemsworld function, is disrupting an element of cultural community, or lifeworld.

Total Quality Management

Total Quality Management (TQM) was mass-introduced to Americans in 1980 by an NBC-TV documentary that examined differences between U.S. and Japanese businesses. This management approach attracted the attention of a number of major American firms, particularly firms that were on the short end of competition with Japanese markets.

TQM is the brainchild of Edward Deming, a management expert whose experience goes back to the early 1930s. Deming was a statistical control engineer in Western Electric's Hawthorne plant when the famous Hawthorne studies were conducted (although he was not involved in them). Later, Deming was a statistical sampling expert for the U.S. Census Bureau. In 1947, General Douglas MacArthur asked Deming to go to Japan to help assess the postwar needs of that country. Deming's experiences with this ravaged economy, and the nature of the Japanese culture, provided him with the foundation from which TQM emerged.

There are four elements in the TQM management approach (Anderson, Rungtusanatham, & Schroeder, 1994; Waldman, 1994; Westphal, Gulati, & Shortell, 1997). First, TQM is customer-focused, emphasizing improvement of processes for both internal and external constituencies. Internal constituencies include workers; external constituencies include suppliers, buyers, and other groups that are related to an organization. TQM devotes considerable attention to identifying the needs and expectations of these constituencies, and of developing products that meet or exceed their needs (Fig. 10.3).

Second, TQM emphasizes continual improvement. It attempts to develop a culture in which people are not satisfied simply with meeting current standards, but rather push to exceed those standards. "Organizations adopting TQM reject the dictum, 'If it ain't broke, don't fix it.' The new dictum becomes, 'If it ain't broke—break it!' if by doing so the process or product can be improved" (Westphal et al., 1997, p. 369).

Third, TQM involves systematic approaches to problem-solving and to finding opportunities for improvement. Its goal is to reduce variation from common standards. The traditional process of quality control in Western industries was to establish an acceptable range of quality; if a product fell within that range, then everything was considered OK. A company might make ball bearings with a diameter of 0.5 mm, but any bearing that had a diameter within a range of, say,

FIGURE 10.3 Four elements of TQM.

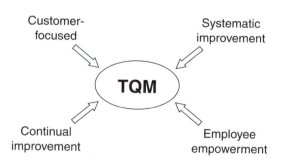

0.498 to 0.502 would be considered acceptable. TQM rejects this, seeking instead to constantly improve the acceptable range.

Fourth, TQM emphasizes employee empowerment. Its proponents argue that continuous improvement requires that employees not only have the skills and motivation to do the job, but that they also have the authority to take action and make decisions. The goal is to bring decision making as close to the actual production process as possible.

TQM represents yet another strategy for strengthening organizational culture, thus enhancing effective productivity. Its proposals to empower employees and to meet the needs of internal constituencies are central to general Culture theory, for example. TQM adds an element that is all too often overlooked by culture gurus, however. It focuses on production as well as on people, and seeks explicitly to find ways to improve that production. Many Culture theorists assume that, if you strengthen the interpersonal dimension of an organization, productivity will follow. Deming and other TQM advocates specifically addressed the production dimension, thus tacitly acknowledging the holistic nature of organizational culture, one that includes all elements of the production process.

ORGANIZATIONAL STRUCTURE AND CULTURE

The physical structure of an organization can have a rather direct effect on its culture. The traditional layout of a public school is called the "egg crate" structure. The structure has a long hallway with a line of classrooms on each side—it looks something like an egg crate, hence the name. Walls between classrooms are typically masonry walls and are sometimes load-bearing, which limits one's ability to alter spaces. In the 1960s and '70s, it was common to use folding partitions in place of masonry walls, but in my experience teachers rarely take advantage of the opportunity they offer to alter spatial relationships and instructional strategies, and prefer permanent walls. The typical classroom door into the hallway has a small pane of glass about the size of a piece of construction paper—a fact that doesn't escape the notice of many teachers. This structure breeds a self-contained atmosphere; teachers cloister themselves and their classes within their secure, anonymous spaces. There is a feeling of independence and autonomy that permits relatively little task-related interaction among faculty. It is something of an intrusion for one teacher to enter the classroom space of another during instruction time, an intrusion that often demands a protocol of apologies and rationale. Teachers can interact during class change, although responsibilities and the chaos of students milling around often preclude it. Interaction, then, is usually restricted to before and after school, lunch periods, and planning periods. Task-related interaction is more probably coordinated through the administrative office than through other channels. Students who wander throughout the facility are more likely to know what is going on in the school than are teachers.

Yet another common structural pattern in schools is called the pod, a structure that is seen more often in elementary and middle schools than in high schools.

In the typical pod structure, classrooms are clustered by grade or teams around a small common area—this is a pod. Pods, in turn, are clustered around a large, common media center. Administrative offices are located behind the media center overlooking the main entrance to the school. The cafeteria and gymnasium are located on the other side of the administrative offices; this not only isolates the noisy functions from the educational function, it permits community access to the gym and cafeteria after hours without having to open the educational wing. While this structure still utilizes self-contained classrooms, the overall ambiance encourages social and task-related interaction. It also facilitates greater community involvement in the school, thus enhancing yet another dimension of school culture.

ROUNDTABLE

The generalizations in the above discussion were limited and circumspect because the impact of structure on culture can be highly individualized. Further, this relationship is often influenced by other factors, such as scheduling patterns. You are, therefore, encouraged to extend these generalizations within the context of your own facility. Analyze the impact that your facility has on your school's culture. How does it impact communication, socialization, social grouping, control structures, group norms and "the way we do things around here," and the general nature of culture (tightly knit, friendly, fractured, etc.)? What factors interact with the relationship between facility and culture in your school?   ▪

CASE STUDY

Richard Snyder (1988) has studied a change event that occurred at Lockheed Aircraft during the 1960s and 1970s. The story of this change is fascinating, and its telling offers useful insights into the nature of organizational culture and how leaders can work with social entities. In 1966, Lockheed decided to manufacture a wide-bodied, medium-range passenger jet to be called the L-1011 TriStar. It almost did not happen.

From the first, setbacks and scandal plagued the TriStar project. The first setback involved the bankruptcy of the Rolls Royce Company, with which Lockheed had contracted to supply engines for their new aircraft. This created a financial crisis that forced massive layoffs at Lockheed; to save the aircraft company, the U.S. Congress had to intervene with a bailout. Then in 1975, when Lockheed was finally crawling out from under this calamity, it became embroiled in a major international scandal in Japan. Lockheed (and other companies) had bribed Japanese officials. The resulting scandal spread all the way to the top of the Japanese government and forced the resignation of Japan's prime minister. As if all this were not bad enough, Lockheed became involved in a bloody competition war with McDonnell Douglas about this time, and the company projects that it lost over two billion dollars in the ensuing hostilities.

During these dark years, the TriStar was being produced at Lockheed's plant in Palmdale, California. In terms of trouble, the Palmdale plant was a microcosm of what was going on in the company as a whole. The plant was unable to maintain its production schedule and was significantly over its budget, it had expensive problems with product quality, and had suffered a long series of management changes. Apparently, the management issue was at the crux of the problem. The plant was well-known in the company for the autocratic and demeaning leadership style of its managers. Workers wrote letters to the president of the company complaining about excessive work, dictatorial leadership, preemptive firings, and public humiliation by managers. It was not unusual for managers to waylay workers on the floor, verbally castigate them before their peers, then summarily fire them on the spot. Fear was widespread, management was out of control, and morale was abysmally low. This created an atmosphere in which there were serious hostilities among departments and among workers. People were afraid to report accurately on the status of projects for fear of management retribution. If problems could not be hidden, then workers attempted to transfer blame to some other individual or department. The Palmdale plant had, to say the least, a dysfunctional culture.

In 1979, Dale Daniels, a respected engineer and manager with Lockheed, was brought in to take over the L-1011 plant. Daniels set about to change the culture of this plant. His leadership style was dramatically different than the one that had plagued the Palmdale plant in its recent past. He began by finding people he could trust, people who shared his philosophy of management, and delegated real authority and responsibility to them. In the past, managers in the plant had no real authority; their decisions and their tenure were subject to the whim and pleasure of their superiors. In a sense, then, actual authority resided only in the plant manager. Daniels changed this by giving his foremen authority that counted.

Shortly after arriving at the plant, Daniels circulated a memo in which he outlined his management philosophy. This list included such aphorisms as, "Don't sell your integrity—it's the only thing that can't be bought;" "You may be better at something than someone else, but you are not better than they are;" "Attack the problem, not the person;" "You don't have to make people do things your way to get performance;" and "When things go wrong, don't shoot the messenger." Saying and doing can be two different things: workers realize this and Daniels understood the pitfalls of not living up to his claims. He knew that you can "attack the problem" a hundred times, but attack the person on the 101st and people will label you with the mistake. He had to live his philosophy and he had to do it consistently.

Daniels believed in management by walking around; he wanted to get to know the people in the plant, to understand the problems of production, and to tap into the "deep level" of plant dynamics. Initially, workers at the plant were skeptical, for walking managers usually meant trouble. Daniels reported that, when he first began to walk about the plant, people would avoid him. They would hide, even run from him. They were afraid of humiliation or accusations. At times, Daniels had to chase workers down, back them into a corner, to talk to them. He persisted, however. He knew he had to reverse the fear, for it was crucial that he tap into floor dynamics in order to help the plant succeed.

Daniels required that his management team exhibit the same administrative attitude. He knew that his efforts to reverse the negative atmosphere would be futile if his managers, many of whom had served under earlier, autocratic superiors, continued to behave as they had in the past. He had one manager in the plant who refused to adopt his (Daniels') more humane approach to leadership, and who continued to treat workers as he had under previous management. Daniels approached this person repeatedly about his behavior without success. He finally had to fire the man. This, however, created a collateral problem, for the firing was inconsistent with his espoused philosophy. Consequently, Daniels took pains to explain his actions to employees, to let them know that he had been faced with problems that were inconsistent with the welfare of other employees and the welfare of the company. He weathered this crisis.

Daniels encouraged workers to report their problems accurately by not punishing them for their failures. He did not allow people to shift responsibilities for problems, requiring them instead to deal forthrightly with solutions. He did not belittle employees and refused to let his management team do so. He required that his management team walk the floor, to tap into the deep level of the organization.

Daniels sought to build teamwork and camaraderie at the plant. He purchased blazers for his management team with TriStar L-1011 emblems emblazoned on them, for example; the managers wore them proudly. Daniels realized that positive morale depended not only on good human relations programs, but on effective task behavior as well. Consequently, he and his team of managers initiated a number of production strategies aimed at increasing productivity and controlling costs; the team became quite proud of their successes.

The results of Daniels' efforts were impressive. The attacks between departments, the employee harassment, and the difficulty obtaining accurate information ceased. The production time per aircraft dropped significantly and costs were controlled. The plant developed an excellent reputation in the industry and its employees were proud of their association with it. When the last TriStar produced at Palmdale rolled out of the hanger in the mid-1980s, the workers organized a major ceremony celebrating the plant's successes and grieving the passing of an era. In the end, the Palmdale plant was entirely different from what it had been at the beginning. ■

PROBLEMS WITH CULTURE THEORY

Culture theory is a powerful and useful metaphor for organizational theorists and practitioners, but this very fact is also its weakness. Culture theory, particularly in its more prescriptive forms (such as transformational leadership and TQM), is so intuitive and so enticing that it has attracted popular culturists who have reduced the theories to simplistic prescriptions and stirring but hollow speeches about will power, heroic leadership, and motivation. These individuals tend to make grandiose and ambitious claims to which no theory could ever possibly rise. For others, Culture theory has assumed an aura of the religious, to the point that lectures on organizational improvement sound more like sermons. Certainly, religions teach principles that are helpful in interpersonal relationships. The problem, however, is that culture prescriptions can become moral imperatives premised on didactic beliefs rather than empirically supportable fact or solid theoretical premise.

The bigger problem, however, is that its faddishness has led many organizations to implement it more as a vehicle for legitimatization than for improvement (Westphal et al., 1997). This is the subject to which we will now turn our attention.

Diary

- Given what you have learned in this chapter, what are some important functions of leadership? In what way does your answer change your previous answers to this question?

- Relate Dale Daniels' success at the Lockheed TriStar L-1011 plant to Theory Z. To transformational leadership.

- The Lockheed case study emphasized Daniels' relationship with people, but it was equally important that he be effective with production. Discuss the importance of production and task behavior to culture.

- Critique the work of modern popular culturalists who preach only a philosophy of motivation and will power.

- Earlier, you were asked to describe what you would do during the first 100 days of a new leadership position. Revisit that discussion in light of the previous case study.

- Describe the culture of your job. What factors influence it, what are its characteristics (norms, values, myths, etc.). If you were the leader, what could you do to make this culture more productive and pleasant?

Recommended Readings

Deal, T. E., & Peterson, K. D. (1991). *The principal's role in shaping school culture*. Washington, DC: U.S. Department of Education, Office of Educational Research and Improvement, Programs for the Improvement of Practice.

Deal and Peterson argue in this book that a principal should be a symbol who affirms values, a potter who shapes via rituals and ceremonies, a poet who uses language to reinforce values, an actor who improvises a school's drama, and a healer who oversees transitions. They illustrate these six points with case studies.

Jones, M. O., Moore, M. D., & Snyder, R. C. (Eds.). (1988). *Inside organizations: Understanding the human dimension*. Newbury Park, CA: Sage Publications.

This is a book of case studies in organizational culture, and is the source of information for the story of the Lockheed TriStar 1011. Other stories in the book delve into Howard Hughes' leadership style, the Girl Scouts, organizational rituals, and the Mormon youth missionary program.

Ouchi, W. (1981). *Theory Z: How American business can meet the Japanese challenge*. Reading, MA: Addison-Wesley.

Ouchi began to study the Japanese management style in 1973 and he reported his findings in this 1981 book, one that has become a classic in the Culture theory literature. He concluded that the Japanese model exhibits three characteristics that American firms do not: subtlety, intimacy, and trust. These characteristics emerge from practices that are dramatically different from those in Western organizations. Japanese firms, for example, often hire employees for life, they are slow to promote, and they expose workers to a wide variety of skills.

Schein, E. H. (1992). *Organizational culture and leadership* (2nd ed.). San Francisco: Jossey-Bass.

Edgar Schein establishes the theoretical framework for Culture theory and relates it to leadership in this book. He argues that culture analysis illuminates subculture behavior within an organization, that such analysis is necessary for management across national and ethnic boundaries, that it is necessary if we are to understand how new technologies affect organizations, and that it is necessary if we are to effectively overcome resistance to change.

Sergiovanni, T. J. (1992). *Moral leadership: Getting to the heart of school improvement*. San Francisco: Jossey-Bass.

Sergiovanni argues that educators understand the need for instructional leaders in schools, particularly troubled schools, but rarely go the next step and ask what kind of leader is needed. Too often, the leader simply perpetuates, or even exacerbates, an existing problem with forceful leadership. Instead, schools need substitutes for leadership. By this he means that teachers should be inculcated with a sense of self-sacrifice, duty and obligation, and group membership.

Sergiovanni, T. J. (2000). *The lifeworld of leadership: Creating culture, community, and personal meaning in our schools*. San Francisco: Jossey-Bass.

In this book, Sergiovanni extends his earlier works into a discussion of systemsworld and lifeworld. Systemsworld, he argues, refers to standardized practices that regulate our lives. Lifeworld is a world of culture, meaning, and significance. The systemsworld, he continues, should serve the needs of the lifeworld.

References

Anderson, J. C., Rungtusanatham, M., & Schroeder, R. G. (1994). A theory of quality management underlying the Deming management method. *Academy of Management Review, 19*, 472–509.

Barnard, C. I. (1938). *The functions of the executive*. Cambridge, MA: Harvard University Press.

Bennis, W., & Nanus, B. (1985). *Leaders: The strategies for taking charge*. New York: Harper & Row.

Burns, J. M. (1978). *Leadership*. New York: Harper & Row.

Deal, T. E., & Peterson, K. D. (1991). *The principal's role in shaping school culture*. Washington, DC: U.S. Department of Education, Office of Educational Research and Improvement, Programs for the Improvement of Practice.

Flanigan, J. L., & Marion, R. A. (1999). *The effects of the Accountability Act on the evaluation of South Carolina's principals*. Paper presented at the Southern Regional Council on Educational Administration, Charlotte, NC, November, 1999.

Foucault, M. (1980). *Power/knowledge*. New York: Pantheon.

Habermas, J. (1987). *The theory of communicative actions: Lifeworld and system: A critique of functional reason* (T. McCarthy, Trans.) (Vol. 2). Boston: Beacon Press.

Halpin, A. W., & Croft, D. B. (1962). *The organizational climate of schools*. Chicago: Midwest Administration Center, The University of Chicago.

Homans, G. C. (1950). *The human group*. New York: Harcourt, Brace & World.

Katz, D., & Kahn, R. L. (1966). *The social psychology of organizations*. New York: John Wiley and Sons, Inc.

Kotter, J. P., & Heskett, J. L. (1992). *Corporate culture and performance*. New York: Free Press.

Kunda, G. (1992). *Engineering culture: Control and commitment in a high-tech corporation*. Philadelphia: Temple University Press.

Leavitt, H. J. (1964). *Managerial psychology*. Chicago: University of Chicago Press.

Maslow, A. (1943, July). A theory of human motivation. *Psychological Review*, 370–396.

Maslow, A. H. (1954). *Motivation and personality*. New York: Harper & Row.

Maslow, A. (1968). Some fundamental questions that face the normative social psychologist. *Journal of Humanistic Psychology, 8*(2), 143–153.

O'Reilly, C. A., & Chatman, J. A. (1996). Culture as social control: Corporations, cults, and commitment. In B. M. Staw & L. L. Cummings (Eds.), *Research in Organizational Behavior* (Vol. 18). Greenwich, CT: JAI Press.

Ouchi, W. (1981). *Theory Z: How American business can meet the Japanese challenge*. Reading, MA: Addison-Wesley.

Pettigrew, A. M. (1979). On studying organizational cultures. *Administrative Science Quarterly, 24*, 570–581.

Pfeffer, J. (1994). *Competitive advantage through people: Unleashing the power of the work force*. Boston: Harvard Business School Press.

Pfeffer, J. (1997). *New directions for organization theory: Problems and prospects*. New York: Oxford University Press.

Schein, E. H. (1992). *Organizational culture and leadership* (2nd ed.). San Francisco: Jossey-Bass.

Seiler, J. A. (1967). *Systems analysis in organizational behavior*. Homewood, IL: Richard D. Irwin, Inc., and The Dorsey Press.

Selznick, P. (1949). *TVA and the grass roots*. Berkeley, CA: University of California Press.

Sergiovanni, T. J. (1992). *Moral leadership: Getting to the heart of school improvement*. San Francisco: Jossey-Bass.

Sergiovanni, T. J. (1994). *Building community in schools*. San Francisco: Jossey-Bass.

Sergiovanni, T. J. (2000). *The lifeworld of leadership: Creating culture, community, and personal meaning in our schools*. San Francisco: Jossey-Bass.

Snyder, R. C. (1988). New frames for old: Changing the managerial culture of an aircraft factory. In M. O. Jones, M. D. Moore, & R. C. Snyder (Eds.), *Inside organizations: Understanding the human dimension* (pp. 191–208). Newbury Park, CA: Sage Publications.

Tagiuri, R. (1968). The concept of organizational climate. In R. Tagiuri & G. H. Litwin (Eds.), *Organizational climate: Exploration of a concept*. Boston: Harvard University, Division of Research, Graduate School of Business Management.

Waldman, D. A. (1994). The contributions of total quality management to a theory of work performance. *Academy of Management Reviews, 19*, 510–536.

Westphal, J. D., Gulati, R., & Shortell, S. M. (1997). Customization or conformity: An institutional and network perspective on the content and consequences of TQM adoption. *Administrative Science Quarterly, 42*, 366–394.

CHAPTER 11

Morality and Organizational Control

Critical theory is so different from what you have studied to this point that one might be tempted to label it as a "paradigm shift," in the sense that Thomas Kuhn (1970) intended for that term. Critical theory is anti-positivistic, as have been the theories discussed in the last few chapters, but it adds a unique twist. Critical theory is not about how to control organizations and increase productivity; Critical theory is about what organizational control does to people. Its advocates argue that even the more humanistic approaches to management (such as TQM) subjugate workers to the interests of a ruling elite. Critical theory exposes abuse by elites and explores alternative, more democratic, and egalitarian models of organization.

In this chapter, students will:

- Re-examine the meaning of the notion of effective leadership.
- Critique traditional approaches to leadership effectiveness, including management by objectives, mentoring, and strategic planning, site-based management, and accountability.
- Develop a research proposal to evaluate possible bias against women in education.
- Develop a sense of, and sensitivity to, morality in educational administration.
- Refine their definitions of leadership in education.

The Structuralist Heritage

Critical theory, like Institutionalism (developed in the next chapter), can trace its roots in organizational theory to the Structuralist perspectives of the 1940s and 1950s. Structuralism was introduced in Chapter 4, and was associated with the works of Chester Bernard and Philips Selznick. We observed that Structuralist theory focused on tension between rational and irrational elements of organizations. Structuralist theory also tended to champion the cause of workers, and it is to this argument that we now turn our attention.

According to the Structuralists, tension between management and workers is due in large part to management's interest in control and increased productivity, and such tension leads to feelings of alienation among workers (see Fig. 11.1). Work can be made more pleasant, as the Human Relationists had demonstrated, but tension and alienation can never be eradicated.

Structuralists turned to the works of Karl Marx to help explain this alienation. Workers, according to Marx, are alienated because they own neither the means of their production nor its product. In agrarian societies, farmers own their land, tools, and harvest—the means and products of their labor. Industrialized societies deprive workers of them. Without the means to produce or access to their products, workers have lost control of their own destinies to a cadre of industrial elites who do own the production tools and the products of worker labor.

The challenge for industrial elites, and organizational theory, is to devise strategies for effectively controlling workers and enhancing their productivity. The elites realized rather early that overt, heavy-handed enforcement of the control relationships (such as was advocated by Machine theorists) tended to create problems of rebelliousness, particularly in the form of labor strikes. Consequently, management searched for substitutes to replace workers' lost sense of control and to placate their feelings of alienation. The Human Relations movement was an early example of such an effort. It attempted to replace lost control of tools and product with inexpensive recognition and praise. Human Relationists involved workers in making decisions that, in reality, had little impact on workflow. Coch's and French's 1948 study in a pajama factory, discussed in Chapter 3, described

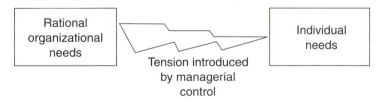

FIGURE 11.1   Structuralists argue that control structures, which are born of rational organizational needs, create tension between managing elites and workers. The result is subjugation of workers.

workers who were involved in decisions about piece rate but who were given no real choice as to whether changes would occur, for example. While such efforts might make the worker's day a bit more pleasant, it could never really overcome the inequities that underlay industrial society.

> By providing an unrealistic "happy" picture, by viewing the factory as a family rather than as a power struggle among groups with some conflict in values and interests as well as some shared ones, and by seeing it as a major force of human satisfaction rather than alienation, Human Relations comes to gloss over the realities of work life. (Etzioni, 1964, p. 42)

Human Relations, then, is not so much a strategy for worker inclusion as it is a strategy for manipulating workers. Two Human Relations consultants reported a story in a 1956 book for managers (quoted in Etzioni, 1964) in which they unwittingly underscore this point:

> The president of an organization said, "Do you mean to tell me a stock boy can help me manage my business?" It is certainly not impossible that the stock boy could give the president some ideas, but the president is thinking of the stock boy sitting on the board of directors. This is not intended, and anyway the stock boy would be extremely uncomfortable. But a visit with the stock boy and some of his fellow workers for an exchange of opinions and experience *would give the president some ideas of how to manage the stock boys* (italics added; Jennings & Jennings, 1956, p. 81).

Clearly the understanding and intent conveyed by these consultants is one of manipulation rather than inclusion. The method in their madness was control. As they said in the last sentence of the above quote, the visit with the stock boys would give the president some idea how to manage them, not how to involve them. The authors might also have added that a visit would provide the president an effective platform for implanting organizational goals into workers' beliefs system, thus reducing, in the president's favor, discrepancies between rational and irrational systems.

The basic ideas underlying Structuralist theory were revived in the 1970s as Critical theory. Critical theory, however, added a rather liberal political agenda to these basic premises. This is not surprising, given the political mood in Western society during the 1960s and 1970s. During these years, people were concerned about alleged excesses among governmental entities, excesses that were exemplified by the Watergate break-in and the war in Vietnam. This was the time that the large baby boomer generation came of age, and youth tends to be somewhat liberal in its political leanings. Critical theory, with its emphasis on the rights of the exploited and downtrodden, was a natural fit for this generation.

Critical theory has remained somewhat on the fringe of organizational theory because of this radical leaning and because of its "in-your-face" challenge to the status quo, however. Its in-your-face personality has been its own worst enemy, preventing it from achieving its intent. "Eschewing a strategy of co-optation or even coexistence, some variants of Critical theory demand different forms of theory and empirical analysis—qualitative, interpretive work as contrasted with quantitative analysis, as one instance" (Pfeffer, 1997, p. 188).

In the late 1990s, however, Critical theorists found a powerful ally. The prestigious journal, *Administrative Science Quarterly,* devoted its entire June, 1998, issue to this subject, thus reflecting a growing interest in Critical theory among scholars. This special edition of the journal also reflected an interest among academics in how organizations are controlled and in the impact of control mechanisms on the quality of life. As Christine Oliver, editor of *ASQ,* wrote in her "From the Editor" introduction to the June, 1998, issue, "The study of organizational control has a long history in administrative science and yet the need to examine the processes and implications of this phenomenon has never been greater."

Educators are in the front lines of social battles over racism, sexism, and other manifestations of prejudice in our society. We struggle with state and local control over the classroom, control that seems to many to have become increasingly insistent over the last two decades. Thus, whether or not we agree with the political agendas that haunt Critical theory, it is important that we come to terms with the issues it raises.

ASSUMPTIONS UNDERLYING THE CRITICAL THEORY PERSPECTIVE

As you have gathered by now, a core theme of Critical theory has to do with power and control and their deleterious effects on workers. All the theories discussed up to this point deal with control and how it can benefit efficiency, productivity, and effectiveness. At their naked core, however, they are about how to control workers and wring profits out of them. Ultimately then, according to Critical theorists, organizational theory serves the interests of those who own profits rather than those who produce those profits. As Jermier (1982) has argued,

> . . . most of the undesirable features of modern capitalistic society are not mentioned by organizational theorists, presenting the appearance of value neutrality, but in actuality masking a politically conservative bias. This compromises the social function of the field to the point where organizational theory serves primarily the dominant interest of capital, rather than society at large. (p. 204)

Organizational theory, from this perspective, is about how owners of the tools and the profits can establish, maintain, and enhance their elite position in society. However, as we shall see, the ultimate goal of the elites is not so much profit (if one is a billionaire, what is an extra million or two?); rather, it is power for power's sake.

ROUNDTABLE

To this point, organizational theory has been based on the assumption that "effective" leadership means getting the job done well. How might a Critical theorist define effectiveness? What implications might this have for your evolving definition of leadership?

Control and Efficiency

The dominant assumption behind most theories of organization is that organizational activities are, and should be, devoted to the enhancement of efficiency and effectiveness. Culture theory, for example, states its premise as one of increased effectiveness by means of strong cultures and involved participants. As William Ouchi (1981) put it, Theory Z (his variation of Culture theory) "suggests that involved workers are the key to increased productivity" (p. 4).

Critical theorists do not dispute the importance of profits, but argue that profits play second fiddle to power. Indeed, the desire for power is so strong that elites would even sacrifice productivity for it (this is called the power preference). As Pfeffer (1997) stated, "control, not efficiency, is the objective of organizing arrangements and . . . when there are trade-offs involved, efficiency concerns are frequently subservient to the achievement of control over the labor process" (p. 180).

Evidence of this falls into four categories (Pfeffer, 1997):

1. Although democratic group-based organizations have a track record of increased productivity, this strategy is less widespread than one might expect given its benefits; forms that involve fundamental realignment of power are even less widespread. Furthermore, where democratic strategies are said to be implemented, they often fail to extend real power to workers, despite claims to the contrary. I once had a discussion with a teacher that illustrates this point. Her school had implemented a policy-mandated, site-based management program and she was a member of the school's budget committee. Her principal told the group that they had plenary control over the allocation of money in the school. After some discussion, this teacher asked the principal, "What would you do if we allocated money to something with which you disagreed?" Without even a pause he replied, "I would overrule it." This story should resonate with most educators. The principal's rationalization was one that is heard frequently: he is ultimately responsible for everything that goes on within the school and must, consequently, maintain veto power. Perhaps this principal did not trust his teachers, as is implied by his response; more likely, however, the principal was simply unwilling to relinquish discretionary power, despite the fact that doing so likely would have benefited the school and made his job easier.

2. Critical theorists cite, as further support of the preeminence of power, evidence that managers seek to extend their control over the labor process even when there is no compelling reason to do so. As Dogbert, the evil consultant in the cartoon strip "Dilbert," put it, "Management is like an organism that needs to survive and grow. Employees are your fertilizer." They point in particular to resistance among the power elite to unionization despite evidence of many positive and few negative effects of unionization on productivity (Freeman & Medoff, 1984).

3. An inordinate amount of money is dedicated to control mechanisms. Many businesses now invest heavily in surveillance equipment, for example. In education, large portions of a school district's budget are allocated to central office and school-level administration (Carroll, 1982; Geske, 1983), despite

evidence of neutral or even negative returns on administrative expenditures for student achievement (Flanigan, Marion, & Richardson, 1996).

4. Finally, Critical theorists point to efforts by controlling elites to deskill workers and transfer those skills to management. Knowledge is a source of power, and those who possess it can resist subordination. The knowledge that university professors possess is so complex and in such demand that they can enjoy a significant level of autonomy and self-governing power—despite the fact that they typically operate within a bureaucratic structure. K-12 teachers likewise enjoy a certain amount of autonomy, particularly with instructional strategies. This autonomy has been assailed in recent years, however, by legislative actions of school boards and state lawmakers that mandate skill expectations and classroom instructional activity. Perhaps the best example of this is competency-based education, in which classroom instruction is based on results obtained by students on criterion-referenced tests. Criterion-referenced tests measure a student's performance on a set of clearly defined objectives. In competency-based education, teachers use such tests to identify weaknesses of individual students and tailor instruction to address those weaknesses. From the perspective of Critical theory, this reduces education to a small set of skills that anyone—educator and lay person—can master. It reduces the significant complexities of instruction and curriculum to a handful of measurable objectives—it ignores the art of teaching and defines it instead as a science (and a rather simple science at that). Such simplification reduces the lay person's dependence on professional expertise—teaching is deskilled—and control over the classroom is transferred from the professional to the controlling elite who mandated the competency-based approach. A variation on this involves control over discretion and autonomy rather than control over expertise. Ruling elites control teachers' autonomy by controlling, among other things, their time (with time-on-task regulations or through control of scheduling), curriculum (with curriculum guides), access to resources, and by limiting library holdings (banning books).

The Velvet Glove of Control

Critical theorists observe that management strategies have become so sophisticated in recent decades that subordinates are dominated and oppressed without realizing what is happening to them. Jermier (1998) argues that "societies control their members by clothing the iron fist of power in a velvet glove" (p. 236). Pfeffer (1997) adds,

> There is irony in the fact that the Taylorist system, with its emphasis on the analysis of work processes, has been perfected not by separating the planning of the work from its doing, as Taylor had proposed, but rather by having the workers participate in their own control and design their own work processes. (p. 183)

In other words, elites control subordinates by giving them a false sense of self-control—the velvet glove.

Total Quality Management (TQM), which was discussed in the chapter on Culture theory, is a good example of this. TQM focuses on continual improvement of products and processes, and emphasizes empowerment of employees by giving them authority to take action and make decisions. Pfeffer (1997) argued that "because workers are involved in a process of continually improving (increasing the productivity) of their own jobs, there is a much more complete form of control achieved than in a more traditional hierarchy" (p. 183). TQM seeks to infuse subordinates with the goals of the organization (to create what Chester Barnard, 1938, called a moral imperative for organizational goals) and then allow workers to control their own progress toward those goals. This strategy controls the minds of workers rather than directly controlling their behaviors; but, of course, by controlling the mind, one indirectly controls the behavior. Perhaps you have been in manufacturing plants where the aphorisms of TQM are displayed on walls with raised bronze lettering or framed plaques. This is salesmanship in which the preferences of elites are being sold to workers. Like the pajama factory workers in the Coch and French (1948) study discussed previously, workers are led to believe they are real participants in the organizational function when, in actuality, they are merely serving goals that are sold to them by elites.

Social Class

Perhaps you have wondered, as have Critical theorists, why it is often the administrators, rather than the talented or the intelligent, that profit in our society. In higher education, professional expertise is the core competency of the university, but it is not unusual for non-academic university administrators to make higher salaries than many of the professors in that school. Authors typically receive only 10 to 15% of the sale price of their work. Researchers who produce life-saving drugs profit relatively little compared to the profits received by the administrators who market those drugs. This is not to say that these professionals are always poorly paid; it is rather to say that the big bucks tend to go to ruling elites who exploit the labors of highly skilled people. The Einsteins of the world are not always the people who benefit from their own brilliance; rather, profits go to a class of elites who have managed to establish control over the products of brilliance. They do so by controlling the tools with which brilliance expresses itself, and by controlling the infrastructure that distributes the products of brilliance.

This suggests, and Critical theorists propose, that capitalism creates class-based societies in which workers are exploited by elites, despite rhetoric about democracy and egalitarianism. Critical theorists claim further that elites often collude to propagate their own corporate ends. They may conspire, for example, to control school boards, political candidates, and other such legislative entities. Some years ago, a man in my hometown ran for a position on the school board. Shortly after announcing his candidacy, he was phoned by a local physician who "summoned" this gentleman to appear before him for an interview. The candidate realized that this physician was an important power broker in our town. The candidate was something of an individualist who was not easily controlled, thus he did not "pass muster" before his interrogator. He placed seventh out of nine candidates for the three school board positions in the subsequent election. He had failed to solicit the support and significant infrastructure of the ruling elite. We refer to such power groups as "political machines," and there are numerous examples in political history—the Daley machine in Chicago in the mid-20th century, for example. Critical theorists would refer to them as an elite class that consolidates power through class solidarity.

These ruling classes function within, and by means of, organizations as well. Palmer (1983) argues that organizations are the agents of elites and that they use interlocking directorates to link their interests. Whitt (1980) found similar solidarity within the elite class in a study of referenda in California regarding five transportation issues in the 1960s and 1970s. He observed that "even though there is good reason to expect that, for each issue, some companies would favor it and some would oppose it, the money in every case is virtually *all on one side or the other of the issue*" (pp. 105–106).

ROUNDTABLE

Ruling class solidarity arguments have been criticized: some, for example, point to hostile takeovers of organizations as evidence that the ruling class is not as unified as some Critical theorists believe. What other arguments or personal experiences can you provide to support or contradict the class solidarity argument? ▪

Mistreatment

Mistreatment is the inevitable result of the exploitation by ruling elites of workers. Karl Marx wrote of it in economic terms, arguing that the separation of workers from the means and profits of their production degrades individuals, subjects them to petty totalitarian control by business elites, and converts them into a miserable extension of organizational machines (Marx, 1972). Modern-day Marxists have expanded this concept beyond Marx's more limited economic model to include societal oppression in general. Thus, they write of oppression not only of laborers, but also of women, minority races, handicapped individuals, and the poor as well.

Knowledge Is Not Neutral

Critical theorists argue that ruling elites consolidate their power in part by controlling the commerce of knowledge. Knowledge, they argue, cannot be neutral; all scientific endeavors serve some prejudices or interests. A survey of public attitudes toward education that asks about approval of sex education curricula, while neutral about attitudes on this issue (assuming the question is asked in a neutral way) expresses a bias by the very fact that it asks this question and does not ask other possible questions. It suffers the dual sins of commission and omission: commission because it states indirectly that sex education is of sufficient importance to be included in the survey; omission because it states indirectly that unasked questions are not sufficiently important to be included. If the survey did not ask, for example, whether respondents feel that school curricula are oriented toward the male experience rather than the female experience, then it implies that this issue is not worthy of exploration. Critical theorists do not suggest by such criticism that surveys and research in general should not be conducted; rather, they suggest simply that all scientific endeavors reflect the same type of prejudice.

This being true, the only way that scientists can honestly deal with it is to express their biases up front and openly advocate those biases. If researchers are advocates of teacher rights, then they should admit that bias and should openly seek to support that position with their research. Carol Shakeshaft and Irene Nowell (1984) put it this way: "It is important to understand that all research reflects particular world views . . . . Of paramount importance is the ability to recognize bias and explain the methods and findings in ways that make it unmistakably clear to the consumer just what that bias is" (p. 188).

This of course raises the question: How can one be objective yet openly express a bias? Critical theorists deal with objectivity in two ways (Jermier, 1998). First, they propose that objectivity is served by debate and critique. When a researcher publishes a paper or presents one at a conference, colleagues subject his or her work to debate. Only well-constructed, defensible arguments will survive. Second, Critical theorists suggest that objectivity is served by efforts to identify elements of reality that traditional research overlooks. Traditional research, they argue, focuses only on the "party line" of the elite. Such research lacks objectivity because it fails to fully reflect the rich diversity of life. Such issues as gender oppression are realities of life that are rarely explored by traditional researchers. Shakeshaft and Nowell (1984) argued, for example, that Abraham Maslow (whose hierarchy of needs was discussed in Chapter 3, as was Shakeshaft's critique of the hierarchy) failed to account for the feminine experience in deriving his famous hypothesis. Critical theorists attempt to identify and address such omissions, thus bringing greater reality (and resultant objectivity) to social study.

Similarly, the words and language structures that we use in inquiry influence our sense of reality and objectivity, and serve to maintain the control of one group by another. Women were once trapped in subservient roles by terms such as "girls" and "Mrs.," each of which conveyed a sense of inferior or secondary relationships. Men, by contrast, were not called "boys" (unless they were Black, in which case the term served another of society's prejudices), and "Mr." reflects nothing about marital status.

Since science inevitably serves someone's prejudice, and perceptions of reality are inevitably dominated by language anyhow, there can be no universal or global theories that describe social behavior. That is, theory is not reality; rather, it is the product of prejudices and the agendas of those in control. Noted postmodern philosopher Michel Foucault summarized this by referring to the "inhibiting effect of global, totalitarian theories." He spoke of the idiographic nature of knowledge by labeling it as "perspectival, requiring multiple viewpoints to interpret a heterogeneous reality" (see Eve, Horsfall, & Lee, 1997, p.10). Theory, from this perspective, serves little use because it is grounded in one's perspective rather than in absolute reality.

ROUNDTABLE

A devil's advocate would argue that the research license this perspective extends to Critical theorists is unconscionable. It would seem to endorse irresponsible editorializing in the name of science and encourage spurious claims that are not supported by theoretical premise. In the absence of theoretical control, it could unshackle a witch hunt mentality that permits researchers to pursue only the moralisms of the majority (a problem with which we struggle even with theoretical controls). Researchers would be hesitant to do research that might contradict orthodoxy about a favored "suppressed class," for example. That is, one might argue, research based on morality throws open the doorways to moral intolerance. Our current system may provide imperfect control over bias, but it is better than the indirect controls of Critical theory. Take sides and debate the issue. Should researchers openly express and pursue their biases because, ultimately, they can't be avoided, or should they try to limit their impulses with theory-based research? You will find that the issues are complex and difficult to resolve. ∎

CRITICAL THEORY AND TRADITIONAL LEADERSHIP STRATEGIES

Critical theorists have critiqued a number of traditional management strategies. The strategies include management by objectives (MBO), mentoring, strategic planning, empowerment and team-based decision making, and enhanced technology. Five themes can be identified in these critiques (see Fig. 11.2). Critiques of MBO have argued that managers manipulate personal worldviews. Discussions of mentoring describe how guided self-examination fosters compliance. Strategic planning is seen as a way to control language and reality. Team-based decisions enable co-optation because management controls the goals that guide

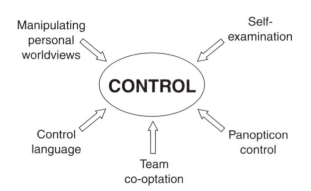

FIGURE 11.2   Subtle control strategies in modern organizations.

team behavior. Finally, enhanced technology extends the threat of surveillance with minimal actual surveillance.

Management by Objectives

Management-by-objective strategies require workers to formulate individual work objectives, with input from their administrators, at the beginning of an evaluation cycle. At the end of that cycle, workers report the degree to which objectives were achieved, and their performance evaluations are based on their level of success. Critical theorists argue that MBO is simply a ruse for advancing the power preferences of managers. Workers are not really in control of their goals because objectives must meet the approval of administrators who veto goals not in line with managerial preferences. Workers are led to feel they are in control, however, thus they willingly march to the corporate drumbeat.

MBO, according to critical theorists Mark Covaleski, Mart Dirsmith, James Heian, and Sajay Samuel (1998), objectifies and transforms the individual into a manageable and self-managing subject. With management strategies like MBO, "Power seeps into the very grain of individuals, reaches right into their bodies, creates their gestures, their posture, what they say, how they learn to live and work with the other people" (Foucault, 1979, p. 28). Managers accomplish this by shaping workers' worldviews (and, consequently, their goals) around organizationally endorsed norms. Worldviews are shaped by the knowledge that others are formally and informally watching them and judging them against these norms. As Covaleski and his colleagues (1998) put it, "Writing, documentation, marking, and notation are the media by which subjects are objectified, individualized, rendered visible, and subjected to the norm" (p. 297). According to Foucault, as quoted in Covaleski (1998, p. 297),

> . . . the judges of normality are present everywhere. We're in the society of the teacher-judge, the doctor-judge . . . it is on them that the universal reign of the normative is based; and each individual, wherever he may find himself, subjects to it his body, his gestures, his behavior, his attitudes, his achievements. (Foucault, 1979, p. 304)

Stated a bit differently, MBO produces a feeling among workers that their very sense of worth is judged against corporate norms. It creates something of an organizational big brother ambiance that says, "The organization is the arbiter of real and unreal, good and bad. If you don't conform to this worldview, you are flawed, an outsider." This whole idea is also akin to the highway rat packs discussed at the beginning of Chapter 10: the interactive dynamics of that phenomenon take over an individual's psyche and make him or her part of something bigger. From the Critical theorist's perspective, however, it is the ruling elite, using strategies such as MBO, that controls the perceptions that are processed by such interactive dynamics. The sense of being judged tends to permeate actors' psyches, thus colonizing their worldview and even their sense of self.

A school principal who values dedication and long hours, for example, will tend to evaluate teachers consciously and subconsciously against this norm. He or she will subtly reward teachers who meet expectations regarding dedication level with friendship and respect; those who don't meet expectations will find these rewards withheld. This principal will expect dedication to be reflected in MBO goals, and will document teachers' progress relative to those aspirations. He or she might summarize end-of-year evaluations with statements such as, "You rarely left before 5 p.m.; I appreciate your dedication," or "I noticed you get antsy when teachers meetings are long; you need to show more commitment to the things we're trying to accomplish in those meetings." These teachers will feel that they are being watched and that their behaviors are constantly being evaluated against the norm of dedication. They are forever looking over their shoulder, so to speak, and this mentality will permeate and affect their behaviors. This leads to self-compliance, not compliance associated with force but rather compliance that comes from the cumulative impact that a constant sense of being watched brings.

Mentoring

In educational mentoring, novice or weak teachers are paired with experienced, strong teachers who guide and monitor their progress. Such mentors may be, but usually are not, responsible for formal, end-of-year evaluation.

Mentoring, according to Covaleski and his colleagues (1998), creates pressures similar to those created by MBO, but adds another important dimension: self-examination. The process is akin to confession, which requires "that the inner truths of one's self be both discovered through self-examination and expressed outwardly through speech so as to affirm and transform oneself" (Covaleski et al., 1998, p. 297). With mentoring, such self-examination is guided by an incumbent who has bought into the corporate line and who will protect corporate preferences. The mentored individual is led by this mentor in self-reflection about how he or she is progressing relative to corporate expectations. A new teacher, for example, may have learned highly effective techniques in college for teaching reading. The teacher's mentor, however, will not necessarily lead self-reflection about how well the individual is teaching reading per se; rather, the mentor will encourage reflection about how well the novice is teaching reading the way the district expects it to be taught. Thus, the new teacher is converted from a professional individual into a district clone.

Strategic Planning

Strategic planning is a rational approach to planned change. Jerald Hage (1980) has identified four stages in the change process that are useful for describing strategic planning: *evaluation* (the identification of performance gaps); *initiation* (identification of radical solutions for the performance gap); *implementation;* and *routinization* of the implemented solutions. Strategic planning, which is not unlike the Dewey decision-making process discussed in Chapter 2, is described by Porter (1980) as an important and powerful force for organizational change, and by Ansoff (1965) as an effective mechanism for exercising direct control of organizations through established goals.

Critical theorists argue that strategic planning controls organizational behavior by, among other things, controlling the language by which organizational participants define their activities. Strategic planning "provides and sanctions legitimate forms of discourse and language and thus serves as a mechanism of knowledge that produces new understandings of the organization" (Oakes, Townley, & Cooper, 1998, p. 258). Oakes and her colleagues described how this happens using Bourdieu's discussions of field and capital. "Field" is defined as the "totality of relevant actors," and "those organizations that, in the aggregate constitute a recognized area of institutional life: key suppliers, resource and product consumers, regulatory agencies and other organizations that produce similar services or products" (DiMaggio & Powell, 1983, p. 148). "Capital" refers to the primary medium of commerce in a field. In a business organization, the primary medium of commerce is money. The medium of commerce for a museum, however, would logically be culture. In education, the medium of commerce is instruction. Field and capital are interrelated. Fields describe the arena within which conflicts over the nature of capital occur; capital determines the relative power relationships of the members of a field. The education field includes, among other things, teachers and school boards. Teachers might define educational capital in terms of well-rounded, broadly educated students; school boards might define capital in terms of achievement test scores and lowered budgets. The group—teachers or school board—that controls the capital of education will dominate the power relationships in the field.

Strategic planning is a vehicle by which a field's capital is defined, and it does so by controlling the language of goals. The goal, "Students in this district will excel in math and reading achievement," would logically lead to the objective, "The average achievement score of students in this district will be in the top 15% of achievement scores for students in the state within three years." The language of this goal spawns objectives that play to the preferences of school board members. If a goal were, "Students in this district will graduate with skills needed to effectively participate as adults in community life," then a related objective might be, "middle school students will participate at least twice a year in multidisciplinary learning experiences that prepare them for real-life work experiences." The language of this goal plays to the preferences of teachers in this hypothetical district.

More generally, the language of the goals in a strategic planning document influences not only the objectives of the organization but the worldviews, or minds, or participants as well. If teachers can be conditioned to automatically equate education with objective achievement, then their classroom behaviors will be focused on strategies that enhance achievement test scores. School boards can achieve such control over teachers' worldviews and behaviors by conveying appropriate expectations of the strategic plan development process, and by rejecting any school plans that are inconsistent with those expectations. The board members could, of course, develop the strategic plan themselves, thus assuring that it reflects their preferences, but teachers' worldviews are more readily influenced if they themselves go through the process. By doing so, they get a false sense of having controlled the process and are more likely to psychologically commit to the wording generated in the document they produce.

Empowerment and Team-Based, Decentralized Decision Making

Team-based, decentralized decision making and empowerment is a management strategy in whcih workers are given increased control over production decisions. It is generally based on the assumption that any normal human would welcome the opportunity to assume greater control over his or her work and will consequently work more effectively if given such control. Popular forms of this strategy include Total Quality Management, Theory Z, and Transformational Leadership, all of which we examined in the chapter on Culture theory. In education we call it "site-based management." Ezzamel and Willmott (1988), drawing from the works of Katzenbach and Smith (1993) and Marchington (1992), argued that "Teamwork is currently being championed as a way of replacing inflexible, dehumanizing, bureaucratic mechanisms with more humanistic, involving, culture-ideological methods of coordinating productive activity" (p. 358).

Consistent with Chester Barnard's arguments about moral imperatives, team-based management strategies seek to "re-align individual motivation with organizational rationality" (Mueller, 1994, p. 386). That is, they seek to convert workers' attitudes, beliefs, and activities in ways that make them more productive and that align them with organizational goals and managerial preferences (organizational rationality). Consequently, while team-based management is, on the surface, empowering and sensitive to worker needs, it ultimately serves instead the control preferences of owners and managers. The bone that this strategy tosses to workers is rather large, but it is still a bone, according to Critical theorists. As Ezzamel put it,

> . . . teamwork practices can disempower employees by strengthening managerial control and intensifying work activities in the name of progress and the more effective management of "human resources". . . . Teamwork can conceal or dissemble a variety of unsavory features of work organization, including coercion masquerading as empowerment and the camouflaging of managerial expediency in the rhetorics of "clannism" and humanization. (pp. 358–359; see also Knights & Willmott, 1987)

Critical theorists have concluded that team-based management strategies are effective at increasing productivity, but argue that they may do so at the expense of worker morale and level of stress—hence, they are exploitative. Ezzamel and Willmott argue that exploitation may not only oppress, it may also alter workers self-concepts and personal preferences. Not all workers see themselves in a "them-us" struggle with management. They may not really care about control and who has it. They may, however, take pride in being efficient or in producing a quality product, or they may find friendships with other workers to be rewarding. These preferences can be disrupted by team-based decision making.

Ezzamel and Willmott examined the implementation of team-based management in a British manufacturing plant. The plant had previously been organized around a piece-rate strategy in which machinists at the plant were paid according to their individual performances. Under the new plan, workers were organized into small teams and bonuses were given to all team members on days when the team exceeded by a certain percentage its established average production quota. This placed pressure on individuals who preferred to work at a "normal" rate (perhaps they had no family commitments or other needs that would make the bonus lucrative). It placed those who wanted the bonus and who otherwise prided themselves in the speed at which they could work in the uncomfortable position of having to cajole slower working machinists. Workers were simultaneously deprived of reward for personal effectiveness and at the same time placed in a conflictive relationship with friends. They were deprived of the very things that made work rewarding for them.

RESEARCH TOPIC

Site-based management in education is popular because it at least appears to return decision-making power from legislative bodies to teaching professionals. It is also popular because of the increased productivity experienced by businesses that adopt such strategies: it is assumed that similar returns will accrue to education. Proponents argue that teachers desire greater control over the management of their schools, that greater control will lead to increased commitment, and that increased commitment will translate into better education. Ezzamel and Willmott did indeed find increased productivity in their study of garment workers, but found also that machinists did not necessarily desire greater control and that the new strategy frustrated basic worker preferences and placed increased pressure on their performance. An interesting study could look at similar dynamics in an educational setting. One might ask questions such as: Does site-based decision making improve teacher commitment and productivity? Do teachers welcome increased managerial control? Does site-based management disrupt other teacher preferences? Does site-based management truly relinquish control to teachers or does it merely give the appearance of decentralized control?

Ezzamel and Willmott found that fiscal accounting systems in place at the plant they examined played an important role in production control. The team-based strategy was expected to return a fiscal profit to the organization; indeed, the new organizational pattern was implemented not because of humanistic concerns for workers, but rather because stakeholders in the organization were alarmed by decreased profitability and were demanding dramatic actions to address the problem. Management responded by distancing themselves from the decision-making process, but in reality they were able to maintain control over worker behavior through the bonus system. The bonus system left the workers with few real options regarding the nature of their work, and placed greater stress on their performance than had been the case under the old system.

By controlling the ultimate goals of the work group (bonuses and productivity), management controlled what Bourdieu (1993) called "the commerce or capital of the organization" (we discussed this a little earlier in this chapter). Such control appeared to be more complete under team-based management than it had been under the old piece-rate strategy. At least under the old strategy, there was room for commerce in friendship and workmanship; the new strategy assailed that commerce had strengthened the primacy of the fiscal commerce.

RESEARCH TOPIC

Investigate whether accountability plans and testing programs (or some similar program) have a similar effect in education—do they represent a struggle over control of educational capital? To conduct this study, you will need to identify the commerces that teachers in the target research organization prefer, and describe how accountability or testing programs alter those preferences. How does this transform how and what students are taught? This research might be associated with the site-based research topic suggested a few paragraphs ago (accountability or something similar may accompany site-based management). ■

Enhanced Technology

Critical theorists suggest that a primary question of modern management is: How do you achieve control without appearing to control (Senge, 1990; Sewell, 1998)? Foucault has argued that domination is enforced through language and symbols. He also proposes that self-control among workers can be enforced through overt and covert surveillance (Foucault, 1977).

Foucault illustrates his point with a story about the design of prisons in the 18th century. Prisoners were placed in cells that were arranged in a circle around a central guard tower (Bentham, 1995). Guards in these prisons were able to observe prisoners without themselves being seen. One or two guards could not observe all the prisoners all the time, but this was not a problem because the prisoners never knew when they might be viewed. They behaved not because they were being watched, but rather because they knew they *might* be watched. They never knew whether deviant behavior would be punished, so they learned to play it safe and behave all the time. Foucault referred to this as "panopticon." We discussed this in the earlier section on management by objectives, but didn't give it a label at that time.

Modern forms of surveillance function on the panopticon principle. Technology provides managers with a wide range of highly sophisticated surveillance options. These include video cameras, audio monitoring of telephone transactions, the ability to track Internet usage, monitoring keystroke speed of data entry personnel, random drug tests, and electronic monitoring of speed and mileage on trucks and buses. Some school districts, for example, have placed dummy video cameras on their school buses; these dummies are replaced periodically with real cameras. Students never know when they are being videotaped; thus, the camera is a constant threat to them.

Less obvious forms of panopticon surveillance are also available. Standardized test results, and the implications for reputation associated with poor scores, are yearly threats hanging over educators. The threat of surprise visits from administrators will tend to keep people in line, as will the fear that a colleague will report deviancy. All these threats foster the internalization of behavior, and with internalization or self-control comes eventual acceptance of expected behavior as normative. If, for example, authorities claim that a given behavior is appropriate for teachers, and if they occasionally monitor for compliance, then many teachers will eventually internalize that behavior and even come to expect it of others. A principal may use his or her legalistic and legitimate authority to label business-like dress as proper and right for teachers. This declaration carries authority, particularly if the principal is respected, for respect makes one something of an arbiter of good and bad, right and wrong. That is, such a person has the capacity to manipulate the language of norms, and consequently can shape perceptions of reality. Further, teachers know that they are being watched by this principal and that failure to dress as expected could lead to sanctions. These forces are conditions for eventual, if not immediate, acceptance and internalization of the dress norm. Further, teachers will not only expect it of themselves, but will expect it of each other, thus bringing social pressure—yet another form of panopticon surveillance—to bear on deviancy (Sewell, 1998, differentiates between vertical surveillance that is initiated by superiors, such as video cameras on school buses, and horizontal surveillance, referring to peer pressure and peer monitoring).

As of 1990, more than 10 million workers in the United States were subject to some form of electronic performance surveillance (Pfeffer, 1997). Such surveillance covers not only the performance of low-skilled workers but high-skilled workers as well. Patterns of prescription-writing by physicians can be tracked, as can teacher, school, and district-level performance on student achievement and other such issues. In 2000, for example, Georgia was developing a policy for monitoring discipline activities of teachers and requiring that teachers attend classes on discipline if they seek to remove two students from their classrooms within a year.

Pfeffer (1997) cites evidence that electronic performance monitoring increases stress, decreases job satisfaction, increases feelings of social alienation, and increases the tendency to believe that the quantity of work is more important than quality. He further cites evidence that computer monitoring increases performance on simple tasks but decreases performance on complex tasks. He proposes that the feeling of control electronic surveillance gives to managers is deemed more important to them than the problems it raises, however. This is consistent with arguments earlier in this chapter that control is more important to managing elites than profits, and that, given a choice between the two, managers will sacrifice profits before control.

 ## ROUNDTABLE

Are such control strategies used by educational administrators (consciously or subconsciously) to perpetuate subtle forms of racial or gender bias? Explain. Identify administrative activities that are motivated more by the desire to control than by the desire to achieve goals. Outline personal strategies for controlling these impulses.

FEMINIST CRITICAL THEORY

The Critical perspectives discussed to this point have focused on domination of the powerless, but there are other forms of discrimination as well. One major Critical theory tradition focuses on the subjugation of females by a male-dominated world. We have already covered examples of this argument. In Chapter 3, we looked at Shakeshaft and Nowell's critique of Maslow's hierarchy of needs, and in Chapter 5, we examined their critique of Getzels' and Guba's model of social systems. The basic thrust of their arguments regarding these important models of organization is that researchers ignored the feminine perspective. Shakeshaft and Nowell label such research as "androcentric," defined as the

> . . . elevation of the masculine to the level of the universal and the ideal; it is an honoring of men and the male principal above women and the female. This perception creates a belief in male superiority and a value system in which female values, experiences, and behaviors are viewed as inferior. Viewing the world through this male lens has not only affected theories in the social sciences, but has shaped reality in organizational behavior theories as well. (1984, pp. 187–188)

According to Critical theorists, the issue of power between genders is never neutral. Even studies that do not mention gender are guilty—the very omission of gender from an analysis contributes to the domination of women by men. As Dorothy Smith (1978) wrote,

> . . . We are talking about the consequences of women's exclusion from a full share in the making of what becomes treated as our culture. We are talking about the consequences of a silence, an absence, a non-presence. What is there—spoken, sung, written, . . .—and treated as general, universal, unrelated to a particular position or a particular sex as its source and standpoint, is in fact partial, limited, located in a particular position, and permeated by special interests and concerns. (p. 283)

A large body of work by feminine Critical theorists has addressed the stereotyping of gender roles in our society. Such stereotyping has locked women into less prestigious jobs, prevented them from rising to positions of authority and power, and has even tended to label jobs dominated by women as less prestigious than those dominated by men. In 1991, several colleagues and I performed (but did not publish) a secondary analysis of survey data we had collected from school principals in South Carolina, and found that women dominated most of the new principal positions in the state (there were more women with five or fewer years experience than men). However, men dominated the new high school positions; the number of new hires in middle schools was about evenly divided between men and women, and the large majority of new hires in elementary school was female. High school principalships on average carry higher salaries than do elementary principalships, and at least in some quarters the high school position is more prestigious than the elementary one. In fairness, we were unable to control for experience in our analysis—males may have had more administrative experience and were consequently more competitive for the high school positions. If so, however, this would raise the question of why women had only recently been allowed to gain such experience. How ever we interpreted it, our data pointed to the previous absence of women in school management and the current (as of 1991) exclusion of women from more prestigious and higher paying administrative positions. On a more positive side, our results suggested that this inequity may be changing.

Feminine theorists have also explored inequities in pay between men and women. A number of studies have found that, after controlling for such things as years of service and educational background, women are less likely to have high-paying jobs than are men. Further, women tend to make lower salaries than men at the same hierarchical level (Feber & Kordick, 1978; Fox, 1985). Pfeffer and Davis-Blake (1987) reported that

> . . . salaries for both male and female college administrators decreased as the proportion of women in administrative positions in a given college or university increased and that in colleges and universities that paid less, the proportion of women administrators increased over time more than in settings in which pay was higher. The explanation was that women's work was socially devalued, and it had become taken for granted or institutionalized to pay less for "women's jobs." (Pfeffer, 1997, p. 187)

Feminine theorists have criticized the divide in organizational theory between organizational life and family life or other relationships. Part of Carol Shakeshaft and Irene Nowell's critique of Maslow's hierarchy of needs (1984) was based on this issue. Women, they argue, accord greater importance to affiliation and attachment than do men, and such need demands a different perspective of motivation than would be required for male counterparts.

> The effect of [Maslow's] conceptualization of the levels of needs which motivate people lead women to believe that their self-actualization is prescribed by sex-role fulfillment or sex-role denial; it leads men to devalue the experiences of hearth and home; and it denies both sexes participation in the full range of human expressions. (1984, p. 194)

The implication of Maslow's writing, they contend, is that women in business can be fulfilled only if they adopt male models of management behavior, and deny their feminine needs.

Feminine theorists call for organizations to be less hierarchical and bureaucratic and to adopt a more consensual style of decision making. Managers, they argue, need to learn to listen to what different constituencies within an organization say they need rather than deciding themselves what is needed. They need to be more receptive to the expression of feelings and emotions, and should respect the family commitments of workers. Martin, Knopff, and Beckman (1998) argue that a feminine-oriented organization would be characterized by egalitarianism, low division of labor, employment based on commitment to feminist agenda, minimal role segregation by gender, participative leadership styles, control by internalized values reflecting feminist ideology, decentralized decision making open to renegotiation, emotional openness, and high concern for private life.

Martin, Knopff, and Beckman (1998) examined the feminist managerial style at the Body Shop International, a large and successful private business. This organization is managed and staffed largely by women; its management style promotes the controlled expression of emotions, what the authors called "bounded emotionality." Bounded emotionality "encourages the expression of a wider range of emotions than is usually condoned in traditional and normative organizations, while stressing the importance of maintaining interpersonally sensitive, variable boundaries between what is felt and what is expressed" (p. 436). The goal is to foster the psychological well-being of workers and their families. The researchers found that Body Shop workers frequently discussed interpersonal issues with coworkers, that emotions emerged naturally but that expression of emotions was tempered by sensitivity to the emotions of others, and that ambiguous or contradictory emotions, values, and tensions were tolerated. Most employees enjoyed a strong sense of being a part of the organizational community. The authors concluded that a feminist-oriented organization is not at all unrealistic.

Emotionality, however, at times led to tensions and the erosion of mutual understanding. Further, there was pressure placed on workers to conform to the ideals of bounded emotionality—manager's performance evaluations were even based in part on demonstrated ability to express emotional empathy and sensitivity—but some employees preferred greater emotional distance and were uncomfortable with this. Further, the organization's survival needs often clashed with its feminist goals. A tendency to expect long hours and high-pressure performance emerged that conflicted with its emphasis on family, for example.

Rebecca Bordt (1998) has examined the structure of nonprofit organizations run by women in New York City. She sought to determine whether such organizations would reflect the goals of feminist theorists. She found that these organizations were different from the bureaucratic structures typically associated with male dominance, but that this difference did not reflect a feminist agenda. Rather, the nonprofit organizations that she examined fell into one of two categories: they were either "pragmatic collectives," which had the look and feel of professional organizations with shared values and autonomy, or they were too small to divide labor to any significant degree. Feminist ideology, Bordt argued, had little to do with the way these organizations were structured. There were, however, interesting differences based on the type of clientele served—nonprofits that served minority populations, for example, were more likely to emphasize networking and coalition-building.

RESEARCH TOPIC

Examine a school with which you are intimately familiar to determine the degree to which its organizational structure and management reflect male-oriented perspectives, and the degree to which female faculty (which typically constitute a large percentage of the faculty in k-12 schools) have influenced or ameliorated the structure and management of that school.

LEADERSHIP AND ORGANIZATIONAL MORALITY

Critical theory is at heart about morality; thus, we should pursue this topic explicitly. Critical theorists argue that social organizations serve an elite class at the expense of a subjugated class, and that women, ethnic minorities, and other such groups are systematically excluded from full and satisfying participation in society. Organizational management is structured for efficient production and for control of subordinates, and is not structured to provide fulfilling work experiences for workers. In effect, Critical theorists charge that elites are immoral and self-serving.

Ethicists and theorists such as Douglas (1995), Duska (1998) and Pfeffer (1997) argue that this assessment may be oversimplified. Ethical and non-ethical behavior exist on two dimensions: an individualistic dimension, which focuses on personal or selfish needs; and a corporate dimension, in which individuals accept responsibilities for broader community welfare. The individualistic dimension revolves around personal liberty, or the right of the individual to life, liberty, and property. Self-interest is at the heart of things. This perspective maintains that people make moral decisions based on self-serving preferences. Cooperative activity, where it exists, is not driven by altruism but by the fact that, in the given case, it is in the individual's interest to be cooperative.

Self-serving people will avoid cooperative activities from which they could benefit in the hopes that others will pick up the slack. Economists call this the "free-rider" hypothesis. An individual may choose not to contribute to public radio, for example, believing that he or she can reap the benefit of others' contributions.

The self-serving personality tends to be opportunistic. Williamson (1985) defined opportunism as overtly non-ethical behavior.

> By opportunism I mean self-seeking with guile. This includes but is scarcely limited to more blatant forms, such as lying, stealing, and cheating. Opportunism more often involves subtle forms of deceit. . . . More generally, opportunism refers to the incomplete or distorted disclosure of information, especially to calculated efforts to mislead, distort, disguise, obfuscate, or otherwise confuse . . . (p. 47, as quoted in Douglas, 1995, p. 107)

Opportunists, like the free rider, can benefit only in environments where others are cooperating for common goals, however. If everyone in society were opportunistic, there would be little to exploit, for production requires cooperation. Further, opportunists must be relatively free of group demands in order to profit. Opportunists in highly interdependent relationships—where every individual's profit is a product of the group's well-being—gain nothing, for they steal from themselves (Douglas, 1995). If you steal from those who help you put food on your table, then you ultimately deprive yourself of food.

Critical theorists portray elites as opportunists. They cooperate only to advance the cause of elites against workers, and they serve personal needs at the expense of the needs of the underclass in society. But, ethicists ask, is it really logical to portray the dominant preference of the large number of individuals who occupy power positions in any given society as self-serving? They contend that morality is more complex than this, and that corporate responsibility is an equally, if not more, important force in social systems.

The corporate perspective on moral behavior differs from the selfish, economic model in its core assumptions. As described by Etzioni (1988) and Pfeffer (1997), individuals pursue goals of pleasure *and* they pursue goals of duty or values; that is, they are motivated both by self-interest and by responsibility. Individuals engage in activities that satisfy both (values and pleasure). Most people don't behave for selfish reasons alone; they also behave according to their value systems and their perceived responsibilities for the well-being of others. Teachers, it is commonly understood, don't teach just for money; many teach because they feel called to do so. Values and personal preferences are not mutually exclusive pleasures; each feeds the other. People derive pleasure from giving as well as from receiving.

Pfeffer (1997) offers research evidence that people act according to values and commitment to community rather than for self-interest alone. Barry (1978), for example, reported that 30 to 40% of variation in voting activities can be accounted for by scores on a scale of moral obligation. In a study of political opinions, Sears and Funk (1990) found that only about a quarter of the self-interest terms in a regression equation met even minimum standards of statistical significance, while political values accounted for a significant proportion of the variation in opinions. Hornstein, Masor, and Sole (1971) found that two-thirds of the participants in a study of honesty returned lost contributions to a fictitious institute doing research in medicine. Pfeffer also took exception to the free-ride hypothesis. Quoting Etzioni, he said,

> A large number of experiments, under different conditions, most of them unfavorable to civility, show that people do not take free rides, but paid voluntarily as much as forty percent to sixty percent of what economists figure is due to the public till if the person was not to free ride at all. The main reason: the subjects considered it the "right" or "fair" thing to do. (Etzioni, 1988, p. 59)

Pfeffer concluded, "Social and individual values matter in understanding behavior and are often more powerful predictors than simple conceptions of self-interest" (p. 77).

Pfeffer makes a strong argument that people are basically moral entities motivated in part by self-interest, but in larger measure by concern for others, by values, and by sense of duty to community. Critical theorists, however, argue that elites are motivated by profit and by power, and they pursue these ends by exploiting the powerless. Even seemingly benign management tools, such as empowerment and team responsibility, are felt to serve management at the expense of the worker.

There can be no question that control is an important motivating force in our society, but the implication that control is a consuming force, that elites are motivated exclusively by self-interest and express little or no duty to workers, or that control *prima facie* is evil, is overstating the issue. Even Frederick Taylor, who is perhaps the epitome of elitist excess in Critical theory literature, was concerned about the well-being of workers. As we observed in Chapter 2, Taylor stated in the opening paragraphs of his 1911 book, *Principles of Scientific Management,* "The principal objective of management should be to secure the maximum prosperity for the employer, coupled with the maximum prosperity for each employee" (Taylor, 1911, p. 1). He believed that this was the most important aspect of his entire management philosophy, and he called it a "Mental Revolution" (Wrenge & Greenwood, 1991). Similarly, to reduce the empowerment proposals of Culture theorists or the Situational Leadership proposals of Contingency theorists to a selfish common denominator is to deny the complexity of the human experience and to reduce it to simple base instincts.

The question of organizational morality might better be boiled down to this: How can we assure maximum gratification for all participants (individual and corporate pleasure), and still assure maximum productivity (the capitalistic preference)? We do, after all, live in a capitalistic society, and that model of commerce has served the well-being of nearly all its participants—although granted, to varying extents. Even Critical theorists have been forced to deal with the reality of competition: in the study of the management of the Body Shop by Martin, Knopff, and Beckman (1998) discussed earlier, the feminist agenda was forced to come to grips with the need for financial survival, for example. As ethicist Ronald Duska (1998) has argued, ethical discourse about business

> . . . must take place within the context understandable to business people. For example, if one ignores the context of a capitalist society, one can see advertising as almost universally manipulative, but in the context of capitalism which creates needs, advertising is essential for the growth of the How much better off will the entire society be without the productivity capitalism and advertising spurs? . . . what is needed is a realistic evaluation of the culture of business and the concept of justice that governs it. (p. 715)

Perhaps the Culture theorists of the last chapter, with their emphasis on empowerment and participation, have it more nearly correct than the Critical theorists will admit.

LESSONS FROM CRITICAL THEORY

Even those who feel that Critical theorists have overstated the immorality of traditional organizational theory and Western production strategies must admit the importance of the issues addressed by these theorists. Critical theorists argue that a moral organization must seek to enhance the "good life" of all its employees and must strive to be a responsible member of the world community. Organizational theorists should seek to listen to the needs and experiences of all constituencies, but, as Etzioni argues, they must also seek to understand how these needs and experiences can converge into community rather than how they diverge. Critical theory would suggest that those of us who prepare leaders and organizational researchers should teach these students to be critical of their personal motives—do actions reflect an inner desire to control or do they serve the corporate good of the organizational community, for example? Critical theory encourages us to understand who controls the commerce of education and whether the commerce that we practice is actually good for students and society. Critical theory makes us aware of our subtle and not-so-subtle prejudices. It should certainly make us cautious of our theories, for, as has been argued throughout this book, theory is not reality itself. Even so, well-reasoned theory is a far better guide for understanding, and indeed for moral knowledge development, than is seat-of-the-pants musing. In summary, Critical theory challenges us to be sensitive to our motives and the impact of our actions when we make leadership decisions.

Diary

- Given what you have learned in this chapter, what are some important functions of leadership? In what way does your answer change your previous answers to this question? Consider, particularly, how Critical theory might redefine leadership effectiveness (this was the subject of one of the Roundtables in this chapter).
- Managerial morality is a major focus of this chapter, and you are encouraged to reflect on your own moral leadership perspective. Reflect first on how you define morality within an educational leadership context. What are some of the moral issues that education must face? What current practices in education need to be changed? What is your disposition toward control and how can you control that disposition? What are some alternative, moral ways that leaders can behave? Will you, as a leader, have the courage to make such changes? Describe your leadership morality philosophy.
- I imagine that, for most of us, control is a difficult thing to relinquish. Critical theorists argue that control is more important to managers than profits, and that managers seek to extend control even when it is not in the best interest of the organization to do so. Consider the following questions: Is control, indeed, that all-consuming? Should a school principal maintain veto power over all decisions in his or her school on the assumption that the principal is ultimately responsible? How important is control to you, and how easy is it for you to genuinely delegate control to others?
- What is the dominant capital of your organization and who controls that capital? Provide evidence to support your position. If control of capital is vested in the bureaucratic or legislative structures of your institution, that capital is probably oriented to such things as budget or test scores. In what ways do such rather narrow foci hinder effective production, and why do they hinder effectiveness? Relate your discussion of this last question to Mintzberg's arguments on professional bureaucracy, which was presented in Chapter 9.

Recommended Readings

Etzioni, A. (1964). *Modern organizations.* Englewood Cliffs, NJ. Prentice-Hall, Inc.

Etzioni's book, *Modern Organizations,* is recommended for two reasons: (1) it is an important classic in the field of organizational theory; and (2) its discussion of Structuralist theory, a major predecessor of Critical theory, is unequaled.

Jermier, J. M. (1998). Introduction: Critical perspectives on organizational control. *Administrative Science Quarterly, 43*(2), 235–256.

This is one of the most comprehensive and readable explanations of Critical theory that I was able to find (unfortunately, Critical theorists seem to suffer from an inability to communicate with the novice reader). Jermier begins by explaining the basic concepts that underlie Critical theory. He then applies the Critical theory perspective to two classics of Western literature, George Orwell's *1984,* and Aldous Huxley's *Brave New World.* Jermier's article introduces this special issue of *Administrative Science Quarterly* dealing with Critical theory. Although the rest of this issue is not as accessible as Jermier's article, it is equally as edifying; thus, I would recommend that you not stop with this first article.

References

Ansoff, H. I. (1965). *Corporate strategy: An analytical approach to business policy for growth and expansion.* New York: McGraw-Hill, Inc.

Barnard, C. I. (1938). *The functions of the executive.* Cambridge, MA: Harvard University Press.

Barry, B. (1978). *Sociologists, economists, and democracy.* Chicago: University of Chicago Press.

Bentham, J. (1995). *The panopticon writings.* London: Verso.

Bordt, R. L. (1998). *The structure of women's nonprofit organizations.* Bloomington, IN: Indiana University Press.

Bourdieu, P. (1993). *The field of cultural production.* New York: Columbia University Press.

Carroll, S. J. (1982). Search for equity. In W. W. McMahon & T. G. Geske (Eds.), *Financing education: Overcoming inefficiency and inequity* (pp. 237–266). Urbana, IL: University of Illinois Press.

Coch, L., & French, J. R. P. (1948). Overcoming resistance to change. *Human Relations, 1,* 512–533.

Covaleski, M. A., Dirsmith, M. W., Heian, J. B., & Samuel, S. (1998). The calculated and the avowed: Techniques of discipline and struggles over identity in big six public accounting firms. *Administrative Science Quarterly, 43,* 293–327.

DiMaggio, P. J., & Powell, W. W. (1983). The iron cage revisited: Institutional isomorphism and collective rationality in organizational fields. *American Sociological Review, 48*(2), 147–160.

Douglas, M. (1995). Converging on autonomy: Anthropology and institutional economics. In O. E. Williamson (Ed.), *Organization theory: From Chester Barnard to the present and beyond* (pp. 98–115) New York: Oxford University Press.

Duska, R. (1998). Book review: Organizational ethics and the good life. *Administrative Science Quarterly, 43*(3), 713–719.

Etzioni, A. (1964). *Modern organizations.* Englewood Cliffs, NJ: Prentice Hall, Inc.

Etzioni, A. (1988). *The moral dimension: Toward a new economics.* New York: The Free Press.

Eve, R. A., Horsfall, S., & Lee, M. E. (Eds.). (1997). *Chaos, complexity, and sociology.* Thousand Oaks, CA: Sage Publications.

Ezzamel, M., & Willmott, H. (1998). Accounting for teamwork: A critical study of the group-based systems of organizational control. *Administrative Science Quarterly, 43,* 358–396.

Feber, M. A., & Kordick, B. (1978). Sex differentials in the earnings of Ph.D.s. *Industrial and Labor Relations Review, 35,* 550–564.

Flanigan, J. L., Marion, R. A., & Richardson, M. D. (1996). Causal and temporal analyses of increased funding on student achievement. *Journal of Research and Development in Education, 30,* 222–247.

Foucault, M. (1977). *Discipline and punish: The birth of the prison.* London: Allen & Lane.

Foucault, M. (1979). *Discipline and punish.* Harmondsworth, England: Penguin.

Fox, M. F. (1985). Location, sex-typing, and salary among academics. *Work and Occupations, 12,* 186–205.

Freeman, R. B., & Medoff, J. L. (1984). *What do unions do?* New York: Basic Books.

Geske, T. G. (1983). Educational finance policy: A search for complementarities. *Educational Evaluation and Policy Analysis, 5*(1), 83–96.

Hage, J. (1980). *Theories of organization: Form, process, and transformations.* New York: Wiley Interscience.

Hornstein, H. A., Masor, H. N., & Sole, K. (1971). Effects of sentiment and completion of a helping act on observed helping: A case for socially mediated Zeigarnik effect. *Journal of Personality and Social Psychology, 17,* 107–112.

Huxley, A. (1932). *Brave new world.* New York: Harper & Row.

Jennings, E., & Jennings, F. (1956). Making human relations work. In E. C. Bursk (Ed.), *Human Relations for Management* (pp. 32–85). New York: Harper.

Jermier, J. (1982). Infusion of critical social theory into organizational analysis: Implications for studies of work adjustment. In D. Dunkerly & G. Salaman (Eds.), *The international year book of organizations studies 1981.* Boston: Routledge and Kegan Paul.

Jermier, J. M. (1998). Introduction: Critical perspectives on organizational control. *Administrative Science Quarterly, 43*(2), 235–256.

Katzenbach, J. R., & Smith, D. K. (1993). *The wisdom of teams: Creating the high-performance organization.* Boston: Harvard Business School Press.

Knights, D., & Willmott, H. (1987). Organizational culture as corporate strategy. *International Studies of Management and Organization, 17*(3), 40–63.

Kuhn, T. S. (1970). *The structure of scientific revolutions* (2nd ed.). Chicago: The University of Chicago Press.

Marchington, M. (1992). *Managing the team: A guide to successful employee involvement.* Oxford: Blackwell.

Martin, J., Knopff, K., & Beckman, C. (1998). An alternative to bureaucratic impersonality and emotional labor: Bounded emotionality at the Body Shop. *Administrative Science Quarterly, 43*, 429–469.

Marx, K. (1972). *Capital* (Originally published in 1867). New York: Dutton.

Mueller, F. (1994). Teams between hierarchy and commitment: Change strategies and the 'internal environment'. *Journal of Management Studies, 31*, 383–403.

Oakes, L., Townley, B., & Cooper, D. J. (1998). Business planning as pedagogy: Language and control in a changing institutional field. *Administrative Science Quarterly, 43*(2), 257–292.

Ouchi, W. (1981). *Theory Z: How American business can meet the Japanese challenge.* Reading, MA: Addison-Wesley.

Palmer, D. P. (1983). Broken ties: Interlocking directorates and intercorporate coordination. *Administrative Science Quarterly, 28*, 40–55.

Pfeffer, J. (1997). *New directions for organization theory: Problems and prospects.* New York: Oxford University Press.

Pfeffer, J., & Davis-Blake, A. (1987). The effect of the proportion of women on salaries: The case of college administrators. *Administration Science Quarterly, 32*, 1–24.

Porter, M. (1980). *Competitive strategy: Techniques for analyzing industries and competitors.* New York: Free Press.

Richardson, M., & Marion, R. (1991). South Carolina's Education Improvement Act: Is it working? Paper presented at the Eastern Educational Research Association (Spring, 1991), Boston.

Sears, D. O., & Funk, C. L. (1990). Self-interest in Americans' political opinions. In J. J. Mansbridge (Ed.), *Beyond self-interest* (pp. 147–170). Chicago: University of Chicago Press.

Senge, P. M. (1990). *The fifth discipline: The art and practice of the learning organization.* New York: Random House.

Sewell, G. (1998). The discipline of teams: The control of team-based industrial work through electronic and peer surveillance. *Administrative Science Quarterly, 43*, 397–428.

Shakeshaft, C., & Nowell, I. (1984). Research on theories, concepts, and models of organizational behavior: The influence of gender. *Issues in Education, 11*(3), 186–203.

Smith, D. E. (1978). A peculiar eclipsing: Women's exclusion from male culture. *Women Studies International Quarterly, 3*, 283.

Taylor, F. (1911). *The principles of scientific management.* New York: Harper.

Taylor's famous testimony before the Special House committee. (1926). *Bulletin of the Taylor Society, 11*(3-4), 95–196.

Whitt, J. A. (1980). Can capitalists organize themselves? In C. W. Domhoff (Ed.), *Power, structure, research* (pp. 97–113). Beverly Hills, CA.: Sage Publications.

Williamson, O. E. (1985). *The economic institutions of capitalism.* New York: The Free Press.

Wrenge, C. D., & Greenwood, R. G. (1991). *Frederick W. Taylor, the father of scientific management: Myth and reality.* Burr Ridge, IL: Irwin.

CHAPTER 12

Pressures that Shape Organizations

OVERVIEW AND CHAPTER OBJECTIVES

New Institutionalism, the subject of this chapter, is closely related to Phillip Selznick's proposal—and that of Structuralism in general—that organizations are defined by tensions between their stated, formal goals and their irrational constituents. Selznick argued that such tension forces organizations to compromise who and what they are. New Institutionalism suggests that irrational social sensibilities are the driving force behind organizational decisions. According to Institutionalists, it is more important for organizations to *appear* effective than to *be* effective. They apply this thesis to explain such things as the spread of fads, the effect of culture on patterns of organization, and isomorphism.

In this chapter students will:

- Understand the premises underlying Institutional theory and how it relates to other anti-positivistic theories.
- Develop a research proposal that seeks to understand how cultural differences influence different patterns of schooling.
- Develop a research proposal that seeks to explain the spread of innovation in education in terms of institutional mimicry.
- Explain how institutional and technical pressures influence different organizations differently.
- Understand how the language of a culture affects organizational assumptions.
- Develop a research proposal on differences in how early adopters and late adopters implement innovation in education.
- Suggest reasons why incompetent people sometimes rise to leadership positions.

- Explain how legislative action is influenced by, and influences, perceptions of social reality.
- Refine their personal perspectives of leadership.

BACKGROUND

Phillip Selznick's brand of Institutional theory (what some have called Old Institutional theory) was introduced in Chapter 4. Selznick defined organizations as living, adaptive, and social systems rather than as Taylorian mechanical systems, and argued that the sociologist's job is to understand the organizational personality.

Selznick, like Chester Barnard and Talcott Parsons, was a Structural theorist. Amitai Etzioni (1964) defined the gist of Structuralism when he wrote:

> It is in exploring the "harmony" view of the Human Relations writers that the Structuralist writers first recognized fully the organizational dilemma: the inevitable strains—which can be reduced but not eliminated—between organizational needs and personal needs; between rationality and non-rationality; between discipline and autonomy; between formal and informal relationships; between management and workers. (p. 41)

Selznick's unique contribution to Structuralist theory was his analyses of the impact of nonrational organizational activities on formal organizational goals. To survive, an organization must often subjugate its formal goals to nonrational internal and external pressures—pressures that have more to do with needs, wants, and personalities than with logic and effectiveness. Nonrational activity within the organization comes from individuals whose needs and desires get in the way of organizational goals. External environments likewise pose irrational demands that may frustrate an organization's rational strivings. Thus, an organization, itself struggling with nonrational, internal compromises, "strikes bargains with its environment that compromise present objectives and limit future possibilities" (Scott, 1987, p. 64).

Selznick wrote that one learns about organizations by analyzing the frustrations and compromises that organizations make with nonrational pressures. Theorists should study the critical organizational decisions, the coping strategies that shape a system's structure and give it a distinct personality. "The pattern of these critical decisions, viewed over time, results in the development of a distinctive character structure for each organization" (Scott, 1987, p. 65). Selznick refers to the process by which an organization develops such personality as "institutionalization." To become institutionalized is to become "infused with value beyond the technical requirements of the task at hand" (Selznick, 1957, p. 17). That is, organizations do things that serve the needs and pressures of nonrational constituents as well as the rational needs of efficient operation.

In 1956, Burton Clark illustrated the usefulness of Selznick's model in an analysis of an adult education program in Los Angeles. This program's professed goals were to provide cultural and intellectual education for adults in the region.

The program was not well-supported, however, and only those parts of the program that could attract students were retained. Other important programs had to be scrapped—a compromise with economic reality. Selznick himself analyzed America's Tennessee Valley Authority project and militarism in what was then the USSR. Zald and Denton (1963) applied his arguments in analyzing the transition of the YMCA from a religious program for the poor into a more secular program for urban youth.

Selznick's work has been criticized for its tendency toward exposé. His study of the TVA project in the 1940s, for example, told how the project was compromised by local influences; in a sense, it read like a newspaper investigation. As Charles Perrow put it, Selznick's "major message is that the organization has sold out its goals in order to survive or grow" (1979, p. 182). Richard Scott adds that "although cynicism seems often justified, this early work stimulated by Selznick's conception appears to go out of its way to inspect the seamy side of organizational life" (1987, p. 67). Selznick's later works moved away from the organizational exposé to explorations of how leaders can protect organizational goals against nonrational pressures (see particularly Selznick, 1957). The leader, he argued, makes critical decisions that help define institutional values, thus assuring that the needs of the organization are served.

Selznick's work on leadership provided a bridge to modern perspectives of Institutionalism. These modern perspectives began to appear in the organizational literature in the 1970s, and by the 1990s had become a powerful force in organizational theory. These recent works focus on the emergence of value and consensus from social dynamics.

THE NEW INSTITUTIONALISM

One could say that Contingency theory is about efficiency and effectiveness preferences, Population Ecology is about adaptive preferences, Critical theory is about control preferences, and modern Institutionalism is about social preferences. By this I mean that, according to Institutional theory, organizational structure and behavior are more the products of social beliefs and fads than of economic rationality. Frederick Taylor, the famous Scientific Management expert, argued that organizational tasks should be carefully structured to produce maximum efficiency; Institutional theorists argued that task behaviors are forged instead by social sensibilities and beliefs. As Selznick said in 1992, "The underlying reality—the basic source of stability and integration—is the creation of social entanglements or commitments" (p. 232). Thus, a principal's decisions are guided by what society, parents, training, and professional organizations say is acceptable and proper. Football coaches make calls and shape strategy based in part on what will please fans (ground plays may reliably eat up the yardage, but the bomb pass is the topic discussed around the water cooler the next day). Businesses shape their strategies to accommodate the demands of moral trends in a culture. The way systems are organized and structured is determined by prevailing beliefs about how work should be structured at the time of their founding—public education, for example, is structured in large measure around the prevailing business precepts of the 1910s and 1920s. The way professors of educational administration teach their classes is determined in large measure by accrediting agencies. In short, social pressures shape reality and propriety, which in turn shape the way organizations are structured and run.

Institutionalism and Social Legitimacy

An organization must be perceived as credible and "mainstream" to achieve support from its public. Institutionalism is the process by which systems achieve legitimacy, or the "generalized perception that the actions, activities, and structure of a network are desirable and appropriate" (Human & Provan, 2000, p. 328). Schools hire state-certified teachers because certified teachers are credible and legitimate. A school that hires, say, high school graduates would not be perceived as legitimate and would not be supported by the public. Similarly, colleges and universities hire Ph.D.s as professors; to do otherwise is to risk being branded as rogue or educationally suspect. If the public is convinced that phonics is the most appropriate way to teach reading, a school achieves legitimacy by offering phonics instruction. When TQM became popular among businesses in the 1980s and 1990s, many organizations jumped on the TQM bandwagon less because of established evidence that it would improve effectiveness and more because it conveyed an aura of legitimacy (Westphal, Gulati, & Shortell, 1997).

Rules that specify standards of behavior are a source of organizational legitimacy. Rules convey a legal right to make decisions and they imbue decision makers with legalistic authority. Rules gain legitimacy because of their historical roots (they often codify the way things "have always been done"), and because they are often the result of some form of consensus or majority decision.

Education is a source of legitimacy, and schools are key purveyors of institutionalization within a society. Because of a long history of commitment to education in Western society, because of indoctrination about the importance of education, and because of significant accomplishments by educated people, education is highly respected. In the United States, Noah Webster, Horace Mann, and others convinced a budding nation that education was the key to its future, and this message is embedded in our collective souls. The fruits of educated people are constantly before us—great inventions, world-changing theories and theorists (such as Einstein and Newton), and astounding accomplishments such as heart transplant surgery and other technological advancements. Such history and accomplishment breed a respect for the educated person that translates into legitimacy for organizations who can recruit such people.

Professional associations and accrediting agencies provide legitimacy to organizations. Schools seek accreditation by the Southern Association of Schools and Colleges (SACS) because such accreditation enhances their reputations. At one time in the United States, school districts could be "de-legitimized" by being blacklisted by the National Education Association. Toothpaste makers display the American Dental Association seal of approval because it legitimizes their products. Advertisers legitimize their products with the Good Housekeeping Seal of Approval.

Fads and images are sources of legitimacy, and both are very obviously social constructs. People who wear the "right" clothes to an interview are more likely to get the job than are those who don't. Male professors may enhance legitimacy by sporting tweed jackets with leather elbow patches that portray the "professorial" look. Legitimacy comes from having the latest trend in technology or from implementing the latest trend in management. Fads and images do not necessarily make one more competent—one could have the most expensive guitar and still be a bad guitar player, or wear the most expensive suit and still be a poor candidate for a given job. Fads and images are socially constructed, rather than actual, reality. To be without them, however, would convey an image of nonlegitimacy.

WHY SCHOOLS LOOK SO MUCH ALIKE

Institutional theorists argue that pressures to be socially legitimate impel related organizations toward isomorphic states, or states in which structure and activities look alike (DiMaggio and Powell, 1983). Thus high schools across a culture tend to look and act quite similarly (for much the same reason that high school students tend to dress and act alike), as do universities, airline industries, banks, and fast-food restaurants.

However, Contingency theory makes similar predictions: organizations operating in the same environment, thus subject to the same contingencies, will adopt similar strategies—that is, isomorphism can just as easily be explained by more positivistic theories. To determine which theory is correct, Gooderham, Nordhaug, and Ringdall (1999) hypothesized that Contingency theory would predict similar structure across different cultures, while Institutional theory would predict different structures. If environmental contingency is the dominant force shaping organizations, then similar contingencies will produce similar structure, regardless of cultural context. If Institutional dynamics such as different cultural expectations are dominant forces in shaping organizations, then organizations will look different across cultures despite similar contingencies.

> Whereas the broad rational model implies that there will be no cross-national differences beyond those that are ascribable to factors such as varying firm size and differing industries, the institutional model assumes dissimilarities not only in relation to industry differences but also dissimilarities rooted in the idiosyncratic national institutional regimes surrounding firms. (p. 508)

Their findings supported Institutional theory. They found four clusters of management styles among the European nations examined: The United Kingdom was broadly receptive to different management styles, Norway and Denmark leaned toward collaborative styles, Germany was relatively unreceptive to new styles, and the Latin nations of France and Spain adopted unique variants of management practices. The authors ascribed these patterns to differences in the

legal and political environments of the different nations and to different normative expectations about organizational legitimacy (particularly expectations regarding labor-management relationships).

Cornelis Lammers and David Hickson (1979) defined similar cultural differences among organizational types in 1979:

> A *Latin* type, exemplified by French, Italian, and Spanish organizations, is characterized
> by relatively high centralization, rigid stratification and sharp inequalities among levels,
> and conflicts around areas of uncertainty. An *Anglo-Saxon* type, exemplified by British,
> United States, and Scandinavian organizations, is marked by more decentralization, less
> rigid stratification, and more flexible approaches to the application of rules. And a *tra-
> ditional* type, found in third-world, developing countries, is characterized by paternalis-
> tic leadership patterns, implicit rather than explicit rules, and lack of clear boundaries
> separating organizational from non-organizational roles. (Scott, 1987, p. 131)

RESEARCH TOPIC

This study of cultural differences among organizations can be replicated in a more localized
population. United States researchers, for example, might explore the normative impacts of
Hispanic populations on school activities and structures, and how this differs from the structure and activities of schools dominated by other cultures, such as Anglo-Saxons, African-
Americans, or Native Americans. The Lammers and Hickson study could serve as a starting
point in formulating premises and hypotheses. Be aware that, for a within-nation study, the
different organizations examined will be subject to similar legal and political expectations. According to Lammers and Hickson, this is a powerful institutional force, thus the variations observed will be different and perhaps more subtle than those discussed above.   ■

The Engines of Similarity

Institutional theorists Paul DiMaggio and Walter Powell (1983) identify three general sources of isomorphic pressure: coercive pressures, mimetic pressures, and
normative pressures. These are the engines of isomorphism, the specific reasons
why schools (and other classes of organization) across a culture are structured
and behave so much alike.

Coercive Pressure   Coercive pressures are typically associated with the legal and
political expectations of a state or nation. Public Law 94-142, which mandated
equal access to public education by handicapped children in the United States,
has had a profound isomorphic impact on the way schools structure their programs for exceptional children. One could go to just about any public school in
the U.S. and find that the structure and activities for exceptional children in that
school are largely the same as those in any other school in the nation. Mandates
from the U.S. Supreme Court regarding disciplinary suspension (*Goss v. Lopez*,
1975) have forced all schools in the nation to draft nearly identical student suspension policies that permit suspension without formal hearings for up to nine

days. On a more subtle side, political expectations and pressure regarding achievement test scores affect the way curriculum is structured in American schools.

Rules and regulations are sources of coercive pressure that, like all Institutional pressures, owe their existence more to legitimacy preferences than to a rational search for enhanced effectiveness. An institutional perspective of rules, called the "Institutional theory of action" by March and Olsen (1989), looks at how legitimacy preferences assume the form of rules to both constrain and enable organizational decisions and action. Rules, according to this argument, represent the codification and legalization of beliefs, social and organizational values, and popular sensibilities. Rules are the product of an organization's history and its "knowledge, capabilities, beliefs, values, and memory" (Ocasio, 1999, p. 386). They are based on an organization's beliefs about what is effective and appropriate behavior, its values and the values of its culture, its understanding about effective organization, its particular state of knowledge and ability, and its memory of its founding and past experiences. Reliance on rules lends an aura of authority and legitimacy to the organization, decreases conflict, and increases the likelihood that action will be taken in response to issues. Rules lead to inertia because they stabilize and routinize organizational action. Reliance on rules will continue even when there is evidence that they are counterproductive or that change is needed.

Coercive pressure also comes from accrediting institutions such as SACS and NCATE. Such institutions provide an organization with legitimacy in return for compliance with their mandates.

Mimicry Pressure   Richard Scott (1987) wrote:

> We seek to behave in conventional ways . . . that will not cause us to stand out or be noticed as different . . . we attempt to imitate others whom we'd regard as superior or more successful. One principal indicator of the strength of such mimetic processes is prevalence: the number of similar individuals or organizations exhibiting a given form or practice. (p. 45)

Students in a high school tend to mimic the dress of the currently popular music groups; this mimetic tendency is so strong that it constitutes, in effect, a dress code. School districts tend to mimic programs that are successful in other districts. Sports coaches tend to mimic strategies that have been successful for other coaches. DiMaggio and Powell (1983) argue that mimicry is most evident in organizations that are dealing with uncertainty; for example, school districts that have been unable to find ways to increase test scores will likely seek out and imitate programs that are effective in other districts.

RESEARCH TOPIC

Examine several innovations implemented by schools or legislators and make the argument that those changes were based more on mimicry pressures than on rational decision making. A good development of this question will require interviews with key actors in the decision-making process.

Organizational theorists have compared mimicry to the genetic process by which traits are passed from generation to generation in a biological population. The genetic system is a portfolio of templates, general models of how a biological system is to be structured. Noted biologist Richard Dawkins (1976) argues that social systems have a similar structure that he called "memes." Memes are loosely defined as cultural content. Just as biological structure is the product of genetic blueprints, social behavior is the product of cultural blueprints, or common understanding of how things should be and how reality is to be defined.

Organizational theorists have described mechanisms by which cultural memes are translated into organizational structure and behavior. Arthur Stinchcombe wrote in 1965 that organizational structure is the result of a process he called *imprinting,* or the transfer through learning, social pressure, rules of behavior, norms, and such, of information from one organizational generation to the next.

Normative Pressure   Finally, organizations tend to look alike because of normative pressures. These pressures refer to a taken-for-granted or assumed character of social life. Zucker (1983) noted that

> . . . institutionalization is rooted in conformity—not conformity engendered by sanctions . . . nor conformity resulting from a 'black-box' internalization process, but conformity rooted in the taken-for-granted aspect of everyday life. . . . Institutionalization operates to produce common understandings about what is appropriate and, fundamentally, meaningful behavior. (p. 5)

Why do people on an elevator face the door and speak in hushed whispers? Why do we walk down the right side of a hallway? Why do clocks run clockwise instead of counter-clockwise? Why do we eat our entrée before our dessert? No reason, it's just the way our culture has agreed to do things. It is "conformity rooted in the taken-for-granted aspect of everyday life." Why do we organize schools into grade levels? Why do we assign letter grades on report cards? Why do schools have principals? Why do we categorize curricula into subject matter instead of integrating various topics? Why do we divide the high school day into 50-minute periods? Why do we organize elementary school students into ability reading groups? Is it because that's the best way to do things, or is the answer because that's the way we've always done things? Participants in a culture agree on proper ways to do things. We take it for granted that there is defensible rationale behind our behaviors, when in fact we often decide on propriety first and rationale second.

Bridges

Organizations exist within two types of environments: a technical environment and an institutional environment (Meyer & Scott, 1983). An organization exchanges goods and services with its technical environment. This environment revolves around profits and productivity; thus, it fosters the development of rational structures and activities. It is characterized by exchanges of money, tech-

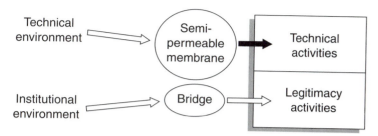

FIGURE 12.1   Technical activities are buffered from environments by semipermeable membranes that allow only a select subset of the environment into the system. By contrast, the Institutional environment is allowed full access to the system's activities by means of bridges.

nology, people, and expertise. The open system model in Chapter 5 illustrates the organization's relationship with its technical environment (see Fig. 5.1). Sergiovanni (2000) referred to this environment as the systemsworld; Burns (1978) called the organization's relationship with it "transactional activity."

Institutional environments, by contrast, are composed of rules, normative expectations, and other such isomorphic pressures; organizations must conform to this environment in order to receive legitimacy. This environment rewards socially approved structures and activities over quantity or quality of output.

An organization typically buffers itself from its technical environment—that is, it screens out undesirable inputs. Open systems theory labels this mechanism the "semipermeable membrane" (Fig. 12.1). Schools, for example, screen applicants for faculty positions. Organizations do not buffer inputs of the institutional environment, however. Schools adopt instructional fads largely without customizing them, and they implement rules without altering their intent (typically they have no choice in this second example). Different organizations become isomorphic in structure and in behavior because they accept rules and normative expectations from the environment as is, without modification by semipermeable membranes.

Bridges are cultural assumptions or requirements that mold organizations around institutional expectations. Scott (1987) identifies four such bridges (see Fig. 12.2). He calls them:

- Categorical Conformity, or taken-for-granted categories of people and activities that shape the way organizations pattern their structures and activities. Universities distinguish among teaching, research, and service activities; high schools distinguish between college-bound and technical courses. Such distinctions are built into our language and define reality for us. Organizations that fail to organize themselves about such categories are not accorded legitimacy by the society that speaks in these vocabularies. Schools that blur the distinction between student and teacher, for example, would likely be considered irrational or irresponsible.

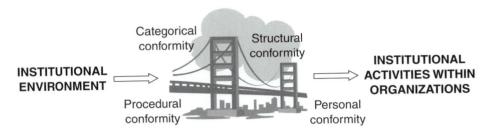

FIGURE 12.2   The four bridges between environment and institutions.

ROUNDTABLE

Try to mentally place yourself into an environment that has a different vocabulary of structure than does the environment with which you are familiar. If you are a public school student, perhaps this environment distinguishes between mentor and mentored instead of teacher and student; it speaks of business managers, master teachers, and teachers instead of principal and teacher; and it makes no distinctions among students by academic track. If you are a higher education student, perhaps your environment distinguishes mentor and mentored, deans are required to teach, science faculty must have minor appointments in a humanities or social science field, and vice versa, and core upperclass courses are structured around participation in a mentor's research. How do you suppose your school would organize itself and what sort of behaviors would it exhibit?

- Structural conformity reflects a society's beliefs about how organizations should be structured. Public schools organize into grade levels, and universities into disciplines, because of such beliefs.

- Procedural Conformity refers to pressure on organizations to conduct their business, or procedures, in certain specified ways. Meyer and Rowan (1977) identified the root of this pressure as the "rational myth," society's beliefs about how systems can be most effectively organized.

- Personal Conformity refers to beliefs about the type of worker who must perform given tasks. Such personnel are a primary building block of organizational structure, thus their characteristics determine the structure and activities of the system. Teachers are certified for certain curricular areas—math, English, social studies, etc.—and this fact pretty much defines the way schools will be structured. The building blocks of education are constructed and influenced primarily by a society's educational preparation system. They are also influenced by licensure procedures and by public expectations about the way schools should be structured (categorical conformity).

TECHNICAL AND INSTITUTIONAL DIMENSIONS OF ORGANIZATION

Meyer and Scott (1983) propose that certain types of organizations are influenced more by technical environments and others are more influenced by institutional environments (see Fig. 12.3). Organizations with highly structured activities, like cotton mills, would be more attuned to their technical than their institutional environments, for example. They would not be immune to legitimacy pressures, but legitimacy might not be as important as productivity. Further, productivity may be a key element of legitimacy for such organizations. Other organizations, by contrast, are quite sensitive to legitimizing pressures. Political parties, for example, invest significant resources into finding out what the public favors and disfavors. Technical and institutional environments, according to Scott, are negatively correlated, but not strongly so (mixed cases are entirely possible).

ACTIVITY

Figure 12.3 represents technical and institutional environments as the axes of a coordinate graph. Locate the following organizational types on that graph. Discuss your reasons for each placement. Scott's placement and rationale is at the end of this chapter (Fig. 12.4).

Utilities	Restaurants	General manufacturing	Banks
General hospitals	Schools	Pharmaceutical companies	Churches
Mental health association	Health clubs	Legal agencies	

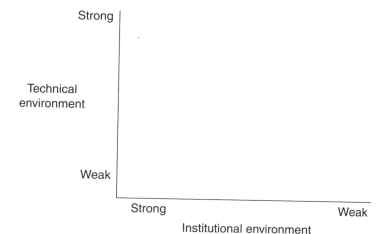

FIGURE 12.3   Coordinate graph of the technical and institution dimensions of organizational environments.

From W. Richard Scott, *Organizations: Rational, natural, and open systems,* 2nd ed. Copyright © 1981. Reprinted by permission of Prentice Hall, Inc.

FROM TECHNICAL TO INSTITUTIONAL

An important hypothesis of Institutional theory is that the first organizations to adopt innovation do so for technical, effectiveness reasons, while later adopters do so mainly for institutional reasons. For example, Institutional theory predicts that the first organizations to engage in strategic planning in the 1980s did so to be more effective. They were selective in the strategies they adopted, tailoring them to the needs of the organization (they buffered the technical system). As strategic planning became popular, however, organizations jumped on this bandwagon because it made them appear modern—it gave them legitimacy. These organizations adopted a one-size-fits-all model that often did little for their effectiveness but did wonders for their image.

RESEARCH TOPIC

Conduct a qualitative study of a public school system or university that engaged in strategic planning and reorganization during this fad. Through interviews with key participants, test the hypothesis that late adopters do so to achieve legitimacy rather than effectiveness. Determine (1) if there were clear, documented reasons (as opposed to rationalizations) for the changes; (2) whether reorganization strategies were specifically tailored to the needs of the organization; (3) whether reorganization actually led to greater effectiveness and efficiency; and (4) whether, over the ensuing years, the organization tended to revert to some semblance of its original structure. Answers to these questions will indicate whether the system adopted the fad for technical or institutional reasons.

There is a temptation to pursue this hypothesis into areas that are too global or complex to be adequately analyzed. Zucker (1983), for example, argued that organizational form itself is a function of the institutionalization process:

> Initially, organizational form was adopted rationally to handle large-scale production and to create predictable conditions of work. . . . However, as the organizational form gained legitimacy . . . it became a taken-for-granted element, so it was unthinkable for a new business . . . to take place *not* located in an organizational structure. (p. 20)

Scott (1987) does not find this argument convincing. "Zucker's data are too sparse to support this broad a conclusion, and one can cite many instances of political and even religious systems being informally structured long before large-scale production systems developed" (p. 199). Narrower arguments, he continues, are better supported.

Most of the studies of this hypothesis are narrower in scope than is Zucker's study. Westphal, Gulati, and Shortell, for example, have examined the implementation of Total Quality Management in over 2,700 U.S. hospitals. "The results show that early adopters customize TQM practices for efficiency gains, while later adopters gained legitimacy from adopting the normative form of TQM programs" (Westphal et al., 1997, p. 366). Tolbert and Zucker (1983) examined the diffusion of civil service reforms between 1880 and 1935, and found that early adopters were motivated by technical or economic needs, while later adopters responded to the growing social legitimacy of these programs.

LEADERSHIP

Institutional theory focuses on the relationships and connections among social actors rather than on individual behavior. It suggests that we can best understand the events in our lives from the perspective of our social interactions rather than our individual behavior (Pfeffer, 1997). Promotions, for example, are less a product of individual competence and more a product of one's position in a social structure. The people with whom one associates affect job attitudes. Status is related to social contacts. Similar truths hold at the organizational level as well. An organization's survival, for example, is dependent on the strength of its network with other organizations (Marion & Bacon, 1999; Pfeffer & Salancik, 1978). Social interactions are the vehicle for, and source of, social constructs that undergird the institutionalization process. Promotions, job attitudes, status, and other such organizational dynamics, then, are related to beliefs we bring to the table rather than the reality of a given situation. A principal may base a teacher's evaluation more on opinions about the group he or she associates with than on the actual competence of the teacher. Peer review committee members whose sense of academic propriety is influenced by their interactions with peers who focus on, say, "practical" preparation of school administrators may judge a promotion candidate whose forte is research as unrealistic or insufficient. Alternatively, peer review members may interact in ways that lead them to construct negative personal attitudes about that person, attitudes that lead them to vote negatively for an otherwise competent individual. In each of these examples, an individual's or group's actions are driven by socially constructed, rather than actual, reality; this is the essence of Institutional theory.

ROUNDTABLE

In the introduction to this chapter, it was suggested that Institutional theory can help us understand why technically incompetent people sometime rise to leadership positions (school principals who were poor teachers, for example). Can you now answer this question from an Institutional theory perspective? ▪

The mere knowledge that socially constructed reality may influence decisions, sometimes inappropriately, should be a cautionary or moral note for educational leaders. Institutional theory suggests a more direct prescription for leadership behavior, however. Leadership, according to the Institutional premise, is a process of influencing social reality. This contrasts starkly with more traditional definitions that revolve around technical competence, such as efficient and effective management. Leaders are people who can mold and dominate the social constructs, the perceptions of reality, of others. They can convince others to subscribe to their goals and objectives. They can manipulate vocabularies of structure in ways that foster structures and activities they desire. They can maneuver social interactions in ways that portray them as effective to their superiors and their subordinates. They can extend their control over their organizations by manipulating symbols of reality and propriety. They can effectively utilize rules and regulations to manipulate reality and beliefs. They can make people believe that success has been achieved, even when concrete reality suggests otherwise. They can capture credit for successes they and their organizations had little real influence over.

ROUNDTABLE

Consider this definition of leadership within the context of your own leadership performance. How effective are you at manipulating socially constructed reality? What do you need to do to improve? Can a person who depends more on manipulating socially constructed reality than on being technically competent really succeed as a leader? Is technical competence really all that important in educational leadership, and in what ways is it more important that leaders be effective at dealing with constructed realities? Referring to the categorizations in Figure 12.3 (an earlier activity), argue that organizations subject to strong institutional but weak technical demands are likely to value leaders who can manipulate reality, and vice versa.

INSTITUTIONALISM AND CRITICAL THEORY

Institutional theory is about legitimacy; Critical theory is about controlling the commerce of legitimacy: the two perspectives overlap. Oakes, Townley, and Cooper (1998), for example, argue that elites extend their control over workers by manipulating institutional pressures. "Although the term `control' is rarely used explicitly, institutional theory focuses on the ability of the institutional field to influence or control organizational functioning" (p. 259). Oakes and her colleagues examined a struggle over the capital of the provincial museums and cultural heritage sites in Alberta, Canada. Capital, in this case, referred to the museum personnel's definition of culture and heritage. The government sought to rename and re-legitimize the cultural focus of museums in Alberta. Officials introduced a business planning process that emphasized profits. In order to be profitable, the planning emphasis would force museums to drop exhibits that failed to attract sufficient numbers of viewers and to make structural and organizational changes that catered to commercial goals. At one museum, for example, there was a struggle over whether to pave an access road: the government saw it is a way to attract more visitors while curators and museum patrons wanted to maintain the authenticity of the museum.

The authors argued that business planning is "one of the most pervasive and taken-for-granted mechanisms for organizational control . . . its rationale draws implicitly or explicitly on a control model of power" (p. 270). It can be used as an "iron fist" of control (to use a term introduced in the chapter on Critical theory), or it can take the form of more subtle methods of control. Its subtle side operates by manipulating interests and shaping values of those who must create and implement the business plan. "Power need not involve coercion or conflict but may involve reconfiguring positional and organizational identities, vocabularies, and values" (p. 271). Bourdieu and Wacquant (1992) label this form of control "symbolic violence," defined as "violence which is exercised upon a social agent with his or her complicity" (p. 167). It's like a condemned man who is forced to tie his own noose, and in doing so grows to appreciate and support the hanging process.

Oakes and her colleagues argue that business plans redirect the focus and vocabulary of a debate; through such redirection they control the building blocks of structure and behavior. If one can refocus a debate around profits, then one puts unspoken limits on the possible solutions that will emerge out of that debate. Business plans construct the reality within which the debate is couched; thus, the elites who support the plans win before the debate is ever concluded. In the Oakes study, museum managers were required to submit business plans and were directed to revise submissions that failed to conform to a governmental "template." That is, the debate was controlled, and its vocabulary was mandated, by coercive pressure. The required business plans engaged museum personnel in activities that undermined their own capital (symbolic violence). Managers reported having less time to devote to their original objectives (the maintenance of cultural artifacts) because of the time they were devoting to creating and revising business plans and to implementing their objectives. Museum personnel were forced by the business planning process to refocus their reality around, and to traffic in a vocabulary of, making profits.

RESEARCH TOPIC

In Chapter 11, you were encouraged to explore whether such things as accountability plans and testing programs represent struggle for control over educational capital. In this chapter, you are encouraged to define this struggle in terms of Institutional theory. In what ways do accountability plans and testing programs, like the business plan in Oakes' study, manipulate the socially constructed reality of educators and redefine sources of educational legitimacy? Reflect on the positive and negative impacts this has on technical effectiveness in education.

TWISTS UPON TWISTS: A SUMMARY

Mark Mizruchi and Lisa Fein (1999) offer an interesting twist on—and a good vehicle for summarizing—Institutional theory. They argue that Institutional theory itself has become institutionalized. Academic writers cite one another to support their theses (as amply demonstrated in this book). Mizruchi and Fein observe, however, that it is not unusual for writers to cite work without carefully reading it—or even reading it at all. Consequently, authors add meaning and understanding to classic works that are influenced by current, rather than the original author's, perceptions of reality. "Virtually any work in which an author reexamines classic texts will reveal a series of widely assumed truths that turn out to be false" (p. 654). This raises the possibility that ideas, over time, cease to accurately reflect the author's original intent and cater instead to popular social constructs. We saw this earlier, in Chapter 2, in the discussion of Frederick Taylor: writers typically portray Taylor with his less humane concepts about efficiency and fail to understand his genuine concern that workers should share in the fruits of their productivity. We saw it again in Chapter 3 in the discussion of Elton Mayo. Textbooks have long taught that the Hawthorne studies demonstrated that people respond positively to novelty; however, a review of the original documents shows that novelty was somewhat low on the list of reasons that Mayo's participants cited for their behavior. Such pseudo-truths "often form the basis of subsequent works, leading to even further distortion of the original classic" (Mizruchi and Fein, p. 654). This leads to selectively presented knowledge "that fits in with currently held paradigms" (Adatto & Cole, 1981, p. 151). The "Hawthorne effect," for example, is an important component of current research folklore, but this concept is a modern construct and was not, contrary to popular belief, a primary conclusion of Mayo's original Hawthorne studies.

Mizruchi and Fein examined how writers have similarly institutionalized the work of a classic in Institutional theory: DiMaggio and Powell's 1983 article, "The Iron Cage Revisited: Institutional isomorphism and Collective Rationality in Organizational Fields." They found evidence that a significant, number of scholars misrepresented this study by overemphasizing their discussion of mimetic isomorphism while underemphasizing other components of DiMaggio and Powell's thesis (coercion and normative pressure). This has led to a situation in which researchers ignore plausible alternative explanations of their observations. "When authors assume that only voluntary mimicry accounts for an organization's behavior, without considering alternative explanations, including coercion, then one may be providing a limited picture of the phenomenon" (Mizruchi and Fein, p. 680). That is, even with Institutional theory, we tend to force ideas into socially constructed molds.

This rather simply summarizes the theme of Institutional theory, even if it does some violence to its details. Institutional theory is about how social systems (fields) construct reality, reality that is, in some cases, substantially different from concrete reality. It's about how such constructed reality emerges, shapes behavior and structure, and causes isomorphism. It's about how innovation is adopted by early users for technical reasons and by late users for institutional reasons. It provides insights into leadership behavior, and even offers prescriptions for how "effective" leaders behave. Finally, it begins to key us in to the nature of the emergence within interactive social networks—the emergence of new structures, of novelty, of beliefs—and this is the theme of the next chapter.

INSTITUTIONAL AND TECHNICAL ENVIRONMENTS REVISITED

In this section we return to the activity presented earlier in Figure 12.3. Scott's (1987) categorizations are presented below (Fig. 12.4). Scott argued that organizations such as utilities, banks, and general hospitals are subject to strong institutional and technical pressures.

> On the one hand, there are requirements that utilities produce energy, water, and other basic commodities effectively and reliably; on the other, there are equally strong demands that they conform to regulations governing safety, distribution, pricing, pollution control, employment practices, and so on. In general, organizations in this cell carry out tasks that combine complex technical requirements with a strong "public good" component. (p. 127)

Manufacturing organizations are influenced more by technical than institutional pressures. Pharmaceutical companies and similar health manufacturing firms are a major exception to this, for their operations raise issues of health and safety. Professional service organizations, like schools, tend to be subject to strong institutional pressures but weak technical pressures. Organizations that provide personal services, like restaurants and health clubs, are typically only weakly influenced by either environment.

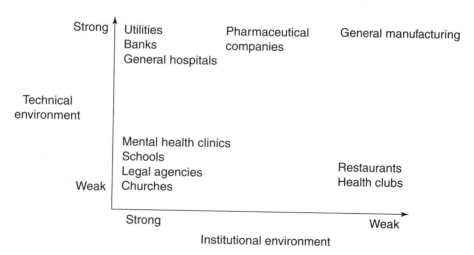

FIGURE 12.4   (Figure 12.3 Completed) Relationship between the technical and institution dimensions of organizational environments.

From W. Richard Scott, *Organizations: Rational, natural, and open systems,* 2nd ed. (Englewood Cliffs, NJ: Prentice Hall, Inc., 1987), p. 126. Copyright © 1987 by Prentice Hall, Inc. Adapted by permission.

ROUNDTABLE

As you just saw, Scott argued that schools are subject to strong institutional but weak technical pressures. What sort of institutional pressures influence public education? Make the argument that, contrary to Scott's analysis, schools are subject to at least somewhat strong technical pressures. ∎

Diary

- Given what you have learned in this chapter, what are some important functions of leadership? In what way does your answer change your previous answers to this question?
- Describe similarities and differences between Critical theory and Institutionalism.
- We will be discussing the diffusion of innovation in the next two chapters, and those discussions will draw in part from Institutional theory. To prepare for that discussion, summarize what you now know, and what you can derive from this chapter, about the diffusion of innovation across a system such as public education.
- Describe several of the isomorphic pressures in education's field.
- Select one of the four bridges between environment and institution (described earlier) and describe that bridge as it applies to education. What specific mechanisms, structures, or dynamics related to that bridge impact the institutionalization of education? For example, the quality indicators of the Southern Association of Colleges and Schools (SACS) represent a procedural conformity bridge that affects the way schools design curriculum and the way teachers teach. How does SACS manage to reach in to the classroom in such a pervasive way?
- Describe the field and capital of your institution. How, and in what ways, do the actors in that field influence the capital of your institution?

Recommended Readings

DiMaggio, P. J., & Powell, W. W. (1983). The iron cage revisited: Institutional isomorphism and collective rationality in organizational fields. *American Sociological Review, 48*(2), 147–160.

"The Iron Cage Revisited" is considered one of the classics of the "new" Institutional theory. In it, DiMaggio and Powell present the three institutional forces that influence isomorphism: coercive, mimicry, and normative pressures. This article can also be found in W. W. Powell & P. J. DiMaggio (Eds.), *The new institutionalism in Organizational analysis* (pp. 63–82). Chicago: University of Chicago Press.

Gooderham, P. N., Nordhaug, O., & Ringdall, K. (1999). Institutional and rational determinants of organizational practices: Human resources management in European firms. *Administrative Science Quarterly, 44,* 507–531.

Contingency theorists argue that organizational structure and behavior are functions of certain contingencies, such as the nature of raw materials and environmental volatility. If true, then all organizations in all cultures that produce the same commodity should look alike, for they all would experience similar contingent pressures. Gooderham et al. analyzed similarities and differences among organizations in Europe to see if this were true. They found significant differences across different cultures. They argue that Contingency theory fails to explain these differences and attribute the variations, instead, to institutional forces such as culture and national regulations.

Mizruchi, M., & Fein, L. (1999). The social construction of organizational knowledge: A study of the uses of coercive, mimetic, and normative isomorphism. *Administrative Science Quarterly, 44*(4), 653–683.

Mizruchi and Fein argue that knowledge itself changes over time in response to changing perceptions of reality and importance. They support this thesis by examining how Institutional theorists themselves have compromised DiMaggio and Powell's classic, "The Iron Cage Revisited," to suit their own shifting emphases. Institutionalists have emphasized mimicry pressures beyond the importance accorded it by DiMaggio and Powell. The authors suggest that this misemphasis has led researchers to overlook alternative hypotheses that may have further illuminated our understanding of social processes.

Oakes, L., Townley, B., & Cooper, D. J. (1998). Business planning as pedagogy: Language and control in a changing institutional field. *Administrative Science Quarterly, 43*(2), 257–292.

Oakes et al. merge Institutional theory with Critical theory to describe how the language of governmental business plans altered perceptions of reality among cultural museums in Alberta, Canada. This article should be of interest to the student of organizational theory not only because of the findings, but because it suggests research designs that might be productively imitated by students of educational theory. A student might draw on Institutional and Critical theories, for example, to describe the impact of legislative policies, such as accountability laws, on the capital of education.

Westphal, J. D., Gulati, R., & Shortell, S. M. (1997). Customization or conformity: An institutional and network perspective on the content and consequences of TQM adoption. *Administrative Science Quarterly, 42,* 366–394.

Westphal et al. describe how institutional forces and network membership influence adoption of Total Quality Management (TQM) strategies. They found, as have other researchers, that early adopters of innovation such as TQM do so for effectiveness, while late adopters do so for legitimacy. They found further, however, that this is influenced by network relationships. Late adopters who are associated with organizations that have adopted TQM, for example, are more likely to adopt it than are organizations in non-adopting networks.

References

Adatto, K., & Cole, S. R. (1981). The functions of classical theory in contemporary social logical research: The case of Max Weber. *Knowledge and society: Studies in the sociology of culture, past and present, 3,* 137–162.

Bourdieu, P., & Wacquant, L. (1992). *An invitation to reflexive sociology.* Oxford: Polity Press.

Burns, J. M. (1978). *Leadership.* New York: Harper & Row.

Clark, B. (1956). *Adult education in transition.* Berkeley, CA: University of California Press.

Dawkins, R. (1976). *The selfish gene.* New York: Oxford University Press.

DiMaggio, P. J., & Powell, W. W. (1983). The iron cage revisited: Institutional isomorphism and collective rationality in organizational fields. *American Sociological Review, 48*(2), 147–160.

Donaldson, L. (1996). *For positivist organization theory: Proving the hard core.* London: Sage Publications.

Etzioni, A. (1964). *Modern organizations.* Englewood Cliffs, NJ: Prentice Hall, Inc.

Gooderham, P. N., Nordhaug, O., & Ringdall, K. (1999). Institutional and rational determinants of organizational practices: Human resource management in European firms. *Administrative Science Quarterly, 44,* 507–531.

Goss v. Lopez, 419 U.S. 565 (S. Ct. 1975).

Hall, R. H. (1991). *Organizations: Structures, Processes, and outcomes* (5th ed.). Englewood Cliffs, NJ: Prentice Hall, Inc.

Human, S. E., & Provan, K. G. (2000). Legitimacy building in the evolution of small firm multilateral networks: A study of success and demise. *Administrative Science Quarterly, 45,* 327–365.

Lammers, C. J., & Hickson, D. J. (1979). A cross-national and cross-institutional typology of organizations. In C. J. Lammers & D. J. Hickson (Eds.), *Organizations alike and unlike: high institutional and interinstitutional studies in the sociology of organizations* (pp. 420–434). London: Routledge & Kegan Paul.

March, J. G., & Olsen, J. P. (1989). *Rediscovering institutions: The organizational basis of politics.* New York: Free Press.

Marion, R., & Bacon, J. (1999). Organizational extinction and complex systems. *Emergence: A journal of complexity issues in organizations and management, 1*(4), 71–96.

Meyer, J. W., & Rowan, B. (1977). Institutionalized organizations: Formal structure as myth and ceremony. *American Sociological Review, 83,* 340–363.

Meyer, J. W., & Scott, W. R. (1983). *Organizational environments: Ritual and rationality.* Beverly Hills, CA: Sage Publications.

Mizruchi, M., & Fein, L. (1999). The social construction of organizational knowledge: A study of the uses of coercive, mimetic, and normative isomorphism. *Administrative Science Quarterly, 44*(4), 653–683.

Oakes, L., Townley, B., & Cooper, D. J. (1998). Business planning as pedagogy: Language and control in a changing institutional field. *Administrative Science Quarterly, 43*(2), 257–292.

Ocasio, W. (1999). Institutionalized action and corporate governance: The reliance on rules of CEO succession. *Administrative Science Quarterly, 44*(2), 384–416.

Perrow, C. (1979). *Complex organizations: A critical essay* (2 Foresman.

Pfeffer, J. (1997). *New directions for organization theory: Problems an* Oxford University Press.

Pfeffer, J., & Salancik, G. R. (1978). *The external control of organizations: A dence perspective. New York: Harper & Row.

Scott, W. R. (1987). *Organizations: Rational, natural, and open systems* (2nd ed.). Engl Cliffs, NJ: Prentice Hall, Inc.

Selznick, P. (1957). *Leadership in administration*. New York: Harper & Row.

Selznick, P. (1992). *The moral commonwealth: Social theory and the promise of community*. Berkeley, CA: University of California Press.

Selznick, P. (1996). Institutionalism "Old" and "New." *Administrative Science Quarterly, 41*, 270–277.

Sergiovanni, T. J. (2000). *The lifeworld of leadership: Creating culture, community, and personal meaning in our schools*. San Francisco: Jossey-Bass Publishers.

Stinchcombe, A. L. (1965). Social structure and organizations. In J. G. March (Ed.), *Handbook of organizations* (pp. 142–193). Chicago: Rand McNally.

Tolbert, P. S., & Zucker, L. G. (1983). Institutional sources of change in the formal structure of organizations: The diffusion of civil service reforms, 1880–1935. *Administrative Science Quarterly, 28*, 22–39.

Westphal, J. D., Gulati, R., & Shortell, S. M. (1997). Customization or conformity: An institutional and network perspective on the content and consequences of TQM adoption. *Administrative Science Quarterly, 42*, 366–394.

Zald, M. N., & Denton, P. (1963). From evangelism to general service: The transformation of the YMCA. *Administrative Science Quarterly, 8*, 214–234.

Zucker, L. G. (1983). Organizations as institutions. In S. B. Bacharach (Ed.), *Research in the sociology of organizations* (Vol. 2, pp. 1–47). Greenwich, CT: JAI Press.

sures that Shape Organizations

nd ed.). Glenview, IL: Scott,

prospects. New York:

resource depen-

wood

299

Encouraging Innovation and Building Fitness

John Holland opened his book, *Hidden Order* (1995), with a provocative question: How do cities, with all their complexity and their many services, evolve without central coordination? It seems a trifling question until you think about it: cities are exceedingly complex entities serving hundreds of thousands, or even millions, of people, yet relatively few of their services and functions are centrally coordinated. Some bureaucracy with a massive strategic plan does not introduce bagel shops, but if you want bagels, you can find them in just about any city. If you want a foreign car, computer services, pet grooming, anchovies, a 10-penny nail, if you need supplies for the services you provide, if you need related services to support the product you sell, they can all be obtained. There are no governmental queen bees sitting around conference tables saying, "We need bagels and pet grooming on 4th and Vine." Natural selection does nothing to cause bagel shops to appear in a given city, it only helps determine which of several bagel shops will be successful. Nor are bagel shops fortuitous but accidental mutations, as natural selection would have to argue. Cities, with their myriad of interdependent services, are far too complex to be the product of either rational pre-planning or accidental mutation.

How, then, do cities emerge? One could ask the same thing about innovations, ideas, fads and rumors, and organizations—where do they come from and what makes some thrive while others die? And how does all this complexity happen without central coordination? The answer to this, and similar questions, is what this chapter is about.

The short answer is interaction. The theories that describe interactions involving massive networks are called Chaos and Complexity theory; they are called this not because they are hard to understand, but rather because they describe complex interacting systems. Chaos is a general theory of interacting systems; Complexity is a more specific theory of interacting and adaptive systems. The former is more descriptive of physical systems such as weather or turbulence; the latter is derived from Chaos but is more descriptive of biological and social systems.

Chaos and Complexity perspectives are natural, albeit unique, extensions of the theories we have examined thus far. They illuminate questions that Institutional theory, Population Ecology, and Loose Coupling hint at but fail to develop, and they ask questions that previous theories have failed to perceive, questions such as:

- How can accidental mutation (the foundation of Population Ecology) possibly account for all the rich and sophisticated diversity of social forms found in a society?

- How do complex structure and activity emerge, often unbidden and unexpected, from social and organizational activity? How, for example, do social movements, fads, rumors, technologies, informal groups, and organizational alliances emerge without central, intelligent coordination?

- How might different coupling patterns contribute to organizational fitness (Loose Coupling theory generally attributes fitness to loose patterns of interaction)?

- Why do seemingly healthy social systems—like the former USSR—sometimes disappear almost overnight?

- Why do good ideas sometimes languish while bad ones thrive?

This chapter explores these issues, and more. In it, students will:

- Describe activities in their schools in terms of interactive dynamics and emergence.

- Explore the role of leadership in emergent behavior.

- Understand the nature of fitness and how it evolves.

- Explore the emergence of incompetent behavior in education and how leaders can counter such emergence.

- Critique market competition assumptions that underlie educational initiatives such as school choice, vouchers, and charter schools.

- Evaluate emergent dynamics in an educational setting and devise strategies for reversing counterproductive emergent behaviors.

- Refine their definitions of the function of leadership in education.

OVERVIEW OF CHAOS AND COMPLEXITY THEORIES

Chaos and Complexity theories of organization, like many of our social theories, have roots in the sciences. Chaos theory is a science of turbulence. Its researchers discovered in the 1960s that, to their surprise, unpredictable behavior is not always random behavior; rather, many highly complex activities exhibit a structure and pattern that could not be observed before the computational capability of computers. Prior to that discovery, no one even imagined that stability and unpredictability could coexist. Scientists had assumed, for example, that weather would yield to accurate prediction if a stable pattern could be discovered in its dynamics: stability yields prediction. The first Chaologist, Edward Lorenz, uncovered the very pattern meteorologists had been seeking, but he also found that weather was still unpredictable (Lorenz, 1964). Unpredictable pattern has come to be called Chaos.

Chaologists found that the prediction problem in systems like weather runs deeper than previously imagined. What they discovered was that two nearby points in an interactive, nonlinear system, points that are behaving according to normal, positivistic rules of cause and effect, will not remain spatially correlated with one another. Shoot two balls, one after the other, out into a pinball machine, and they will follow two quite different trajectories. We can measure the balls' initial positions along with the force that acts on them, we can calculate the trajectories with equations that normally are quite good at predicting, but still their trajectories diverge unpredictably. They don't follow the paths that the equations say they will. The problem, it turns out, is that there are inevitably very small, logically insignificant differences in exactly where the pinballs start, and those tiny differences are magnified by the curved surfaces that interact with the balls. In the same way, small perturbations, something as minor as the flapping of a butterfly's wings, can reverberate throughout an interactive system with dramatic ultimate effect (thus, this phenomenon is called the "butterfly effect"). Knowing the state of a nonlinear system today, then, gives you little or no information about its state tomorrow because we can never know its precise initial position. Knowing the stock market today does relatively little to help you determine where it will be in a month. Chaotic systems just do not hold information very long; thus, they are ultimately, thoroughly unpredictable.

Chaotic events, such as weather or fads, can change suddenly and often without warning. The relationship between cause and effect in nonlinear systems is not smooth and constant—as when a governmental body slowly increases class size year after year without perceptible change in student achievement until finally one or two more students cause a precipitous decline in scores (see Ferguson, 1991). Chaos theory has been used to explore such nonlinear changes in decision making (Sterman, 1988), planning (Cartwright, 1991), economics (Arthur, 1989; Curtis, 1990), workforce productivity (Guastello, 1992), and classroom behavior (Doll, 1989).

Chaos theory is useful for explaining physical-like interactions, the types of things that go on in weather patterns and fluid turbulence. It does not account for adaptation and intelligent behavior, so its applications in social systems are somewhat limited. Researchers bridged this limitation in the 1970s and 1980s with a derivative theory that came to be called Complexity theory.

Complexity theory, like Chaos, is a science of large interactive networks and nonlinear cause and effect. Unlike Chaotic systems, Complex systems make rational, deliberate changes in response to their environments; further, their dynamics are more settled than are those of Chaotic systems (human behavior, a complex system, rarely exhibits the wildly turbulent characteristics of a hurricane, for example). Complex behavior lies somewhere between relatively unchanging stability and constantly changing Chaos; for this reason, it is often referred to as the Edge of Chaos. This location permits it the best of two worlds: its relative stability allows it to accumulate information (in a Chaotic system, information is quickly lost to butterfly effects), while its Chaotic side allows it to experiment with invention, or precipitous, nonlinear change. Like Chaos, Complex systems function according to regular rules of cause and effect, and because they do not fluctuate as wildly as Chaos, these rules permit some degree of predictability—hence, the successes of Contingency and other positivistic theories. Even so, they do have their nonlinear sides and they will produce anti-positivistic surprises from time to time.

Complexity's Place in Organizational Theory

Chaos and Complexity theories, then, are about interactions among different actors and how that interaction generates both innovation and fitness. As applied to social systems, these theories are a bit of an enigma because they cannot be categorized clearly as positivistic or anti-positivistic. They propose, that law-like, positivistic behaviors can produce unlaw-like, anti-positivistic results, that determinism creates both predictable and unpredictable behavior. Like the anti-positivists, they challenge assumptions of linear relationships between contingencies (such as raw material or subordinate readiness) and organizational structure; yet they propose that relationships between contingency and structure, while nonlinear, are usually rather stable. In a way, Chaos and Complexity theories suggest that positivism and anti-positivism are not the diametric opposites reflected by their definitions. They suggest instead that the forces over which positivists and anti-positivists debate—the material and nonmaterial, determinism and nondeterminism, predictable and nonpredictable—should be understood together, not separately. It is, when one thinks about it, a practical proposal: social behavior is simply too complex to fall exclusively into one or the other of the positivistic/anti-positivistic camps. Social behavior is indeed stable, but it is also capable of surprises. There is a regular relationship between contingency and outcome even though that relationship is nonlinear. Leaders must adjust to contingencies, but they also have latitude in how they run organizations. Complexity theory will help us understand the positivistic/anti-positivistic debate as two sides of the same thing, to understand how together these two social realities interact to create organization.

Complexity theory is more generally applicable to social systems than is Chaos and will consequently be the main focus of this chapter. Complexity is rather closely related to theories of social networks. Network theory can trace its roots back at least to the era of sociograms in the 1950s and 1960s. Sociograms are charts that graphically represent relationships among individuals in a group. Education students from that time, for example, were taught to ask children who their three best friends were, then use that data to construct sociograms, or profiles of social structure in their classes. Those modest beginnings blossomed into theories of social and organizational network, and it is with this that Complexity can best be identified. We cannot say Complexity is the direct descendant of

FIGURE 13.1
Relationship between
Complexity theory and
other anti-positivistic
theories.

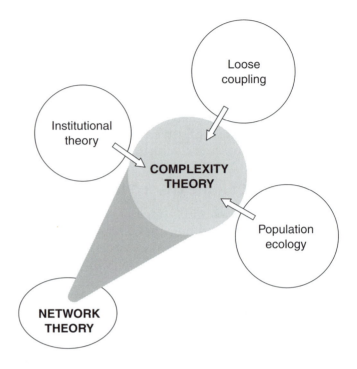

network theory because Complexity didn't evolve in the social science, it emerged and evolved in the physical and biological sciences. Even so, network theory does provide a natural niche for Complexity (see Fig. 13.1).

Perhaps the most important of the early network theories in organizational analysis is Resource Dependency. This theory, which was popular in the 1970s and 1980s, proposes that organizations depend on transactions with their environments (i. e., other organizations) for survival, and that the nature of an organization's environmental relationships determines its structure and behaviors (Pfeffer & Salancik, 1978). Organizations seek to control these relationships in order to reduce uncertainty and to avoid dependent relationships (as when another organization monopolizes a needed raw material). They achieve this with such strategies as alliances, mergers, cartels, interlocking directorates, and by integrating or diversifying their markets. Other theorists have explored networking as a means of integrating information and power (Barge, 1994). It has been used to explain such things as diffusion (Burt, 1992; Westphal, Gulati, and Shortell, 1997), failure (Human and Provan, 2000), minority influence (Westphal and Milton, 2000), and product or organizational status (Podolny, 1993).

Complexity theory looks at such interactions more globally. Whereas Resource Dependency predicts the deliberate creation of associations to help an organization control its environment, for example, Complexity predicts that associations are the natural result of adaptive interaction. That is, associations need not be deliberately created for specific purposes as Resource Dependency argues. Such natural, unplanned emergence has the same impact as its more deliberate cousins: it provides the system with fitness. But Complexity theorists offer greater insight into the dynamics of organizational fitness and the emergence of fitness than have Resource Dependency theorists. Further, Complexity theory argues that networks are the source of creativity and surprise, and on this point they supplant not only deliberate perspectives of creation (like Resource Dependency), but offer alternative explanations to natural selection as well.

Complexity borrows from, or is related to, other anti-positivistic theories. It borrows from Population Ecology because it argues that organizations assume stable forms that change sluggishly with the environment, and because it incorporates natural selection to help explain fitness. It borrows from the coupling perspectives of Loose Coupling, but unlike Loose Coupling, Complexity theory explores the dynamics and fitness contributions of multiple coupling patterns.

Complexity theory is closely related to Institutional theory. Institutionalism is about the spread of institutional isomorphism while Complexity theory is about the spread of fitness—and to Complexity theory, fitness includes institutional legitimacy. Further, network dynamics, which are at the core of Complexity studies, have lurked in the background of Institutional research and at times have even been overtly examined by its researchers (see, for example, Westphal, Gulati, and Shortell, 1997).

Complexity theory integrates and refocuses elements of these various traditions into its own unique perspective to explore the emergence, growth, stability, and demise of organizational forms and behaviors. Like many of its intellectual predecessors and relationships, it is about describing the general dynamics, the mass movements and behaviors, that characterize organizations, and is not primarily a prescription for leadership behavior. As has been the case in previous chapters, we will, nonetheless, explore implications for leadership; what we find will be, like the theory itself, different than anything we have seen before.

EMERGENCE

Complexity is about the emergence of things. It is a theory of where ideas and structures come from, of how surprises occur, how failure occurs, and how organizations grow strong. It provides guidance to leaders about how they can encourage new ideas and innovations, how they can change their organizations for the better, and how they can build and maintain strong organizations. Over the next three sections we will examine the emergence of cooperation, innovation, and, finally, fitness.

The Emergence of Cooperation

The notion of "field" was introduced in our discussion of Critical theory (see, for example, Oakes, Townley, & Cooper, 1998). The same idea is useful here. Field was defined by Dimaggio and Powell (1983) as "a totality of relevant actors;" it is "those organizations that, in the aggregate constitute a recognized area of institutional life: key suppliers, resource and product consumers, regulatory agencies and other organizations that produce similar services or products" (p. 148). Organizational fields are networks of related, interacting systems; they could be defined as a group of organizations, a group of departments or hierarchical levels, or a cluster of organizational roles. The key is that the systems in a field influence one another in some way.

Fields are composed of units whose fitness or cognitive beliefs are interdependent such that change in one unit potentially affects the state of the others. Participants in a field are coupled with links of varying strength: some are tightly coupled, some moderately so, some are only weakly coupled. The field within which the automobile industry exists includes buyers and suppliers, gas stations, auto repair shops, insurance agencies, a system of highway laws, road construction companies, and so forth. Each of these industries potentially influences, and is potentially influenced by, the state of other actors within the field. The price of gasoline can affect the market for automobiles; the decision of policy-makers can affect the way cars are built.

Correlation and Isomorphism The engine that underlies the emergence and cohesion of fields is called "correlation" (Prigogine, 1997). Correlation is a process in which social actors accommodate each other's needs by compromising bits of themselves. They compromise on worldviews, beliefs, structural forms—they even compromise their individual fitness, all for the good of the whole.

Correlation will cause participating actors to look like one another. It is said that older married couples tend to look alike; this observation is likely influenced by personality similarities that have evolved over the years of the couple's relationship. Westphal, Gulati, and Shortell (1997) found that organizations in a network likewise tend to "look alike" because of their common adoption of leadership strategies (in their case, the organizations tended to adopt the similar form of TQM). They refer to this as isomorphism.

Institutional theorists attribute organizational isomorphism to a search for socially constructed legitimacy. Its engine is normative, mimicry, and procedural pressure (DiMaggio and Powell, 1983). The perspective of Complexity theory, by contrast, revolves around fitness, with interactive, correlational adjustment as its engine, but this too leads to isomorphism. Organizations adjust their production and leadership strategies to accommodate the fitness needs of other organizations within their network (correlation). The degree of isomorphism that results is related to the level of coupling that binds the organizations. Highly coupled systems experience a high degree of correlational pressure and isomorphism, while loosely coupled systems experience little correlation.

CAS The discussion of networks and fields leads us to a core concept in Complexity theory: the Complex Adaptive System, or CAS. A CAS is an interactive network of actors (see Fig. 13.2). It emerges because of the accommodations people make when they interact.

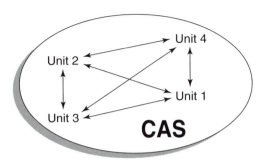

FIGURE 13.2   The correlation of individual units leads to the emergence of CAS.

John Holland (1995) uses the term "aggregate" to describe mutually accommodating clusters, and his terminology allows us to be more specific about the nature of CAS. For our purposes, an aggregate is the smallest social or organizational unit from which an organizational field is constructed. An aggregate might be defined as an informal group, a department, a division, or even an organization, depending on the observer's needs.

Aggregates interact and correlate with other aggregates to form larger social networks called "meta-aggregates." This term will be used to refer to specific contractual (or noncontractual but mutually agreed upon) cooperative relationships among aggregates. An organization (aggregate) and its customers (another aggregate) interact to create a meta-aggregate, as do the different organizations in a cartel or different departments in a division. Meta-aggregates are the subject of Resource Dependency theory, described earlier.

Relationships among meta-aggregates are less formally defined or direct than are relations among aggregates. Two meta-aggregates are linked when the state of one is related to the state of the other. Meta-aggregates are often linked because of common dependency on a related industry or on other meta-aggregates. Interdependent meta-aggregates are called meta-meta-aggregates, and constitute our definition of field (see Fig. 13.3). The automotive industry field (gas stations, insurance companies, etc.) described earlier is a meta-meta-aggregate. Meta-meta-aggregates might be linked by a technology such as instruction. Schools, teacher preparation institutions, tort liability (negligence) laws, and insurance regulations, for example, are all linked by a common relationship with education, and, along with other such associations, constitute a meta-meta-aggregate or field. One meta-aggregate is not necessarily linked formally to the other, but events in one potentially impact the other. One could conceive, for example, that school violence could influence tort liability laws in a given state, which could, in turn, affect negligence insurance regulations and the law curriculum in administration preparation programs.

Units, whether aggregates or meta-aggregates, are coupled by varying levels of bonding: some are tightly coupled, some are loosely coupled, and then there is everything in between. This bonding diversity discourages, but does not totally prevent, "cascading damage" (most cascades get trapped in loosely coupled

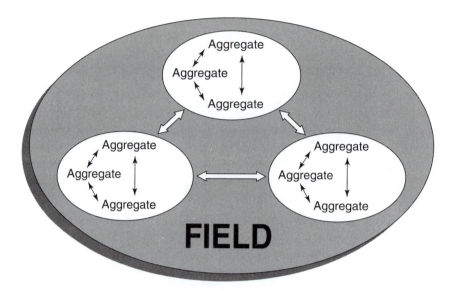

FIGURE 13.3 Aggregates interact to form meta-aggregates, and meta-aggregates interact to form meta-meta-aggregates, or fields.

dead ends). Complexity theory suggests that dominant bonding patterns are moderately coupled, particularly those within meta-aggregates (fields may be a bit more loosely coupled but still lie within the moderate coupling range). Coupling strength is defined by Loose Coupling theorists as (1) the time it takes for changes in one unit to affect another unit, and (2) the degree of influence that changes in one unit exert over another. Complexity theorists add that coupling is a function of the number of units a given unit is influenced by or influences.

The Emergence of Innovation

Complexity theory helps explain how surprises, such as fads, innovations, programs, educational emphases, and community demands, emerge. Darwin and Spencer claimed that these happen because of accident and natural selection; Complexity theorists argue that innovation emerges from cauldrons of interacting aggregates. Like fields, innovation is a product of the nature of that interaction and of the surprises that characterize nonlinear events.

To understand, we must clarify the nature of social cause and effect. Traditional, linear notions of one-way causality, where B responds directly and proportionately to causal agent A, are not sufficient to explain what goes on in Complex systems. Instead, social causality emerges out of interacting networks with multiple, circular chains of events where causes become effects and effects become causes. In this cauldron, aggregates combine and recombine with one another to create new aggregates and meta-aggregates, and occasionally nonlinear surprises emerge to change the whole nature of the cauldron.

Complexity theorists call this process "autocatalysis" (Kauffman, 1993). Autocatalysis means that events catalyze themselves. Existing aggregates interact to create new aggregates, much like chemicals interact to form new substances (the correlation principle). These new aggregates interact with one another and with other existing aggregates to create more aggregates or, more likely, meta-aggregates. At some point, the interactive dynamics create one or more catalysts, something that speeds up interactions. In a sense, this catalyst supplements mutation. Catalysts often speed up the process by hastening the production of the original aggregates that started the whole process.

The emergence of the microcomputer is a good example of autocatalysis. The original units of the microcomputer included transistors, printed boards, microprocessors, cathode ray tubes, and LEDs. In the 1960s and early 1970s, the potential of these (and other) units was explored individually and in combination with one another. The combinations in particular yielded a variety of new forms, such as the handheld calculator and "intelligent" toys. These advances catalyzed the development and improvement of the original units and the emergence of newer, even more sophisticated applications. The handheld calculator, for example, catalyzed the further development of the microprocessor and of data storage technology. In 1976 a hobby company, Micro Instrumentation and Telemetry Systems (MITS), pulled together these various pieces and created the first microcomputer, the Altair. Unit-level interactions catalyzed higher-level products and sophistication, which catalyzed, in turn, further development of the original components and of the higher-level components. Higher-level interactions led to even higher-level products, and so on. Eventually, all this collapsed together and the microcomputer emerged. For many, the micro appeared almost out of nowhere—technology took a giant and unexpected leap forward—but the dynamics that led to this leap forward had been brewing for years. Once they achieved critical mass, it was inevitable that micros would happen.

RESEARCH TOPIC

Describe an event in your organization in terms of interactive dynamics. Perhaps your school has had a successful year in sports, or you have been doing well recently in your standardized test scores, or perhaps, on the flip side, your test scores are dismal or you are a school of higher education that has difficulty recruiting high-achieving students. Identify the components (people, activities, events) that contribute to your success or failure. How do they catalyze, or fail to catalyze, one another (both success and failure can be catalyzed)? What can a leader do to help catalyze the emergence of positive, effective structures and behaviors? The type of questions you might ask include: Does the booster club lack leadership and how is that lack affected by, and affect, the team's performance, or the coach's and the school administrator's leadership styles? To what extent is student performance on achievement tests affected by the stability or lack of stability of the student population (transience), programmatic initiatives, staff profile, and so forth?

Organizational Failure Failure happens for the same reasons; the major difference is that with failure, networks collapse rather than emerge. An organization is supported by its networks: its aggregates, meta-aggregates, and meta-meta-aggregates. These networks are normally quite robust and can resist damage effectively. However, when damage accumulates, when detrimental events interact with one another, when problems cascade from one system to another, a critical mass of problems can be achieved that cause the collapse of the network and, consequently, the organization.

A colleague and I studied this phenomenon among nonprofit organizations (Marion & Bacon, 1999). One of the nonprofits we examined had once been a robust, strong organization. Its cascade to failure began when a new leader made significant changes in the core organizational structure (the aggregate). These changes led to the loss, within a short period of time, of all but one staff member, forcing the hiring of workers who were unfamiliar with the organization and its service area (meta-meta-aggregate). Changes were also made in the structure of the board of directors (meta-aggregate), and again, within a short period of time, all but two resigned or retired and were replaced with people who were unfamiliar with the organization and its services. The massive losses in the aggregate and meta-aggregate disrupted or weakened numerous alliances with meta-meta-aggregate systems (community clubs, medical service institutions, schools, churches, businesses, other nonprofits, state agencies, etc.). Even so, this nonprofit appeared on the surface to thrive, despite its underlying deterioration. Then the director resigned two and a half years after assuming the job for reasons unrelated to what was happening in the nonprofit. The director believed the organization was strong when he left: it had a budget that would sustain it for a month and several fundraisers were scheduled. The network, which at one time was quite strong, had enough residual robustness to appear strong, but in reality it had been weakened significantly. The director's departure was the final straw and the organization folded within four months. For many (including the director), the failure came as a surprise, seeming to come out of nowhere. The system looked strong because fitness does not decline in direct proportion to damage: a system's networks can make it look strong right up to the end. Failure is the collapse of networks, and that tends to occur nonlinearly; it happens suddenly, when one more piece of straw is added to the pile.

The Emergence of Fitness

Organizational fitness, and the emergence of fitness, is a function of networks, and network fitness is related to the coupling patterns that unite individual aggregates. As we saw above, when coupling patterns are weak, the organizational network is jeopardized. As we shall see, when network linkages are too strong, fitness is likewise jeopardized. Strong networks require moderate levels of coupling among aggregates, meta-aggregates, and fields.

Organizations that are strongly coupled must juggle the needs of a number of different actors. Any change in one aggregate affects the fitness of a lot of other aggregates; thus, it is difficult to find a change that accommodates everybody's fitness needs. This is because of conflicting constraints: what is good for one may not be good for another (we introduced this earlier in Chapter 2, the section on hyperrationality). If a curricular change in a high school's math department negatively impacts the curriculum of the physics department, you have a conflicting constraint. If an organization is weakly coupled, this is not a big problem; if it is strongly coupled, with each department directly affecting many others, this is a big problem. You might say it's like having a room full of jealous prima donnas waiting for role assignments, and trying to make them all happy. It will be very difficult to find a compromise that satisfies everyone's ego. Organizational units aren't necessarily prima donnas, but what is good for one may very well be detrimental to one or more others, and finding compromises that maximize fitness in a strongly coupled network can be daunting.

In systems with no coupling among aggregates, there are no conflicting constraints because there are no interactions. Of course, there is no organization either, but that is beside the point. In this scenario, all that needs to be done to assure maximum fitness of the organization is to optimize fitness one unit at a time. No one unit's state affects any other unit's state, so there are no differences to work out. For weakly coupled organizations (each department only affects, say, one other department), the conflicting constraints are likewise manageable, with only limited constraints. The organization must make some compromises, but system units are still largely on their own and the limited interdependencies demand little coordination—each unit can essentially do its own thing. Therein lies a problem, however: there is little incentive for the units to get their acts together or to increase their level of fitness. This is inertia without any incentive to change. Such organizations tend to stagnate, and their survival may be at risk (Marion & Bacon, 1999).

In moderately coupled systems, the constraints are more complex but still manageable. The organization will have to work harder to find a good combination of solutions to the conflicting constraints in its networks, but this only forces them to find quality solutions. They can't stop with the first solutions that come along, as they would in weakly coupled networks. There is sufficient looseness in coupling patterns to enable coordination, but sufficient tightness to make coordination difficult and force quality compromises; sufficient looseness to foster individual innovation and sufficient interdependency to enable network exploitation and development of innovations. Such systems are strong and vibrant.

Tight Coupling, then, creates problems of coordination and makes it difficult to find fit compromises. Stuart Kauffman (1995) has labeled this the "Stalinist limit dilemma," referring to Stalin's efforts to centrally coordinate the economy of the USSR. In such a system, change is difficult to implement because of massive conflicting constraints, and the system typically becomes frozen in a low fitness state. The Stalinist limit system is overly stable; units interact in a highly predictable manner, and change rarely if ever occurs. Loose Coupling also creates problems of coordination but for different reasons: without substantive interdependency, there is little incentive to coordinate. There is also little incentive to improve one's fitness. Kauffman called this the "Leftist Italian dilemma," referring to the numerous, uncoordinated political parties in Italy. The Leftist Italian system is chaotic; different units interact in a seemingly random manner, and changes tend to occur spontaneously and without warning. Kauffman relates all this to patchwork quilts: the Stalinist limit is like a quilt with one large patch while the Leftist Italian pattern is like a quilt with many small patches.

Moderately coupled systems lie between these extremes. They are sufficiently coupled to permit coordination and encourage innovation, and sufficiently loose to permit change and innovation. Such systems must make compromises among conflicting constraints, but the patterns of constraint are not so complex that fit compromises are difficult to find. The search for fit compromises is challenging, but a resolvable challenge is invigorating. These systems exist at the edge of chaos, that balance between stability and chaos.

The Evolution of Fit Organizations

Young, emerging networks operate with a somewhat different set of rules than do mature organizations. Fitness in mature organizations is threatened by tight networks of interdependency; fitness in young networks requires them. For young, developing networks, tightly coupled interdependency does not lead to frozen stability as it would in mature networks; rather, it leads to massive cascading change. Young, emerging aggregates must vigorously search for fitness or they risk dying before they even get a start on life. Because their parts are so highly interconnected, a change in one part of the aggregate can easily reverberate throughout the aggregate, thus emerging systems tend to change rapidly and dramatically. One can readily see this in the rapid growth and learning of young children. In organizations, this process is aided by natural selection, which helps the system choose between fit and unfit options.

As an aggregate matures, its pool of possible fitter states dwindles and fitness depends increasingly on the ability to cooperate and compromise. Tight, extensive networks, with their massive, chaotic changes, begin to become a liability. At this point, natural selection begins to favor fewer actors and gradually increasing looseness in networks (Kauffman, 1993). Changes become less dramatic and less frequent as the network winnows competitors and seeks accommodation among its remaining components. Eventually, at maturity, the system reaches a moderately coupled state with a manageable (but still challenging) number of interacting aggregates and meta-aggregates.

The mature state must be sufficiently interdependent and must contain enough competitors to enable future change, for over-stability can be just as debilitating as the continued chaos of immaturity. Fitness requires that systems are neither too stable nor too chaotic—fitness exists in the in-between, edge of chaos state. Its stability is dynamic rather than stagnant.

Fit, dynamically stable networks—aggregates, meta-aggregates, and fields—represent a balance in yet another way. No one unit within the network achieves optimal fitness; each must give up something in order to find a compromise that serves the whole. Complexity theory is not a throwback to the pre-Open Systems days when theorists assumed that leadership's role is to find optimal solutions to organizational problems. Optimal solutions cannot exist in a system of conflicting constraints. Fit networks have achieved the best state they can given the conflicting needs of all aggregates remaining in the network. Individual fitness is compromised for the good of the larger network.

LEADING COMPLEX ORGANIZATIONS

It is clear from all this that one of leadership's important roles is to build networks. Leaders should initiate, encourage, catalyze, make connections, and, as appropriate, should leave matters alone.

Let's take this last point first. Complex dynamics are bottom-up phenomena. That is, order emerges naturally out of unrehearsed interactions among actors and aggregates. Complex systems do well when they engage in a relatively unencumbered search for fitter states. Emergence is difficult to plan or control, and when effort is expended to control it, unanticipated outcomes are not uncommon (outcome uncertainty has been a key feature of organizational theories since at least the 1960s). Complexity theory proposes that, when searches are directed from the top down, a system will likely settle into only moderately fit states. Systems must be relatively free to interact with other systems until good fitness strategies are found.

Bill McKelvey ("The gurus speak," 1999), referencing theorist Yaneer Bar-Yam, has said that, when an individual controls group behavior, the group behavior can be no more complex than that individual. He argues from this that leadership theorists are wrong in advocating such things as heroic leadership or visionary leadership—the person who single handedly leads the organization to production Utopia. Such leaders shut down emergent behavior by controlling it. "In a rapidly changing world," McKelvey continues, "what chance is there that the leader has the right vision at the time, or the right level of technology, and so forth? Very little chance" (p. 77).

All this is not, however, a call to return to laissez-faire management. Experiences with Spencerian philosophy in the late 1800s and early 1900s demonstrate that indiscriminate fitness searches can lead into undesirable territory. But clearly it rejects Taylorian-like control. What it advocates is leadership that prods, encourages, complexifies, advocates, symbolizes, and most of all, sees the systemic picture.

Effective leaders of complex systems are technically competent at the tasks they perform and they help those for whom they are responsible to be technically competent as well. Technical competence in school leadership includes competent instructional leadership, the ability to solicit resources for the school, effective interpersonal skills, the ability to manage programs, and the ability to manage resources. Even though complex dynamics select effective fitness strategies for organizations, the actors in those organizations must be effective at exploiting the capabilities of the strategy.

Beyond this obvious fact, effective leaders learn to manage and develop networks. They foster and cultivate interdependencies within and without the school. As Regine and Lewin (2000) concluded in their ethnographic study of leadership in a dozen U.S. and UK industries operating according to Complexity principles, "Leaders generally felt that it was their responsibility to enrich connections in the system—that is, to forge new connections where none existed or to improve existing connections" (p. 10).

Complexity theory's definition of a school's external network would include elements that one might not necessarily imagine. Certainly it includes the obvious elements: parents, school boards, local clubs, and such. These are the elements that make up a school's meta-aggregate, and they are readily identified. A school's strength arises from its meta-meta-aggregate (or field) as well, however. These elements may include the local community college, informal community groups, book sales representatives, educators in other districts, professional organizations, service clubs, and arts groups. The respective impacts of these groups certainly vary, and the attention devoted to cultivating various relationships would likewise vary. Regardless, the interactive fingers of the effective school should spread wide and far.

Leadership's role in network construction is twofold: to directly engage in network-building activities (as we have been discussing) and to catalyze network-building. A catalyst is a person who indirectly fosters network construction. The leader can perform this role through delegation (by asking an assistant principal to work with social clubs in the school district, for example), by providing encouragement and resources to subordinates (such as enabling teachers to attend conferences), or by simply not interfering in network construction.

Leaders also catalyze network development by becoming what John Holland (1995) has called a "tag." For our purposes, a tag is defined from two related perspectives. First, a tag is a feature that separates an aggregate from other aggregates. It makes the aggregate distinctive and definable. If the eight ball on a billiard table had a colored stripe like many of the other balls on the table, it could not be readily distinguished. The fact that it is black sets it apart. Similarly, an aggregate needs a distinguishing feature to set it apart from other aggregates. Second, a tag symbolizes the aggregate. It is the flag around which everyone rallies; it is the philosophy that binds people together. Winston Churchill was a symbol—tag—of Great Britain's spirit during World War II. Churchill did not fight the war, but one can hardly think of the Battle of Great Britain without thinking of him. He was a symbol of the sacrifice and the spirit of the British people, the symbol that united Great Britain.

Most leaders play less dramatic roles than do leaders like Churchill, but the role of tag is nonetheless potent even in modest endeavors. The catalyzing school principal might serve as tag for instructional excellence; the catalyzing dean might serve as a tag for a school's research excellence and its teaching reputation. Such tags articulate a system's personality for its inhabitants and for its public. Tags rally subordinates around the organization's ideals. They solicit resources to support goals, they engage others in goal-based activities, and they build meta-aggregates and meta-meta-aggregates that support the goals and that extend the system's influence.

Leaders of complex organizations drop seeds of emergence. Bill McKelvey poses the question, "How do we actually do leadership in a way that fosters emergent structure in a firm without the leader somehow creating a bunch of passive fol-lowers following some vision" ("The gurus speak," 1999)? They do it by identify-ing knowledge centers within an organization, by encouraging them to do creative things, and by getting them to communicate with one another. Leaders encourage people to try things, then to evaluate and change their experiments. The complex leader doesn't closely control, for controls limit the organization's potential; rather, the complex leader creates organized disorder in which dynamic things happen at multiple locales within the system. This leader seeks to spawn emergent behavior and creative surprises rather than to specify and control organizational activities.

 ## ACTIVITY

If you work in a k-12 environment, try a little experiment. Recruit a few relatively popular students to participate in this activity. Ask each to do something a bit idiosyncratic for a week or two—perhaps walk around with their fingers hooked in their belt loops, wear their clothing a bit differently, or introduce a new idiom into their vocabulary (such as us-ing the word "spontaneous" in place of the word "cool"). They should, of course, be sworn to secrecy about what is going on, and they should all be doing the same thing. Predictably, this fad should spread; your task is to observe how it spreads. It should spread first to the group (aggregate) to which your co-conspirators belong. If you're lucky, it will soon spread to aggregates that are fairly closely associated with the first aggregate, and eventually to more distant aggregates. Your co-conspirators are tags in this experiment. They are the catalysts that get the fad moving, that drop the seeds, and keep them grow-ing. They are metaphors for leadership. When the experiment is complete, report what happened to your organizational theory class. Discuss the implications for leadership be-havior. Given your results, what does it mean to "drop the seeds of emergence?"

This activity would make an interesting research paper, but you will need to develop well-planned qualitative strategies for tracking the spread of the fad. ▪

Leadership and the Emergence of Group Personalities

Leaders need to be attuned to the "personalities" of the aggregates that evolve within an organization. Group personality, like innovation, ideas, and movements, is an emergent dynamic; it emerges from interactions among people and between people and activities, and is dependent on, among other things, the climate of the organization, the capabilities and beliefs of participating actors, and the na-ture of the tasks that actors perform. Leaders foster the development of effective group personalities by discouraging the evolution of behaviors that hinder ef-fectiveness, such as interpersonal conflicts, mediocre work habits, or boring work. This is a tricky task for, as we have discussed, interactive dynamics are highly complex and idiosyncratic; they resist top-down control and at times seem to have a mind of their own. That is, attempts to suppress negative behavior can make matters worse. Perhaps the leader can try a positive approach by interject-ing a dynamic, innovative attitude into organizational activities (dropping the seeds of emergence). The leader should certainly serve as a tag and a catalyst for the productive atmosphere desired.

ROUNDTABLE

Incompetence, as a group personality, is particularly difficult to address. Justin Kruger and David A. Dunning (1999) of Cornell University have investigated incompetence and people's perceptions of their own competence. They found that incompetent people don't realize they are incompetent, for the skills needed to *judge* competence are the same as the skills needed to *be* competent. Thus, a person who is poor at telling jokes is oblivious to that fact, and people who are poor at day trading persist in losing money in that activity. In fact, they report, people who do things poorly are usually more confident of their abilities than people who do things well. The researchers concluded that such people probably fail to learn from their life experiences because they rarely receive negative feedback about their performance. Even if people do receive such information, they often are not led to understand *why* their performance is suboptimal. Further, incompetent people seem unable to benefit from comparisons with competent people because they lack the skills needed to spot competence.

Incompetent people, then, convince themselves that they are competent, thus making it difficult for leaders to rectify incompetence. The situation can be exacerbated when incompetent individuals aggregate into a "mutual admiration society," or group personality. They reinforce one another's skills, or lack thereof, thus creating a culture of incompetence. How would you deal with incompetent group personalities?

ORGANIZATIONAL INERTIA AND FITNESS—A DIFFERENT TWIST

"Fitness" is the ability to glean sufficient resources from the environment to meet survival needs. Fitness can be defined either as production efficiency or in terms of irrational ideational forces (such as institutionalism, politics, or control). Fitness in a state's office of education, for example, could be as much a function of image as of effective productivity. Fitness is about survival, and whether survival means playing political games or enhancing efficient production is determined by the situation.

Traditional Fitness: Decreasing Returns

Traditional theory presumes that organizations must grow and adapt in order to maintain fitness. Inertia is good to a point, but organizations that are too set in their ways risk getting out of step with their environments. School failure, for example, is typically attributed to educational systems that are overburdened with incompetent and unchanging teachers or curricula that fail to address today's needs. They fail society because they are inertial.

This assumption is based on a philosophy that is deeply ingrained in the Western mindset (Waldrop, 1992). This philosophy associates fitness with decreasing returns and competition. Decreasing returns means, for example, that a second glass of lemonade is not as desirable as the first, and that increasing a ship engine's torque after a certain speed is surpassed will produce a negligible increase in speed. In economics, it means that an organization can tap only so much of a market before demand for its product levels off. Because market share is finite, organizations typically share a market with other producers and other ideas. Ford, for example, shares the automobile market with other car manufacturers, and its internal combustion engine shares the market with ideas about better engines—it even shares the market with potentially radical technologies such as electric cars. To maintain market share, an organization must be competitive—it must explore new ideas and must produce ever better engines. It cannot let up or it will lose its market, just as a ship would quickly lose speed if it cut its engines. Competition and decreasing returns, in this scenario, are central to strong, growing economies.

Poor schools, then, are poor because they have no incentive to improve (competition). Public schools have a virtual monopoly on education, and monopolies stifle improvement and create mediocrity. Society's challenge, then, is to either break this monopoly or find ways to force education out of its overstuffed malaise.

Complex Stability and Fitness: Increasing Returns

Brian Arthur (1989), of the Santa Fe Institute for Study of Complexity, argues that fitness is a product of increasing, rather than decreasing, returns, and that monopoly is good rather than bad. Increasing returns means that things grow without apparent end. A rock rolling down a snowy incline and accumulating mass represents increasing returns, as does a feedback loop between a microphone and speaker. In economics, it refers to situations in which a system attracts some resources, those resources spark the accumulation of additional resources, and the process continues ad infinitum. That is, a system gains an advantage within its environment and that advantage gains it more advantage and so on—to them that has shall be given more, so to speak.

Increasing returns tends to shut down competition and to close out alternative solutions because it favors just one or two approaches to a given problem. Proponents, for example, argue that increasing returns pretty well precludes electric cars unless something radical happens (oil becomes uncomfortably expensive or electric power demonstrates unequivocal superiority, for example)—gas engines dominate the market and cannot easily relinquish that dominance. Organizations are fit because such dominance allows them to thrive and accrue environmental resources, not because they are the better idea. This is stability, but not the stability of decreasing returns. Stability, for decreasing returns advocates, means finite shares of the market; for increasing returns advocates, it means unchangeable dominance of the environment.

Arthur offers four reasons why a dominant, rather than better, idea may prevail in the market place (see Fig. 13.4). These reasons are similar to those offered by Population Ecologists for inertia, but this time the focus is on fitness rather than competitive disadvantage. First, the high costs associated with setting up a

FIGURE 13.4 Reasons for stability and for fitness; Arthur's four, plus one.

production strategy or changing to a new strategy are incentive to keep doing what one is currently doing, even if more effective strategies are available. Related to this, the unit costs of an organization's products decrease as its output increases, thus making it even more unlikely that a new idea or technology will readily replace an existing strategy. It is an almost universal fact that the first units produced under a new production strategy will cost much more than units produced with an established strategy. When CD burners first appeared on the market, they were almost prohibitively expensive; this was due at least in part to high production costs. Only when production increased did the costs drop.

Second, becoming proficient with a new way of doing things typically involves a learning curve; thus, the first units produced under a new strategy could very well be less effective and dependable than units produced under an old one. For example, teachers who modify their instructional procedures may be less effective while they work out the bugs than they were before with their old instructional techniques.

Third, Arthur argues that when an organization changes its technology or production strategies, it often threatens the well-being of other organizations. Such dependent organizations will resist industry changes that affect their survival. For example, numerous automobile-related industries—such as oil distributors, repair shops, and filter producers—depend on the gas engine standard and would resist changing that standard.

Finally, there may be an expectation or belief that a prevailing strategy will dominate the future; thus, there is reluctance among consumers to try something new. The Microsoft Windows® operating system currently dominates its market, and most consumers believe it will dominate well into the future. Consequently, they are unlikely to assume the risk of adopting a different system.

A variation of Arthur's third point gets even closer to the heart of Complexity theory's definition of fitness. Organizational fitness is directly related to robust, interdependent networks. VHS tapes are not a stand-alone success; this industry's success was built on the proliferation of VHS players, the use of VHS by the home movie distribution industry, VHS cameras, and so forth. It is a story of interdependency and network. An organization is fit when it is a part of a network (field) of related organizations, each of which depends on the network for its well-being and each of which supports the network's well-being in return.

Fit networks control their environment and inhibit the emergence of upstarts that would challenge their stability and fitness. They don't necessarily conspire to do this; it can happen naturally via mechanisms such as those that Arthur discussed. Once fit networks are established, it is often prohibitively expensive to break out of the network commitments and adopt a new production strategy or technology. For the home video industry to switch exclusively to the emerging DVD technology, for example, it would have to dismantle widespread commitments to VHS and create a new network of interdependencies around DVD. Individuals would have to throw out their VHS players and invest in DVD players. This would require that they sacrifice the ability to record unless they maintained a dual system. DVD movie cameras are just beginning to appear, so people would still have tape-based home movies. Video stores would have to convert totally to DVD movies and face big losses in their existing VHS stock. The iron oxide industry would take a big hit. All this is not to say that DVD technology will not dominate the market eventually, it's just that the VHS meta-meta-aggregate will be tough to topple, for its networks of support are extensive and robust.

Fitness from this perspective does not necessarily come from having a better technology; rather, it comes from having an initial advantage. A gas-driven automobile won a popular cross-country race at the beginning of the 20th century against competitors that included steam-driven engines. This catapulted the gas-driven engine into prominence and gave it a popular advantage that steam engines could not overcome (who's to say that if a steam-driven auto had won, we wouldn't have developed that technology and be driving a completely different type of car today).

Not all organizational strategies can dominate their environments like this, however. While fitness is based on robust networks of interdependencies, some networks depend on exchanges that are neither costly nor permanent. Such networks can change readily, for change does not threaten the network or the organization. The music industry, for example, readily changed in the 1950s from a big band standard to a rock and roll standard. This was possible for a variety of rather obvious reasons. It costs little for consumers to change their tastes: they were going to buy new music anyhow, and it cost them the same to buy rock and roll records as to buy big band records. Similarly, the shift was not expensive for the recording industry: they used the same machinery and technology they had used before. Many existing musicians were affected, but their resistance had little impact on the change.

ROUNDTABLE

School Choice is a popular issue in American politics. Its advocates suggest that parents should be allowed to select the school, private or public, that their children attend, and that public funding should follow their children. They ground their arguments in the free market (decreasing returns) philosophy: if schools have to compete for funding, then education will improve. Debate this assumption. Explore alternatives suggested by increasing returns and decide which perspective is likely correct. Consider two competing schools, one perceived as poor and the other perceived as being good. Will competition force the poor school to improve? ∎

POSITIVISM OR ANTI-POSITIVISM?

We can now pull together these arguments about Complexity theory and shed further light on the positivism/anti-positivism debate that has been discussed in the last part of this book. Complexity theory suggests that human discretion, which is at the core of the debate, is either enabled or constrained by network characteristics.

The point can be graphically represented as a contingency table (Fig. 13.5). The two dimensions of this table are degree of network complexity (scope and level of interdependency) and cost of changing the network.

Four organizational forms are defined by the dichotomization (into high and low) of these variables. The Type 1 organization (high complexity, high cost) is committed to an extensive, well-developed network of systems. Further, it would be expensive, in real costs and network integrity, to adopt a new strategy or technology. The automobile industry, for example, is part of a large and established aggregate, meta-aggregate, and field, thus its network commitments are complex. Its fixed assets are expensive, therefore not readily replaced, and the gas-driven engine it has adopted as its standard has a high level of legitimacy and acceptance. This type of organization is stable and concentrated (by concentrated, I refer to its level of dependence on other systems).

Leaders in Type 1 organizations have relatively little discretion over the structure, activities, and technology of their operations. These are pretty well determined by network commitments and legitimacy. If the automobile industry were to change its production strategy, for example, it would likely disrupt relationships with hundreds of product and service suppliers who are themselves structured for the existing production strategy. This would reduce the fitness of both the network and the automobile industry itself. Selfish change under such conditions hurts everyone, including the selfish party. Type 1 systems, then, resist dramatic change and would logically be best described by positivistic determinism.

Type 2 organizations (high complexity, low cost) are moderately stable but still concentrated. They have extensive networks but those networks are based on a technology that is relatively inexpensive. Leader discretion is somewhat restrained by network commitments but, since the cost of change is low, they do have some latitude in their decision making. This organization is less strongly

COST OF CHANGING

	High		Low	
	Form:	Stable, concentrated	*Form:*	Mod. stable, concentrated
High	*Discretion:*	Low	*Discretion:*	Low/moderate
	Change resistance: likelihood:	High Low	*Change resistance: likelihood:*	Moderate Moderate
	Innovation complexity:	High	*Innovation complexity:*	Moderate
	1		**2**	
	Form:	Mod. unstable, dispersed	*Form:*	Unstable, dispersed
Low	*Discretion:*	Moderate	*Discretion:*	High
	Change resistance: likelihood:	Moderate Moderate	*Change resistance: likelihood:*	Low Low
	Innovation complexity:	Moderate	*Innovation complexity:*	Low
	3		**4**	

NETWORK COMPLEXITY (row label at left: High / Low)

FIGURE 13.5   Effect of network complexity and cost of change on organizational form, change, and technology.

restricted by contingencies than are Type 1 systems. It is somewhat resistant to change but still somewhat likely to change. Its networks have created a relatively sophisticated technology but the tendency of this organization to change more readily than do Type 1 organizations means that emerging technologies are sometimes aborted before they can achieve their full potential. The music industry is an example of this type of system.

Type 3 organizations (low complexity, high cost) have immature or vestigial networks but expensive production processes; they are moderately unstable and dispersed (low levels of interdependency). Leadership discretion is limited only by the costs associated with change; if the organization has the desire and the money, then there is little external pressure to prevent it from changing. Like Type 2 systems, this organization is only moderately determined by contingencies. Also like Type 2 systems, it is moderately resistant to change, moderately likely to change, and has moderately complex technologies.

Type 4 systems (low complexity, low cost) are not part of developed networks and have low-cost technologies and production strategies; they are unstable and dispersed. Leadership discretion is high; thus, of the four organizational types, they are most strongly described by anti-positivistic theories. Their resistance to change is low but they are not likely to change because there is no network (and consequently no legitimacy) pressure to do so. Since there is limited network interaction, their technology will be relatively undeveloped. Locally owned restaurants in small towns exemplify a Type 4 system.

ROUNDTABLE

Where would you place education in this chart? Explain.

THE FIFTH DISCIPLINE

Peter Senge's book, *The Fifth Discipline* (1990), has been one of the more popular management books of the 1990s. Senge recognized the practical implications of Complexity theory and expressed a kinship between his work and that of researchers in this discipline in a panel discussion at the Second International Conference on Complex Systems in 1998.

> Most of what's talked about in a conference like this is dynamic complexity . . . by dynamic complexity I do mean things like emergence. I mean situations where cause and effect are not close in time and space, where in the behavior of a complex, non-linear system, the areas of most significance are very often very distant from the symptoms of the problem. ("The Gurus Speak," p. 79)

Senge's arguments are grounded in the same premise that grounds Complexity theory: organizations must be understood systemically. This means stepping back and seeing the forest rather than merely seeing more trees. Senge put it this way:

> A cloud masses, the sky darkens, leaves twist upward, and we know that it will rain. We also know that after the storm, the runoff will feed into groundwater miles away, and the sky will grow clear by tomorrow. All these events are distant in time and space, and yet they are all connected within the same pattern. Each has an influence on the rest, an influence that is usually hidden from view. You can only understand the system of a rainstorm by contemplating the whole, not any individual part of the pattern.
>
> Business and other human endeavors are also systems. They, too, are bound by invisible fabrics of interrelated actions, which often take years to fully play out their effects on each other. Since we are part of that lacework ourselves, it's doubly hard to see the whole pattern of change. Instead, we tend to focus on snapshots of isolated parts of the system, and wonder why our deepest problems never seem to get solved. (1990, pp. 6–7)

Systemic thinking requires that we look beyond personalities and events, that we look for underlying structures of organizational dynamics and individual behaviors. By structures, Senge means inter-relationships among such things as communities, resources, social structures, knowledge, and normative expectations.

"Learning-disabled" organizations have difficulty thinking systemically. Such organizations focus on localized events rather than the systemic implications of behaviors. Participants in learning-disabled organizations, for example, tend to invest themselves in their specific roles and cannot perceive their systemic (meta-aggregate and field) membership. As we observed in the chapter on Contingency theory, organizations differentiate to deal with complex environments, but differentiation leads to ego-investment and conflict—they focus on position and self. When people don't see themselves as part of a problem, they will opt out of their part of the solution. They assume that the problem, and the enemy, is "out there," and if only "out there" would shape up, there would be no problem.

Actors in a learning-disabled organization often have a take-charge mentality—they are proactive, to use an overused buzzword of the 1990s. The problem is, they are more likely to be proactive about taking care of self than about systemic solutions. This, Senge argues, is reactivity rather than proactivity. It is aggression toward "the enemy out there" when, in reality, the enemy is within. Effective proactivity works to cure the problems we share; take-charge personalities battle the very system that supports and nurtures them. Systemic problems are distant from their myopic piece of the world, thus they address their problems by, in effect, attacking themselves—and they praise their tail-chasing behavior by calling it proactive.

Senge described learning-disabled organizations with a parable of the boiled frog. If you put a frog into hot water, it will struggle to escape. If you put the frog into room temperature water, then slowly raise the water temperature to boiling, the frog will accept matters quietly. Similarly, as organizations get into increasingly hotter water, they often simply acclimate rather than deal with underlying, systemic problems. Detroit's big three automakers in the 1960s and 1970s did not react to Japan's slowly growing intrusion into the American market until it was too late. Public education in the United States may be exhibiting the same dangerous malaise in the face of growing interest in home schooling, vouchers, and charter schools. We need to learn to slow down, Senge argues, and see the subtle, gradual processes going on around us in order to avoid the frog's fate.

Systemic thinking is not as difficult as it sounds, but it does require a nonlinear, rather than linear, perspective on life. Simply put, one must learn to look for forests instead of trees. As Senge explained, there is "detail complexity" and "dynamic complexity." Detail complexity refers to all the local events, actors, and activities that comprise a dynamic. Detail complexity is a bunch of organizational "snapshots" that one attempts to memorize and to understand. One can drown in such detail; there can be simply too much to keep up with or to process. This leads to inaction rather than action, a sense that "it is all too much for me to deal with." Dynamic complexity, by contrast, is a process and a whole, and one can develop the ability to see patterns in a whole just as one can see patterns in even complexly involved movies. True, cause and effect are subtly related in complex dynamics; they are typically separated in time; and the way to deal with cause-effect relationships is not always immediately obvious; indeed, it may even be counterintuitive. Dynamic complexity means that an action may have one effect in the short run and a totally different effect in the long run. It means that one's activities can affect systemic behavior in unobvious, unpredictable, or even unseen ways. But dynamic complexity is a holistic system, thus once we learn to think systemically, all this becomes manageable and intuitive.

To think systemically, to understand dynamic complexity, one must, according to Senge, understand a few simple principles. The first is that today's problems come from yesterday's solutions. Social and organizational behavior are like a balloon: if you squeeze air out of one part of the balloon, it will simply show up in another part. The teacher who punishes racial intolerance does little more than drive it into some other form of expression; he or she has not dealt with the underlying, systemic problem that created the intolerance. The university administrators who reduce middle management to save money will likely see expenses increase elsewhere. The passage of lottery bills to solve immediate funding problems in education may make it more difficult to get the public to accept tax increases to solve more fundamental, long-term funding needs.

The second of these principles is, "The harder you push, the harder the system pushes back." Senge calls this "compensating feedback"; it exists "when well-intentioned interventions call for responses from the system that offset the benefits of the intervention" (1990, p. 58). In Chapter 5, we observed that a leader's efforts to change one subsystem of organizational behavior may elicit responses from other subsystems that tend to neutralize the change (return to homeostasis). This is what Senge is talking about here. If university administrators crack down on student drinking on campus, students will compensate by going off campus to drink. This increases the administrator's problems, because now students are combining drinking and driving. The administrator pushes, and the system pushes back.

Third, nonsystemic intervention can sometimes cause behavior to become better before it becomes worse. By this Senge means that short-term, local solutions to systemic problems may produce immediate benefit, but the systemic problem continues to fester, and once the local cure wears off the problem may be even worse than before. He points in particular to political solutions—making the boss look good, or building one's powerbase. Hersey and Blanchard (1993) called this "getting the job done," or success-oriented behavior—opting for short-term gain at the expense of long-term health.

Fourth, faster is slower. A complex system can develop only so fast, and to push it beyond its natural limits is to court problems. Although Senge doesn't say it, Complexity theory in general suggests that a lot of interrelated systems must be brought along in a growth dynamic. Enduring relationships must be forged and other subsystems must make collateral changes; that is, growth and maturity is a network dynamic rather than an individual dynamic. If the network isn't given time to develop along with the individual, then the individual is left hanging with a weak infrastructure.

Fifth, cause and effect are often separated by time and space. What we do today may not produce its biggest effect for years, or may produce an effect at an unexpected location. When the effect does occur, we tend to look for causes in proximal events and cannot perceive the history that created the problem.

Sixth, small changes can produce big results, but the area of highest leverage is often the least intuitive. Some have called systems thinking the "new dismal science" because it teaches that the most obvious solutions don't work or only help in the short term. One often cannot change a system by pushing it to do better; rather, one changes a system by finding leverage points that remove barriers to growth and improvement, and the leverage may not be something you would normally envision.

 ## CASE STUDY

A nonprofit organization I occasionally help needs an additional program director, but its fund-raising efforts haven't grown as anticipated and the organization is putting off hiring the new person. Meanwhile, the current personnel are overworked trying to keep up with demand. It is intuitive, and seemingly safe, to get the money first, then hire the new person; we do that in our personal finances and it makes sense to do it in business. The intuitive solution may be the wrong one in this case, however.

This organization is in a growth spiral. Their strength lies in their service to families and in their programs. The organization has built a reputation for caring and helpful service, thus the number of programs has increased dramatically over the 15 years of its existence, and this in turn has strengthened its core mission of service and programs. This reinforcing cycle is represented by spiral A of Figure 13.6 which was created using instructions provided by Senge (1990). The growth of this mission, however, led to increased workload, which placed pressure on the system's ability to deliver programs (spiral B). Spiral A, then, drives spiral B, but if B slows down, it can limit the growth of A—hence, it is a "limit cycle."

The growth of program offerings in spiral A also generates revenues (spiral C). In the past, revenues have made it possible for the organization to increase its workforce to meet the demand for new programs. Losses in spiral C can slow growth in A, thus it also is a limit cycle.

This organization has grown to the point that its ability to provide services is stressed (spiral B), but the board is reluctant to commit to added personnel until revenues are more certain. The slowdown in the revenue cycle, then, puts the breaks on the growth of personnel. Meanwhile spiral A continues its growth, thus placing additional demands on spiral B. The resulting overload of B threatens the integrity of the organization's core mission of service and programs (spiral A)—the organization may have to delay certain services, for example, or overworked personnel may not be as effective as before. This could eventually damage the reputation of the system and set up conditions for a downward spiral in the entire system.

The board of directors is hoping to leverage spiral C by enhancing fund-raising, but if they fail to increase revenues before service decline becomes critical, they could find it difficult to do so, for service problems could depress donations. The better, but less intuitive, leverage is in spiral B: increase organizational capacity by hiring a new person even if this temporarily overextends the budget. This will strengthen the core mission (spiral A) and ultimately create more programs that should result in increased revenues (spiral C).

FIGURE 13.6 Growth in a nonprofit service organization.

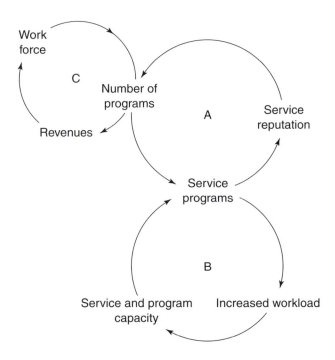

In a different example, a teacher has a class of Hispanic and English-speaking students and is trying to teach English to the Hispanic students and Spanish to the English students. Recently, however, students in both groups have lost interest in language studies and there is growing hostility between the groups. The teacher, obviously, needs a leverage point to reverse this downward spiral.

The class' dynamics are represented by Figure 13.7. The goal is to teach language skills and, as a side benefit, to teach tolerance and understanding between the cultures. The language training is embodied within instructional procedures that are intended to promote spiraling proficiency (spiral A). Students are exposed to one another's cultures, thus fostering appreciation and understanding (spiral B).

In the example, however, both cycles are spiraling down: proficiency is declining or stablizing because students are insulating themselves from instructional efforts; appreciation is declining, causing students to insulate themselves from one another's culture. The obvious response is to leverage instruction, perhaps by varying instructional approaches or demanding greater attention to studies. For teachers who fail to think systemically, who fail to see the relationship between language studies and cultural respect, this might be the only solution evident. It is likely, however, that students will ignore or even resist such efforts. The better leverage point is a bit distant from language instruction in the appreciation and understanding cycle. The teacher might leverage this by planning a spring vacation tour in Mexico or by forming cooperative, diversely structured learning groups charged with planning creative culture experiences. By leveraging interest and respect, student acceptance of language instruction should follow. ▪

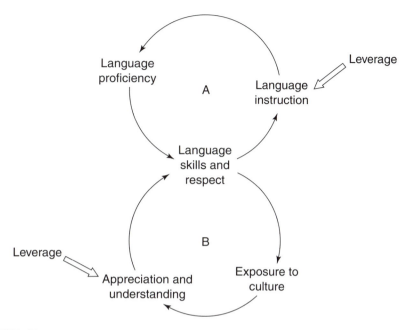

FIGURE 13.7   Model of a language and culture curriculum.

 RESEARCH TOPIC

In an earlier activity, you were asked to identify a particular event in your organization and analyze it in terms of interactive dynamics—perhaps you could evaluate an increase or decrease in standardized test scores, for example, or difficulty recruiting quality students (in higher education). Supplement that analysis with your insights from Senge's work.   ▪

In a way, Complexity theory brings closure to the anti-positivistic image of organization. Each of the theories examined under this rubric has looked at different, but overlapping, sides of organization. Strategic Choice created a general guiding image of loose relationship between leadership and organization. Population Ecology looked at how this looseness translates into generic forms. Cultural theory argues that social forces dominate organization, and Critical theory states that control is more the driving force in organizations than is effectiveness. Institutional theory argues that the driving force is legitimacy. Finally, Complexity theory argues that effectiveness is still the issue, but that it is the product of interaction and compromise. Complexity theory calls for leaders who can maintain a systemic perspective, who understand the nonlinear relationships between cause and effect, who can foster and tend to networks, who drop seeds of emergence, who symbolize. It calls for leaders who can make sense of complexity.

Diary

- Summarize your thoughts on the Roundtable discussions that were proposed in this chapter.
- Given what you have learned in this chapter, what are some important functions of leadership? In what way does your answer change your previous answers to this question?
- We observed in this chapter that leaders should "drop the seeds of emergence." What are some ways that educational leaders can do this?
- What can leaders do to help emerging ideas, behaviors, or structures move toward fit maturity?
- In Chapter 8, a Roundtable in the section on garbage can theory asked, "If organizational dynamics make little or no rational sense, if decision making is irrational and organizations are so loosely structured as to defy control, of what use are administrators?" Does the perspective in this chapter offer new ways to answer that question?
- What are some things leaders can do to discourage the emergence of negative and counter-productive behaviors and structures, or to deal with them if they do emerge?

Recommended Readings

Arthur, W. B. (1989). The economy and complexity. In D. L. Stein (Ed.), *Lectures in the Sciences of Complexity* (Vol. 1, pp. 713–740). Redwood City, CA: Addison-Wesley.

Brian Arthur argues that the economy is better described by increasing returns than by decreasing returns. Increasing returns means that it is not necessarily the best that will rise to the top of the competitive heap, it is the system with the initial advantage.

Holland, J. H. (1995). *Hidden order.* Reading, MA: Addison-Wesley Publishing Company.

John Holland, referred to by some as the father of the field of genetic algorithms, describes how Complex Adaptive Systems (CAS) interact to generate order. His discussion of aggregates and tags can be found in this book.

Kauffman, S. A. (1995). *At home in the universe: The search for the laws of self-organization and complexity.* New York: Oxford University Press.

Kauffman discusses patches (Stalinist Limit, Leftist Italian, etc.) and change in the last chapter of this book.

Kruger, J., & Dunning, D. (1999). Unskilled and unaware of it: How difficulties in recognizing one's own incompetence leads to inflated self-assessments. *Journal of Personality and Social Psychology, 77*(6), 1121–1134.

This article is not about Complexity theory; rather, it is about incompetence and failure to recognize one's lack of skills. It was referred to in one of the Roundtables, and the subject is important to leaders who want to foster the emergence of effective, rather than counterproductive, behaviors and structures.

Lewin, R. (1992). *Complexity: Life at the edge of chaos.* New York: Macmillan Publishing Company.

This is one of a handful of books that popularized Complexity theory in the early 1990s; it is probably still the best introduction to the subject available. Lewin discusses the subject through interviews with key researchers in the area, including Chris Langston, Stu Kauffman, John Holland, and Craig Reynolds.

Marion, R. (1999). *The edge of organization: Chaos and complexity theories of formal social organization.* Newbury Park, CA: Sage Publications.

This book examines many of the same organizational theories discussed in the current text, but it reinterprets them in relationship to Chaos and Complexity theories. Its goal is two-fold: to weave nonlinear dynamics into the fabric of social dynamics, and to develop a theory of Complex dynamics in social organizations.

Marion, R., & Bacon, J. (2000). Organizational extinction and complex systems. *Emergence: A Journal of Complexity Issues in Organizations and Management, 1*(4), 71–96.

This article applies Complexity theory to organizational failure. Three non-profit organizations are examined using qualitative strategies: one is a strong and viable organization, one of the organizations has failed, and the third has been weak for all of its existence. The authors conclude that failure results from a decline of, or chronic weaknesses in, the organization's aggregates, meta-aggregates, and meta-meta-aggregates (fields).

Senge, Peter M. (1990). *The fifth discipline: The art and practice of the learning organization.* New York: Random House.

Peter Senge provides a comprehensive blueprint for managing dynamically complex organizations. His model outlines strategies for leveraging systemic problems and building learning organizations. A major goal is to help readers see both the forest and the trees, as Senge put it.

The gurus speak: Complexity and organizations. (1999). *Emergence: A Journal of Complexity Issues in Organizations and Management, 1*(1), 73–91.

This article is a transcription of a panel discussion among experts on organizations and Complexity theory at the 1998 International Conference on Complex Systems. Speakers include Bill McKelvey, the director of Strategy and Organization Science at the Anderson School at UCLA; Henry Mintzberg, professor of Management at McGill and author of *The Structuring of Organizations: A Synthesis of the Research;* Peter Senge, author of *The Fifth Discipline;* and Yaneer Bar-Yam, president of the New England Complex Systems Institute.

References

Arthur, W. B. (1989). The economy and complexity. In D. L. Stein (Ed.), *Lectures in the Sciences of Complexity* (Vol. 1, pp. 713–740). Redwood City, CA: Addison-Wesley.

Bak, P. (1996). *How nature works.* New York: Copernicus.

Bak, P., Tang, C., & Wiesenfeld, K. (1989). Self-organized criticality: An explanation of 1/f noise. *Physical Review Letters, 59,* 381–384.

Barge, J. K. (1994). *Leadership: Communication skills for organizations and groups.* New York: St. Martin's Press.

Barnard, C. I. (1938). *The functions of the executive.* Cambridge, MA: Harvard University Press.

Burt, R. S. (1992). *Structural holes: The social structure of competition.* Cambridge, MA: Harvard University Press.

Carlson, R. O. (1965). *Adoption of educational innovations.* Eugene, OR: Center for the Advanced Study of Educational Administration, University of Oregon.

Cartwright, T. J. (1991). Planning and chaos theory. *Journal of the American Planning Association, 57*(1), 44–56.

Curtis, R. K. (1990). Complexity and predictability: The application of chaos theory to economic forecasting. *Futures Research Quarterly, 6*(4), 57–70.

DiMaggio, P. J., & Powell, W. W. (1983). The iron cage revisited: Institutional isomorphism and collective rationality in organizational fields. *American Sociological Review, 48,* 147–160.

Doll, W. E., Jr. (1989). Complexity in the classroom. *Educational Leadership, 47*(1), 65–70.

Ferguson, R. F. (1991). Paying for public education: New evidence on how and why money matters. *Harvard Journal on Legislation, 28,* 465–498.

Flanigan, J. L., Marion, R. A., & Richardson, M. D. (1996). Causal and temporal analyses of increased funding on student achievement. *Journal of Research and Development in Education, 30,* 222–247.

Guastello, S. (1992). Population dynamics and workforce productivity. In M. Michaels (Ed.), *Proceedings of the annual chaos network conference: The second iteration* (pp. 120–127). Urbana, IL: People Technologies.

Hersey, P., & Blanhechard, K. H. (1993). *Management of organizational behavior: Utilizing human resources* (6th ed.). Englewood cliffs, NJ: Prentice Hall.

Holland, J. H. (1995). *Hidden order.* Reading, MA: Addison-Wesley Publishing Company.

Human, S. E., & Provan, K. G. (2000). Legitimacy building in the evolution of small firm multilateral networks: A study of success and demise. *Administrative Science Quarterly, 45,* 327–365.

Kauffman, S. A. (1993). *The origins of order.* New York: Oxford University Press.

Kauffman, S. A. (1995). *At home in the universe: The search for the laws of self-organization and complexity.* New York: Oxford University Press.

Kruger, J., & Dunning, D. (1999). Unskilled and unaware of it: How difficulties in recognizing one's own incompetence leads to inflated self-assessments. *Journal of Personality and Social Psychology, 77*(6), 1121–1134.

Lewin, R. (1992). *Complexity: Life at the edge of chaos.* N̶ Company.

Lorenz, E. (1964). The problem of deducing the climate from th̶ *Tellus, 16,* 1–11.

Marion, R. & Bacon, J. (1999). Organizational extinction and complex s̶ *gence: A Journal of Complexity Issues in Organization and Management, 1*(4), 71–

Oakes, L., Townley, B., & Cooper, D. J. (1998). Business planning as pedagogy: L̶ guage and control in a changing institutional field. *Administrative Science Quarterly, 43*(2), 257–292.

Pfeffer, J., & Salancik, G. R. (1978). *The external control of organizations: A resource dependence perspective.* New York: Harper & Row.

Podolny, J. M. (1993). A status-based model of market competition. *American Journal of Sociology, 98,* 829–872.

Prigogene, I. (1997). *The End of Certainty.* New York: The Free Press.

Regine, B., & Lewin, R. (2000). Leading at the edge: How leaders influence complex systems. *Emergence: A Journal of Complexity Issues in Organization and Management, 2*(2), 5–23.

Rogers, E. M., & Rogers, R. A. (1976). *Communications in organizations.* New York: The Free Press.

Senge, P. M. (1990). *The fifth discipline: The art and practice of the learning organization.* New York: Random House.

Sterman, J. D. (1988). Deterministic chaos in models of human behavior: Methodological issues and experimental results. *System Dynamics Review, 4*(1–2), 148–178.

The gurus speak: Complexity and organizations. (1999). *Emergence: A Journal of Complexity Issues in Organizations and Management, 1,* 73–91.

Waldrop, M. M. (1992). *Complexity: The emerging science at the edge of order and chaos.* New York: Simon & Schuster.

Westphal, J. D., & Milton, L. P. (2000). How experience and network ties affect the influence of demographic minorities on corporate boards. *Administrative Science Quarterly, 45,* 366–398.

Westphal, J. D., Gulati, R., & Shortell, S. M. (1997). Customization or conformity: An institutional and network perspective on the content and consequences of TQM adoption. *Administrative Science Quarterly, 42,* 366–394.

ing Innovation and Building Fitness

w York: Macmillan Publishing

o governing equations.

stems, Emer-

n-

96.

331

Educational Organizations

When all is said and done, this book is about change. A number of related themes have wound their way through these chapters: leadership has been a pervasive theme (every chapter has included material on this). We have discussed conflict, organizational structure, motivation, preferences, communication, decision making, organizational learning, environment, culture, and complexity. But change (or, at times, its antithesis, stability) has lurked throughout. It is appropriate, then, that this last chapter is about change; it allows us not only to expand this important topic, it provides us with a summary of the book.

This chapter will be organized around two broad perspectives of theory: positivism and anti-positivism. Positivistic change assumes a rather close, regular relationship between contingency and outcome, and, consequently, it assumes some level of predictable control over organizational behavior. Positivistic change tends to be prescriptive; that is, it prescribes specific leadership behaviors for specific organizational contingencies. Anti-positivism, by contrast, assumes much less of a regular relationship between contingency and outcome, and argues instead that organizational behavior is a product of idiosyncratic preferences. Further, it perceives organizations as generally too complex, their goals too ambiguous, and their environments too unpredictable to permit close control of the change process. Anti-positivistic change models, then, tend to be non-prescriptive and often lean toward description, but as usual, we will seek prescriptive guidance in these models.

In this chapter, students will:

- Explore positivistic and anti-positivistic perspectives of the change process.
- Evaluate case studies relative to these different perspectives.

- Develop research proposals regarding variations in implementation of innovation between early and late adopters.
- Examine the role of leadership in the emergence of change.
- Refine their definitions of the function of leadership in education.

POSITIVISM AND CHANGE

Let's clarify something before we begin: given sufficient power, humans can physically change things. We have it within our power to place computers within public school classrooms, restructure our organizations, throw people out of office, pass laws that affect our lives, force people to accommodate those who are deprived or handicapped, and to change the way teachers teach. Organizations can take over other organizations, fire their employees, and revise their organizational philosophies. We can organize projects for predetermined ends. Positivists presume, and elaborate on, these capabilities.

Anti-positivists do not necessarily contradict such capabilities. Rather, they question whether such changes always achieve their formally stated ends; they question whether we are motivated primarily by rational goals; they question whether individual leaders can, after all, really know what is best for an organization; and they argue that social and environmental forces often do emasculate leadership intent. Social systems often produce unintended consequences, their actors are motivated by irrational preferences, they are often too complex to understand, and they often frustrate the best efforts of leaders.

Positivists sometimes presume that simple acts, such as placing computers in schools, are sufficient to create deep-level change. They presume that we control the future, or that change and improvement are synonymous. They assume that change is the property of the change agent and ignore the power of history and interactive dynamics. And every now and then they are right. Humans are, after all, the major actors in the change process, and our deliberate efforts often have a significant impact on events. So let's examine positivistic strategies and see what can be learned.

Scientific Management and Change

The Scientific Management proponents, Frederick Taylor, Frank and Lillian Gilbreth, and even modern ergonomics focus on efficiency and on the separation of planning from production. Scientific Management considers change to be the property of those who plan. Planners make the decision to change, they weigh its pros and cons, and they are responsible for its success or failure. In essence, change affects only the planner, and production personnel have no stake in its stresses. Production is merely the "machine" that performs the tasks of the planners.

Given this, the soldiering incident reported by Frederick Taylor (discussed in Chapter 2) must have come as quite a surprise to him. In that incident, you'll recall, Taylor had attempted to implement efficiency changes, but those changes were vigorously resisted by workers who wanted to control their own work. Taylor saw worker control as counterproductive, arguing that work must be standardized around scientific principles. The workers saw standardization as an attempt to increase their workload without increasing their pay, and did everything they could to sabotage Taylor's effort.

The battle, however, boiled down to a matter of control, and herein lies an important issue of change. Scientific Managers (and later, bureaucracies) attempt to centralize change, but workers tend to resent being told what to do. Centralized change breeds resentment, affects morale and motivation, and fosters resistance. The separation of planning from production epitomizes what Karl Marx was talking about when he lamented the separation of people from the tools and the products of their livelihood.

Taylor proposed that this divestiture be offset by increasing the worker's share of the profits of their labors. This makes him something of a Marxist enigma: he simultaneously devalued life from the Marxist perspective by depriving workers of their tools, and enhanced life by proposing that workers share in the products of their work. Even so, the more immediate concern of workers in Taylor-based factories during the 1920s and 1930s was still the control issue, and often the mere rumor that a plant was going to adopt Taylorian methods was sufficient to arouse the threat of strike. Taylorian change was too heavy-handed—it was an iron fist, to use the terminology of Critical theory. Problems with the Taylorian approach to change taught organizational scholars that they needed to seek more subtle, velvet-glove approaches, and to a large extent that was what the Human Relations movement (and indeed all subsequent approaches to change) was all about.

Power-Coercive Planned Change

Robert Chin (1967) examined change that results from the application of authority and force. He labeled it "power-coercive planned change," referring to change that is enacted by fiat and enforced by coercion and sanctions. This approach is commonly used by legislative agencies and underlies the implementation of a number of programs aimed at public education, such as exceptional children and federal remediation programs. It is not restricted to legislative initiated change, of course; indeed, it is a common source of change in business and in governmental institutions, such as public schools and universities. Power-coercive change does not seek support from those who must implement the change; it typically does not involve them in decision making about the change; and it certainly does not extend to them the power of veto over change. Typically, such change generates significant resentment in the initial stages, but a sufficiently powerful elite can prevail. In time, people will accept the change, despite the heavy-handed implementation. Resentments don't last, and people move on to be replaced by others who know nothing of the imperious behavior that generated the programs.

Power-coercive change is probably most successful when power elites allow subordinates to make some decisions about how to implement it. The implementation of Title I remediation programs in the United States during the 1960s is a case-in-point. These programs provided funding to public education for remediation in reading and math for low-achieving students. Congress wisely decided not to mandate certain details of the implementation, such as how money would be distributed within a school district or just how student eligibility would be determined. The authors of the bill felt, correctly, that implementation would more likely succeed if districts were given some flexibility to address local needs. The Title I program was subsequently hailed as one of the more successful federal efforts to influence public education in the United States, and much of that success is attributable to the flexibility in the program.

Power-coercive change suffers at least two major weaknesses. First is the fact that centrally determined and coordinated change typically fails to anticipate the significant complexities of organizations. Such change often addresses a localized element of a broader organizational dynamic; this sets up the change for failure and sets up the organization for unanticipated outcomes. Peter Senge (1990) argues that the problem is a failure or inability to think systematically. We tend to compartmentalize problems, he states, and fail to understand how these problems relate to the entire organizational dynamic.

The second problem with power-coercive change is that it demands long-term effort. One's natural tendency is to assume that change is over once it is implemented. In reality, change is rarely complete at that point. Power-coercive change agents must stay on top of things for extended periods of time, otherwise organizations may gravitate back to their pre-change status. In Chapter 5, we referred to this as "movement toward homeostasis." In Chapter 6, we argued that change that is inconsistent with organizational contingencies will tend to return to the state demanded by those contingencies. In Chapter 9, we observed the staying power of organizational inertia. If change agents ease their pressure prematurely, their efforts may be partially or even totally reversed.

Human Relations and the Lewinian Approach to Change

Human Relations was, in many ways, a counterpoint to the excesses of Scientific Management. It involved workers in the planning process, where Scientific Management separated planning from production. It understood the importance of worker morale and investment, where Scientific Management saw workers as tools of production. Nonetheless, Human Relationists were probably little better at extending real control over work processes to workers, for they tended to give workers more the appearance rather than the substance of involvement. It was, according to Critical theorists, more of a velvet glove of control, but the glove regardless covered a fist.

Kurt Lewin's (1952) approach to change exemplifies the Human Relations perspective. His approach capitalizes on the power of informal groups within any given organization (the same sort of informal groups that so potently opposed

Taylor's efforts in the soldiering incident). Lewin argued that workers are more likely to accept change if they participate in the decision-making process and come to group agreement about the necessity and the scope of change. He and others demonstrated that such strategies promote greater acceptance, shorter learning curves, enhanced morale, and longer-lasting attitudinal changes. While successful in many situations, this approach failed in conditions that were influenced by strong external forces, such as labor unions. It was also later criticized for its underlying goal of enhancing managerial control to the ultimate detriment of worker welfare.

Psychological Change

Another school of thought within the Human Relations movement focused on worker psychology and sought ways that those psychologies could be manipulated to produce satisfaction and, by extension, to promote climates in which change can flourish. This approach assumed that dissatisfaction or low morale is the property of the affected individual, and that managers need only find strategies for improving such depressed states of satisfaction and motivation. Such strategies include improved working conditions and enhanced recognition.

The practice of seeking psychological reasons for low morale and productivity, however, encouraged an attitude that, ultimately, morale was a personality issue. Consequently, improved morale comes about when individual psychological problems are resolved. Organizational theorists Daniel Katz and Robert Kahn (1966) wrote that, in the 1960s, it became faddish among organizations to send workers to "t-group" workshops for such problems. T-group analysis attempted to change individuals, to reconstruct them from the inside out and return them to their organizations as more productive and effective workers. The strategy made several potentially fatal assumptions. It assumed that:

1. the individual could be changed;
2. the changes will become permanent parts of the individual's personality;
3. the individual will carry the changes with him or her back to the workplace;
4. the worker's colleagues will accept and respond to the changed personality;
5. the colleagues will make collateral changes themselves; and
6. the organizational pressures that helped create the original personality and the pattern of interactions with colleagues that fed the problem will no longer be potent forces.

This is brittle logic, and it takes only one broken link to disrupt it. Personality is the product of complex interactions with complex histories; consequently, it is not easily changed and certainly is intractable to efforts that ignore the social context of personality. Managers definitely have an obligation to try to improve conditions that feed individual dissatisfaction and to be tolerant of idiosyncrasy. But they can't always expect to change organizations through the often impossible task of changing only individuals.

The Heroic Leader

Warren Bennis and Burt Nanus (1985) state that they wrote their book, *Leaders,*

> In the belief that leadership is the pivotal force behind successful organizations and that, to create vital and viable organizations, leadership is necessary to help organizations develop a new vision of what they can be, then mobilize the organization change toward the new vision. . . . The main stem-winder [in organizational transformation] is the leadership. The new leader . . . is one who commits people to action, who converts followers into leaders, and who may convert leaders into agents of change. (pp. 2–3)

This is "heroic" leadership. It is the proactive person who charges out front and valiantly leads his or her troops to "victory" over organizational goals. It is the visionary, the person who rises above organizational activities to see the big picture, then infects followers with that vision.

Proactive, heroic leadership is the topic of most guru books. The guru's answer to problems caused by skyrocketing social and organizational complexities, explosive communication technologies, and internationalization of market perspectives is heroic, visionary leadership. A key element of this perspective is the mission statement, an ambitious declaration that reflects the desired future of the organization. Mission statements are banners that heroic leaders bear, flags that infuse the very being of organizational actors. Heroic leaders are captains who bravely and charismatically guide their organizations through treacherous waters to the safe harbors defined by mission statements. Advocates point to leaders such as Winston Churchill, Franklin Roosevelt, Dr. Martin Luther King, Jr., and Lee Iacocca to illustrate their points.

But heroic leadership may not be quite all it is stacked up to be. Ronald Corwin (1987) argues that, while visionary and intelligent leadership is certainly important, change is a complex process that involves more than just good leadership. It involves, for example, timing. Heroic leadership is powerless when the timing is wrong—it is doubtful, for example, that Dr. King would have made much impression 50 years before his time, or that Horace Mann could have launched the common school movement in 1750, 100 years before his time. It's all a matter of timing.

Heroic leaders may have the skills needed for one stage of a change process but not another. They may be excellent visionaries and communicators, but lack the managing skills needed to see a task through, or their skills may be suited for one set of conditions but not for subsequent conditions. John F. Kennedy was undoubtedly good at stimulating excitement in American politics, but it took someone of Lyndon Johnson's abilities to squeeze cooperation on social legislation from the U.S. Congress. George Patton was highly effective during WWII, but his hostility toward the USSR may very well have been a liability during the Cold War.

Change requires, Corwin continued, significant support from subordinates and stakeholders—George Bush, for example, was successful in the Gulf War because of broad support from other world leaders and public opinion. Eisenhower was surrounded by competent leaders and massive resources during World War

II. Heroic leadership typically thrives because of favorable historical contexts. The integration movement in the United States can trace its roots to court cases as early as the 1850s and certainly to cases that were heard in the 1930s and 1940s—Dr. Martin Luther King, Jr. inherited the movement, he did not originate it.

Simply put, heroic leadership often succeeds only because conditions allow it to succeed. As Peter Senge (1990) observed, Leo Tolstoy argues this point eloquently in his masterpiece, *War and Peace:*

> "But whenever there have been wars, there have been great military leaders; whenever there have been revolutions in states, there have been great men," says history. "Whenever there have been great military leaders there have, indeed, been wars," replies the human reason; "but that does not prove that generals were the cause of the wars, and that the factors leading to warfare can be found in the personal activities of one man . . ." For the investigation of the laws of history, we must completely change the subject of observations, must let kings and ministers and generals alone, and study the homogenous, infinitesimal elements by which the masses are led. . . . It is obvious that only in that direction lies any possibility of discovering historical laws; and that the human intellect has hitherto not devoted to that method of research one millionth part of the energy that historians have put into the description of the doings of various kings, ministers, and generals.

Strategic Planning

Strategic planning is yet another tool of the heroic leader. Strategic planning, along with its almost obligatory companion, reorganization, are rather popular change strategies because of their emphasis on rational, proactive leadership. Such planning involves analysis of current organizational conditions to identify structural and organizational problems, formulation of goals and strategies for addressing the problems, and implementation of those strategies. Strategic planning is a variation of Dewey's decision-making model (discussed earlier) but with modern clothing.

Strategic planning was popular in the last decade of the 20th century for a variety of apparent reasons, some of which serve perceptual, rather than rational, needs. The following summarizes some of these needs:

- In a period of tight budgets and vigorous competition, when organizational mission statements all too often aspire to lofty and probably unattainable goals such as "cutting-edge technology" and "world-class operations," strategic planning permits organizations to showcase their aspirations and make themselves look mean and lean. It portrays the organization as in control of its present and its future; it leaves the impression among managers, policymakers, and the public that something has been done about "the problem;" and it wins support from fiscally conservative legislatures. But this is show rather than substance. It provides legitimacy without requiring the organization to actually *do* anything about its problems.

- Strategic planning can be (Critical theorists would say it is) a strategy for solidifying leadership control, of showing who is who in the organizational and environmental pecking order. It is a statement that says management—like the shaman at primitive rain dances—is potent and in control.

- Strategic planning lends an aura of the rational to organizational activities. It rationalizes the elimination or consolidation of positions. It legitimizes changes in production strategy. However, change of the magnitude often witnessed in strategic planning and reorganization typically upsets existing networks of accommodation, and launches long periods of readjustment. Reduced productivity may offset gains from enhanced efficiency, morale may be depressed, and overall effectiveness may be compromised.

- Strategic planning may seek improvements and innovation in the quality of production. Microcomputers or distance learning may be injected into classrooms, or new accounting procedures may be introduced into a business management department. The degree to which such change is accepted, however, may depend on whether it is perceived as a move to extend administrative control or an effort to help workers. In 1977, Michael Moch and Edward Morse evaluated the impact of 12 technological innovations in 1,000 hospitals. They found that those changes designed to facilitate diagnosis and treatment were accepted by the staff, while those perceived as improving administration control, such as efforts to better monitor expenses, were less acceptable.

Corwin (1987) argues that strategic planning assumes change "can be controlled by opportunistic managers who are wise enough to find the right strategies" (p. 204). It assumes that leaders possess sufficient knowledge and wisdom to adequately evaluate present conditions and enough foresight to project future conditions. Such omnipotence is unlikely in any but the more stable situations, and even then, it may be difficult to accurately evaluate the nature of future problems. Strategic planners often just decide on a course of action and pray that they've called the future correctly. In this regard, strategic planning is merely a way to make one's guesses look credible and authoritative.

Finally, as Senge has argued, even when intervention associated with strategic planning has an impact, managers may not learn from that outcome. The true impact, for example, may emerge too far in the future to be associated in management's mind with the original strategic plan. Many of the managers who implemented the original intervention may no longer even be around. We have short memories, and by the time our interventions bear fruit (whether good fruit or bad), our minds are off on a dozen or so new projects. I've often wondered what happens to five-year plans once completed; I'm willing to bet that many can't even be found by the time their projections are supposed to have reached fruition.

Open Systems

Open Systems theory introduced theorists to the importance of understanding how change impacts interactive sets of systems—that is, it introduced us to systemic thinking. Chapter 5 provided an illustration of systemic change involving the introduction of computers into a public school classroom. It was argued that such a change immediately affects the classroom's technological subsystem and sets a number of dynamics into motion that will involve other subsystems, including subsystems that exist outside the school. A principal's failure to deal with these dynamics, it was argued, may derail the change effort. Perturbations such as this place strain on other subsystems; those subsystems must either adapt or they must neutralize the change (this is called "returning to homeostasis"). It is not unusual that they do the latter.

To avoid neutralization, we argued in Chapter 5 that teachers need to be shown how to organize classroom activities, how to integrate computers into their existing curricula, how to manage classroom logistics, and how to make computers a part of the instructional flow. Budgetary line items should be dedicated to training, software purchases, equipment purchases and repair, network maintenance, and such. Buildings may need renovation. Teachers should be involved in decision making; they should have opportunities to attend conferences and workshops; their creativity should be encouraged. Parents should be sold on the change, and policy support from the school board should be sought.

Systemic thinking is an important aspect of models of change that followed its introduction in the 1960s. It is particularly important to Complexity theory, which examines the dynamics of holistic systems. Peter Senge (1990), whom I have labeled as a Complexity theorist, has made systemic thinking a central part of his writings. He argues that business and other human endeavors

> . . . are bound by invisible fabrics of interrelated actions, which often take years to fully play out their effects on one another.
>
> Since we are part of that lacework ourselves, it's doubly hard to see the whole pattern of change. Instead, we tend to focus on snapshots of isolated parts of the system, and wonder why our deepest problems never seem to get solved. Systems thinking is a conceptual framework, a body of knowledge and tools that has been developed over the past fifty years, to make the full patterns clearer, and to help us see how to change them effectively. (p. 7)

ANTI-POSITIVISM AND CHANGE

Anti-positivism is premised in large measure on three assumptions:

- Humans are semirational beings who are at least as equally disposed to pursue personal preference as they are to pursue rational, organizational preferences;
- This is OK because there is a somewhat loose relationship between leadership behavior and organizational outcome anyhow; and
- Much of organizational behavior is too complex to be rationalized to any great extent.

Anti-positivists argue that humans do not make rational choices. We are influenced by our egos, by politics, by the need to be considered legitimate, and by the limits of our knowledge. We find solutions and seek problems on which to use them. We often take credit for success we had little to do with and sometimes dodge responsibility for problems we had everything to do with. We run our organizations to satisfy our personal needs or in conformance with somewhat personal conceptions of what organization should be. We are typically unable to see the big picture and respond instead to local events. We assume simple causation when, in reality, causation is quite complex.

But, the logic continues, this doesn't matter because organizational success is loosely coupled with leadership behavior. Anti-positivists point to the fact that structural contingencies such as leadership explain no more than 50% of organizational behavior (Donaldson, 1996). This leaves considerable room for leadership discretion, for mistakes, personal preferences, or for ego.

All this is a good thing because organizations are too complex to understand anyhow. Stuart Kauffman (1995) argues that

> Despite the fact that human crafting of artifacts is guided by intent and intelligence, both processes often confront problems of conflicting constraints. . . . I suspect that much of technological evolution results from tinkering with little real understanding ahead of time of the consequences. . . . [W]hen problems are very hard, thinking may not help that much. We may be relatively blind watchmakers. (p. 202)

If organizational success were not loosely related to leadership behavior, we'd be in a good deal of trouble. The best we could do would be to structure simple organizations because anything of any complexity would be unmanageable. We need latitude to be imperfect in order to run large, complex systems.

To the extent that all this is true, we delude ourselves with our detailed planning initiatives, our glorification of direct intervention by leadership, even our belief that leaders control and guide organizations. And if even only somewhat true, it suggests that we need to think about change in unique ways, and that is what this section is about.

Six perspectives of organizational change are imbedded within these definitions of anti-positivistic logic, and each will be discussed in turn over the next few pages. The first two come from Strategic Choice theory: one derives from Learning theory and the second from the Loose Coupling argument. The third perspective on change relates to Population Ecology's arguments about Darwinian adaptation. We will then discuss change from the perspective of Culture theory, then Institutionalism. The final perspective of change to be examined is actually a hybrid of positivism and anti-positivism, and relates to Complexity theory.

Learning Theory and Loose Coupling

One might assume that learning and change are somewhat synonymous; after all, people alter their behavior based on learning. But there is irony here: learning also limits change. The more people learn, the more they become set in their ways. The problem can be described with a fitness landscape metaphor. Imagine a landscape of peaks. Some are tall, some short, and there is everything in between. Each peak represents a fitness strategy, and we, or our organizations, choose one of those peaks to climb (master). As one approaches the top of a fitness peak, options for improvement decrease, however. You can't turn around, for that means less fitness, yet you are near the top and there is little left to learn. Going to another peak (change) is expensive and you would have to start the learning process all over again. As we said, learning limits change.

Learning results in gradual improvement in performance. It is what one does as he or she climbs a fitness peak, learns the ropes, and becomes proficient. Learning is, to a large extent, guided by trial and error, much like natural selection. A person in a new role stumbles around a bit, tries out techniques learned in school or in a previous job, looks at how role models (if available) handle the job, and works on convincing everyone he or she is competent. As neophytes find strategies that demonstrate some degree of success, they refine and repeat them. Slowly, a repertoire of reasonably useful strategies for dealing with the job evolves. This is learning, and it is also change.

But learning does not exhibit the sort of panache we usually associate with change. We tend to think of change as something dramatic—a new look, or a new way of doing things. Dramatic change is peak-hopping, or strategy-changing, while learning is peak-climbing, or strategy-refining (referring to the fitness landscape metaphor). Peak-hopping change invalidates peak-climbing change to a degree that is roughly related to the extent of disruption associated with the hop. If, for example, a reorganization redefines roles and responsibilities, then much of what workers learned in their previous roles would be obsolete. This would render participants at least temporarily less effective than they had been before. If an assistant principal for discipline were to change disciplinary strategies, that person would likely be less effective while he or she learns the new approach— the assistant would have to climb a new fitness peak.

Learning is often codified as rules and regulations. Rules represent the conversion of what we learn into standard, dependable behavior. If university officials learn that college-age students respond well to experiential learning, they might implement a rule that requires internships for all students. If they learn that morning classes are cluttering the course-offering schedule, thus making it difficult for students to get all the courses they need, they may pass regulations regarding schedule distribution.

Rules do not necessarily beget more rules, however—they do not grow exponentially (Schulz, 1998). Like fitness peak-climbing, each new rule limits future options and reduces the number of new rules—and new learning—available to us. Thus, as systems become more proficient at what they do, fewer rules, and less learning, are generated. Organizations typically break out of this rut only when environmental change presents new choices. The popularity of home schooling in the 1990s, for example, forced public education to rather dramatically revise oversight and attendance regulations that had been virtually unchanged for decades.

Loose Coupling and Change

The nature of interaction and interdependency in an organization affects change. Weick (1976), for example, observed that loosely coupled interdependency permits local adaptation and experimentation without disruption of an entire organization. That is, change happens best if it starts in small, relatively unencumbered subsystems.

Howard Aldrich (1979) illustrated this point with the story of watchmakers Hora and Tempus. You will remember from the earlier chapter on Loose Coupling theory that Hora tried to assemble all the pieces of a watch simultaneously, while Tempus assembled a watch in smaller, easier to manage modules. Weick's intent, in part, was to underscore the importance of working with small, independent components when attempting to construct something new. His point is that change is easier to manage one small piece at a time.

Weick inadvertently makes another important point with the story, however, one that segues into our discussion of complexity and change a few paragraphs from now. Different innovations that emerge in different subsystems may eventually find one another and collapse together into something bigger and better than the individual innovations alone. An experiment with a tutoring program for athletes in a university and an initiative to teach Ph.D. students how to teach, for example, could find one another to the greatly enhanced benefit of both.

Loose Coupling offers a solution to the dilemma posed by Learning theory: the seemingly inevitable stultification of learning, particularly when the environment offers no challenges. Units operating relatively independently will typically behave in different ways and do different things, and these differences could provide sufficient variation to challenge the system. If every person and every department marches lockstep to the same beat, then obviously there is no challenge and learning will eventually limit choices, as Learning theorists suggest. But if each unit has enough freedom to do somewhat of its own thing and sufficient interdependency to influence a few other units, then the units will perturb one another and help perpetuate vibrant learning.

CASE STUDY

The implications of thinking about change in these ways (learning and coupling) can be illustrated with the following story. You have worked with an abbreviated form of this story in a Roundtable in an earlier chapter; we will expand it here to illustrate not only learning and loose coupling, but subsequent perspectives of change as well.

The superintendent in a school district with which I was once associated decided that all elementary reading programs should adopt a competency-based organizational strategy. The plan called for administering a criterion-referenced achievement test at the beginning of each school year. By the middle of October, teachers would receive printouts from the testing company that listed the strengths and weaknesses of each of their students on about 130 specific reading competencies. Students were to work individually on the weaknesses identified in their profiles. The goal was for every student to master every objective for the given grade level by the end of the school year.

During the spring prior to implementation of this program, teachers were given inservice training on the basic strategies. They were told to assemble a box of learning materials organized by objective. Worksheets, games, and exercises were placed behind dividers representing each of the objectives on the criterion-referenced test administered at the beginning of the year. The district put together a "make and take" lab at a central location in the district where teachers could get ideas and materials for their skills boxes. The intent was for students to receive assignments each Monday based on identified weaknesses, then, during reading period each day, they would work on pertinent exercises from the skills box. At the end of a period of time (usually one week), students would take an interim test for the specific skills on which they were working. The results were used to update the skills chart and to plan subsequent assignments.

The program was pushed for three years, then quietly dropped. The superintendent and his curriculum supervisors misunderstood what could be considered anti-positivistic cautionary maxims: don't assume that an organization and its members will eagerly hop to your bidding, and don't assume that planning is the initial step in change. The first maxim is derived from the Loose Coupling assertion that organizational behavior is loosely connected to leadership activity. It's not that subordinates are mean-spirited and proto-naturally resistant, or that they are "set in their ways," or that they are "slow." It is rather this whole loose coupling complexity thing that afflicts organizations. A system is not tightly coupled to the boss' will because a whole complex of issues go into making the organization the way it is. Systems are structured as they are because the learning process has made them that way. Their structures are the product of a historical process that struggled with problems and challenges, in which compromises have been struck with a complex environment and an uncertain raw material, and in which a host of supporting structures have emerged as support. Given all these forces, a superintendent's will is sometimes merely spit in the wind. For a leader to ignore history and all its constructed complexities, to say in effect "damn the torpedoes, full speed ahead," is naïve.

In this story, teachers had a long, reasonably successful history of teaching using homogeneous reading groups; textbooks and supplementary materials were oriented to that style of teaching; universities prepared them for that teaching strategy; parents expected it. Instructional strategies were a product of something much bigger than the superintendent's will—leader and structure were loosely coupled. Instruction was not going to be changed with the wave of a superintendent's wand. Loose coupling can be a powerful adversary, and in this case it lived up to its potential: it ravished the superintendent's initiative.

That doesn't necessarily mean organizational systems cannot be changed; it does mean that one must deal with (among other things) the learning process and loose coupling. The superintendent in this story failed on both counts, and this brings us to the second maxim: don't assume that planning is the first step in change. I don't mean by this that planning should not occur or that change should occur spontaneously before any thought is devoted to it (nor do I preclude this possibility, however); rather, I suggest that planning is a continuous learning process. Planning does not occur once, with its product considered immutable mantra. Effective planning incorporates ongoing learning. The future is simply too uncertain to be mastered in a single, upfront planning session, no matter how intelligent the planners. Leaders can plan where they want to go and can lay general guidelines for getting there, but their plans should be sufficiently flexible to allow for learning. As they experience their initiatives, they will learn more about them—the details will begin to emerge. Their early, idealistic thoughts will not be up to dealing with the rich complexities they will experience along the way, and the subsequent sophistication and understanding they develop should be used to revise and refine plans. Leaders should even be open to scuttling their plans if it becomes clear that they will not work.

The superintendent in this case study was hardly flexible. For starters, he tried to deal with the whole system as if one unitary strategy would work in every school, every grade, and every class. Similarly, he assumed that general speeches and inservice programs, a one-size-fits-all sales effort, would suffice to change opinions and create an attitude of acceptance among teachers and administrators. For him, there was one definitive plan and only one message to be delivered: the message that he and his supervisors had constructed a priori. The superintendent gave a positive, encouraging speech in the district-wide meeting at the beginning of the year and supported the program at each monthly administrator's meeting. His supervisors periodically visited each school to deliver the message anew and to answer questions about the plan itself (e.g., "Is there money to buy product X?" or "Do you think this game I have found is appropriate for objective 52?"). They were not there to explore ways to modify and improve the program.

That is, the superintendent ignored the power of learning. He did not allow the district to capitalize on its experience with competency-based education. He asked teachers to abandon much of what they had learned in their past experiences about instruction and to develop new skills. He declared that the new ways of doing things were fully mature and needed no development—in effect, he limited the learning process to the preordained model. This virtually assured that, barring bootleg initiatives on the part of individual teachers or principals, the program would be no more complex or sophisticated than he, from his ivory tower, could make it.

The story of Hora and Tempus suggests that the district might have done better to create a general plan of action, then encourage individual schools to develop the basic ideas, to see what they could make of the general plan. Teachers in this scenario would be given the latitude to adjust and learn. The supervisors would not be in the untenable position of authority police and would instead become interunit bridges. They would share experiences in one school with teachers in other schools—they become carriers of ideas. They would serve to bring units together into a moderately coupled system rather than a tightly coupled one. Their job in this proposal would be to foster interaction rather than compliance. This system takes advantage of the opportunities offered by natural coupling patterns rather than trying to dominate those patterns.   ▪

Darwinian Organization

Population Ecology theory argues that change is Darwinian, that the environment judges organizational events, rewarding those that improve organizational survivability and sanctioning those that don't. Much of the work in Population Ecology has looked at just how organizations adapt to different environments.

A primary reason for labeling Population Ecology as anti-positivistic is its claim that environment and structure are loosely related, thus organizations have evolved into a handful of generalized types. Positivists, particularly the Contingency theorists, argue that there is a continuum of organizational forms, each adapted to its particular environmental inputs. Population Ecologists argue that there are typologies of organizations just as there are typologies of life (genera, families, etc.). Henry Mintzberg (1979) identified five such typologies: simple forms, machine bureaucracies, adhocracies, divisionalized forms, and professional bureaucracies. We will, of course, focus on the professional bureaucracy.

In Chapter 9, we discussed the fact that professionals deal with highly complex issues and their responsibilities demand specialized, extensive knowledge. Such complexity is not open to traditional bureaucratic controls with rules and regulations: professional knowledge is far too complex for that. Consequently, professionals standardize their own behavior through their university training programs, their conferences and publications, and their interaction.

Problems arise from two facts, however. First, clients are typically not in a position to know whether a given professional is making competent judgments about services offered to them, and second, the system tends at times to be difficult to change. Laypeople do not usually have the skills needed to recommend improvements. Legislators, school boards, and public opinion can unintentionally hinder education with simplistic solutions to highly complex problems.

Further, professionals possess a high degree of autonomy that is difficult to penetrate. The trustees of a university may mandate instructional changes, but when professors get behind closed doors (and behind academic freedom laws), they can typically, and for the most part should, do as they judge appropriate. Professionals are often relatively independent of one another. They make their own decisions and formulate their own plan of action. They make cooperative decisions democratically but each member is usually free to ignore the decision of the group. That is, professionals are rather loosely coupled with one another. This serves the professional bureaucracy, for autonomy is well-suited to dealing with complex problems. But loosely coupled systems can be a bear to change. In the extreme, it means that change must occur one professional at a time.

Let's place all this into a little different perspective. What Mintzberg is referring to, using Population Ecology terminology, is inertia—the extended state that emerges between periods of change in an organizational species' life-span. Stasis does not necessarily mean that an organization is out of touch with its environment. More usually, it means that the organization is strong and vibrant. It has learned how to perform effectively and will inevitably outperform new ideas that are touted as "in touch." Open classrooms in the 1960s were considered in touch with the latest in organizational technology; literature-based reading instruction was considered in touch with the technological reality of reading instruction in the 1990s. Both succumbed to the traditional way of doing things. The reason was not that these were bad ideas; rather, the reason, in large part, was that teachers could perform more effectively with the old ways of instructing. They had developed traditional classroom instruction and phonics-based instruction to the point where the upstarts simply could not compete. Organizational structures need stability to develop effectiveness, and change is not instinctively desirable. To put this more bluntly, the reflexive change mode on which many leaders build their reputations may actually inhibit, rather than enhance, organizational productivity. One might do better to build up current structures and strategies instead of replacing them.

Change agents then, according to Population Ecology, should not automatically assume that an inertial organization is maladaptive or unproductive. One should understand that, even if the organization is a bit out of touch with the environment, even if there is a seemingly better strategy in the wings, one may very well serve the organization better by staying with, and strengthening, the current structures. "Better" ideas don't always have a long shelflife (remember 8-track tapes or ROM chip software cartridges?). Conversion cost may be quite high and the learning curve quite steep. The existing structure may appear ineffective only because it hasn't been in place long enough for workers to have mastered it, in which case change would merely compound the problem. And being somewhat out of touch is not necessarily a bad thing. Population Ecology is premised in part on the assumption that the environment is quite forgiving and organizations need not maintain one-to-one correspondence with it to be successful (hence, the generic structural archetypes, like Mintzberg's professional bureaucracy and simple bureaucracy, rather than a continuum of organizational types).

Leaders should judge, however, when inertia ceases to be an asset and an organization needs to be shaken up. Yet breaking out of an inertial state is hardly an inconsequential task. Inertia not only fosters effectiveness, it also fosters the capacity to resist change. Professionals such as professors or physicians would likely sidestep attempts to force change on them, and inclusion strategies like TQM conflict with professionals' strong sense of autonomy (this may be less true of public school teachers, who tend to enjoy a bit less autonomy than university professors; nonetheless, they too are difficult to change). Mintzberg (1979) argued, consequently, that,

> Change in the Professional Bureaucracy does not seep in from new administrators taking office to announce major reforms, nor from government technostructures intent on bringing the professionals under control. Rather, change seeps in by the slow process of changing the professionals—changing who can enter the profession, what they learn in its professional schools (ideals as well as skills and knowledge), and thereafter how willing they are to upgrade their skills. Where such changes are resisted, society may be best off to call on the professionals' sense of responsibility to serve the public, or, failing that, to bring pressures on the professional associations rather than on the Professional Bureaucracies. (p. 379)

In many ways, perhaps the best agent for changing the professional bureaucracy is the professional bureaucracy itself. Professionals, almost by definition, are structured to seek new knowledge, and they often pave the way into change for the rest of society. Professionals are sensitive to hostile or changing environments and possess structures that allow them to change from within when the environment demands it. Education professionals, for example, have accrediting agencies created by, and comprised of, professionals themselves, and these agencies are powerful vehicles of change. These accrediting agencies are responsive to public dissatisfaction with the perceived state of education and work to implement changes that improve productivity among professionals.

Higher education professionals have responded to the emergence of nontraditional students during the last decades of the 20th century with evening classes, offcampus classes, and distance learning. Public schools have embraced technological advances such as the microcomputer. They have made transitions to middle school structures and, in high schools, to block-scheduling strategies such as A-B scheduling (extended periods and class rotation every other day) or 4 × 4 scheduling (four complete courses in extended blocks per semester). They appear to be starting the transition to year-round schooling at the beginning of the 21st century. Education is probably more amenable to change than public opinion and politicians credit it with being, and much of the substantive change comes from within rather than from without.

Cultural Change

Cultural change agents deal with the complex mix of attitudes, beliefs, perceptions, management activities, technologies, organizational structures, histories, rituals, and symbols that make up a given system. The relationships among these various dynamics are stable and enduring, thus difficult to maneuver. Successful change agents have a long-term perspective, are adept at perceiving and manipulating a complex network of symbols and events, and are not deterred by what might be called "organizational mushiness," or sluggish and unpredictable response.

Contingency theory assumes that effective organizations change dynamically with constantly shifting contingencies. Culture theory shifts the focus: effective leadership is about building and managing productive stability (culture). Change is more the process by which that occurs than an end in and of itself. Productive stability might mean an atmosphere of experimentation and institutionalized change— stability can be quite dynamic—but the focus of Culture theory is less on what the culture does and more on the stable values and norms that produce action.

The Culture theory literature is replete with case studies of leaders who fostered stable values and norms within organizations. We looked at the story of how Dale Daniels turned around the culture of Lockheed's Palmdale plant in Chapter 10. Peter Tommerup (1988) compared the rather chaotic, task-oriented leadership style of Howard Hughes at Hughes Aircraft with the more predictable, friendly style of a successor, Pat Hyland, and how these two mythologized founder effects influenced the subsequent culture of that aircraft producer. Terrance Deal and Kent Peterson (1991) relate several stories of how school leaders converted the cultures of their schools.

In achieving these ends, each of the respective leaders trafficked in the cultural elements listed above: norms, values, formal philosophy, rules of the game, climate, embedded skills, habits of thinking, shared meaning and symbolism, myths, and rituals. At times, they deliberately created cultural elements such as rituals and myths, at other times they shaped cultural elements whose emergence was otherwise beyond their control (teachers can take advantage of emergent lingo among teens, for example). Dale Daniels at the Lockheed plant created symbols that built a sense of pride (the blue logo blazers for managers). He defined shared meanings when he published his philosophy ("You may be better at something than someone else, but you are not better than they are," or "Attack the problem, not the person"). He focused workers' pride in accomplishment and work ethics by emphasizing productivity and demanding that subordinates assume responsibility for their failures. Howard Hughes (the Tommerup paper) fostered a myth of idiosyncratic brilliance while Hyland created a myth of humaneness. The principals in Deal's studies turned their schools around by constructing formal philosophies of educational excellence, telling stories of their schools' achievements to reinforce values, and creating rituals and symbols to embed the importance of academics.

In each case, the leaders were patient. Culture is not constructed or changed overnight. One needs a general (as opposed to specific) vision to guide action. Culture leaders work with a large number of interactive events and structures, and understand that they will not control these events so much as they will prod them and clear the way for them—and often they will just go with the flow as if that were what they intended all along. They will build stable habits into the organization—rituals, myths, habits of thinking, shared meanings, symbols, norms and values, and rules of the game. Subordinates will tend to take cues from leaders on these issues. If the leader likes to tell stories about the organization's past, then those stories will likely become mythologized. If the leader repeats activities periodically, they will become rituals. If the leader models certain behaviors and encourages others to model them, the behaviors will become norms. This of course means that leaders must choose their stories and their rituals and their behaviors carefully. It means that the leader must be consistent: one can practice the open-door policy a hundred times but violate it once, and people will remember the violation. Culture is a way of life, and leaders must live that life if they expect others to live it.

Institutionalism

Institutional theorists focus more on *why* change occurs than on *how* it occurs, on explanation rather than prescription. Thus, they write of the institutional pressures that create change but largely ignore the leadership process by which change itself occurs. This depreciation of the role of leadership is more than a matter of focus; it is built into the theory. Scott's (1987) bridging structure hypothesis argues that institutional values migrate into organizational structure and behavior without buffering or modification: generic forms of fads such as TQM or restructuring, for example, are implemented as "canned" programs, so to speak. Thus, Westphal, Gulati, and Shortell (1997) argued that "late adopters [among the 2,700 U. S. hospitals they studied] gained legitimacy from adopting the normative form of TQM programs" (p. 366). They support this by noting that, in a large-scale study by Powell (1995), most organizational features of TQM failed to show any significant performance benefits. Their own study showed similar results. Institutional theorists do not attribute such failure to leadership; rather, they attribute it to the canned program's lack of relevance.

The evidence in Institutional theory literature that organizations tend to *adopt* normative forms of innovation is rather convincing; their evidence that organizations *implement* normative forms is largely non-existent, however. Westphal et al. (1997), for example, observed that, "Researchers have typically treated innovation as a discrete phenomenon, neglecting to examine variation in the form of adaptation itself *or in implementation*" (italics added, p. 366). Westphal and his colleagues attempted to correct this problem for their own research. Instead of asking simply whether TQM had been adopted, they asked CEOs and senior managers in hospitals whether certain TQM practices (such as team structures, statistical tools, quality reports, training, and benchmarking) had been implemented in their programs. Implementation was then related to the number of components adopted, and normative implementation was defined as the degree of consistency among hospitals in what was being implemented.

This effort, while laudable, still failed to get at variations in the way TQM is implemented. Even though a given CEO might claim that, say, team structure had been implemented in his or her hospital, it is reasonable to assume that managers in different departments (and across different hospitals) implemented teaming differently. They would have been influenced, among other things, by their own understanding of TQM, by variations in the willingness and ability of staff members to implement the strategies, by their leadership qualities, by their commitment to TQM, by existing structural features such as degree of formalization and centralization, and by the degree to which their options were restricted by external and internal regulations.

Thus, while hospitals may have adopted TQM in its normative form, without buffering (screening undesirable elements) and modification, the actual implementation process *would* have buffered and modified. Managers may decide to go with a canned innovation, but the way it is actually implemented will inevitably vary across organizations and across departments within an organization. And this brings leadership back into focus.

Variations in how innovations are implemented may partly explain why innovation shows such poor performance benefits among late adopters. Variation would, of course, be observed among early adopters as well, but early adopters also customize innovation to their specific needs. Customized variation is systematic, rather than random, variation, and is undoubtedly rather potently related to performance increments among early adopters.

 ## RESEARCH TOPIC

These hypotheses beg quantitative or qualitative validation, and you may want to tackle this. If you attempt quantitative validation, you will have to find a way to measure not only what is implemented in sample organizations, but how each element is implemented as well. A qualitative researcher may find it prohibitively overwhelming to collect data across different organizations as Westphal did. The same results might be obtained, however, by examining implementation variations across different departments within one organization, and studying the respective performance benefits in those departments.   ■

Westphal's key point remains largely intact: late adopters probably do prefer the benefits associated with an innovation's legitimacy over benefits associated with performance. The suggestion that the normative form of a given innovation will typically provide little performance benefits, however, may not reflect the whole story. At least some of an innovation's potential impact may be modified by variations in the way it is implemented. This fact refocuses attention on leadership qualities and the role of leadership in the change process, and connects Selznick's late 1950s work on leadership's role in maintaining the integrity of organizational goals with modern Institutional thought (Selznick, 1957).

 CASE STUDY

Let's return to the case study on implementation of competency-based instruction developed earlier, for there were some things going on that illuminate what we have just discussed. To review, the superintendent in the case study had adopted a standard competency-based approach to reading instruction for all elementary schools in his district. This program was structured around competencies identified in a criterion-referenced test. Teachers were instructed to individualize instruction based on each student's profile of strengths and weaknesses.

Had an outside researcher asked the superintendent whether the district had adopted the key components of a competency-based program (criterion-referenced tests, skills boxes, mastery matrixes, individualized instructions—much like what Westphal and colleagues asked of hospital CEOs), he would have responded "yes." And it was true, the district had adopted all the right activities. In practice, however, there was considerable variation across schools and across classrooms in the way the program was implemented. Many teachers rejected the program and paid only lip service to its principles. Others adopted the program selectively—the "make-and-take" lab, for example, was popular among some. Most principals were lukewarm in their support of the program, and all were somewhat confused and unsure about how to implement it. One school customized the program by creating mastery profiles for homogeneous reading groups rather than for individuals.

Thus, while the components of a stock competency-based curriculum were adopted by the district, each school implemented the components differently. Many implemented it half-heartedly, some embraced certain components of the program but ignored others, and the one school customized the normative program to meet its needs. The school with the customized program, along with a school in a strongly upper middle-class community, did well on end-of-year testing; but the district as a whole showed little performance benefit.

An outside researcher using research strategies similar to those typically used by Institutional theorists might, as a result, have concluded that the program was adopted more for legitimacy than for benefit. This conclusion is probably true as far as it goes: the superintendent apparently did adopt the program to look good before his board and public. But that is hardly the whole story. The lack of significant performance gain was logically influenced by uneven and spotty implementation, which confounds the conclusions about gains. We have no way of knowing whether the program, if implemented as required, would have produced performance gains or not, for it wasn't really given a chance to show what it could do. The components of a normative competency-based instruction program may have been adopted without buffering or modification by the district, but those components certainly were not implemented without buffering. Consequently, performance gain is not necessarily appropriate evidence of Institutional theorists' claims, which may be better explained by the qualities of the change agent—the "how" of change.   ■

RESEARCH TOPICS

Such attention to leadership's role in the Institutional process raises some interesting questions about the relationship between implementation and adaptation. It suggests that implementation (as well as adaptation) may be a function of whether an organization innovates for reasons of legitimacy or for effectiveness. The following are logical conclusions rather than empirically supported fact, and you may find it productive to explore these issues further.

Institutional theorists argue that early adopters customize their innovations and thus obtain greater effectiveness outcomes than do late adopters. This suggests that early adopters give greater, or more effective, attention to implementation strategies than do late adopters who adopt for reasons of legitimacy. Institutional theorists have not explored the nature of such differences. It may be that implementation by late adopters is less focused because normative innovations are less specific about implementation or because the customization experiences of early adopters force them through a learning process not required of late adopters. Alternatively (or additionally), the greater relevance of customized change to the organization's needs may be more motivating than less relevant innovations.

Legitimacy comes either from the process of innovation or from the expected results of innovation. If it derives from innovation itself, then outcomes, hence implementation may not be particularly important. The mere fact that a state legislature passes a law denying driving privileges to school dropouts says to voters that the legislature is doing something about the dropout problem. The legislature has received legitimization from the law alone, and implementation issues are important only if they contribute to that legitimacy. By the time the results of this effort are available, most have forgotten that the bill is implemented and are interested in some entirely different legislative agenda.

If legitimacy derives instead from the expected outcomes of innovation, policy-makers will place pressure on administrators to successfully implement the innovation but may not provide useful guidance on how to implement it. State accountability acts, for example, may demand that schools show increases in test scores. The way those increases are achieved may not be important to the legislature, thus, predictably, there would be variation in strategy across schools. In this case, the leader's competence as a change agent becomes quite important. The legislature wants the legitimization that comes from being able to say it actually did something about education, and the onus for providing that legitimacy lies with the change agent.   ■

Rain Dances   Organizational "rain dances" (a term suggested by political scientist Murray Edelman, 1967) are things systems do that project an image of doing something without actually doing anything. They provide legitimacy at little cost, thus, they are fodder for Institutional theorists. One may be observing a rain dance when a school board fires its superintendent for poor test scores, leaving the basic problems that created the poor scores untouched, or when legislatures pass anti-tenure laws during periods of teacher shortages. Rain dances portray accomplishment, getting things done; they makes us feel that we are in control of a problem when, in reality, our actions have little to do with the underlying problems. We dance about and create lots of smoke and dazzling lights, but we still have a drought. If something does change following the rain dance, we are quick to credit our efforts; if nothing happens, we often ignore that fact as we plan our next rain dance.

Some states have passed laws that revoke the driving licenses of students who drop out of school or that deny students with poor grades access to sports programs. These laws likely have, at best, a modest impact on the problems they attempt to address, but they make people feel like they have done something about those problems. Lotteries for education can likewise be considered public rain dances. Lotteries typically add three to five percent to a school system's budget, although even this is often drained by legislative cuts in general allocations. Voters, however, are lulled into believing they have taken care of education with their lottery; consequently, general tax increases for education become difficult to obtain.

Changing Complex Systems

In 1989, physicists Per Bak, Chao Tang, and Kurt Wiesenfeld published the results of an elegant and simple experiment in Complexity dynamics. They dropped grains of sand one at a time onto a weight scale. When the scale's platform was full, avalanches of sand spilled over the side and could be measured. Bak and his colleagues observed many small avalanches, a few medium-sized avalanches, and occasionally there would be a very large avalanche.

Bak and colleagues applied their observations to explanations of social and physical change. In his 1996 book, *How Nature Works,* Bak described earthquakes, species extinctions, the economy, traffic jams, and brain functioning with the same dynamics he observed in the sandpile. Bak explained that all such systems are composed of interactive units that support one another, thus providing vibrant fitness to the whole. The grains of sand in his sandpiles are linked such that most perturbations are captured before they can cause large landslides. Similarly, mature social networks are interactively linked in a manner that resists major change and damage. Actors support and depend on one another because damage to one actor can affect one or more other actors.

Mature networks achieve a state of mutual accommodation among participants that provides good fitness for the network as a whole. This compromise may not be optimal for any one actor in isolation, but the benefits of network membership far outweigh selfish need. An individual professor may be able to increase his or her productivity by regularly keeping students an hour longer than the class is scheduled, but the damage to other classes and to the ultimate welfare of students will make the professor unpopular (thus unselected) among students and will foster retribution by colleagues and administration. Perturbations to the scheduling interdependencies in universities are quickly trapped and neutralized, and major cascading damage is avoided, for it benefits the larger network to maintain its fit accommodations.

To be fit, such networks must enable change, however, for the alternative is stultification. Yet this act of accommodation exposes the network to the potential of catastrophic change. The only way to avoid catastrophe is to avoid change altogether, and this cure is worse than the problem. Thus, to be vibrant, adaptive, and fit, networks must accept change, along with the risk (actually the inevitability) that they will one day step over the edge and collapse.

The nature of interaction—moderate (as opposed to loose or tight) coupling, multiple redundancy in the interdependent support structures—assures that most perturbations will remain small and that major perturbations are rare. That is, mature social networks are robust. The moderate coupling permits distribution of innovation and change, but also serves to trap change before it gets out of hand. Multiple, redundant linkages give the network backups upon backups, so if any one system fails, others can take up the slack. Robust systems are hard, although not impossible, to damage.

Now, of course this is good—the edge-of-chaos phenomenon makes us strong and vibrant. But it has its downside: it makes such networks resistant to change—its strength is also its weakness (in this regard, it is like inertia). At the turn of the millennium, internal combustion cars, VCRs, and regular-definition TV enrich our lives, but our lives could possibly be even better with electric cars, DVD, and high-definition TV. Schools do a good job with their current structure and instructional techniques, but laypeople and legislatures are sure we would do even better if we would only listen to them. The problem is, the networks that support existing structures are so entrenched and fit that they are difficult to change. We can't implement high-definition TV overnight because of the expensive infrastructure that supports the existing format for television, and legislatures have a tough time making inroads into educational behavior because of the significant infrastructure that supports the current way of educating.

Given this, we will turn our attention to two questions: first, how do Complexity theorists explain change; and second, how can leaders foster change in robust systems? These questions focus on major, network-changing change. Systems make adaptive changes regularly; it's part of being dynamic and fit—and it's part of what helps them avoid the big changes now being discussed.

To understand how major change comes about, we need to realize that major change often does not come on gradually; rather, it frequently appears full-blown and furious, and almost out of nowhere. The fall of the USSR in 1989 was sudden and, for most people, unexpected. Urban riots usually erupt with little or no warning. The microcomputer revolution in the late 1970s came unexpectedly. The takeover of the U.S. Congress by conservative Republicans in 1994 surprised everyone but seasoned political observers. Stock market crashes are almost always unheralded. Dramatic change often surprises us.

Why? There are two dynamics at play here. First, returning to Bak's sand-pile metaphor, most perturbations are captured before they cascade very far, but occasionally one can catch the system just so, at just the right time, and ravage the whole network. These changes are almost completely unpredictable: the same event may fizzle one day and run everybody ragged the next. Riots, fads, and rumors often emerge in this fashion. The mood of an audience listening to a presentation on, say, a school bond referendum can turn on a dime—a senior citizen, for example, can comment that he or she cannot afford added property taxes and the crowd's sympathy shifts. Small events can have a major impact for no apparent logic—a perturbation just catches the network at the right place and time.

ROUNDTABLE

Given this knowledge, what could one do to help assure that an audience at a bond referendum hearing (or similar meeting) does not turn against the speaker?

The second dynamic is a bit more predictable and more amenable to manipulation. This is because, although it emerges much as the change described in the last paragraph does, it evolves more slowly. It still tends to surprise people because the seeds of this change grow quietly, and the type of change these seeds will eventually lead to may not be evident. How many people bought a transistor radio in the 1960s and thought, "This is going to lead one day to microcomputers," for example? How often have school administrators seen the signs of suicide and tragically not known what they meant until it was too late? The seeds of change are often evident only in retrospect.

According to Complexity theory, the seeds of this type of change emerge independently in different parts of a network and eventually find one another to create larger seeds. Cathode ray tubes, transistors, microprocessors, storage media, and memory chips all evolved independently in the 1940s, 1950s, and 1960s, began to find common ground in the 1960s and early 1970s (in such things as handheld calculators and games), then collapsed together suddenly to form the microcomputer in 1976. This is a common pattern with change. The component pieces emerge separately, the pieces find each other to create simple, then increasingly complex, applications; then, finally, the complex applications find one another and dramatic change explodes onto the scene.

What does this mean for leadership? It means that change agent leadership performs two important roles: it drops seeds of innovation, and it builds interactive networks within which the seeds can grow. Change agents in complex systems are fountains of ideas (their trash cans overflow with solutions, to use a metaphor from Garbage Can theory). They see possibilities wherever they go, and they encourage subordinates to try new ideas. They don't particularly worry about coordination among actors or divisions, and they aren't particularly focused on strategic plans and goal-setting. They understand that, if they attempt to plan and control innovation, it will be no more sophisticated or useful than their own limited vision is capable of—controlled innovation is no more complex or sophisticated that the controller. Interaction, by contrast, can produce some wondrous innovations that we, individually, cannot anticipate.

To make these fortuitous accidents happen, the leader must help build networks within which individual innovations can interact. These networks must not be so tight that every innovation spreads throughout the network, but not so loose that nobody knows what is happening in other areas. In properly tuned networks, any given actor interacts with only a few other actors or is moderately dependent on a number of actors—or some combination of these conditions. Networking is influenced by the way an organization is formally structured, the patterns of control and interdependencies. It is influenced by scheduling patterns—which teachers have break together or eat lunch together. It is influenced by room assignments (who is proximal to whom), curricular demands (interdisciplinary units demand coordination, for example), and facility layout (pod structures, in which three to five classrooms are oriented around a small commons area, foster interaction among the teachers in those classes). Interaction is fostered through committee assignments, common projects or responsibility, and mutual interests. Interaction is fostered by leaders who are comfortable with a bit of chaos in which they are not in control of every event and do not have fingers in every project. It is fostered by leaders who are sufficiently comfortable with their abilities and are sufficiently confident in their subordinates to use the system as a giant analytical system, one that processes information from the bottom up (decentralized) rather than top down (centralized). Such leaders understand that bottom-up systems, with a properly tuned network with a sufficient supply of innovation seeds, can generate complex order and can produce innovations that no one individual could ever conceive.

CASE STUDIES AND ROUNDTABLE

Returning to the case study of the competency-based curriculum discussed earlier, how might you have implemented this innovation, given what we have discussed in this section?

FINIS

This chapter, and this book, pose a challenge to you: sort through the material, weigh the pros and cons of various prescriptions and perspectives, and build your own theory of leadership. How will you deal with change? How will you relate to subordinates? How will you structure your organization to achieve its ends? What is leadership? By what code of ethics will you lead? How do you assure a continuous flow of resources into your organization? How will you relate to your school's environment?

Your answers should not come only from this book. Consider this course to be a source of questions you need to ask, a source of some tentative answers, and a source from which you can structure your thinking as you struggle with questions of leadership. The other course work you take in your degree program, along with your life experiences, will help you flesh out the answers to questions we have raised. A School and Community course, for example, will help you refine your perspective on the school's relationship with its environment, and many of the models discussed in this book (the general systems model, Getzels' and Guba's models, or Senge's systemic cycles) will help you put community relationships into perspective. Principalship, superintendency, or college administrator courses will provide practical backdrops against which you can evaluate and understand these theories. A personnel course will help draw policy and legal boundaries around your perspectives of staff relationships. Practicums or internship classes will give you an opportunity to refine your perspective of leadership. In other words—to draw from the learning theory material in an earlier chapter—use this book as a foundation for your own learning journey. One book cannot teach everything you need to know, and there is a lot of detail you need to develop over the next few years. Consider your program of study, and your subsequent leadership experiences, as a unified experience intended to make you a mature and effective leader.

Build your leadership philosophy from all this. Ten years from now, you may remember Hersey and Blanchard but you probably won't remember the details of their model: even so, their model can influence the way you work with subordinates. You can remember to deal with subordinates based on their state of readiness—new employees need different types of encouragement than do advisory boards, who need different types of support than do seasoned teachers. You may not remember the definition of anti-positivism, but you can remember that leader behavior isn't always tightly connected to organizational outcome, or you can remember to question your preferences, for they won't always be motivated by productivity. You can remember the garbage can maxim: stuff yours as full of solutions as possible and don't worry too much about the illogic that often places solutions before problems. Perhaps the material about building culture struck a chord with you. The Marxist premise that underlies Critical theory may not appeal to you, but surely you are now sensitive to your motivation for being in control and are sensitive to your moral obligations to employees. Some parts of Complexity theory may elude your mastery, but you can remember the charge to drop seeds of innovation and to build networks.

This book is useless if it doesn't help you build your leadership philosophy and shape your leadership style. I have done all I can do toward that end: it is now up to you to process, and do something with, the information in these pages.

Diary

- Summarize your thoughts on the Roundtable discussions that were proposed in this chapter.
- Given what you have learned in this chapter, what are some important functions of leadership? In what way does your answer change your previous answers to this question?

Recommended Reading

Bak, P. (1996). *How nature works*. New York: Copernicus.

In this book, Bak reviews and develops his sandpile experiment, and identifies similar dynamics in events as disparate as brainwave activity, earthquakes, automobile traffic patterns, the economy, and extinctions. He also offers an excellent discussion of the power law distribution.

References

Aldrich, H. E. (1979). *Organizations and environment*. Englewood Cliffs, NJ: Prentice Hall.

Bak, P. (1996). *How nature works*. New York: Copernicus.

Bak, P., Tang, C., & Wiesenfeld, K. (1989). Self-organized criticality: An explanation of 1/f noise. *Physical Review Letters, 59,* 381–384.

Bennis, W., & Nanus, B. (1985). *Leaders: The strategies for taking charge*. New York: Harper & Row.

Carroll, G. R., & Hannan, M. T. (1995). *Organizations in industry*. New York: Oxford University Press.

Chin, R. (1967). Basic strategies and procedures in effecting change. In Edgar L. Morphet (Ed.), *Educational organization and administration concepts: Practice and issues*. Englewood Cliffs, NJ: Prentice Hall, Inc.

Corwin, R. G. (1987). *The organizational-society nexus: A critical review of models and metaphors*. New York: Greenwood.

Deal, T. E., & Peterson, K. D. (1991). *The principal's role in shaping school culture*. Washington, DC: U.S. Department of Education, Office of Educational Research and Improvement, Programs for the Improvement of Practice.

Donaldson, L. (1996). *For positivist organization theory: Proving the hard core*. London: Sage Publications.

Edelman, M. (1967). *The symbolic uses of politics*. Urbana, IL: University of Illinois Press.

Getzels, J. W. (1978). The communities of education. *Teacher College Record, 79*(4), 659–682.

Getzels, J. W., & Guba, E. G. (1957). Social behavior and the administrative process. *School Review, 65,* 423–441.

Getzels, J. W., Lipham, J. M., & Campbell, R. F. (1968). *Educational administration as a social process: Theory, research, and practice*. New York: Harper & Row.

Hersey, P., & Blanchard, K. H. (1993). *Management of organizational behavior: Utilizing human resources* (6th ed.). Englewood Cliffs, NJ: Prentice Hall, Inc.

Katz, D., & Kahn, R. L. (1966). *The social psychology of organizations*. New York: John Wiley & Sons, Inc.

Kauffman, S. A. (1995). *At home in the universe: The search for the laws of self-organization and complexity*. New York: Oxford University Press.

Leavitt, H. J. (1964). *Managerial psychology*. Chicago: University of Chicago Press.

Lewin, K. (1952). Group decision and social change. In G. E. Swanson, T. M. Newcomb, & E. L. Hartley (Eds.), *Readings in social psychology, rev. ed.* (pp. 459 – 473). New York: Holt.

McKelvey, B. (1982). *Organizational systematics.* Berkeley, CA: University of California Press.

Mintzberg, H. (1979). *The structuring of organizations: A synthesis of the research.* Englewood Cliffs, NJ: Prentice Hall, Inc.

Moch, M. K., & Morse, E. V. (1977). Size, centralization, and organizational adaptation of innovation. *American Sociological Review, 42,* 716–725.

Pfeffer, J., & Salancik, G. R. (1978). *The external control of organizations: A resource dependence perspective.* New York: Harper & Row.

Powell, T. C. (1995). Total quality management as competitive advantage: A review and empirical study. *Strategic Management Journal, 16,* 15–37.

Prigogine, I. (1997). *The end of certainty.* New York: The Free Press.

Schulz, M. (1998). Limits to bureaucratic growth: The density dependence of organizational rules births. *Administrative Science Quarterly, 43*(4), 845–876.

Scott, W. R. (1987). *Organizations: Rational, natural, and open systems* (2nd ed.). Englewood Cliffs, NJ: Prentice Hall, Inc.

Seiler, J. A. (1967). *Systems analysis in organizational behavior.* Homewood, IL: Richard D. Irwin, Inc., and The Dorsey Press.

Selznick, P. (1957). *Leadership in administration.* New York: Harper & Row.

Senge, P. M. (1990). *The fifth discipline: The art and practice of the learning organization.* New York: Random House.

Tommerup, P. (1988). From trickster to father figure: Learning from the mythologization of top management. In M. O. Jones, M. D. Moore, & R. C. Snyder (Eds.), *Inside the organizations: Understanding the human dimension* (pp. 319–331). Newbury Park, CA: Sage Publications.

Weick, K. (1976). Educational organizations as loosely coupled systems. *Administrative Science Quarterly, 21,* 1–19.

Westphal, J. D., Gulati, R., & Shortell, S. M. (1997). Customization or conformity: An institutional and network perspective on the content and consequences of TQM adoption. *Administrative Science Quarterly, 42,* 366–394.

INDEX